Collecting Visible Evidence

Jane M. Gaines and Michael Renov, Editors

University of Minnesota Press

Minneapolis

London

A slightly different version of "They Said We Were Trying to Show Reality—All I Want to Show Is My Video: The Politics of the Realist Feminist Documentary," by Alexandra Juhasz, was previously published as "The Politics of the Realist, Feminist Documentary," *Screen* 35, no. 2 (summer 1994): 171–90; reprinted by permission of Oxford University Press. An earlier version of "Phenomenologies of the Surface: Radiation-Body-Image," by Akira Mizuta Lippit, was published in *Qui Parle* 9, no. 2 (spring/summer 1996). A slightly revised version of "The Ethics of Intervention: Dennis O'Rourke's *The Good Woman of Bangkok*," by Linda Williams, appeared in *The Filmmaker and the Prostitute: Dennis O'Rourke's "The Good Woman of Bangkok*," edited by Chris Berry, Annette Hamilton, and Laleen Jayamanne (Sydney: Power Publications, 1997).

Published by the University of Minnesota Press
111 Third Avenue South, Suite 290
Minneapolis, MN 55401-2520
http://www.upress.umn.edu

Library of Congress Cataloging-in-Publication Data

Collecting visible evidence / Jane M. Gaines and Michael Renov, editors.
     p.   cm. — (Visible evidence ; v. 6)
     Papers from three annual conferences held beginning in 1993.
     Includes index.
     ISBN 0-8166-3135-2. — ISBN 0-8166-3136-0 (pbk.)
     1. Documentary films—History and criticism—Congresses.
     I. Gaines, Jane, 1943–   . II. Renov, Michael, 1950–   . III. Series.
     PN1995.9.D6C535   1999
     070.1'8—dc21   99-14043

Printed in the United States of America on acid-free paper

The University of Minnesota is an equal-opportunity educator and employer.

11 10 09 08 07 06 05 04 03 02   10 9 8 7 6 5 4 3 2

Dedicated to the memory of Arlindo Castro
(1948–1997)—scholar, videomaker, musician,
media activist

Contents

Acknowledgments   vii

Introduction: "The Real Returns"   JANE M. GAINES   I

1 ▶ The Spectacle of Actuality   ELIZABETH COWIE   19

2 ▶ Embarrassing Evidence: The Detective Camera and
    the Documentary Impulse   TOM GUNNING   46

3 ▶ Phenomenologies of the Surface: Radiation-Body-Image
    AKIRA MIZUTA LIPPIT   65

4 ▶ Political Mimesis   JANE M. GAINES   84

5 ▶ Damming Virgil Thomson's Music for *The River*
    NEIL LERNER   103

6 ▶ Paradigms Lost and Found: The "Crisis of
    Representation" and Visual Anthropology
    NANCY LUTKEHAUS AND JENNY COOL   116

7 ▶ Domestic Ethnography and the Construction
    of the "Other" Self   MICHAEL RENOV   140

8 ▶ The Parallax Effect: The Impact of Indigenous Media
    on Ethnographic Film   FAYE GINSBURG   156

9 ▶ The Ethics of Intervention: Dennis O'Rourke's
    The Good Woman of Bangkok   LINDA WILLIAMS   176

10 ▶ They Said We Were Trying to Show Reality—All I Want
     to Show Is My Video: The Politics of the Realist Feminist
     Documentary   ALEXANDRA JUHASZ   190

11 ▶ Loving Yourself: The Specular Scene in Sexual Self-Help
     Advice for Women   EITHNE JOHNSON   216

12 ▶ Toward a Phenomenology of Nonfictional Film Experience
VIVIAN SOBCHACK   241

13 ▶ A Bone of Contention: Documenting the Prehistoric Subject
JAMES M. MORAN   255

14 ▶ Subjunctive Documentary: Computer Imaging and Simulation
MARK J. P. WOLF   274

15 ▶ History in a Flash: Notes on the Myth of TV "Liveness"
MARK WILLIAMS   292

16 ▶ Documentary Horizons: An Afterword   MICHAEL RENOV   313

Contributors   327

Index   331

Acknowledgments

This book would not exist were it not for the resurgence of interest in documentary studies that began with the 1990 Ohio University film conference, whose single topic that year (thanks to Jeanne Hall) was documentary. The realization that sufficient interest existed to create an ongoing conference devoted entirely to nonfiction dawned on a group of us awaiting our flights at the Columbus, Ohio, airport. We would like to thank all the individuals and institutions responsible for mounting the Visible Evidence conferences over the years: Jane Gaines at Duke University, 1993; Michael Renov at USC, 1994; Gerald O'Grady at Harvard University, 1995; Brian Winston and Roberta Pearson at University of Wales-Cardiff, 1996; Chuck Kleinhans at Northwestern University, 1997; Bill Nichols at San Francisco State University, 1998; and James Friedman at UCLA, 1999. Of course it is the scholars and practitioners who have attended and shared their insights at each of these events who have made them a success.

We have appreciated the support of the University of Minnesota Press, which has maintained great enthusiasm for Visible Evidence, both the conference and the book series. Special thanks are due to the two editors at the Press who have worked so closely and expertly with us, Micah Kleit and Jennifer Moore.

We wish to dedicate this book to Arlindo Castro, who made a memorable contribution to the 1995 Visible Evidence conference through the brilliance of his presentation and the vibrancy and warmth of his personality. Arlindo spoke of the prospects of hosting a future conference in his hometown, Rio de Janeiro, but that was not to be. His untimely death has saddened all of us who had the privilege of knowing him.

JANE M. GAINES

Introduction
"The Real Returns"

Reality is more fabulous, more maddening, more strangely manipulative than fiction.
:: Trinh T. Minh-ha, *When the Moon Waxes Red*, 1991

At a conference in 1993, scholars gathered to try to decide how or whether to reconstitute an area that seemed to be in danger of falling into theoretical disrepair. Whereas film studies had historically been divided into three "modes"—the theatrical fiction film, the documentary, and the experimental film—these old distinctions were no longer viable. Although film- and videomakers had been creatively scrambling up these modes for several decades, critics had not yet sorted out this mode mixing, let alone addressed the changes that have resulted from the advent of digital technologies. Also at that time, questions of documentary discourse, factuality, and meaning were newly charged in U.S. public consciousness. A little more than a year after the April 1992 announcement of the verdict in what came to be known as the Rodney King trial and the ensuing Los Angeles riots, film studies scholars were still pondering the significance of the trial proceedings for media theory. How could the jury decide to exonerate the white Los Angeles police officers accused of brutally beating black suspect King when the prosecution offered an amateur videotape recording of the actual beating as "evidence"? Hence, the origins of "Visible Evidence," the conference on "strategies and practices in documentary film and video," an event that has been held annually since 1993. The essays in this collection represent a sample of the papers delivered at the first three conferences; taken together, they represent a significant reconfiguration of documentary studies.

To return to documentary is to return again to cinematic realism and its dilemmas. To look back at film theory from the 1950s to the 1970s is to think about the way cinematic realism, first heralded as a technological triumph, became a philosophical problem. Although it is not unusual for one generation of critics to rebel against another, what may be unusual in the case of contemporary film theory is the way a later generation characterized an earlier one as having been taken in by "bourgeois realism," the narrative form that so subtly denies its own devices. Greeted as a scientific breakthrough by André Bazin and Siegfried Kracauer, the new postwar realism was discovered to be something of a fraud by the *Cahiers du Cinéma* critics of the 1970s, because, they argued, realism didn't exactly "reproduce" the real as it said it did. In retrospect, however, it might seem that the *Cahiers* critics may have "overreacted," given that the invocation of "reality" is probably a strategic rhetorical move just as often as it is a deference to empirical fact. The *Cahiers* response, or what has become known as the "critique of realism," however, has continued to be enormously influential in film studies, and it is often invoked to criticize stylistic illusionism and spectatorial naïveté, but also to advance critical distance and a corresponding philosphical position. The point most often made, drawing on philosophical positions in poststructuralist thought outside film studies, is that the problem with the concept of painting, photographing, or "recording" reality is that this assumes that there is a real "out there" in the natural world that can be shown (or that will reveal itself) without the use of linguistic or cinematic signs. Reality outside of cultural signs, as it is so often said, does not exist. In the same general poststructuralist drift, but associated with Althusser more than Derrida, is the concept that any claim to "reality" is a highly ideological move to begin with. Incorporated into apparatus theory, exceedingly important in film studies since the 1970s, this position is neatly summarized in Jean-Luc Comolli and Jean Narboni's statement about the machines themselves:

> Clearly the cinema "reproduces" reality: this is what a camera and film stock are for — so says the ideology. But the tools and techniques of film-making are a part of "reality" themselves, and furthermore "reality" is nothing but an expression of the prevailing ideology.[1]

The machines that produce the signs as well as the signs themselves are both in and of ideology, and documentary filmmaking has been the example par excellence of this, with its techniques of intervention and invisibility, its use of telephoto camera and inconspicuous miking devices designed to capture "raw truth" but finally delivering ideology.[2]

Whereas poststructuralism has had an exceedingly important impact on documentary theory, particularly as it has called attention to the processing and mediating function of cinematic signs, the relationship between postmodern thought and documentary is still in negotiation. Some of the difficulty we face at this juncture has to do with a general vagueness about what constitutes the postmodern, and it is not clear from contemporary critics whether by *postmodern* they mean the indistinguishability between the real and its image or the state in which there is no reality outside representation. How quickly the critique of the excesses of poststructuralism (there is no "outside" to ideology) has merged with the idea that there is nothing but discourse! Whereas the general thrust of the philosophical positions that flowered in the 1970s was one of understanding the odds against resistance in the postwar world (given the thoroughness of the prevailing ideology), the contemporary articulation of the relationship between reality and image is not necessarily informed by a notion of ideology at all. The postmodern indistinguishability between the real and its image always seems in danger of turning into a lament for a time when the two were clearly distinguishable, but in the end it is never exactly clear in this theory whether the breakdown between the real and the imaginary is a good thing or not. Documentary theory and practice are both immediately implicated here, particularly because the tendency to mix documentary footage and fictional enactment seems coincident with the contemporary period so often described as postmodern.[3]

Up until the present, those critics who have written on documentary from the standpoint of Marxist theory have dealt with what might be termed the need for an ultimate reference point (sometimes "the real") by holding out or reserving history and revolutionary struggle as this point. Documentary film criticism, as it has been conceived in the past two decades by critics such as Bill Nichols, Tom Waugh, Julia Lesage, Brian Winston, and others, has always assumed "real historical actors" and revolutionary events.[4] At the same time that this criticism has assumed these historical events, however, it has aggressively critiqued the assumption that even the "reality" of a revolutionary situation could be discovered and brought back to us through technological devices. Describing this strategy, Judith Butler has said that "the options for theory are not exhausted by *presuming* materiality, on the one hand, and *negating* materiality on the other."[5] Her solution to the need to separate these strategies, one commonly used by contemporary culture critics, is to put the questionable term in quotation marks, designating it as contested and setting it aside as an area of debate.

▶
───

"Reality" in Quotation Marks

To some degree, there is really only one way to read the pioneer thinkers Bazin and Kracauer—that is, as though they are capable of employing several notions of "realism" and "reality" at once. André Bazin is then seen as one of the more adept negotiators of these concepts, simultaneously able to give the impression that realism is both achieved through artifice and unproblematically expressed, and able to create the sense that "reality" is found as well as constructed. The critic who said that "some measure of realism must always be sacrificed in the effort of achieving it" can hardly be construed as a naive realist.[6] Also, in Siegfried Kracauer's famous assertion that "what the camera captures is more real than reality itself" one finds a subtle comment on aesthetics whereby the construction surpasses and even comments on its own constructedness. Putting the emphasis in Kracauer's famous statement on the "more real" instead of on the "reality itself" produces a comment on the plurality and the contingency or the relativity of realities.[7]

To reconsider the pioneer film theorists on realism and to assert their critical distance from it, however, is still to distance ourselves yet again from realism, to see ourselves as neither too easily duped by a style that fraudulently "passes itself off as the real" nor too innocently empirical in our attitude toward the world. Perhaps this is why we have been so comfortable with the critique of realism and consequently less inclined to consider either the positive efficacy or the popular attraction of realism. A serious consideration of attraction returns us to "resemblance," one of the more obvious but neglected attributes of documentary, which, nevertheless, as Bill Nichols tells us, is the "central aspect" of the documentary aesthetic.[8] From a contemporary point of view, resemblance, in its long association with realism, is associated with a slavish or easy way of representing and accessing the world. With reference to painting, Bazin expresses his disdain for the kind of imitative art associated with resemblance:

> Freed from the "resemblance complex," the modern painter abandons it to the masses, who, henceforth, identify resemblance on the one hand with photography and on the other with the kind of painting which is related to photography.[9]

Given this disregard, it may be difficult for a twentieth-century skeptic to imagine resemblance historically—to imagine it not as mindless copying of the same, but as a legitimate form of knowledge. Resemblance as a way of knowing is held in low esteem because it seems to offer no comparative dimension and no distance. However, at least two contemporary theorists have devoted some serious consideration to seeing similarity as an epistemology that characterizes earlier centuries—Michael Taussig as he looks at the mimetic mode of ancient cultures and primitive peoples and Michel Foucault as he analyzes sixteenth-century discourses. Foucault describes the empiricism of the sixteenth century as an "Age of Resemblance" in which language and things were rather more inextricable than we would like to see them today. Then a legitimate category of knowledge, resemblance was esteemed as a way of seeing likenesses everywhere in the social and natural worlds. Rehabilitating resemblance as a way of knowing, Foucault makes it somehow modern for us by stripping down the semiotic process to its fundamentals: "To search for a meaning is to bring to light a resemblance. To search for the law governing signs is to discover the things that are alike." Semiotics and hermeneutics he says, are "superimposed" in similitude.[10]

Reading documentary realism has historically been a matter of seeing similarity. Foucault brings us face-to-face with the epistemological problem of documentary, of the sound track that "sounds like" and the image track that "looks like." This problem posed by "lookalikeness," or iconicity, is, of course, endemic to all mimetic technologies. And as it turns out, this is the same basic hermeneutic problem that began to concern Continental theory in the late 1960s (no doubt prodded by the growth of image culture). The problem that I am referring to is none other than the problem of language and its other. In semiotic terms, the difficulty with photographic realism is that it prefers a relation between language and thing that is too close. But never let us think that this relation is too close from the standpoint of ordinary viewers who have historically thrilled to displays of similitude. Reconsidering Bazin's ontology of the real in a pathbreaking essay, Phillip Rosen has considered how this ontology "may have to do with the subject's (viewer's) desire to see similarity."[11] The language/thing proximity is too close from the standpoint of high modernism, for which discourse has always had to stand at a distance from that to which it referred, preferably at an oblique angle. Michel de Certeau elucidates this problem of the estrangement of reality from language:

> Perhaps, too, by holding to the idea of discourse and to its fabrication, we can better apprehend the nature of the relations *that it holds with its other, the real.* In this fashion, doesn't language not so much implicate the status of the reality of which it speaks, as pose it as that which is other than itself?[12]

The otherness of that to which discourse refers puts us in mind of that theoretical companion to resemblance, that problem of the relation to the world that we call *referentiality*. If the central aspect of documentary is resemblance, the defining feature of it has been the exceptionality of its referentiality. Simply stated, according to semiotic theory, there is thought to be a "special indexical bond" between the photographic image and the object in the real world to which the image refers. Much has been made of this bond in documentary theory as well as in cultural studies in general, particularly as defined in the work of Bazin and Roland Barthes. The advantage of this bond is largely rhetorical, given that the defining edge that documentary has over the fiction film is the edge of indexicality, summarized in Bill Nichols's reference to the indexical "whammy." But if it can no longer be said that documentary has "reality" on its side, what can be said of it? Can we at least say that documentary has an inside track on reality, that it has a something, even if it can no longer be said to have a "trace" of the real?

Much is at stake for documentary theory here, and a number of the essays in this collection address this issue of the impossible claim to indexicality, giving us a compendium of cases in which the special indexical relation is in question, from turn-of-the-century x-ray photography to digital computer simulation. Much is at stake because it is a matter of giving up the rhetorical clout that comes with the claim of "evidence" of the real. Arguing in this collection for supplementing documentary theory with a concept of "virtual reality," Jim Moran concludes that "claims to credibility must lie outside the technology producing it," because "documentary reality never lies *within* the image, but always in the discursive field *around* it." Mark Wolf concurs, urging us to abandon or totally revise the notion of indexicality, which is inadequate to describe the representational functioning of the newest of the new mimetic technologies.

▶
_____

Anthropology and Similitude

Anthropology, the field perhaps most thoroughly implicated in the dilemma of the radical otherness of the real in relation to the discourse it eludes, has other stakes in the twin questions of iconicity and indexicality. As three of the contributors to this collection attest, ethnographic media, having undergone a crisis in representation stemming from the very problem of who represents and who is represented, are looking forward as they redefine their "discourse to other" relation. But the crisis in representation has also produced a commitment to looking backward to the practice of ethnographic filmmaking as it was originally defined, and this looking back has produced significant contributions to the debates around cinematic realism, especially as the debates take questions of race and ethnicity into account.

Recently, Fatimah Tobing Rony has reread Robert Flaherty's *Nanook of the North* (1921) as a "cinema of romantic preservationism," dedicated not to anthropological knowledge but to the production of indigenous peoples as trophies and to the capture of their ways of life in nostalgic fiction.[13] Borrowing Donna Haraway's concept of ethnographic taxidermy

Still from *Nanook of the North* (1921).

to define Flaherty's cinema, she addresses at once the question of the film-maker's attitude toward a vanishing people and the question of how arti-fice produces a reality that improves upon the event before the camera, cre-ating an enriched and supplemented real that invites us to take it as true. And it is this supplemented reality that audiences repeatedly prefer. Rony's definition of taxidermy as the "use of artifice [to seek] an image more true to the posited original," hearkening back to Bazin and Kracauer, no doubt sums up the documentary ideal they inspired.[14] But rather than look only at the colonizing impulse in the cinema of romantic preservationism, we should also look at the genuine quest for knowledge about the totally un-known and unfamiliar. A cinema of taxidermy is of course a cinema that plays on the public fascination with likenesses (its attraction to similarity), and the success of that cinema returns us to the function of resemblance as a route to knowledge. Think of the audiences who rushed to "see," as encouraged by the Paramount press books: "See Nanook spear the seal, fight to get it and then eat the raw flesh"; "You'll not even wink your eyes"; "So much interest, so much heart-throb, so many pulse-quickening sensations, you'll sit as if you were hypnotized." Here audiences are attracted both *to* the hoax and *by* the very success of the hoax—by the ability of the maker to produce a perfect illusionistic imitation.[15]

The cinema of taxidermy, a cinema of the fascination with resemblances, has its connotations of prurient looking (looking to see Nanook embalmed), but there is a danger that these negative connotations may overshadow any possibility of seeing cinematic realism as an invitation to knowledge.[16] As I have been suggesting, to see the legitimacy of mimesis and resemblance as routes to discovery is to appreciate an aspect of the documentary aesthetic that has gone unremarked. (And of course this is in direct contradiction to the critique of realism that holds that realism is incapable of delivering analytic knowledge.) Perhaps this aspect has gone unremarked because similarity and resemblance as modes of understanding the world are associated with mass knowledge, or the knowledge of the masses—the ways in which ordinary people learn through yielding to their fascination, a fascination that leads them to public museums, exhibitions, tourist attractions, even circus sideshows. Here, the motion picture is on a par with other performances, natural phenomena, curiosities, and technologies that play on similarity—from Civil War reenactments to flight simulators, from fossils to death masks. (Vivian Sobchack in this collection refers us to the French term for the home-movie mode, *film-souvenir,* which suggests further the interchangeability of movies and curiosities.) Documentary is particularly attracted to freaks of nature and technological wizardry: quintuplets and x rays. In this category, moving pictures are resemblance-as-attraction par excellence. The motion picture's resemblances are both horizontal (in its parallel of the temporality and the panorama of the world) and vertical (in the repetition of images on the celluloid strip, each one of which resembles the next). But of course it is in the remarkable, effortless similarity between the world before the camera and the image that attempts to replicate it that the public has historically found the camera's achievement. Documentary adds to the achievement of the camera and the projector the fascination of congruence and coincidence: the camera was there, history was there. Similarity is a technological wonder!

In her essay here, Elizabeth Cowie gives us the foundation for an understanding of documentary's "spectacle of actuality," a spectacle that has its own pleasures and thrills as well as its contradictory desires. These are the desires for reality in both its recorded and its re-presented forms. And this desire as well as the documentary spectacle posit a knowledge-

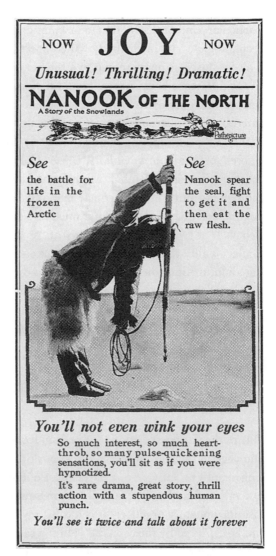

Exhibition for *Nanook of the North* (1921).

seeking spectator. In the documentary mode, reality becomes an attraction, not because it is ordinary, but because it is suddenly strange. The subject of documentary may be buried in everyday life when it is discovered untouched by the camera, but it soon becomes the object of spectatorial incredulity. Thus, to Tom Gunning's understanding of the early detective camera (forerunner of the documentary camera) as an expression of the curiosity of the photographer, we have to add the complementary understanding of the curiosity of the viewer. And we might say that, despite the emphasis on documentary as hard, cold fact, as propaganda and social problem, as a "sobering" discourse, it is also a discourse that elicits a particular kind of fascination, a fascination with the workings of mimetic technologies, only intensified by their spectacularly successful illusionism. This is a fascination increased to a further degree by the alluring question of the difference between reality and fiction, a question raised every time documentary ceases to be just news and becomes entertainment. And the interest of popular audiences in just this question is confirmed not only by reality-TV programming but by the classic documentaries from *Nanook of the North* to *Harlan County, U.S.A.* Helping us out on this point, documentary filmmaker Trinh T. Minh-ha has said, "Reality is more fabulous, more maddening, more strangely manipulative than fiction."[17] Of every commercial documentary film it must be said that there is a "Ripley's Believe It or Not" quality, a quality of "stranger than," and it is this particular quality that invites investigation and knowledge, even a questioning about the imagined world/real world distinction. And this brings me to a point that must be made about the wholesale political dismissal of reality-based forms premised on their inability to achieve analytic distance from the cinematic subject as well as distance from their own aesthetic devices.

▶ ───

Feminist Realism and Documentary

One of the strongest critiques of realism from within film studies was launched in the mid-1970s, a critical position that effectively went unchallenged until recently. In one of the most quoted statements in the first years of feminist film theory, Claire Johnston establishes the platform for feminist documentary practice: "It is idealist mystification to believe that 'truth' can be captured by the camera."[18] In the case of feminist film, it has been the particular "truth" of the oppressed condition of women in patriarchial society that could not be merely "captured" or recorded on film or tape but that had to be manufactured or constructed. Revisiting what she calls the realist feminist debates of the 1970s, Alex Juhasz asks in her essay here about the hard line and the implications for a documentary practice that grows out of political activism, given that Johnston's stated position has been interpreted as effectively producing an unbridgeable divide between women's movement activists and feminist theorists. It is not, however, as though this position was ever "debated" among feminists who theorized and feminists who practiced documentary filmmaking. It is more as though the two groups went their separate ways and feminist filmmakers continued over the span of twenty years to produce an extremely impressive body of work, some of which challenged representation (Jill Godmilow, Martha

Rosler) and some of which did not (Julia Reichert). In retrospect, then, Juhasz asks us to think about those works that did not challenge the aesthetics, about the rhetoric of realism, which she sees as multiple, plural, and capable of much more political efficacy than it has been given credit for over the past several decades. Directly taking on the critique of realism, she says: "'Realism' can function in any number of ways, including, but not limited to, the confirmation, perpetuation, and reflection of bourgeois, patriarchal reality. It can testify to alternative, marginal, subversive, or illegal realities; it can critique the notion of reality." Usefully, she points out that the critique of realism did not arise from within feminism itself. Rather, the challenge to realist aesthetics was imported from the constructivism in vogue in French Continental theory in the 1970s, as I discussed earlier with reference to the *Cahiers* critics.

This is not to deny the importance of constructivist thinking to feminism, a feminism that seems unthinkable when divorced from a concept of the constructedness of gender. And yet feminist philosopher Judith Butler has forced us to rethink even this foundational premise, a reconsideration that has some implications for documentary theory. It is when, in *Bodies That Matter,* she asks us to think about the extreme of radical constructivism that we have to wonder about the realities beyond the reach of constructivism, a position that, as she characterizes it for the sake of argument, "refutes the reality of bodies, the relevance of science, the alleged facts of birth, aging, illness, and death." But almost immediately, she continues, as soon as we consider what would happen if we were to concede these materialities (the body in all of its physiological manifestations, including sexuality), we must think how the very "concession" to the "undeniability" of materiality constructs that materiality.[19] Even if we defer to at least some of the natural world, conceding that it is "the real," even if we give the body the last word, the body cannot speak without benefit of our intervening discourses.

▶──

Looking Back and Looking Forward to Dziga Vertov

> Kino-eye is understood as "that which the eye doesn't see,"
> as the microscope and telescope of time,
> as the negative of time,
> as the possibility of seeing without limits and distances,
> as the remote control of movie cameras,
> as tele-eye,
> as X-ray eye,
> as "life caught unawares," etc., etc.

All these different formulations were mutually complementary since implied in kino-eye were:

all cinematic means,
all cinematic inventions,
all methods and means that might serve to reveal and show the truth.[20]

In the first histories of documentary film, the East never really met the West, but in recent years scholars have increasingly considered Robert Flaherty and Dziga Vertov together, despite controversies that put the two "fathers" of documentary film in stark contrast. Flaherty may be alternately cited positively as the beginning of maker-subject collaboration in ethnographic filmmaking or cited negatively as the start of the tradition of anthropological exploitation of native people.[21] Vertov may have been the inspiration for radical filmmaking in the West, but in the glasnost period, according to Patricia Zimmermann, he has fallen out of favor in the countries of the former Soviet Union, just at the height of his importance as part of an international reconsideration of documentary theory and practice.[22]

Dziga Vertov (aka Denis Arkadievich Kaufman), in both his film practice between 1922 and 1931 and his manifestos from those years, offers new directions for documentary, particularly since he takes us around and beyond a lockstep empiricism while still maintaining a passionate interest in what he terms the "higher mathematics of facts."[23] Vertov had no apparent angst about the nature of "the real," neither did he strive for an impossible objectivity, flaunting his subjectivity along with his politics. One of his favorite modes of shooting, which he called "Life Caught Unawares," was not the antithesis of the staged event, although in this original moment of cinema verité, the viewer did get the feeling that the camera was undetected.[24] Increasingly, particularly as we look at the global invocations of cinema verité, we suspect how much has been lost in the translation of *kino pravda* into cinema verité, and even as we return to Georges Sadoul and Jean Rouch (both of whom liked to claim the credit for this translation), verité is becoming a style and its connotations are already beginning to shift from "political truth" to "real and true."

And finally, Vertov was eclectic. As Zimmermann has described him, he is now revered for the way he has introduced the experimental into documentary. She notes the way he explores the potentialities of the camera, not restricting himself to the most obvious function, that of a recording device that could "compliantly copy and replicate the world."[25] As the first documentary experimentalist, Vertov gives license to that new documentary practice that in recent years has rejected the recording device in favor of, in his terms, "all cinematic means, all cinematic inventions." And so it is that Vertov's definition of the "kino-eye" serves as a table of contents for this collection that features new directions in documentary film and video: cinema as the "microscope and telescope of time," "tele-eye and X-ray eye," and "all methods and means that might serve to reveal and show the truth."

Rewriting documentary film history, Tom Gunning begins with the small detective camera, suggesting that the legacy of surveillance (Vertov's "Life Caught Unawares") has been built into the photographic apparatus from the moment of its invention. This tiny hand camera and its "documentary impulse," there from the beginning, also seems to have discovered its ideal object in the strange urban scene, in the criminal world and the "exotic slums" that invited an early imperial gaze. Further, we have confirmation that the ostensible "mission" of the documentary has historically been tinged with curiosity.

Akira Lippit's contribution to rewriting documentary history consists of a consideration of new mechanical eyes, other technologies that produce images and that *seem* to have a special relationship with the empirical world. Lippit reminds us that the year 1895 produced Röntgen's x ray as well as the Lumière brothers' motion picture camera. The "x-ray eye" that uses light to probe the invisible poses a challenge to the theoretical premises underlying the "positivist camera and its photographic referent," the hardness of evidence and the certainty of the reality that the camera constructs. The very "phenomenology of the real" is questioned by the x-ray process, he says, requiring us to ask, "What is the referent of the x ray?" and "What is x-ray reality?"

Part of the reconsideration of documentary film history must also include taking a hard look at the links between documentary form and radical politics in the spirit of Dziga Vertov. In my own essay, I begin an interrogation of the assumption that socially committed films produced in the West, from John Grierson's *Night Mail* (1936) to Julia Reichert and Jim Klein's *Union Maids* (1976), have automatically produced some kind of consciousness change that leads to activism. I argue that radical filmmaking, whether in relation to the women's movement, the labor movement, or other peoples' struggles, has not adequately considered the politicization of the spectator by visceral means. Specifically, I suggest that we look at the effects of the political documentary on the body, even consider that makers strive to produce in the spectator a "political mimicry" of the radical action portrayed on the screen.

Another aspect of this closer scrutiny of documentary aesthetics reveals that although emphasis has been placed historically on the style of shooting and cutting to produce the famous "perfect illusion of the real," there has been little or no discussion of sound in the classical documentary. In an effort to rectify this omission, Neil Lerner produces a close analysis of the sound track and in particular the Virgil Thomson musical score for Pare Lorentz's *The River* (1934). Despite the much-touted neutrality and objectivity of 1930s documentary imagery, Lerner finds that the sound track to this film carries a highly ideological message. In its instrumentation, rhythms, and melodic strains, he finds a religious subtext that betrays a southern fundamentalist point of view.

Prefacing the trouble in documentary theory and practice at large, the crisis of representation in the field of anthropology has left First World ethnographic filmmakers wondering where to turn their cameras next if they want to abstain from reproducing the Us/Them power differential that has characterized the work of classical ethnography from Robert Flaherty to Robert Gardner. Rather than an end to anthropology, this has meant a renewed effort to use the documentary camera to bridge gaps in understanding, following James Clifford's charge: "It is more than ever crucial for different peoples to form complex concrete images of one another, . . . but no sovereign scientific methodology or ethical stance can guarantee the truth of such images."[26] As contributions to the dialogue on the "new wave" of ethnographic film, three essays in this collection look at innovative camera-subject configurations. Videomaker Jenny Cool's solution to the cultural asymmetry of classic ethnographic filmmaking has been to find subjects closer to home. She describes the subjects of her tape *Home Economics* as so close in cultural proximity to herself and her colleagues that her colleagues could not imagine what she could find to study about the Antelope Valley, California, residents, who were thought to be so thoroughly "known." As Nancy Lutkehaus and Cool describe the new ethnography, it is a study of the "self via a detour through the other," and, as Michael Renov continues the discussion, that study may now begin at home. Renov's discovery of a subgenre he calls "domestic ethnography," based on a close analysis of Su Friedrich's *Sink or Swim* (1990), Sandi DuBowski's *Tomboychik* (1993), and Mindy Faber's *Delirium* (1993), retrieves works that would not have even been considered in terms of documentary theory under the classical definitions, because these works are so aesthetically eclectic. Renov singles out the "shared camera," one of the conventions of this new subgenre that is a clear violation of the aesthetic transparency as well as the traditional "subject-object relations" of the classical documentary camera. In her study of the new indigenous media, Faye Ginsburg hypothesizes that it is this very reversal of traditional positions that is at the heart of the new style that clearly abandons the old formal conventions of documentary. Ginsburg's analysis of media produced by Aboriginal Australians in defiance of First World representations of their culture reveals what might be another subgenre—"reverse ethnography"—as seen in such video work as *BabaKiueria,* in which indigenous people invert the historical roles in a humorous reenactment of colonial "first contact" by playing the parts of the white conquerors. As an example of a work that, in her analysis, belongs "equally to two cultures," *BabaKiueria* is uninterested in the old assumptions about how to study others with the use of recording devices.

It is not only traditional anthropology that is challenged in these essays but traditional feminism. Linda Williams, in her discussion of Dennis O'Rourke's *The Good Woman of Bangkok,* takes on two prohibitions: the documentary prohibition against intervention in the scene before the camera and the feminist prohibition against the voyeuristic stalking of the female subject. Filmmaker O'Rourke has abandoned any pretense of neutrality and not only intervenes in the scene but in the life of the Bangkok prostitute he photographs, first sleeping with her and then buying her a rice farm in an effort to help her find a new way of supporting herself. The surprise comes when feminist Williams champions both O'Rourke's involvement with and his objectification of the prostitute, because, she says, it is as though "staging the voyeuristic elicits resistance to it."

Eithne Johnson offers another challenge to feminist film theory in her analysis of educational self-help films and tapes on female masturbation. Anticipating the possibility that these films in which women are represented as enjoying their own bodies might be "vulnerable to the critique of pornography," she defends them on new ground. Deriving the concept of "counterporn" from Claire Johnston's definition of feminist countercinema as works that challenge the formal structure of classical narrative cinema, she advances the concept as an antidote to both feminist moralism and patriarchial assumptions about women's pleasure.

Vivian Sobchack's phenomenological approach to documentary represents a breakthrough in theories of cinematic identification as well as documentary film and video. Here, *documentary* is defined neither by its object nor by its style of shooting, but by the viewer's "attitude toward the screen." Illuminating the little-known work of Jean-Pierre Meunier, Sobchack starts from his three modes or moments: the fiction film, the documentary film, and the home movie or *film-souvenir.* As Meunier would see documentary consciousness, it is a way of "looking both *at* and *through* the screen," almost as though one were both directly experiencing the event and watching the film of it. To emphasize how it is the viewer who ultimately determines the mode, Sobchack concludes: "One viewer's fiction may be another's *film-souvenir*; one viewer's documentary, another's fiction."

Jim Moran and Mark Wolf offer new perspectives on documentary theory that challenge the assumptions underlying theories of indexicality that depend upon a conventional temporality and a positivist worldview. "What is the proper strategy for representing a dinosaur?" asks Moran. And before we dismiss this question as having nothing to do with documentary theory, he leads us to think about the problem of subjects that, although they existed long before the camera, leave indexical traces in stone. Why the antipathy between documentary and animation, he asks, when special-effects artists and computer technicians are now deeply concerned with the epistemology of the real? Like the enigma of the x ray, we are faced with a "document of the unseen but not unreal" when we look at a computer-generated reconstruction of prehistoric life.

It is the new technologies themselves that force us to rethink existing theories, says Mark Wolf. His elaboration on the concept of "subjunctive documentary," or "what would be or might have been," asks us to consider, among other things, the problem of computer-generated flight simulations and the accuracy with which they represent "real conditions." Knowing more about how digital cameras work—considering, for instance, quantization, scaling, and the significance of the pixel—we realize that the Peircian distinction between index and symbol is less and less clear. We are faced with the need to redefine indexicality completely.

Television, through the "live" broadcast, introduces temporality into its special claim to the real, adding another dimension to the question of documentary indexicality. In its attribute of "liveness," as Mark Williams describes it, television plays on both the immediacy of indexicality and the immediacy of distribution. The ultimate use of liveness is the telecast of the catastrophe, the spontaneous horrors of which lend themselves to the television medium, as Williams demonstrates in his discussion of the WKLA-TV telecast of the Nevada A-bomb test in April 1949. As he says of catastrophe telecasts, they "reaffirm, through their shock value and proximity to death, TV's distinctive access to the Real."

The "Real" returns again and again when we try to define documentary as a distinct mode, and, as Michael Renov shows in the afterword to this book, scholars have recently returned to this area of inquiry, intrigued by the abundance of questions raised by a form that is both attracted to and implicated in "the real." Perhaps we have returned because new technologies have challenged the old definitions. Or perhaps, as Renov explains, it is like Bill Nichols's term for "fascinated documentary looking" itself—it is a drive, a drive in opposition to the fiction film's scopophilia. It is an epistephilia about "epistephilia" that returns us to documentary.

◆ ───

NOTES

1. Jean-Luc Comolli and Jean Narboni, "Cinema/Ideology/Criticism," in *Movies and Methods*, vol. 1, ed. Bill Nichols (Berkeley: University of California Press, 1976), 25.
2. It is important to remember that it is the American cinema direct movement and not the French cinema verité style that Comolli and Narboni criticize in their essay. The tersest explanation of the difference in the two schools can be found in Brian Winston, "Direct Cinema: The Third Decade," in *New Challenges in Documentary*, ed. Alan Rosenthal (Berkeley: University of California Press, 1988). There he says of cinema verité, the more reflexive style: "All it has in common with the American school of 'direct cinema' is equipment" (517). My thanks to Michael Renov for this clarification.
3. One of the better examples of this argument is made by Hayden White in "The Modernist Event," in *The Persistence of History: Cinema, Television, and the Modern Event*, ed. Vivian Sobchack (New York: Routledge/American Film Institute, 1996). White discusses the docudrama as postmodern in the way it can be seen as "placing in abeyance the distinction between the real and the imaginary" (19). The uses of the terms *real* and *imaginary* in this context are his.
4. Bill Nichols, *Representing Reality: Issues and Concepts in Documentary* (Bloomington: Indiana University Press, 1991); Thomas Waugh, ed., *"Show Us Life": Toward a History and Aesthetics of Committed Documentary* (Metuchen, N.J.: Scarecrow, 1984); Julia Lesage, "The Political Aesthetics of the Feminist Documentary Film," in *Issues in Feminist Criticism*, ed. Patricia Erens (Bloomington: Indiana University Press, 1990); Brian Winston, *Claiming the Real: The Griersonian Documentary and Its Legitimations* (London: British Film Institute, 1995).
5. Judith Butler, "Contingent Foundations: Feminism and the Question of 'Postmodernism,'" in *Feminists Theorize the Political*, ed. Judith Butler and Joan W. Scott (New York: Routledge, 1992), 17.
6. André Bazin, "An Aesthetic of Reality: Neorealism," in *What Is Cinema?* vol. 2, trans. Hugh Gray (Berkeley: University of California Press, 1967), 30.
7. The reference is to Siegfried Kracauer, *Theory of Film: The Redemption of Physical Reality* (New York: Oxford University Press, 1960). But see the important recent translation of Kracauer's work that puts this earlier publication into English in a new light: Siegfried Kracauer, *The Mass Ornament: Weimar Essays*, trans. Thomas Y. Levin (Cambridge: Harvard University Press, 1995).
8. Nichols, *Representing Reality*, 28.
9. André Bazin, "The Ontology of the Photographic Image," in *What Is Cinema?* vol. 1, trans. Hugh Gray (Berkeley: University of California Press, 1971), 13.
10. Michel Foucault, *The Order of Things: An Archaeology of the Human Sciences* (New York: Random House, 1973), 29.
11. Phillip Rosen, "History of Image, Image of History: Subject and Ontology in Bazin," *Wide Angle* 9, no. 4 (1987): 10.
12. Michel de Certeau, *The Writing of History*, trans. Tom Conley (New York: Columbia University Press, 1988), 21.
13. Fatimah Tobing Rony, *The Third Eye: Race, Cinema, and the Ethnographic Spectacle* (Durham, N.C.: Duke University Press, 1996), 102.
14. Ibid.
15. See Thomas Gunning, "The Cinema of Attractions: Early Film, Its Spectator, and the Avant-Garde," *Wide Angle* 8, nos. 3–4 (1986): 63–70.
16. Neil Harris has made this point about the genuine curiosity of the late-nineteenth-century viewer, a curiosity stimulated by hoaxes and satisfied by museums, fairs, and other public attractions. See his *Cultural Excursions: Marketing Appetites and Cultural Tastes in Modern America* (Chicago: University of Chicago Press, 1990).
17. Trinh T. Minh-ha, *When the Moon Waxes Red: Representation, Gender, and Cultural Politics* (New York: Routledge, 1991), 39.
18. Claire Johnston, "Women's Cinema as Counter-Cinema," in *Notes on Women's Cinema*, ed. Claire Johnston (London: Society for Education in Film and Television, 1975), 28.
19. Judith Butler, *Bodies That Matter: On the Discursive Limits of "Sex"* (New York: Routledge, 1993), 10.
20. Dziga Vertov, "Kino-Eye," in *Kino-Eye: The Writings of Dziga Vertov*, ed. Annette Michelson, trans. Kevin O'Brien (Berkeley: University of California Press, 1984), 41.
21. For a comprehensive overview of the tradition, see Jan Ruby, "An Anthropological and Documentary Dilemma," *Journal of Film and Video* 44, nos. 1–2 (1992): 42–66.

22. Patricia R. Zimmermann, "Strange Bed-
fellows: The Legacy of Vertov and Flaherty,"
Journal of Film and Video 44, nos. 1–2 (1992):
4–8.

23. Vertov, "Kino-Eye," 84.

24. Seth Feldman, "'Cinema Weekly' and
'Cinema Truth': Dziga Vertov and the Leninist
Proportion," in Waugh, *"Show Us Life,"* 9.

25. Patricia R. Zimmermann, "Soviet Film Theory
and American Documentary," *Journal of Film
and Video* 44, nos. 1–2 (1992): 83.

26. James Clifford, *The Predicament of Culture:
Twentieth-Century Ethnography, Literature,
and Art* (Cambridge: Harvard University
Press, 1988), 23.

ELIZABETH COWIE

[1] *The Spectacle of Actuality*

Documentary film is associated with the serious. It is, in Bill Nichols's words, one of the discourses of sobriety alongside—albeit as a junior player—such discourses as science, economics, politics, education, and the law.[1] Yet, for all its seriousness, the documentary film nevertheless also involves more disreputable features of cinema usually associated with the entertainment film, namely, the pleasures and fascination of film as spectacle. In the documentary film these pleasures arise not through make-believe or fictional enactment but by the re-presentation of actuality. In recording actuality, photography and cinematography address two distinct and apparently contradictory desires. On the one hand there is a desire for reality held and reviewable for analysis as a world of materiality available to scientific and rational knowledge, a world of evidence confirmed through observation and logical interpretation. It is a desire for a symbolic or social reality ordered and produced as signification.[2] The camera eye functions here as a mastering, all-seeing view, as well as a prosthesis, an aid and supplement to vision whereby we are shown a reality that our own human perceptual apparatus cannot perceive. On the other hand there is a desire for the real not as knowledge but as image, as spectacle. Jean Baudrillard argues that "there is a kind of primal pleasure, of anthropological joy in images, a kind of brute fascination unencumbered by aesthetic, moral, social or political judgements. It is because of this that I suggest they are immoral, and that their fundamental power lies in this immorality."[3]

The interrelation of the desire for reality as knowledge and as spectacle in the emergence of photography and cinematography, together with the paradoxes and limits of these pleasures and their relation to identification, is the concern of the following discussion. It has of course been more usual to place this duality across the divide between fiction and nonfiction film, conventionally characterized by film historians as two opposing traditions arising from Georges Méliès on the one hand and Louis Lumière on the other, in which fantasy is set against reality. In contrast, I want to explore the extent to which actuality and documentary films involve us as desiring, as well as knowing, spectators.

The moral—and political—requirement to distinguish between the real and illusory is central to modern Western culture. Psychoanalysis and cinema were contemporaneous developments at the end of the nineteenth century, but while the developments of Etienne-Jules Marey and Lumière were directed toward established modernist goals of science and knowledge in relation to observable phenomena, Sigmund Freud was challenging the assumption of a simple division between the real and the imaginary as well as the correlation of illusion and fantasy as equivalent. Foundational for Freud's new therapy of psychoanalysis was his theory of the unconscious, of a division in the human subject between a domain of consciousness, and a preconscious domain of what can be recalled to consciousness through memory, and an inaccessible domain—the unconscious. The unconscious consists of the material expelled from consciousness: thoughts or wishes that are unacceptable in some way and therefore repressed. This material is not lost, but instead continues to bear on the psyche through mechanisms of return: in dreams, termed by Freud the royal road to the unconscious, and in fantasy; in slips of the tongue; and in symptoms, notably the hysterical symptoms of Freud's first patients and of the "shell-shocked" soldiers of the First World War, which are recorded in *War Neuroses: Netley, 1917, Seale Hayne Military Hospital, 1918* (Pathé, United Kingdom, 1918). This film will be a focal point for my discussion in this essay.

For the human subject, the unconscious and fantasy are psychically very real and produce effects in reality. Indeed, the contagion—as it was often perceived—of shell shock was a contingent reality threatening the war effort of allies and enemy alike while equally undermining the theoretical premises of both traditional physiological psychology and aspects of the new psychoanalysis of the Freudians. As a result of the need to treat men suffering from shell shock, psychiatric medicine in Britain and elsewhere was fundamentally challenged and transformed. Freud's view of the unconscious, however, came to have enormous significance for the understanding of the war neuroses of soldiers in the First World War, largely, Martin Stone has argued, as the result of the article by the psychologist and anthropologist W. H. Rivers, "Freud's Psychology of the Unconscious," which appeared in the *Lancet,* the main British journal of medicine, in 1917.[4] Rivers's account is, as Stone suggests, a very partial and reduced version of Freud's theories, for although he plundered psychoanalysis for its psychodynamic concepts—such as repression, the unconscious, and the notion of mental conflict—Rivers nevertheless centered his etiological account on the emotional world of the battlefield rather than tracing the origins of the hysterical and anxiety states associated with shell shock back to the patient's infantile sexual impulses. Stone also argues that it was the large number of doctors who became familiar with nervous disorders while working in army hospitals with shell shock patients that opened psychiatry to new theories, and in the 1920s several of the standard textbooks were revised to include enlarged sections on the neuroses, together with references to psychoanalysis. As a result, the theoretical orthodoxies of asylum-based psychiatry were overturned while the new forms of psychotherapy led to developments in treatment that were enshrined, finally, in the 1930 Mental Treatment Act in Britain, which promoted outpatient clinics and "voluntary" treatment.[5]

War trauma was the unrepresentable, not only for the soldier and conventional psychiatry but also for psychoanalysis, leading Freud to reorganize his view of the role of the drives and sexuality to propose his most debated and notorious concept of the death drive as an incontrovertible element of the psyche in order to account not simply for aggressivity as such but for the compulsion to repeat and for self-aggression. The French psychoanalyst Jacques Lacan subsequently extended Freud's challenge to the simple division of reality versus fantasy through a tripartite distinction: the real, the imaginary, and the symbolic. None of these terms relates straightforwardly to what is commonly termed everyday reality, and it is in his concept of the "real" that Lacan incorporates those phenomena of human suffering that Freud saw as a death drive.

The medical documentary *War Neuroses,* which is about the work in two British military hospitals in 1917 and 1918 with soldiers displaying hysterical symptoms in response to posttraumatic stress, shows, I will argue, how factual film functions as well as a document of the "real," in Lacan's sense. *War Neuroses* was made as visible evidence, as a spectacle of knowledge, that is, as a *display* of knowledge-categories organized by the discourse of psychological medicine of the time—portraying the men's physical symptoms within medical categories. Presenting a narrative of cure, the film also offers an array of visual "pleasures," both visual "attractions" and visual knowing. In contrast to the knowability of reality and its pleasures, the film also figures something that is uncommunicable in conventional language in its images of the grotesque contortions produced on the bodies of the soldiers. These recorded images constitute indexically the men's symptoms, which are now *medical* categories, and at the same time constitute a *filmic* discourse that represents to us as spectators the disturbed and disrupted minds of the soldiers. The film is therefore fully symbolic and symbolizing. But at the same time these images signify an unrepresented that is also unrepresentable—namely, the absent trauma of war presented in the symptoms of the men displayed for the camera and represented in the battle performed by some of the "cured" men. In this we can discern the repetition, replaying, and re-presenting of the subject's relation to trauma, that is, to the "real."[6] The "real" of *War Neuroses* is not in the film as represented, however, but as representing, that is, insofar as it is a process for the subject-spectator.

Just as the war neuroses demanded a reorganization of conceptual categories within psychiatry following the First World War, so I am seeking to use *War Neuroses* to demand the inclusion in our understanding of documentary film the psychical relation of the spectator—that is, the desire not only for reality represented through symbolic and social discourse, in the visible evidence *War Neuroses* presents, but also a desire for the real, that domain of a compulsive repetition and trauma that comes to be figured in this documentary.

▶ ──

Desiring Reality Re-presented

The desire for a reality held and reviewable had been articulated within science as well as the arts long before cinematography. For Louis-Jacques-Mandé Daguerre, however, the impetus that led him to develop in the daguerreotype a method of chemically recording the image of the world provided in the camera obscura, rather than reproducing it in a painted scene, involved a desire not only to reproduce a realistic view of reality but also to reproduce the spectacle and sensation of views in the real world, as his earlier dioramas had done.[7] The daguerreotype, moreover, also reproduces the evanescent quality of the diorama in its requirement that it be viewed from a certain angle and thus position of view. Only when the daguerreotype is held and viewed from this angle does the image emerge, for if turned slightly the surface appears merely as a vaguely shadowed silvery screen. The daguerreotype therefore produces a now-here, now-gone quality to the image (a quality found, too, in the painterly device of anamorphosis, where a smudge on the canvas becomes, with the next step, a skull in Holbein's *The Ambassadors*). These features suggest that Daguerre is a more important precursor of the moving pictures than Henry Fox Talbot. It is the legacy of the latter, however, that is of an epistemological realism, which theorists and critics have subsequently emphasized.[8]

With the chemical recording of the camera obscura's images, the human observer is displaced by a mechanical seer. Jean-Luc Comolli notes:

At the very same time that it is thus fascinated and gratified by the multiplicity of scopic instruments which lay a thousand views beneath its gaze, the human eye loses its immemorial privilege; the mechanical eye of the photographic machine now sees *in its place,* and in certain aspects with more sureness. The photograph stands as at once the triumph and the grave of the eye.[9]

The overturning of the classical optics of the Renaissance, and with this the decentering of the classical subject of vision, had begun well before the developments of Joseph Nicéphore Niépce, Daguerre, and Talbot. The camera obscura had been the privileged metaphor for the observer's relation to the external world, a relation in which vision is knowledge, and knowledge is seeing.[10] The human eye, however, is now shown to be a limited organ, misleading and imperfect in its observations, and human vision becomes instead a realm of the fallible. A subjectivity of sight comes to the fore at the same time and as a corollary of a heightened scientificity/objectivity of apparatus. Comolli writes:

Decentered, in panic, thrown into confusion by all this new magic of the visible, the human eye finds itself affected with a series of limits and doubts. The mechnical eye, the photographic lens, while it intrigues and fascinates, functions also as a *guarantor* of the identity of the visible with the normality of vision.[11]

Photography, then, concludes the separation of the subjective, human viewer from the new objectivity of mechanized observation.[12] Knowledge of the world is no longer equivalent to human perception. The observer of the camera obscura becomes instead the consumer of an already recorded and reproduced view. Although the "referential" is no longer a domain, a world, knowable through the physical senses and preeminently through sight, the demand for such a referentiality—and with it a realist imperative— continues to be apparent and indeed is central to the emergence of photography and cinematography, which now become, as Comolli suggests, guarantors of the real. Subjectivity is simply a hurdle to be overcome by mechanized modes of vision; thus Mary Ann Doane concludes, "Hence we are faced with the strange consequence that the cinema, as a technology of images, acts both as a prosthetic device, enhancing or expanding vision, and as a collaborator with the body's own deficiencies," for it only succeeds as an appearance of continuous movement because of the limitations of the eye.[13]

Vision may no longer be viewed as the site of understanding, but the conflation between the eye as a mechanisim of sight and the mind or brain as the location of a comprehension of the visible nevertheless remains compelling—as shown by the use of "I see" for "I understand," and its extension in the exhortation "you see" puncturing our everyday speech and by which we invoke the wish and demand for understanding from our addressees. We still want to see with our own eyes even while "knowing" the fallibility of our sense of sight. Located here is the central paradox of our perception of the world, of on the one hand the knowledge that the senses deceive and on the other hand the sense of knowledge that our bodily perceptions afford us, of knowing the world through its smells, sounds, textures, and temperatures, as well as sights. Translated as a mental understanding, this sensory knowledge becomes a representation to the mind through the work of memory-enabling cognition, that is, the matching up of this new sensory information with the learned understanding derived from previous sensory information. A gap, an aporia, exists between sensory knowledge or stimuli and sense itself. The sense of certainty of our sensory experience opens us to the disavowal of our knowledge of the limitations of our senses, of the uncertainty of their sensemaking, so that we still want to see with our own eyes even while knowing the fallibility of our sense of sight. The camera obscura, displaced as the metaphor for a centered subject of knowledge, now plays to this desire. As an apparatus of overlooking, it offers the pleasures precisely of the separation of the body as site of vision and the object of sight, presenting a panorama of the seen world, or so it seems as one gazes upon the curved dish of its screen in which friends, relatives, or strangers stroll, unaware of one's look.[14]

The fixing of such a scene through photography expands the fantasy arising here, of reality beyond oneself but graspable and available to be held in an image. The pleasure of the visual and the desire for the "real" were joined directly with the science of the visible in the stereoscope,[15] which is perhaps a closer antecedent for documentary film than the monocular photograph.[16] The stereoscope is, however, paradoxical in its mode of representation. It does reproduce the vision of the human eye very closely, unlike the photograph and cinema, and the realism and sense of tactility of the three-dimensional stereoscope image can be very vivid.[17] The viewer nevertheless initially has to concentrate hard on bringing into focus the stereoscopic scene, while the eyes held close to the glasses are excluded from any peripheral vision beyond the encased images. As a result, the viewer of the stereoscope is also made fully conscious of the means of production of the viewing process itself. It is here that, Jonathan Crary has argued, the observer is "disciplined," subject to the viewing process effected by the apparatus.[18] The stereoscope thus fails to be fully phantasmagorical or "properly" illusory.[19]

The disjuncture of the stereograph lies not only in its three-dimensionality but also and in some ways more strikingly in the lack of a single point of view, of a focused scene in the photographic or painterly sense. Instead the eye must roam the view, so that it never fully converges as a homogeneous view. The appearance of three-dimensionality, whether in a reproduced scene in the stereograph or in the world directly apprehended, requires a cognitive process—primarily of memory—in order for the spatial relations to be understood. What the stereoscope makes apparent, therefore, as the viewer attempts to bring the scene together, is the very incoherence of vision. It is thus indeed the case that, as Crary argues, each observer is transformed "into simultaneously the magician and the deceived."[20] And this is the very structure of disavowal described by Freud, in which the subject knows very well the truth but all the same believes its opposite.[21] The process of recording both fulfills that wish and brings with it the question of how far the mechanism of recording nevertheless intervenes on reality to transform—and pervert—it.

The problem or possibility that the image lies as well as tells the truth is an issue of theology and philosophy such that it might be hazarded that this dilemma posed by the photographic image is the locus of ambivalent desire—for the true image and for the image that truly shows us things as we wish them to be. It is as well, of course, the locus of anxiety and thus of a repeated returning. Documentary films as recorded actuality therefore figure both in the discourse of science, as a means of obtaining the knowable in the world, and in the discourse of desire—that is, the wish to know the truth of the world, represented by the question invariably posed to actuality film, Is this really so, is it true? In that question is another, namely, the question of, finally, Do I exist? A question that is addressed to an other from whom we seek and desire a response. This is the questioning that psychoanalysis has sought to understand.

▶
_____

The Pleasures of the Spectacle of Reality

Spectacle is part of a long tradition of popular forms, such as the circus or the magical acts of traveling fairs.[22] It is thus opposed to the scientific; the "sight" is viewed not for knowledge but for sensation, which has increasingly been associated with the nonintellectual. But spectacle is also a feature of the high culture of the upper and middle classes in the West, exemplified in the institution in the eighteenth century of the "grand tour" in Europe as the necessary completion of a Northern European young man's education, whereby the viewing of the sights themselves and their visual appreciation was the mark of a gentleman. At the very least, spectacle is a feast for the eyes. We consume the world through our look, appropriating it as meaningful; pleasured by its colors and shapes, we nevertheless form it into social or philosophical meanings or aesthetic experience. Sight-seeing later became a commonplace for the bourgeoisie, whether of objects, places, or peoples in the nineteenth century.[23] The expansion of visuality in the nineteenth century through mechanical reproduction opened up new vistas for visionary pleasures but at the same time posed the dilemma of vision for spectacle or for knowledge, a division between a subjective and experiential engagement with the seen as opposed to an objective and intellectual appraisal.

Spectacle, a sheer pleasure in looking, is typically cited as the key and initial element in cinema's popularity and fascination for audiences, rather than, and in opposition to, narrative. In *The Struggle for the Film*, Hans Richter presents a version of the "urban myth" about the responses of audiences to the first projected films. His story is set in 1923 and involves a Jewish emigrant to Palestine:

> He had few possessions, only an old projector and a single ancient film. With these he installed himself in the poorest Arab quarter of Jerusalem. His film ran for several months. The audience never failed him; indeed, he noticed many faces that returned again and again.
>
> One day by mistake the last reel was run first. Surprisingly, there were no complaints. Even the "regulars" failed to stir. This intrigued the cinema owner. He wanted to find out if anyone objected, and if not why not, so he ran all the reels in any order. No one seemed to mind. "Why?," he wondered in some amazement, and asked one of his oldest customers. It turned out that the Arabs had never grasped the plot, even when the film was shown in the right order. It was clear that they only went to the cinema because there one could see people walking, horses galloping, dogs running.[24]

The foundational role of spectacle for cinematic pleasure was quickly disavowed, however. Instead the pleasures of cinema have become defined as narrative and the standard account of film history is that the thrill of the spectacle of actuality in the new form of imaging gave way to the pleasures of narrative in the fiction film and its more successfully illusionistic world. In Crary's terms, the fiction film is more fully phantasmagorical as— especially in American cinema—the processes of production become hidden in order to sustain more effectively the illusion of a real world up there on the screen, complete and whole and integral. In contrast, the actualities of early cinema invariably betrayed their processes of recording, making the viewer aware of the camera's look, which has preceded her or his own, revealing its "disciplining" of the spectator. [25] Tom Gunning has described early film as a "cinema of attractions" characterized by a showing rather than a telling.[26] Such showing is marked through a display or performance that acknowledges the viewer, notably through the recurring employment of looks at and thus direct address to the camera, and hence by extension to the anticipated future film audience, which disturbs the establishment of narrative illusion. In acted film this might create a complicity of gaze in the sharing of a secret or a joke with the spectator, who is thus drawn into the fictional narration, albeit not as a narrative illusion. In the early actualities "showing" is not quite the same. The look at us so often recorded in actualities may be one or all of three different looks—a gaze at the camera as an extraordinary machine and a wish to see it functioning, or a gaze at the cameraperson, or a look at an imagined future audience. This last look is less likely in the earliest actualities, but it is certainly quickly a feature of actuality filming, as marked by the tendency of people to wave at the camera—a tendency especially disconcerting in World War I film footage of what we would at first perceive as lines of forlorn and desperate refugees walking past the camera, but who, when they suddenly turn and smile or wave at us, transform their relation to us and disrupt our understanding of their victimhood.[27] The disjunction arises not only because the spectator becomes aware of her or his look as well as of becoming the—imagined— object of another's look, but also because such a look rivals the spectacle that is the "topic" of the actuality, for the camera's gaze is narratively undercut when all the bystanders appear quite uninterested in the scene behind them, which we are being shown, and instead are avidly watching the camera. The look back at the camera disturbs the actuality shot by reversing the object of fascination from inside the scene to outside. What must be distinguished here is not an opposition between spectacle and narrative illusionism, but one between a filmic pictorialization—whether acted or actuality—that solicits and addresses the spectator's look for whom it "performs" and a spectacle that confronts or surprises the spectator in her or his looking.[28]

The spectacle of reality involves an entertaining of the eye through form and light in a showing, and an entertaining of the mind in the showing of something known either as familiar or in a new or spectacular way, or something not yet known that thereby becomes the known. The world shown in the actuality of documentary film is presented as knowable, and the terms of its knowability are organized by the film, not by reality. The scenes of reality are posited for our view by their selection, framing, and combination; the spectator is invited to look and, even without titles or voice-over, thereby to understand the seen. The particular knowledge of a documentary film confirms the knowableness in general of the world. What is conjoined here is the pleasure that Freud called "scopophilia," or the satisfaction of the wish to see, and that, as curiosity, is closely associated with the wish to know, or epistephilia, together with an identification as the subject of knowledge.[29]

Curiosity is also central to the scientist's project of knowing the world, as well as to the scientific use of optical devices, including film, in order to "see" what the human eye cannot. In the work of Eadweard Muybridge and Marey, in their search to record physiological movement imperceptible to the human eye, optical devices became prostheses for human sight, enabling us to really know the *moving* object of view, which for Muybridge was especially the human body. The highly acclaimed British series *The Secrets of Nature*, filmed in the 1920s, which used microscope and time-lapse cinematography to reveal the unfolding processes of nature, equally but less pruriently satisfied such curiosity. In curiosity, the desire to see is allied with the desire to know through seeing what cannot normally be seen, that is, what is normally veiled or hidden from sight. Of course, when the desire to see what is normally hidden or forbidden is associated with pleasure rather than science, that desire is more usually termed voyeurism. Two processes can be discerned here. First is the lifting of the veil and the overturning of the physical barrier to sight, of that which prevents knowledge, with all the violence this can imply. Desire is here attached to the barrier rather than the hidden, which therefore cannot wholly be distinguished from nonphysical barriers, namely, moral and social prohibitions. Second, there is the desire to see what is hidden and the knowledge thereby afforded. What may be desired in this coming to know of the hidden is the familiar, the already known, as in the repeated viewing of the now-familiar but still forbidden body of the woman/mother of voyeurism. Alternatively, there is the pleasure and wish to see/be shown the unfamiliar. In documentary films the unfamiliar of the seen has been associated with its sensationalism, as a "cinema of atttractions," presenting the exotic and the horrific, as well as the bizarre and unusual, including the erotics of the sexually strange of other cultures and peoples.[30] Curiosity here implies a seeing without the subject itself being seen or being the object of inquiry, involving a fantasy of mastery. Such pleasure is clearly afforded by documentary film, notably—as has been widely discussed—in the "observational" film, where, as a "fly on the wall," the spectator/camera intrudes or roams with impunity (depending on how one evaluates this) through the scene.[31] This pleasure in overlooking and overhearing the scene is heightened whenever an action not normally seen in public is shown in a film, or when someone exposes her or his feelings or thoughts on film accidentally or without apparent premeditation, which we are therefore led to read as "genuine." Such moments may also be comic or embarrassing and, when caught on home video, have become the material for television comedy shows. A version of

ELIZABETH COWIE

such shows in Britain in the 1960s was called *Candid Camera*; the show currently broadcast is now more accurately titled *You've Been Framed*.

▶ ——————————————————————————————————

Identifying in Reality

Documentaries invoke and require identification—we must identify their facts and their meanings, and we must come into position as addressees of these meanings. It is here—between cognition and communication—that the psychical engagement summarized conventionally by the term *identifi- cation* arises. Identification in the cinema is not all of a piece, however; rather, it involves a number of distinct psychical and cinematic processes.

Cinema produces both a subjection of objects to its gaze and a subjec- tion of the spectator to a gazing that is separate from it and that has gone before the spectator's look to organize the space and the seen. But in the process and time of projection the spectator can take up the position of the camera, adopting its look as her or his own and thus participate as a seeing subject who controls and possesses what is shown. Walter Benjamin, in 1936, commented, "The audience's identification with the actor is really an identification with the camera. Consequently the audience takes the posi- tion of the camera."[32] In documentary film a key device for such identifica- tion has been the "roving" camera, often handheld, which gives the viewer the feeling of being an observer, of "seeing for oneself," hence the term *direct* or *observational* documentary, with all its possible scopophilic plea- sures, as noted earlier.

What is seen is taken to be knowledge, for documentary—rather than simply actuality—film is associated with the serious, and its spectator is posited as a subject of knowledge. Aligned with the controlling discourse of the titles or voice-over within the documentary film, or with the documen- tary investigator who may figure directly in the film, we identify with the "other" of knowledge, a position of mastery. The spectator, however, may take up the position not, or not only, of the discovery of knowledge, in an identification *with* the scientist, but of coming into the knowledge *of* the sci- entist, and thereby to know what has already been organized as knowledge, so that through the documentary I become, or am affirmed as, a member of the knowledgeable culture, identifying with the place of address as the site of a coming-to-know of knowledge. One pleasure, therefore, of the "infor- mation" documentary film is not an identification with the other of knowl- edge but the pleasure of the recognition that the other knows and thus I can know, together with or even alternatively, the reassurance that, for example, science or scientists know, and they know for me.[33]

The emplacement of the viewing subject is also secured by the devices—and pleasures—of the "novelistic" upon which the documentary draws. Stephen Heath and Gillian Skirrow have argued that, as in the novel—the initial apparatus for the novelistic—in the documentary film reality is made over into a story involving "little dramas of making sense in which the viewer as subject is carried along—in which, indeed, the individual becomes 'the viewer,' the point of view of the sense of the programme."[34] The novelizing documentary presents a narrative of cause and effect, creating the security of facts over the terror of fantasy. Verisimilitude is therefore central for the documentary film—just as much as and perhaps more than for the fiction film. The world presented must be believable, it must be like what we expect the world to be in order for the film to sustain our belief in its claim to reality.

Documentary film cannot as easily construct or draw upon the classical devices for verisimilitude in fiction film, namely, narrative causality and psychological motivation. It can, however, unlike the fiction film, establish the terms for the believability of the places and people it shows through the authority and knowledge of a narrator. A greater conviction, and pleasure, is achieved if the documentary can in some measure enable viewers to "discover" this world for themselves, for—as noted earlier—by taking the "observing" camera's gaze as their own, viewers can feel that they are discovering the space and place of the documentary scene themselves. But the mise-en-scène and its social actors will appear to be unrealistic if they do not confirm or conform to the expectations of the viewers. The poor, for example, must appear properly poor in whatever way an audience may currently recognize poverty. Reality—such as the reality of poverty—is coded, it is read through conventionally understood signs. The meaning of reality is therefore variable, dependent on the (changeable) conventions for recognizing poverty, which itself is a socially constructed category.[35] The "believability" of the documentary's world—its verisimilitude—is produced when that world and its people appear recognizable, familiar, and thus—in some sense—as the same as what we already know. The documentary film therefore presents the knowable world not only or necessarily in order to enable us to know the world as the new, but also—and perhaps more often—to know the world as familiar, to find again our known objects.

Identification also involves taking up the position of the social actors presented by the documentary so that we are moved by their stories as if they were our own. The willingness of members of the public to be filmed—whether in more ostensibly serious observational films or in shows such as You've Been Framed—as well as our pleasure in the confessions and humiliations exposed attest to our wish not only to see and hear but also to be heard and seen, for we may identify with the other as heard and as seen in place of ourselves. There arises therefore the pleasure of a certain exhibitionism, though this may also include a certain masochism in thus exposing oneself, while at the same time there is a pleasurable separation, a sadistic pleasure in *not* being the social actor presented.

The close-up, now a ubiquitous feature of documentary as a result of developments in telescopic lenses, and without even the speech of the "character," can lead us to identify on the basis of being what we see. This is the identification involved in what has been termed *infantile transitivism*, in which the small child, seeing another fall and, hurt, start to cry, will also start to cry though not in any pain.[36] Although only momentary, this identification supports the adoption of the social actors in the documentary as stand-ins for ourselves within the scene. Together with the image, the speech of social actors in the documentary, whether direct to camera or in relation to an interlocutor within the film, is central to producing identification. The incorporation of the interview and the "overheard" speech of observational documentary have been major elements in the success of documentary since the 1960s, especially in television documentary. Interviews or moments of speech to camera—however scripted and selected they may be—enable real people to tell their own stories, to give their own accounts of events. It is through this that documentary presents "point of view," that is, the subjective and internal thoughts and feelings of its social actors. Through the interview we can be brought to share their view of the events, to put ourselves in their place(s) in the(ir) world, which the film is showing us, and thus to empathize with them.

A British news broadcast on the war in former Yugoslavia in 1992, for example, included a short documentary item involving an interview with a refugee. In the film, a Croatian housewife, describing her experiences, speaks tearfully about the freezer full of food—her homegrown or homemade produce—that was abandoned as she and her family fled their homes. This detail can draw us to identify, to have the same feeling of loss, not because we are the same, or have had the same experience, but because we can take up the same position as her in relation to loss. The full freezer is a sign of plenty, and of her and perhaps our role—male or female—as provider; but its provisions are now spoiled or stolen and the sign that supported that identity is lost. Moreover, in its place there arises the image of a usurper enjoying what is rightfully hers/ours. Identification, empathy, arises rather than simply pity or sympathy, for we become engaged on our own behalf in the injustice, with all the grief and anger we might feel if we had lost what sustains our identity as providers. Identification here is with her position in a narrative of loss, and our feelings are not, or not only, for the

Croatian housewife but for ourselves and our own losses, whether actually experienced or just feared as a potential threat.

This identification is not the result of a judgment, but in order to be sustained it will require the support of evidence of the believability of the social actor—for example, that the housewife was unjustly deprived. Here again verisimilitude is central, now in the further sense of causality and motivation for the circumstances and actions of social actors. The people in the documentary must appear properly deserving, to be properly victims and also innocent victims insofar as their poverty or starvation is not caused by themselves. Thus, for example, the couple seeking help in order to have a child, to be rehoused, or whatever, must be justified in some way in order that we can empathize, that is, so that we can have such a wish for them. The woman who is seeking in vitro fertilization treatment may seem less deserving if she is unmarried or already the mother of five children. *Their* wish, in order to become *our* wish—that is, in order to evoke our identification—must be "reasonable."

Documentaries afford us another pleasure in identifying, for through them we can engage in situations in which we feel for others in order to assure/reassure ourselves that we are caring people. We thus fulfill a certain ego ideal demand that we are "nice," that we can be touched by human suffering, by the causes and claims of others.[37] For this we require victims, the less fortunate, for whom we can feel.[38] Again, they must be properly helpless, as well as voiceless, or at least voicing only their plight, their suffering, and must not make any overt demands for help. Nor should they be able to provide a sophisticated analysis of their circumstances and its causes, or else they will rival the spectator as knowing subject.

▶

Desire and the Real

The desire for the "real" is the desire for some little bit of absence by which the possibility of presence is affirmed while yet restating loss, absence itself. In *War Neuroses* this "real" is not the war and the death and destruction it wrought, but the *unrepresentability* of war for the subjects of the film, the "shell-shocked" soldiers, and the viewing subjects of the film. What then does Lacan refer to in this concept of the real, and how is it distinguished from his other two concepts, the imaginary and the symbolic? None of these terms maps onto our commonsense notion of everyday reality. Instead, through these distinctions Lacan seeks to show how the human subject, the ego, emerges in a relation of interiority to exteriority through which the child represents itself to itself and to its others—its parents. It is the middle term, the "imaginary," that names the organizing process for this, the moment when the child comes to experience itself as an object distinct and separate from the other significant objects in its life, the mother's breast or bottle and the milk it obtains, and its excretions. Lacan terms this the "mirror stage," using the notion of the mirror image to describe the way the child comes to identify itself with an image of itself, a body image traced by the mirror reflection or by the words and touch of its carers. It is the moment of the precipitation of an I of the ego in the recognizing/identifying with the image as "that's me," but whereby the image is now both the child itself and other to it as an image *of* itself. The child *imagines* itself. Before this, the human infant has been a bundle of experiences of satisfactions and needs. The satisfaction of need—of, for example, hunger—arises externally, whereas the need as such arises internally. The child's cry of discomfort as a result of its hunger becomes a call of demand to be fed when the child connects the sense of satisfaction obtained by suckling with the activities of those caring for it. This call of demand inaugurates fantasy, the imagining of the future satisfaction that will be obtained when the breast/milk arrives, and it inaugurates signification, for the child communicates by its call and it does so in relation to something experienced as absent and that the child wishes to have made present to it—the breast/milk. Retrospectively, the domain of need becomes the "real," as the before of the fantasying of the object of satisfaction in the imaginary. It is therefore quite material, but also unrepresented. In fantasying, the child is representing the object to itself and to the other—the mother—through its cry, which thereby designates the absence of the breast to the child and its demand for it to be made present again. In contrast, the "real" involves absolute and unmediated deprivations experienced as need; it also thereby involves as well absolute satisfactions. The infant is not yet split by an apprehension of itself as needy and satisfied; it simply is either needy or satisfied. It is therefore also prey alternately to annihilation and to bliss, to *jouissance,* as Lacan terms this. In the imaginary the subject demands and thus imagines/fantasizes/represents a possible satisfaction. But, while the breast/milk will satisfy the physical need, the mental relation to demand now established is never fully met; that is, the mental image of need—and therefore of loss and deprivation—is assuaged only at this moment and not forever. Nevertheless, through fantasy the child can imagine things otherwise, and although its satisfactions will always be partial, it thereby subdues the terror of unrepresentable loss, of annihilating deprivation. It is by imagining things otherwise that the child engages with the external world, to which it poses its demands and which, later, it seeks to make respond to its demands. Fantasy covers over loss and absence. The "imaginary" is not simply the domain of fantasy, however, but of social action and interaction—reality in fact.[39] In the "symbolic," Lacan's third element in his tripartite division, the subject's relation to its losses is transformed by its acceptance of loss as an absolute principle. Whether termed castration or lack, what must be apprehended is lack in the Other, and not just lack in the subject itself; in the symbolic the subject identifies as lacking, as at some level forever sundered from the possibility of absolute satisfaction. The symbolic is the social law as it organizes our relations and interrelations of desire—that is, our relations of everyday reality.

For Lacan the apprehension of the "real" is the encounter with the contingent, impossible element of reality that is senseless, that is, unapprehendable as signifying.[40] It is the confrontation with moments in recorded actuality, whether in film or the photograph and stereograph, that separate out from the continous scene, like curdled milk, and somehow undercut the "isness" of the image with a questioning "is it." The givenness of reality and our look that finds and possesses the world through our images is suddenly addressed as such.

▶

Documentary Realities

The desire for reality represented as knowable and the desire for the "real," an absence by which presence is assured yet also questioned, is made clear in *War Neuroses,* which presents the spectator with an encounter with the scientific real, with the novelistic in its stories of cure, and with the realism of the specular figured in its reenacted battle scene. The film was made under the supervision of Dr. A. F. Hurst (later Sir Arthur Hurst) and Dr. J. L. Symns and produced by Pathé Frères. A silent documentary, the auditory is absent from its system of representation, although it retains language in written titles, while the organization of its images and text present an illustration, a demonstration, of a process and an argument—the cure of shell-shocked servicemen invalided home from the trenches of the battlefront in Europe.

The film shows the servicemen displaying a variety of kinds and degrees of shell shock, in particular paralysis of limbs or loss of sight where no organic cause is evident—that is, hysterical conversion symptoms.[41] The term *war neuroses* refers to both the hysterical symptoms shown in the film and more generalized conditions of chronic anxiety, sleeplessness, and nightmares. The first types of symptoms were most typically exhibited by the ordinary soldiers, and it is they who are shown in the film; the latter types of symptoms were experienced by officers and are of course less easy to document visually.[42] The film documents the physical symptoms in moving images in the tradition and conventions established by the French neurologist Jean-Martin Charcot, who displayed the hysterical symptoms of his patients at Salpêtrière from 1892 in a series of photographs. (It was with Charcot that Freud himself had trained.) The film thus functions as evidence (it continues to be shown to medical students) of the physical symptoms of the men and the nature of their paralysis and motor incapacity. The film also shows the alleviation of these symptoms following the use of techniques of suggestion as well as physical therapies, demonstrating the success of treatment through a "before and after" form of presentation.[43] It is thus also historical evidence of the discourses of psychiatry of the time, both of the modes of determining the etiology of disease and of the changing discourse of psychiatry in its incorporation of a psychological approach in the use of suggestion and thus seeing the men's symptoms—precisely, war *neuroses*—as the result of mental rather than physical or neurological factors.[44] (But, curiously and regrettably, the film does not show the process of suggestion used with the soldiers.)

The film incorporates the novelistic in its story of cure, which serves to narrate both the story of the doctors who cure and the stories of the servicemen themselves. We are shown Private Meek, aged twenty-three, in a wheelchair, oblivious to his paralysis (still 1),[45] whom we next see walking and supervising basket making, his prewar craft. We see Private Preston, aged nineteen, with amnesia, word blindness, and word deafness except to the word at the sound of which he scrambles under the bed (stills 2 and 3). Other men with various disabilities and symptoms are shown, including facial spasm, hysterical dancing gait, swaying movement and nose wiping tic, and hand contracture persisting thirty-five months after a wound near elbow. Still 4 shows two men both compulsively talking in speeches with hysterical gait, the younger man unaware that he is mimicking the older man. Still 5 shows the latter now walking normally, reading from a book. Stills 6, 7, and 8 show a case of "hysterical pseudo-pseudohypertrophic muscular paralysis," in which the man is crippled by his fixed arched back—seen seminaked in the first two scenes and later fully dressed, cured. The men are subsequently seen cured, walking, talking, and no longer convulsed by muscular spasms. A number of scenes then show the men on the hospital farm, digging and plowing. A narrative world is thus introduced of work and of the lives to which the men can return, healthy. Comedy is introduced as well with the private who, though now cured, still cannot dig properly—as we are shown—and who instead becomes the hospital librarian, for as a civilian he had been a bookseller. The film's medical account of cure is followed by scenes of celebration as the men prepare

Still 1.

Still 2.

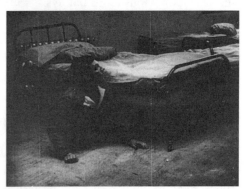

Still 3.

Still 4.

Still 5.

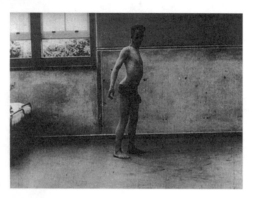

Still 6.

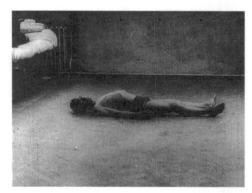

Still 7.

Still 8.

Still 9.

Still 10.

Still 11.

Still 12.

Still 13.

Still 14.

food for a party, constructing an oven in which to roast a whole pig (stills 9–11).[46]

The film's coda, presenting a reenactment for the camera by the newly cured men of a trench battle, implies the successful abreaction of the trauma of shell shock (stills 12–14). At the same time it displays to medical colleagues, to the War Office, and to the military authorities in charge of the hospitals the effectiveness of the treatments shown. The film's visible evidence functioned, therefore, for the discourses of psychiatric medicine and for governmental agencies, not only the War Office but also the Ministry of Pensions. The curing of the men was vital to the national interest not so much in relation to the war effort, for most of the men would not return to active military service, but in relation to the cost of medical care for the men and in relation to public morale and concern for relatives suffering shell shock, as well as in relation to postwar costs of disability pensions. During the war two hundred thousand men were discharged from service as a result of disability due to war neuroses, and at least eighty thousand shell shock cases passed through army hospitals. The development of outpatient facilities after the war was a direct response to the flood of more than a hundred thousand cases of former servicemen experiencing a range of mental and physical symptoms of war neurosis, which reached a peak in 1922. The Ministry of Pensions was forced to set up more than a hundred treatment centers in an effort to cope with the situation, and even as late as 1939, on the eve of the Second World War, the state was still paying out two million pounds a year to victims of war neuroses.[47]

The military reenactment presented in the film's coda is striking for its successful filmic realism—that is, verisimilitude—in portraying a battle. For example, it carefully creates the effect of smoke trails from falling mortar shells, although many of those used in the First World War produced no such smoke trail, making bombardment difficult to portray visually in film. This poses questions as to the extent to which conventions for the representation of such scenes were already established, for example, by *The Battle of the Somme*, released in August 1916, which itself has been seen as drawing upon the battle scenes in Griffith's *Birth of a Nation* (1915).[48] At the same time, *War Neuroses* constitutes an extraordinary document of remembering by the formerly shell-shocked infantrymen. The men enact themselves as soldiers moving out of trenches to attack the enemy under shell fire; they thus play out the scene of trauma that had caused their bodies to act outside of their intellectual knowledge and control—producing their hysterical symptoms. The unconscious is figured by its absence—the battle is a conscious act for the camera—just as it was absent in the medical documentation of their bodily symptoms. The reenactment is an enactment of their cure. The horror of their war experiences is signified in a performance of *successful* soldiering, in contrast to the documenting of the signifying of the horror of war in the hysterical symptoms the men had earlier displayed. Thus precisely because it is *fictionally* enacted, the *reality* of war is given representation. At the same time, while the "real" of trauma remains absent, it is figured in the picturing of cure that is the mimetic double of the source of the disorder—the battle. Two knowledges jostle side by side: the *before* of the men's traumatization through war that is represented *after* as cured in the enacted battle. This acted battle now successfully endured produces an oscillation between two realities, for the cure never fully displaces its cause—the war—which itself is used to signify the cure. The "after" of symbolization never fully displaces the "before" of the "real," however. War is here not only a documentary reality; it also functions metaphorically to figure the scene of a psychological encounter for the men—it is a metaphor of the trauma of the "real." This *mock* battle serves terrifyingly well, therefore, to demonstrate the relation of the real and the symbolic whereby the "before" of the "real" is the *effect* and not the cause of the "after" of symbolization, namely, war as a product of the civilized democracies of Europe.

NOTES

1. Bill Nichols, *Representing Reality: Issues and Concepts in Documentary* (Bloomington: Indiana University Press, 1991), 3–4. Nichols argues that "these systems assume they have instrumental power; they can and should alter the world itself, they can effect action and entail consequences." Such discourses are opposed to the world of make-believe; instead, they assume a relation to reality that is direct and transparent. "Documentary, despite its kinship, has never been accepted as a full equal" (3–4).

2. This is not the same as desiring to know the true functioning of social reality, for if, as Slavoj Žižek argues, "we come to 'know too much,' to pierce the true functioning of social reality, this reality would dissolve itself. This is probably the fundamental dimension of 'ideology': ideology is not simply 'false consciousness,' an illusory representation of reality, it is rather this reality itself which is already to be conceived of as 'ideological.'" *The Sublime Object of Ideology* (London: Verso, 1989), 22.

3. Jean Baudrillard, *The Evil Demon of Images*, trans. Paul Patton and Paul Foss (Sydney: Power Institute of Fine Arts, University of Sydney, 1987), 28. Evil and immorality are invoked not in relation to morality versus sinfulness, but in a Manichaean opposition of rational and irrational (43).

4. I am drawing here on Martin Stone's excellent reevaluation of British psychiatry and the development of modern psychiatric practices as a result of the unprecedented medical requirements of the war neuroses of soldiers in "Shellshock and the Psychologists," in *The Anatomy of Madness: Essays in the History of Psychiatry,* ed. Roy Porter, William F. Bynum, and Michael Shepherd (Cambridge: Cambridge University Press, 1985), 242–71.

5. Ibid., 244.

6. Hal Foster, in his discussion of repetition in Andy Warhol's works, describes the paradoxical role of the real: "Somehow in these repetitions, then, several contradictory things occur at the same time: a warding away of traumatic significance *and* an opening out to it, a defending against traumatic affect *and* a producing of it." *The Return of the Real* (Cambridge: MIT Press, 1996), 132.

7. Daguerre first established himself as a scene designer and was famous for the realistic spectacle he portrayed through his sets. He later constructed the diorama—a room entered through a dark corridor in which was displayed painted scenes on transparent cloth that, as a result of the manipulation of light, appeared to change from day to night or sun to storm. By contrast, Henry Fox Talbot recounts that he was drawn to discover a means by which to chemically record the image produced by the camera obscura as a result of frustration with his efforts to record the image by his own hand. I am grateful to Jon Carritt for pointing out the connections among Daguerre's work in the theater, his dioramas and his painting, and his development of the daguerreotype.

8. In the context of cinema the desire for reality re-presented has been described most forcefully in the writings of André Bazin: "Only a photographic lens can give us the kind of image of the object that is capable of satisfying the deep need man has to substitute for it something more than a mere approximation, a kind of decal or transfer. The photographic image is the object itself, the object freed from the conditions of time and space that govern it. No matter how fuzzy, distorted, or discolored, no matter how lacking in documentary value the image may be, it shares, by virtue of the very process of its becoming, the being of the model of which it is the reproduction; it *is* the model." *What Is Cinema?* vol. 1, trans. Hugh Gray (Berkeley: University of California Press, 1967), 14.

9. Jean-Luc Comolli, "Machines of the Visible," in *The Cinematic Apparatus*, ed. Stephen Heath and Teresa de Lauretis (New York: St. Martin's, 1980), 123.

10. As Jonathan Crary has noted in his discussion of the emergence of a new scientific account of the optics of the eye and its transformation of the place of subjectivity: "But whether it is Berkeley's divine signs of God arrayed on a diaphanous plane, Locke's sensations 'imprinted' on a white page, or Leibniz's elastic screen, the eighteenth-century observer confronts a unified space of order, unmodified by his or her own sensory and physiological apparatus, on which the contents of the world can be studied and compared, known in terms of a multitude of relationships." *Techniques of the Observer* (Cambridge: MIT Press, 1993), 55.

11. Comolli, "Machines of the Visible," 123–24.

12. It is this split that Bazin values, for by encountering the objectivity of the photograph human vision can be brought to see anew, to see again, what convention and daily cares cause to be overlooked. *What Is Cinema?* 15.

13. Mary Ann Doane, "Technology's Body: Cinematic Vision in Modernity," *Differences: A Journal of Feminist Cultural Studies* 5, no. 2 (1993): 5.

14. I am referring here to the large installations

at seaside resorts and spectacular locations in which several persons at a time could enter and view the reflected images of the scenes and people outside.

15. Unlike photography, the stereoscope was the direct development of scientists. Invented by Charles Wheatstone, it was developed by Sir David Brewster with the aim of democratizing knowledge of real phenomena and opposing illusory magic. Crary, *Techniques of the Observer*, 133.

16. Viewers might be large upright boxes containing a series of cards that could be rotated in front of the binocular lenses, or they might be smaller, handheld viewers on the model of opera glasses.

17. The contemporary American writer Oliver Wendell Holmes, inventor of the Holmes stereoscopic viewer, presented an enthusiastic case for the stereograph: "The first effect of looking at a good photograph through the stereoscope is a surprise such as no painting ever produced. The mind feels its way into the very depths of the picture. The scraggy branches of a tree in the foreground run out at us as if they would scratch our eyes out. The elbow of a figure stands forth so as to make us almost uncomfortable. Then there is such a frightful amount of detail, that we have the same sense of infinite complexity which Nature gives us." "The Stereoscope and the Stereograph," *Atlantic Monthly*, 1859, reprinted in *Classic Essays on Photography*, ed. Alan Trachtenberg (New Haven: Leete's Island,1980), 77.

18. There is in Crary a nostalgia for a lost possibility of embodied visuality when he writes of the triumph of modernism as a domain of the machinery of the spectacle that depends "on the denial of the body, its pulsings and phantasms, as the ground of vision." (*Techniques of the Observer*, 136.) Modernity, having enabled a subjectivity of vision to emerge through embodying the seer, rationalizes it through measurement and colonizes this new space of "subjectivity" for its own visionary disciplining. For in the "dissolution of the boundaries that had kept the subject as an interior domain qualitatively separated from the world," new forms of power also arose such that "modernization demanded that this last retreat be rationalized" (148). The stereoscope for Crary exemplifies this rationality and disciplining while also displaying it, unlike cinema. Yet "this last retreat" is itself a feature of the modern that comes into existence only because of the discourse of rationalism, which must pose a nonrational or irrational beyond itself.

19. Ibid., 132. Crary argues that the stereoscope was displaced by photography, "a form that preserved the referential illusion more fully than anything before it. Photography de-

feated the stereoscope as a mode of visual consumption as well because it recreated and perpetuated the notion that the 'free' subject of the camera obscura was still viable" (133). This does not seem to have been the case, however. Reese V. Jenkins notes that although the popularity of stereographs and stereoscopes declined in the United States during the late 1870s and early 1980s, it revived strongly with the introduction of mass-production methods. He cites the popularity of these forms as continuing until at least 1914, well after the emergence of cinema. *Images and Enterprise: Technology and the American Photographic Industry, 1839–1925* (Baltimore: Johns Hopkins University Press, 1975), 60.

20. Crary, *Techniques of the Observer*, 133.

21. The concept of disavowal was developed by Freud in his analysis of fetishism; see Sigmund Freud, "Fetishism" (1921), in *The Standard Edition of the Complete Psychological Works of Sigmund Freud*, vol. 21, ed. and trans. James Strachey (London: Hogarth, 1974).

22. It is also central to performative popular forms, such as carnivals and religious processions.

23. The visual as spectacle was also central to discourses of the sublime in the eighteenth century, both in relation to an aesthetic experience of landscape and in relation to the represented in art. What is invoked in the notion of the sublime is, in contrast to the beautiful, the power of the image or the seen, which is experienced as awesome or terrifying. It is so insofar as it is a sensible experience that lies outside sense or meaning. Edmund Burke, *A Philosophical Enquiry into the Origin of Our Ideas of the Sublime and the Beautiful*, ed. Adam Phillips (Oxford: Oxford University Press, 1990); Immanuel Kant, *Critique of Judgement*, trans. Werner S. Pluhar (Indianapolis: Hackett, 1987).

24. Hans Richter, *The Struggle for the Film: Towards a Socially Responsible Cinema* (Aldershot: Scolar, 1986), 41. Richter drafted this book in the 1930s, but it was published much later.

25. Noël Burch defines spectacle as the primary characteristic of the "primitive mode of production" of early cinema that confronts the spectator as an externality, as well as opposing the closure and transparency of the "institutional mode of production" of classical narrative. It is this that he values in early film. "A Primitive Mode of Representation," in *Early Cinema: Space-Frame-Narrative*, ed. Thomas Elsaesser (London: British Film Institute, 1990), 220–27.

26. Thomas Gunning adopted the term from Eisenstein, for whom "attractions" were theatrical and visual events and effects that

"aggressively subjected the spectator to 'sensual or psychological impact.'" "The Cinema of Attractions: Early Film, Its Spectator, and the Avant-Garde," *Wide Angle* 8, nos. 3–4 (1986): 59.

27. Such actions are seen, for example, in *Prigionieri Della Guerra*, Italy, 1995, dir. Yuervant Gianikin, Angela Ricci Luchi, made by Museo Storico di Trento and Museo della Guerra di Rovereto and Commune di Rovereto using Russian and Austro/Hungarian film footage from the First World War.

28. Ben Brewster and Lea Jacobs do not see what they describe as the pictorialism of the theatrical picture as inimical to narrative cinema, but rather as one of its modes. They question the distinction of a "cinema of attractions" as more than a form of exhibition. *Theatre to Cinema* (Oxford: Oxford University Press, 1977), 215.

29. Scopophilia and epistephilia are, for Freud, components of the human drive, that is, what impels the subject in relation to objects of desire. The wish to see may be active (voyeurism) or, as Freud emphasizes, it may be passive, in the wish to be seen (exhibitionism). The passive wish is satisfied in the cinema through identification with the seen displayed to us, so that the spectator becomes the seen image. Here arises the pleasure of that psychical engagement summed up more or less well by the term *identification*. This will be the focus of discussion in the next section.

30. Two contradictory desires can be involved in this encounter with the unfamiliar: either a mastery of the new and unknown or a repeated encounter with the impossibility of mastery, of knowledge and sense making. The latter, which as noted earlier might also be called the sublime and which is therefore not necessarily simply satisfying, is as well the experience Freud names as the "uncanny," and which can be related to Lacan's notion of the real. For Freud, the uncanny is the emotion associated with the return of the repressed and, specifically in his analysis of Hoffman's tale "The Sandman," of the Oedipal wishes involved in the castration complex. The uncanny confronts the subject—unconsciously—with the impossibility of its desire and the terror of its losses as a "castration." For Lacan, the disturbance in the image or story is the little bit of the real, of the senseless, intruding into the picture or narrative that disturbs its ordering. Sigmund Freud, "The Uncanny" (1919), in *The Standard Edition of the Complete Psychological Works of Sigmund Freud*, vol. 16, ed. and trans. James Strachey (London: Hogarth, 1955).

31. See, for example, Trinh T. Minh-ha, "The

Totalising Quest of Meaning," in *Theorizing Documentary*, ed. Michael Renov (New York: Routledge, 1993), 95; Brian Winston, *Claiming the Real: The Griersonian Documentary and Its Legitimations* (London: British Film Institute, 1995), 205–18.

32. Walter Benjamin, "The Work of Art in the Age of Mechanical Reproduction," in *Iluminations*, trans. Harry Zohn (London: Fontana, 1968), 230. This view has also been adopted by later theorists, including Laura Mulvey and Christian Metz.

33. In Lacanian terms, this is an affirmation that the Big Other knows, and thus that it does not lack; this is termed by Lacan an *imaginary relation*, whereby lack in the other, though not in the subject her- or himself, is disavowed. This is discussed more fully below.

34. Stephen Heath and Gillian Skirrow, "Television, a World in Action," *Screen* 18, no. 2 (1977): 58. In their analysis of the British television documentary *Yesterday's Truants* (World in Action, Granada, 1976), they argue: "Summoned as citizen into a world of communication to receive particular communications, the individual must be held into the programme, *entertained* as well as occupied. Hence the organising movement of "Yesterday's Truants" with its scenes, its rhymes, its multiple times, varied yet narrated into coherence through the basic idea, the fascination with identity, with the lives of the truants. The novelistic is a veritable process of identification in a quite simple sense of finding, reviewing, staging, voicing *identifying* in terms of lives, multiple times fused in that basic vision which supports the whole viewpoint definition" (58).

35. The importance of conventions of representation can be seen in Raoul Ruiz's documentary film *Great Events and Ordinary People* (France, 1979), in which the middle-aged, middle-class, and articulate woman who declares that after finishing her shopping she will be voting for the Communist candidate—for she belong to the French Communist Party—appears unverisimilitudinous to a British audience, for whom in the 1970s Communists were male and working-class.

36. Lacan took this term from the work of Charlotte Bühler in order to describe the moment in what he has termed the *mirror stage* when the child takes others as its imagos, giving rise to the formation of the ego as such. The transitivist identification with the image of the face is but a moment, for in film, whether fiction or documentary, the movement of the camera and thus of the narrative in the shift from close-up to medium shot of the figure, for example, or to the object of her or his glance, breaks the viewer's absorption in the image of the other and opens her or him to the chain of signification

and the movement of desire for the *next* image, *another* image, a *different* image. Jacques Lacan, "The Mirror Stage," in *Ecrits: A Selection*, trans. Alan Sheridan (London: Tavistock, 1977), 5. This is discussed again later.

37. The ego ideal is the image of the self that one should be or become in order to be likable, valued. Renata Salecl has described this aspect of caring as the "second tear," drawing on Milan Kundera's discussion of kitsch in *The Unbearable Lightness of Being* (London: Faber, 1986): "Kitsch causes two tears to flow in quick succession. The first tear says: How nice to see children running on the grass! The second tear says: How nice to be moved, together with all mankind, by children running on the grass! It is this second tear which makes kitsch kitsch" (250–51). Salecl comments: "To paraphrase Kundera, in the case of the Bosnian refugee girl, one could say that the first tear runs when we see the picture of the poor girl and the second tear runs when we, together with all mankind, are moved by the fact that we are compassionate." *The Spoils of Freedom: Psychoanalysis and Feminism after the Fall of Socialism* (London: Routledge, 1994), 139.

38. Brian Winston has addressed the "victim" tradition in documentary in "Documentary: I Think We Are in Trouble," in *New Challenges for Documentary*, ed. Alan Rosenthal (Berkeley: University of California Press, 1988), 30.

39. Žižek argues that "reality" is a fantasy construction that enables us to mask the "real" of our desire. *The Sublime Object of Ideology*, 45.

40. Jacques Lacan, *The Four Fundamental Concepts of Psycho-Analysis* (Harmondsworth: Penguin, 1977), 55. Lacan notes that the real "first presented itself in the history of psychoanalysis in a form that was in itself already enough to arouse our attention, that of the trauma" (54).

41. Physical trauma—such as the experience of war as in *War Neuroses*—is not the cause but the occasion for the hysterical symptom, a moment when the traumas of reality become the trauma of the "real," when something in the "assault" is unassimilable, unhandleable, that is, unrepresentable. Freud terms this afterwardness of affect *Nachträglichkeit*. Hysteria, whether the bodily conversion symptom of what is now called posttraumatic stress disorder or the neurotic symptoms of hysterical identification, is a response to the trauma of the lack in the subject and in the other and is therefore also the trauma of sexual difference for both the man and the woman.

42. W. H. Rivers accounted for this difference by reference to the different training procedures of the two groups of men, likening the drill

training of the ordinary soldier to hypnosis, whereas the man of the officer class—educated in the main at public schools (that is, in the English system, privately)—comes into the army "with a long course of training behind him which enables him successfully to repress, not only expressions of fear, but also the emotion itself." "War Neurosis and Military Training," in *Instinct and the Unconscious: A Contribution to a Biological Theory of the Psycho-neuroses* (Cambridge: Cambridge University Press, 1920), 209.

43. The technique of suggestion involved simply implanting in the patient's mind the certainty of his cure, achieved by the preparatory assurances of nurses invoking the curative powers of the doctor/officer, followed by a session with the doctor/officer in which he affirmed that the soldier would shortly be cured. The use of suggestion was accompanied by physical treatments, which are shown in the film, involving the manipulation of limbs. Psychoanalytically, suggestion is understood as involving a transferential relation to the doctor as father figure and in a role of authority. Although the technique produced spectacularly rapid results, as *War Neuroses* demonstrates, such cures frequently proved short-lived. Hypnosis was also used, but, as indicated in *War Neuroses*, the curative effects were also not often long-lived, and the technique was difficult for doctors to learn; morever, patients were frequently not suitable subjects. The treatment at Netley and Seale Hayne is described by Drs. Hurst and Symns in "The Rapid Cure of Hysterical Symptoms in Soldiers," *Lancet* (Aug. 3, 1918).

44. British neurology up to this time had been predominantly materialist, and the response of such doctors as Sir Frederick Mott was that the soldiers' symptoms represented a neurological response to the physical effects of shell blast. But symptoms of shell shock, as it was subsequently but misleadingly called, were also arising in men who had not been directly exposed to physical factors such as shelling, and it was apparent after the war that only a small proportion of shell shock victims had suffered organic damage to the central nervous system. In response, such traditionalists marshaled the second account of mental illness in the nineteenth century, namely that of "tainted" heredities. Shell shock, however, occurred so widely, even among the "volunteers" and officers, considered to be the "best" genetically, that such an approach was fundamentally discredited. Martin Stone argues, therefore, that the process of "medicalisation of the mind" characterized by the "invention of the neuroses" at the level of medical discourse suggested by D. Armstrong (in "Madness and

Coping," *Sociology of Health and Illness* 2 [November 1980]: 296) was propelled by the concrete problem confronting the medical establishment, namely, shell shock. "Shell-shock and the Psychologists," 248.

45. This is described as "complete retrograde amnesia, hysterical paralysis, contractures, mutism and university anaesthesia dating from February 1926. . . . September 1918, complete recovery, patient runs down flight of steps and waves his arms."

46. Such scenes are possibly a convention of war documentaries at the time; a similar scene of soldiers off duty appears in *British Troops in Italy* (United Kingdom, 1918), involving the comic plucking of a chicken for cooking.

47. Stone, "Shellshock and the Psychologists," 246, 248.

48. As suggested by Michael Hammond in "Education or Entertainment: Public and Private Interpretations of *The Battle of the Somme* (1916)," in *Non-Fiction British Cinema*, ed. Alan Burton (London: Flicks, forthcoming).

TOM GUNNING

[2] *Embarrassing Evidence: The Detective Camera and the Documentary Impulse*

If they knew what I wear when I walk in the street,
It should be quite a terror to people I meet;
They will fly when they see me, and ne'er stop to chat,
For I carry a camera up in my hat.
:: anonymous poem in *Punch*, circa 1887[1]

The British scholar Stephen Bottomore, in his tireless research into the cultural context of early cinema, discovered that in the first decades of cinema there was a virtual explosion of accounts in short stories, newspapers, dramas, and even early films in which a movie camera captured either a moment of private indiscretion or evidence of a crime. In these narratives, this filmed evidence was then screened in public, embarrassing or incriminating the culprit.[2] As I have pointed out in previous articles, this prevalent myth of the initial reception of cinema derives its power from a dramatic series of oppositions.[3] Private and furtive acts become public and exposed. The apparatus of the cinema allows this passage from private to public space, and its role as simultaneously witness and record endows it with a juridical effect, providing both evidence of wrongdoing and the occasion for judgment and punishment. The viewer of the film negotiates this propulsion of private deeds into public exposure, positioned as both voyeur-witness and moral judge through the surrogate apparatus. But the power of this fantasy of potent vision also contains its inverse, the paranoia of constant surreptitious surveillance. The enclosure of private space becomes porous and uncertain. This mythic reception of the invention of cinema reflects a growing awareness of a society increasingly based on surveillance in which technology stimulates a fear of constant observation based, like Bentham's panopticon, on a concealed apparatus of vision. The peculiarly modern sense of the self as composed on a fragile borderline between public and private became threatened in these accounts with a drama of collapse triggered by making visible to all that which one would hope to conceal.

This myth of early cinema reveals anxieties as well as expectations that the apparatus of the cinema held in the era of its emergence. In this early period, actuality films constituted the main product of the cinema rather than fiction filmmaking, and the motion picture camera itself remained the focus of attention. This essay, then, will deal less with film images than with the apparatus itself, viewed not as a transcendent subject-manufacturing, -influencing machine, but as a product and transformer of social relations of power and observation, negotiating new relations between the private and the public, and creating new notions of propriety and the body. All of these issues, I believe, subtend much of documentary film and photography. They also reflect back on the primal fantasies and anxieties that the apparatus of the camera generated when it was taken out of the studio and turned on the activities of daily life.

Modern surveillance techniques may provide a basis for the paranoia found in these early accounts of unwitting observation, but the bulky nature of the early movie camera and the noisy and relatively attention-grabbing process of cranking it made it an unlikely choice for surreptitious photography. But this fantasy of observation and exposure derives from more than a social anxiety founded in an almost prescient awareness of new forms of social control. These narratives of concealed photography simply extended to the motion picture camera, the *latest* photographic novelty, the purpose behind the invention of the *previous* major innovation in still photography—the detective camera.

After the initial invention of still photography, the greatest technical transformation of this new medium came in the 1870s and 1880s, with a series of interlocking innovations. The replacement of the previous wet collodion photographic plates by, first, gelatin dry plates and, later, roll film allowed both a simplification of the photographic process and a mastery of instantaneous photography. The greater simplicity of the apparatus and the reduced exposure time possible with faster emulsions allowed a major innovation in camera design: the *hand camera,* small and light enough to do without the tripod, which had guaranteed not only support but steadiness of image in the era of heavier cameras and slower emulsions.[4]

This combined simplicity and portability put cameras literally in the hands of an enormously larger segment of the population, creating a new, more extensive realm of amateur photography to compete with the already established professionals, as well as challenging already established amateur traditions of the older generation. It also allowed the photographer, amateur or professional, to have a new attitude toward subject matter, an

The latest photographic innovation: the hand camera, unobtrusive, nearly invisible.

ability to penetrate into terrain previously difficult to navigate with bulky equipment and to capture spontaneous action quickly and simply. For most of us today, this revolution is associated with the word *Kodak,* the neologism and trademark that George Eastman devised for his new cheap hand camera aimed directly at this new type of amateur photographer, who no longer had to worry about preparation or development of the film concealed inside the black box, but simply "pushed the button."[5] However, the innovation of the hand camera was originally known by a different name, the *detective camera,* the first general term for an instantaneous handheld camera, of which the Kodak was only the cheapest and most commercially successful example.[6]

Why was the hand camera originally called a detective camera? So far I have found it easier to trace the effacing of this term than its origin, but I believe that the suppression of the term *detective* is as revealing as its appearance. Already by 1890 a reaction had set in among amateur photographers against the use of the term introduced less than a decade before. An article in the *American Amateur Photographer* published in April 1890 declared:

The name Detective should be dropped from the photographic vocabulary at once and forever. The word savors too much of devious ways and shady practices to be retained by any true lover of the camera. But against the term "Hand Camera" there lies no such objection.[7]

Three years later, in the same journal's "Index Rerum Photographia," a lexicon of photography that hoped to be authoritative, one found under the term "Hand Camera" the following statement: "Formerly called detective, a name that should be conveyed at once to the dead past and be forgotten."[8]

The change in name indicates a change in use and intended user. The hand camera was apparently originally seen as a specialist camera whose small size, instantaneous exposure, and ease of operation allowed it to be used unobtrusively or even surreptitiously. If not designed for the professional photographer primarily, it seemed to target professionals in other fields—the police photographer, the private eye, or the muckraking journalist. But it was its popularity among amateurs that made the hand camera more than a specialist camera and subsequently greatly enlarged the field of amateur photography. The need to suppress the term *detective* indicated the expansive success of the format. The proper use of the hand camera was now seen to lie primarily in amateur travel photography. *American Amateur Photographer* announced in 1890 that the hand camera "is now almost an indispensable part of the outfit of every tourist and summer boarder." The new camera, the article added, "hastens the coming of the time when the whole world will lie within easy reach of one's hand."[9] We can see here a very clear semiotic redefinition of a technological device in both terminology and use. From a device whose name inscribes its power to make visible hidden practices, the camera gains a more neutral name and a less devious purpose.

An ambivalence about the potential of this new form of camera was evident from its first appearance. In 1887, the French amateur photographic journal *L'Amateur Photographe* greeted the small-format Photoeclair camera by saying:

> In summary, the advantage of this camera lies in how easy it is take a photograph suddenly without encumbering equipment, and at the same time with a rapidity of pose and a finesse of execution that could rival the best models of our well-known manufacturers.

But the journal expressed concern about possible uses of this hand camera:

> Any person one meets could be photographed without suspecting it in the least, even against their will. . . . without doubt, alas, blackmail could be undertaken in this manner. It is certain that the general use of this little camera could take some very bad turns, just as it could render inestimable services, informing

equally police officers and amateur spies. Is this a reason to despise it, and isn't this true of all innovations?[10]

One might speculate that the emergence of the detective camera and its initial popularity owed a great deal to this earlier voyeuristic appeal. The plain box of the Kodak camera and other handheld models like it was designed not only for simplicity and portability but for unobtrusiveness. To a generation for whom the camera had been visually identified by its tripod and bellows, the nearly neutral oblong of the 3¼-by-3¼-by-6½-inch box of the Kodak did not *look* like a camera.[11] What seems today like purely functional design at the time of its appearance looked more like camouflage.

This concept of a camera that increased its ability to capture images of reality not only by its portability and speed of exposure but through its unobtrusive appearance provided the inspiration for the most flamboyant

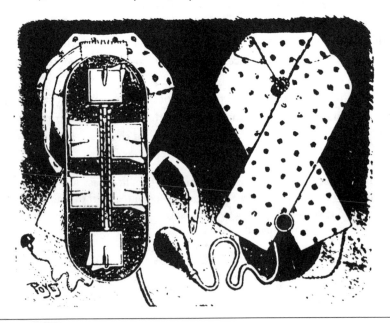

Advertisement for camera concealed under a cravat.

detective cameras, those disguised as other objects. Particularly for the years 1884 to 1894, the British registry of photographic patents is filled with descriptions of detective cameras masquerading as other objects or designed to be concealed on the photographer's person. Cameras were fashioned to resemble watches, revolvers, bags or purses, books, the knobs of walking sticks, opera glasses or binoculars, picnic baskets, cigar cases, matchboxes, and bowler hats.[12] The operator of a detective camera could have kept it not only under his hat, but concealed behind a cravat; under a vest, with the lens fashioned to look like a button; or up his sleeve.[13] While some of these patent specifications may never have led to commercially viable cameras, there survive a sufficiently large number of advertisements for vest, watchcase, and cravat cameras to indicate that more than a mad inventor's fancy lay behind this flurry of disguised cameras.[14]

While the use of detective cameras by actual detectives, whether police or Pinkerton men, labor spies or the agents of political reaction (like the czarist spies in Eisenstein's *Strike,* who record political agitation with a camera concealed in a watchcase) remains a topic in need of further research, there is clear indication that detective cameras were used to provide documentation for certain forms of social discourse, as well as journalistic investigation. David Francis has shown me a set of lantern slides produced and marketed in Britain at the turn of the century titled "Slum Life in Our Great Cities," whose printed lecture announced: "The set of lantern slides for which this Lecture was written have been photographed direct from Life in the slums, by means of a special Detective or Hand Camera."[15]

The detective camera allowed the gathering of documentary evidence, and its images were used in a format that clearly parallels later social film documentaries: the reformist lecture illustrated by magic lantern slides. As Maren Stange has shown in her treatment of Jacob Riis, many of the most famous images of American documentary photography were originally presented as stereopticon slides in the context of accompanying lectures. As Stange puts it: "The lectures embedded the evidentiary image in an elaborate discourse offering simultaneous entertainment and ideology, and from this the photograph, no matter how seemingly straightforward its reference, never stood apart."[16]

Stange's placing of Riis's images within the tradition of the illustrated lectures reveals a great deal about the position of the reformist documentary photographer as well as the camera's unique role in gathering evidence. Riis's rhetorical position as lecturer mediating the images of slum life he collected to a middle-class audience was modeled on another direct ancestor of the documentary film, the travel lecturer, such as John Stoddard or Burton Holmes, who interwove oral accounts of foreign travels with projected images (stereopticon slides and later films) of exotic locales.[17] Riis's use of "the language of tourism" in a social context fashioned a powerful ideological effect for his audience. As Stange effectively puts it:

> His evocation of spectacle and tourism in regard to New York's slums used the rhetoric and its associations for purposes akin to those of the western imperialists. Riis' representation of the touristic point of view offered a "respectable" perspective on the photographs he showed; in addition it helped him further flatter his audience, implicitly assuring them that they were the "half" designated by history and progress to colonize and dominate.[18]

The slum tour's congruence with the colonialist voyage and exploration has been noted by a number of social historians of literary urban narratives during the nineteenth century. Accounts of urban investigations in the nineteenth century provided vicarious voyages for "respectable" audiences into the burgeoning urban slum jungle. Those writers whom Judith Walkowitz has described as the "urban explorers" of nineteenth-century London also "adapted the language of imperialism to evoke features of their own cities. Imperialist rhetoric transformed the unexplored territories of the London poor into an alien place both exciting and dangerous."[19] John F. Kasson has shown how this tradition of urban exploration created a minor nineteenth-century literary genre, centered on the revelation of the dark hidden side of the metropolis, exemplified by works such as *New York by Gaslight*.[20] Riis's illustrated article "Flashes from the Slums" and his public lectures clearly referenced this genre, literalizing their frequent contrast between darkness and revealing illumination with the magnesium flash used with his camera.[21] George G. Foster, author of *New York by Gaslight*, claimed to let his readers "penetrate beneath the thick veils of night and lay bare the fearful mysteries of darkness in the metropolis," uncovering "the underground story" of life in New York City.[22] Kasson also compares these exposés of the seamy side of urban life to colonialist voyages:

> Regarding this "underground story" as a dark continent, populated by "primitive" natives, urban explorers typically set out upon their safaris at night, accompanied by police officers and lanterns to map the region of poverty, vice and crime as a first step to eradicating it.[23]

The emerging discipline of anthropology (with its ties to colonial exploration) undoubtedly provided a context in which the recording of details of daily life (which otherwise might seem unworthy of notice or smack of simple snooping) could gain a respectable veneer. However, a new fascination with daily life and a nearly prurient interest in uncovering scandalous or otherwise deviant material also played an important role in the genre's popularity.

Although the metaphor of explorer undoubtedly applies, the detective, dedicated to uncovering concealed deception and operating frequently through his mastery of disguise, seems an equally relevant term of comparison for this form of urban voyeurism focused not only on penetrating and mapping the urban wilderness but on uncovering wrongdoing and gathering evidence. As Dana Brand has shown (with the aid of Walter Benjamin and Edgar Poe), the gaze of the nineteenth-century urban spectator transformed from the casual observation of the stroller-observer *flaneur* of the early part of the century into the penetrating surveillance of the detective as the urban environment became more alien and less legible.[24] The detective, as Benjamin has indicated, intensified the *flaneur*'s power of observation and at the same time concealed this newly focused gaze under an appearance of idleness.[25] This structure of penetrating vision shrouded in the disguise of the everyday reveals how appropriate the term *detective camera* was for an apparatus that recorded evidence so unobtrusively and yet so faithfully.

The lecture accompanying the lantern slides for "Slum Life in Our Great Cities" reflects starkly the imperialist gaze of the urban explorer as well as the devious scrutiny of the detective. Lacking Riis's reformist impulse, the lecture focuses the images of slum dwellers through the lens of middle-class outrage and disdain, repeatedly remarking on their lack of hygiene, their laziness, and their supposed preference for a life of squalor. Its tone of sanctimonious censure (such as a shocked reaction to a photograph of a little girl with a jump rope, which it cites as evidence of "the little regard paid towards the sacredness of the Sabbath day" in the slums)[26] sets a moral gulf between the photographer and viewers of these images and the subjects captured by the detective camera. The act of seizing these images is clearly understood as a dangerous appropriation within an alien environment:

> It need scarcely be mentioned that this was a work of no small difficulty, and at times of danger also; for many of the inhabitants in these districts strongly object to have their portraits taken, or to be photographed or noticed in any way. The photographer was several times threatened, and at others taken for a detective officer.[27]

Although several of the images in this series of lantern slides clearly indicate awareness on the part of the subjects that their pictures were being taken, the surreptitious detective camera played an essential role in seizing these images from the recalcitrant subjects through subterfuge. Beyond the voyeuristic pleasures and satisfaction of curiosity these views offered to their middle-class audiences, the lecture's only call for reform came with its claim that drink supplied the major cause of poverty and squalor. One slide of a slum woman is accompanied by this commentary:

> What a sad picture is this. Look at the female on the right. Quite young but what a wreck. How dirty, how degraded looking, how ugly a debauched drunken life has made her, what an idle slouching gait she has, a fearful commentary on the text, "The way of transgressors is hard."[28]

In his appropriation and condemnation of this image of a working-class woman, the lecturer directs attention not only to setting and environment, but also to bodily posture and appearance, aspects a detective camera could claim to capture directly. This interrogation of the body not only reflects the colonialist attitude of this slum voyage, but more particularly invokes middle-class codes of body propriety, which, as we shall see later, were brought to a point of crisis through other uses of the hand camera. As Kasson has indicated, etiquette books in the nineteenth century instructed their middle-class readers that bodily posture must be constantly controlled precisely because it is so revealing. *The Mentor,* published in 1885, proclaimed: "Not only is a man's walk an index of his character and his grade of culture, but it is also an index of the frame of mind he is in."[29] The detective camera allowed bodily language to be captured for display and comment, and even condemnation.

With the detective camera, the urban adventurer could emerge from the slums with object lessons of working-class debauchery and bad posture to be shown to a comfortable audience. The claim was made that such revelations could transform slum life (presumably through lobbying for stricter regulation of saloons), and the detective camera gathered the evidence needed to support this temperance argument. The lecture accompanying the opening image claimed:

> It will be noticed in the series of pictures taken that in almost every one a public-house or vaults are present, so numerous are they that it is hardly possible to point the detective camera in any direction without encountering one. Oh, that every gin palace had its plate glass windows down to the ground, and the interior open to the gaze of passersby. Surely many a trembler on the brink of vice, awed by the publicity, would fear to commence the career of drunkenness and crime.[30]

The detective camera becomes a panopticon of "publicity" acting out this fantasy of full-length plate-glass windows through photographic exposure and visibility.

If one use of the detective camera lay in the exploration of the world of the underclasses for purposes of social criticism (ranging from the truly progressive "sneak work" Lewis Hines undertook to get pictures of child

Image of slum inhabitant from the magic lantern lecture "Slum Life in Our Great Cities."

laborers for the National Child Labor Committee to the reactionary moralistic slumming evident in the lantern lecture quoted above),[31] the other end of the picture-snatching spectrum wormed its way into the lives of the rich and famous. The impetus here was frankly commercial, particularly by the turn of the century, when new techniques of picture reproduction allowed the rise of a photographic press. According to English scholar Nicholas Hiley, in Great Britain the *Penny Pictorial Magazine* in 1899 featured a regular page titled "Taken Unawares: Snap Shots of Celebrated People."[32] Although the sale and exhibition of photographs of famous people, as in Mathew Brady's *Gallery of Illustrious Americans*,[33] had been the cornerstone of commercial photography for decades, these earlier images had involved studio portraits, which, as Hiley points out, involved lengthy negotiations between the photographer and his subject, with the subject retaining ultimate control over his or her image.[34] Robert E. Mensel quotes a turn-of-the-century American photographic journal declaring that photographs of celebrities taken without their knowledge (and therefore without their control) were bought by periodicals and commercial shops at a price "fully twice as much . . . as for the conventional photographs made in the studio."[35]

The somewhat fanciful disguised cameras described earlier, then, did function as actual tools of the trade for many news reporters. Cameras concealed under hats became so common in British courtrooms that one reporter recalled, "Those of us in the know used to watch the hats rise slightly when anything happened."[36] Indeed, it was this fascination in publishing private moments of citizens that, as Mensel points out, occasioned in the United States a new consideration of the legal "right to privacy."[37] This new legal concept was argued in a definitive manner in 1890 by Samuel Warren and future U.S. Supreme Court justice Louis Brandeis in the *Harvard Law Review* in 1890. Their call for a new interpretation of the law was sparked by the social change brought on in part by the hand camera. The authors warned that "instantaneous photographs and newspaper enterprise have invaded the sacred precincts of private and domestic life; and numerous mechanical devices threaten to make good the prediction that 'what is whispered in the closet shall be proclaimed from the house tops.'"[38] The fantasy of private drama made public that haunted the turn of the century appears to be less a private paranoia than a defining social drama of modernity.

Therefore, while the middle-class audience of "Slum Life in Our Great Cities" or even of Riis's lectures could enjoy a voyeuristic position of privilege insulated from what Riis described as "the vulgar sounds and odious scents and repulsive exhibitions" to which the photographer adventurer was subjected in gathering the images,[39] they nonetheless experienced new anxieties about photography's ability to expose disturbing or unattractive aspects of their own private lives, or undermine their own sense of propriety and privacy. If the detective camera could be used for the observation and moral condemnation of the recalcitrant inhabitants of the slums, it could also turn its lens unexpectedly onto the daily life of the average middle-class citizen. The amateur photographer targeted not only the rich and famous but also those around them—whether passersby on the street, friends, or family members. Without going as far as the blackmail feared by *L'Amateur Photographe*, such images could cause embarrassment and discomfort. This possibility of capturing one's companions unaware undoubtedly contributed greatly to the initial popularity of the detective camera, but it also drew the censure of an emerging amateur photographic culture. As Warren and Brandeis's article made clear, new technologies of reproduction could unravel traditional conceptions of the formal public self, while breaching the privileged precincts of privacy.

The hand camera, then, brought on nothing less than a social revolution that affected the legal definition of self and privacy as well as the nature of embodied social behavior. The popularity of images of both the famous and the abject taken unawares revealed ambivalent ideas about the relation between truthfulness and propriety. Mensel quotes a photographic journal's claim that the hand camera could penetrate to a person's true and sincere character, rather than presenting a carefully arranged public persona: "The beauty of the invention [the hand camera] is that the victim is thoroughly unsuspicious. He does not know his picture is being 'took,' consequently the character is all preserved."[40] But if the camera could capture that moment when the body's guard was down, when the truth of a character was rendered visible through the subject's being unaware of the camera's gaze, then the photograph could stage the conflict between one's bodily existence and the creation of a social self for all to witness.

With this peculiarly modern threat, we see how a sense of self, bodily existence, and public life were redefined by the introduction of the hand camera. Reactions to the first detective cameras reveal concern over the loss of control over one's own image it could introduce. The French journal *L'Amateur Photographe* described the threat of being photographed by a detective camera concealed behind a cravat, without the subject's permission or desire—or possibly even awareness—as a sort of modern fate: "Your face never before captured on sensitive emulsion is now in his [the photographer's] possession, say what you will. It was written: You shall be photographed."[41]

Being photographed unawares entailed a new awareness of one's own body brought on by the possibility of instantaneous photography outside the portrait studio. Even outside the slums, the detective camera could reveal a body that violated the protocols of nineteenth-century etiquette. In 1886, a journal printed a complaint from a Belgian man who described his shock on seeing photographs of himself taken at a beach resort by a detective camera:

> I had no difficulty in recognizing myself. But what photographs they were. Certainly not such as might be calculated to tickle my vanity. In the first photograph, I was shown at the very moment of entering the water, and my face reflected all too clearly the sensation of the first contact with the cold sea-water. Really, one would not approach a lady with such gestures on shore.
>
> The second picture had been taken while I was blowing out a mouthful of water which I had involuntarily gulped in, while my facial expression made it obvious that my taste buds had been stimulated in a far from pleasant way.

In the third picture, I resembled a bedraggled poodle rather than a civilized man. I emerged from the sea, dripping wet.[42]

Although hardly sufficient basis for blackmail, such surreptitious photographs could provide a blow to Victorian self-esteem and give unwelcome evidence of a less-than-civilized and all-too-bodily existence. They contrasted sharply with the dignified poses and carefully defined identities contained in studio portraiture and the bodily control recommended by nineteenth-century etiquette manuals. These manuals prescribed careful body management, restraint of facial expressions, and the concealment of all bodily functions as signs of proper behavior.[43] The Belgian's shocked expression at the cold water, gestures unsuitable for approaching a lady, and especially his spitting out of the water captured by the detective camera would all exclude him from the realm of proper behavior in a public place. But here lay the fascination offered by the detective camera: a novel and possibly scandalous, yet titillating revelation of the everyday life of the body, outside of traditional protocol. A correspondent for the *Photographic Times and American Photographer* in 1888 reported that amateur photographers flocked to Coney Island, where "during the bathing hours, a half dozen cameras may be seen at almost any time, pointed at the half-nude and innocent bathers, at a time when they are not in a position to be perpetuated by the camera."[44]

Further, the camera's gaze in effect broke one of the strongest behavioral taboos, that against concentrated visual attention directed at a stranger. To stare at a woman in public, Kasson notes, "was to violate her modesty and assault her honor."[45] And even encounters between people of the same gender required a disciplining of the eye, particularly if one saw something amiss, some aspect of the private self inadvertently peeking out in public. The *Illustrated Manners Book* declared, "The rule is imperative that no one should see, or, if that is impossible, should seem to see, or to have seen, anything that another person would choose to have concealed, unless indeed it is your business to watch for some misdemeanor."[46] In other words, only a detective could participate in such rude observation, and his professional skill lay in his ability to watch without appearing to watch, like the operation of a camouflaged detective camera.

The detective camera enacted a social rudeness and indiscretion, violating the norms of proper behavior, but accomplished this by obeying the single most important public virtue, discretion—at least at the moment of photography. The detective camera, with its camouflaged stare, could release fantasies of broaching social taboos, often invoking scenarios of both erotic and criminal encounters. An anonymous poem published in *Punch* inspired by the announcement of a detective camera concealed under a hat contained these verses:

> Should I meet when I chance to be taking the air,
> With a lady who looks so surpassingly fair;
> If I wish to preserve her sweet face by the sun,
> Why, I just pull a string, and the photograph's done.
> If I'm stopped in the street—that may happen you know—
> By a robber whose manners are not *comme il faut*
> His identification should never be hard
> There's my neat little photograph in Scotland Yard.[47]

It would seem that photographs that violated social decorum provided a common motivation for the amateur use of detective cameras, one that was harshly condemned by the growing institutionalization of amateur photography on the grounds of violating both the art of photography and simple good manners. Under the heading "Ethics of the Hand Camera," the *American Amateur Photographer* in 1891 quoted Andrew Pringle declaring:

> Here let us say that we have nothing to do with so-called "detective" cameras. We do not consider that anyone has the right to steal a photograph of another person, except as an adjunct to an ordinary view; and most certainly we have no right to snatch a photograph of a person in any compromising position or circumstances. Persons walking the streets are objects of public view, and conduct themselves with a knowledge that they are so, but to us it appears the height of impertinence to take surreptitious shots at, for instance, ladies bathing and unaware that they are the victims of such indecent officiousness. A man who steals an exposure on any person, in any position at all compromising, richly deserves a horsewhipping.

The journal indicated its agreement with this position and added a sort of photographic golden rule that the owner of a hand camera "should hold it as a matter of conscience never to make an exposure on a person in circumstances under which he would not himself wish to be photographed."[48] In another article carried in the journal a year earlier, an author claimed the true possibilities of the hand camera were in danger of being lost if it was "degraded into a means of caricaturing one's friends by securing them in various ludicrous or uncomely postures." Of the use of photography to display an unintended lack of bodily management, the author commented, "Nothing can be more contrary to the spirit of our gentle art."[49]

The hand camera offered a powerful new means to negotiate the division between public and private behavior so central to Victorian and modern capitalist society, and thereby created new anxieties about the success of this balancing act. It offered a new form of indiscretion in which one's own image might, like Peter Schlemihl's shadow, be stolen from one

Artist's rendering of one type of camera concealed under a hat.

without one's knowledge, and in which one might encounter oneself in unfamiliar bodily postures that violate the protocols of etiquette and civilized behavior. These disturbing possibilities were emblazoned in the device's original name, the *detective camera,* a name that so boldly displayed these possibilities that it was soon abandoned as indiscreet and the growing ranks of amateur photographers were advised of the unethical nature of such photography and to shun the term. However, the repression of this practice and rubric does not mean that it did not leave an important imprint upon the practice of documentary photography. Further, the initial scandalous fascination exerted by the hand camera—its penetration of private life, its ability to capture aspects of which its subjects were unaware—

remained a powerful component of photographic documentary, whether in still or motion photography, as well as fueling the recent popular entertainment use of video surveillance.

I believe that tracing the origin of the hand camera does more than simply root the documentary impulse in pure nosiness (although it may be useful to recall the *curiositas* that underlies documentary). This curiosity shapes a particular conception of the camera, whose technical design allows a certain way of seeing and gathering evidence. It is not simply the supposed neutrality of the camera that must be interrogated, but the historically specific fantasies of knowledge and power that this apparatus embodies and produces. The targeting of daily life, of self-betraying postures and the language of the body, as an area of investigation, as well as the subsequent containing of this curiosity under the rubric of "camera ethics," constitutes an important archaeology of the documentary impulse. I believe these issues still loom before us.

The turmoil that a detective camera could cause, not during a slum voyage but within a middle-class household, provided material for many popular narratives, as Bottomore has indicated, including the 1908 Biograph film *Bobby's Kodak,* starring Bobby Harron, who later played the lead in the modern story of *Intolerance.* The plot of this short comedy parallels the archetype that Bottomore has isolated, only substituting a Kodak for a motion picture camera.

Having received a new hand camera as a gift from his father, Bobby at first takes family photos. But, as the film's publicity bulletin tells it, "family groups and grandpas are a bit tame for our neophyte Daguerre. He yearned for something more spicy and piquant."[50] The boy then creeps around the house unobserved, camera in hand, capturing moments of impropriety: the cook in the kitchen kissing the cop on the beat, his mother in the bedroom stealing money from his father's pants pockets. He even makes a trip to his father's office and snaps him embracing his typist. As the bulletin puts it: "Click goes the infernal machine and the damaging evidence is recorded."[51] Bobby's snapshots are then prepared as stereopticon slides and arranged for an evening of family entertainment. The showing begins with the anodyne family portraits, but then proceeds to the embarrassing evidence, moving upward in the social hierarchy from domestic servant to wife and mother and finally overturning the self-important image of the paterfamilias. The evening's entertainment ends with papa taking a swipe at Bobby, but the film reserves the true punishment for the apparatus itself. In an emblematic final scene, the father, framed in medium shot, destroys the camera with a hatchet, ending the film.

This Biograph comedy falls into an already well-established genre of

BOBBY'S KODAK

Papa's Present Proves a Prejudicial Portent

LENGTH, 518 FEET.   PRICE, 12 CENTS PER FOOT.

We have often heard of, if not really experienced, the disastrous results of presenting to the young son and heir a tool-chest. What devastation lies in his wake—crippled chairs, wrecked tables, four-inch spikes through the piano top, and most inartistic handcarving on everything wooden about the house. We all know of these terrors, which are certainly heartrending, but are mild indeed compared with the malignant mischief brewed by giving the youngster that sinister, pernicious instrument, a snapshot Kodak. Such was the ill-advised, injudicious procedure of the leading old gentleman of this Biograph comedy.

Good, kind Papa brings home the Kodak for Bobby, and at once instructs him how to work it. First the family is arranged and a snap taken; then baby, grandpa and so on. Bobby has now gotten a pretty clear idea of the thing and resolves to go it alone—and he did with a vengeance. Family groups and grandpas are a bit tame for our neophyte Daguerre. He yearned for something more spicy and piquant, and his yearning was soon appeased. Going to his dad's room, where paterfamilias is indulging in a quiet nap, he sees mamma dear, extracting the loose change from papa's pockets—Great! Click goes the infernal machine and the damaging evidence is recorded. To the kitchen he is drawn by this evil genius, the Kodak, and there finds Maggie and the Cop brightening their condition of social ostracism with apple pie and kisses. Here is a chance of a lifetime. Click, and the villainous work is done. Later in the day papa's office is visited. Pa has a pretty typewriter, and you know it is often necessary for the boss and typist to sit in close proximity, that there may be no slips in the dictation. Well, just as Bobby appears at the door, papa—but let us be charitable and draw the curtain. However, again that peace-lacerating click. Oh, horror! Is there no help? Great Jove send forth thy thunderbolts and crush to smithereens this calamitous Pandora's Box; but, no, the fates do not intercept and Bobby takes his noxious negatives to have them made into Stereopticon Slides.

Bobby now becomes the star of an evening's entertainment at home. Great preparations have been made, and the family and friends of the family are assembled to see the stereopticon show. On the sheet hung in the parlor are thrown, first the family groups and Grandpa. Then comes the episode in the kitchen, to the embarrassment of poor Maggie, followed by the mortifying disclosure of mother's subtle act at dad's pockets. Ah, ha! Papa gloats, but for short duration, for the piece de resistance is yet to be shown, and when it is—well they say photos and figures never lie, and this photo is so truthful that the figures look like twenty-three for papa. It shows him and his typist participating in the Soul Kiss. Ten thousand furies! Dad makes a swipe at Bobby, overturns the Stereopticon, and with a hatchet smashes into bits the impish box of tricks—the Kodak. Photographically this film is perfect, and the situations are sure to elicit a succession of laughs terminating in a yell.

No. 3388   CODE WORD—Reveladora.

Produced and Controlled Exclusively by the

American Mutoscope & Biograph Co.

11 East 14th Street, New York City

PACIFIC COAST BRANCH,   116 North Broadway,
Los Angeles Cal.

Biograph Bulletin's description of the 1908 comedy *Bobby's Kodak*, starring Bobby Harron.

early film stories of mischievous boys. It reenacts in a sense the suppression of the detective camera and its causes. The betraying camera is now in the hands of a boy whose mischief marks his distance from full adult acculturation and discipline, from the realm of manners and proper behavior. The camera itself bears the brunt of greatest rage, portrayed as an agent of domestic disruption if allowed to fall into the wrong hands. But the very pleasure of the film (and its recognizable place as an ancestor of television's domestic situation comedy) also reveals the strong attraction that the temptation of documenting ordinarily concealed aspects of daily life still exerts. To what extent does it reveal an unacknowledged drive behind the documentary impulse, as well as America's home videos?

NOTES

1. Quoted in Leonard de Vries, *Victorian Inventions* (London: John Murray, 1991), 112.
2. Stephen Bottomore, "Le Theme du temoignage dans le cinema primitif," in *Les Premiers ans du cinema Français*, ed. Pierre Guibbert (Perpignan, France: Institute Jean Vigo, 1985), 155–61.
3. Tom Gunning, "What I Saw from the Rear Window of the Hotel Follies Dramatique," in *Ce que je vois de mon cine*, ed. Andre Gaudreault (Paris: Klincksieck, 1988); and Tom Gunning, "Tracing the Individual Body AKA, Photography, Detectives and Early Cinema," in *Cinema and the Invention of Modern Life*, ed. Vanessa R. Schwartz and Leo Charney (Berkeley: University of California Press, 1995).
4. Basic accounts of the development of instantaneous photography and its apparatuses can be found in Beaumont Newhall, *The History of Photography* (New York: Museum of Modern Art, 1964), 83–96; Reese V. Jenkins, *Images and Enterprise: Technology and the American Photographic Industry 1839–1925* (Baltimore: Johns Hopkins University Press, 1975), 36–96; and Brian Coe, *Cameras: From Daguerreotype to Instant Pictures* (New York: Crown, 1978).
5. See Jenkins, *Images and Enterprise*, 111–20.
6. Coe, *Cameras*, 41.
7. W. H. Burbank, "Hand Cameras," *American Amateur Photographer* 2 (April 1890): 136.
8. John H. Janewas, "Index Rerum Photographia," *American Amateur Photographer* 5 (October 1893): 493.
9. W. H. Burbank, "The Danger of Hand Camera Work," *American Amateur Photographer* 2 (September 1890): 327, 328.
10. "Le Photo-Eclair," *L'Amateur Photographe*, February 1, 1887, 69 (my translation).
11. The dimensions of the Kodak are given in Jenkins, *Images and Enterprise*, 114.
12. *Patents for Inventions, Abridgment of Specifications Class 98 Photography* (London: Her Majesty's Stationery Office, periods A.D. 1884–89, 1889–92, 1893–96, 1897–1900). I cite the following patents: 1893, 21,727, Imray, O. (watch); 1894, 16,091, Smyth, H. (revolver); 1895, 19,128, Thompson, W. P. (bag or pouch); 1886, 7121, Lowdon, G. (book); 1891, 13,686, Campell, A. (walking stick handle); 1891, 2725, Sanders, W. (opera glass); 1888, 11,300, Harrison-Dearle, S. G., and Ashcroft, T. H. (picnic basket); 1886, 12,571, Lancaster, W. J. (cigar case, matchbox, etc.); 1890, 20,931, Jekeli, K. F., and Horner, J. (hat).
13. See *Patents for Inventions*, 1890, 12,766, Bloch, E. (scarf tie); 1886, 9655, Allison, H. J. (vest button); 1893, 18,412, Marsh, J. (up a sleeve).
14. See advertisement in *American Amateur Photographer* 1 (August 1889) for C. P. Stirns Concealed Vest Camera.
15. "Slum Life in Our Great Cities" (printed lecture to accompany a set of lantern slides), preface, p. 4. My great appreciation to David Francis of the Library of Congress, Division of Motion Pictures and Recorded Sound, for sharing this document with me. According to Steve Humphries in *Victorian Britain through the Magic Lantern* (London: Sidgwick & Jackson, 1989), 85, this series was produced by Riley Brothers of Bradford in the 1890s.
16. Maren Stange, *Symbols of Ideal Life: Social Documentary in America 1890-1950* (Cambridge: Cambridge University Press, 1989), 2.
17. For accounts of the travel lectures of Stoddard and Holmes, see X. Theodore Barber, "The Roots of Travel Cinema: John L. Stoddard, E. Burton Holmes and the Nineteenth-Century Illustrated Travel Lecture," *Film History* 5, no. 1 (March 1993): 68–84.
18. Stange, *Symbols of Ideal Life*, 17–18.
19. Judith R. Walkowitz, *City of Dreadful Delight:*

Narratives of Sexual Danger in Late-Victorian London (Chicago: University of Chicago Press, 1992), 18.

20. John F. Kasson, *Rudeness and Civility: Manners in Nineteenth-Century Urban America* (New York: Hill & Wang, 1992), 74–82.
21. Stange, *Symbols of Ideal Life*, 6.
22. Quoted in Kasson, *Rudeness and Civility*, 78.
23. Ibid.
24. Dana Brand, *The Spectator and the City in Nineteenth-Century American Literature* (Cambridge: Cambridge University Press, 1991), 79–105.
25. Walter Benjamin, "The Paris of the Second Empire in Baudelaire," in *Charles Baudelaire: A Lyric Poet in the Era of High Capitalism* (London: Verso, 1983), 41.
26. "Slum Life," slide 11, p. 8.
27. Ibid., preface, p. 4.
28. Ibid., slide 29, p. 14.
29. Quoted in Kasson, *Rudeness and Civility*, 123.
30. "Slum Life," slide 1, p. 5.
31. On Lewis Hines, see Alan Trachtenberg, *Reading American Photographs: Images as History, Mathew Brady to Walker Evans* (New York: Hill & Wang, 1989), 201.
32. Nicholas Hiley, "The Candid Camera of the Edwardian Tabloids," *History Today* 43 (August 1993): 17.
33. On Brady and the commercial and cultural significance of photographs of famous people, see Trachtenberg, *Reading American Photographs*, 43–52.
34. Hiley, "The Candid Camera," 16.
35. Robert E. Mensel, "'Kodakers Lying in Wait': Amateur Photography and the Right of Privacy in New York, 1885–1915," *American Quarterly* 43, no. 1 (March 1991): 31.
36. Quoted in Hiley, "The Candid Camera," 18.
37. See Mensel, "'Kodakers Lying in Wait.'" I want to thank my colleague James Lastra for drawing my attention to this aspect of the

detective camera and to Mensel's article. A further consideration of the effect these concepts had on modern conceptions of the self can be found in Stacey Margolis, "The Public Life: The Discourse of Privacy in the Age of Celebrity," *American Quarterly* 52, no. 2 (Summer 1995): 81–101. Laws covering public photography varied from country to country. An article in the *Photographic Times* 27, no. 1 (July 1895): 60, titled "Photographing Abroad" indicated that laws in France and Germany were very strict about "promiscuous photographing of people on the streets or at the seashore in summertime." I thank Mark Sandberg for this reference.
38. Samuel D. Warren and Louis D. Brandeis, "The Right to Privacy," *Harvard Law Review* 4, no. 5 (December 15, 1890): 195.
39. Quoted in Stange, *Symbols of Ideal Life*, 16.
40. Quoted in Mensel, "'Kodakers Lying in Wait,'" 31.
41. Leo, "Revue des nouveautes photographiques," *L'Amateur Photographe*, September 15, 1890, 360 (my translation).
42. From *De Natuur*, 1887, 172; quoted in de Vries, *Victorian Inventions*, 112.
43. Kasson, *Rudeness and Civility*, 123–26.
44. Quoted in Mensel, "'Kodakers Lying in Wait,'" 33.
45. Kasson, *Rudeness and Civility*, 127.
46. Quoted in ibid., 126–27.
47. Quoted in de Vries, *Victorian Inventions*, 113, 115.
48. "Ethics of the Hand Camera," *American Amateur Photographer* 3 (June 1891): 230.
49. Burbank, "The Danger of Hand Camera Work," 328.
50. "Bobby s Kodak," Biograph Bulletin no. 123 (February 10, 1908), reprinted in Kemp Niver, *Biograph Bulletins 1896–1908* (Los Angeles: Locare Research Group, 1971), 336.
51. Ibid.

AKIRA MIZUTA LIPPIT

[**3**] *Phenomenologies of the Surface:*
Radiation-Body-Image

Nothing is more fragile than the surface.
:: Gilles Deleuze, *The Logic of Sense*, 1990

During the night of July 23–24, 1895, Sigmund Freud dreamed of "Irma."
Following a near-catastrophic misdiagnosis earlier that year, Freud's confi-
dence had been greatly shattered. The case, which almost resulted in the
death of Emma Eckstein, had reopened Freud's primal wound, rupturing the
delicate tissues that separated, in Freud's thought, the psychic from the organic body. The crisis had threatened the very foundation of Freud's theory
of repression. On the night of July 23–24, then, Irma appeared before Freud
with the "solution" to this crisis. The "dream of Irma's injection," which
Freud would later claim had revealed to him "the secret of dreams," marks
not only a critical moment in the history of psychoanalysis—it was the first
of his own dreams that Freud submitted to analysis—but also Freud's anx-
ious desire to visualize the unconscious.[1] That is, against the uncertainties
that assailed his nascent theory of the unconscious, Freud felt the pressing
need to offer a material figure or image of the psychic apparatus. The
dream work, constituted by signifiers of visuality, promised such a figure.
The "Irma dream," in particular, suggested the possibility of a virtually impossible spectacle, an opportunity to observe the psychic apparatus in motion. Freud offers the following account of his dream:

> *A large hall—numerous guests, whom we were receiving.—Among them was*
> *Irma. I at once took her on one side, as though to answer her letter and to*
> *reproach her for not having accepted my "solution" yet. I said to her: "If you*
> *still get pains, it's really your own fault." She replied: "If you only knew what*
> *pains I've got now in my throat and stomach and abdomen—it's choking*
> *me"—I was alarmed and looked at her. She looked pale and puffy. I thought*

to myself that after all I must be missing some organic trouble. I took her to the window and looked down her throat.[2]

Peering into Irma's throat, into the recesses of her body, Freud is confronted by a series of abstract forms: "a big white patch . . . whitish grey scabs . . . some curly structures which were evidently modelled on the turbinal bones of the nose."[3] In fact, Freud dreams of—is dreaming of—perceiving visually the source of Irma's disorder, that is, the unconscious. The gesture can be seen as an attempt to secure the unconscious in the visual field of the most exemplary of visual indices, the human body. It is, of course, a nervous phantasy, one that would haunt Freud throughout his career.[4] Yet the dilemma is clear: the anticipated birth of psychoanalysis had been complicated by the return of a repressed corporeality. Organic and psychic disturbances were vying for supremacy in Freud's own turbulent psyche: "I thought to myself that after all I must be missing some organic trouble." In the dream, Irma's interiority appears to obstruct Freud's view of the unconscious. Or rather, Freud had compressed Irma's psyche onto the surface of her interiority. The result of Freud's condensation leads, according to Jacques Lacan, to a paradox: it effects a formless image, an image of formlessness. Lacan writes:

> There's a horrendous discovery here, that of the flesh one never sees, the foundation of things, the other side of the head, of the face, the secretory glands *par excellence*, the flesh from which everything exudes, at the very heart of the mystery, the flesh in as much as it is suffering, is formless, in as much as its form in itself is something which provokes anxiety. Spectre of anxiety, identification of anxiety, the final revelation of *you are this — You are this, which is so far from you, this which is the ultimate formlessness.*[5]

What is even less clearly defined, perhaps, is the identity of the formless *you,* its proper topography. For in the end, it is not Irma's unconscious that returns the look from inside, but rather Freud's own. The locus of Irma's dream body provides the opening for Freud to encounter himself, the site of his own subjectivity deposited and reflected, as it were, in Irma's depths—a displaced unconscious incorporated by Irma's dream body. The radical gesture of searching the other's body for the residues of oneself articulates a wish that carries, as do all unconscious thoughts, its antithesis: the desire to lose oneself in the other's body, to be dissolved in the body of the other. The discourse of that wish, Lacan argues, points toward a profound *senselessness*: "It is just when the world of the dreamer is plunged into the greatest imaginary chaos . . . that the subject decomposes and disappears. In this dream there's the recognition of the fundamentally acephalic character of the subject, beyond a given point."[6] The wish for dissolution would, within four months of Freud's dream, be fulfilled as a photographic phenomenon: the x ray.

The desire to transgress the surface of the body, to be dissolved in the body of another and encounter its interior *as interiority* would have a profound impact on the evolution of psychoanalysis, but also on the nature of representation, especially that of the human body. The x ray in particular, with the fluid inside-outside vantage point it yields, would, like psychoanalysis, participate in the erosion of a subjectivity that had sustained Western science and art in the age of the Enlightenment.

The Enlightenment project, which Ernst Cassirer characterizes as an epistemological movement acutely aware of and fascinated by the contours of the limit, reached a crucial threshold on November 8, 1895, when Wilhelm Conrad Röntgen discovered the x ray.[7] The Enlightenment had determined, in its pursuit of limits, the parameters of a singular subject bound by the desire to expose and appropriate the world around it. The "Enlightenment," write Max Horkheimer and Theodor Adorno, "is totalitarian."[8] That is, the logic of the Enlightenment, what Horkheimer and Adorno refer to as "the mastery of nature," required a master-subject who stood outside the limit, unaffected and, in the Kantian sense, disinterested. That dialectical subject defined itself in its encounters with the limit. The persistence of limits, in turn, maintained the viability of such a subject. With the appearance of the x ray, however, the subject was forced to concede the limits of the body, erasing the limit against which it claimed to be outside. For the x-ray image, with its simultaneous view of the inside and outside, turned the perspective of the spectator-subject inside out. Regarding the fragility of inside spaces, Gilles Deleuze writes: "In this collapse of the surface, the entire world loses its meaning."[9] Against the field of x-ray vision, the Enlightenment had exceeded the function of the classical subject: the traditional subject was now inside the frame, an aspect of the spectacle. This, in turn, produced a kind of blindness that necessitated the advent of a phenomenological supplement. According to Linda Dalrymple Henderson, Röntgen's discovery of the invisible rays "clearly established the inadequacy of human sense perception and raised fundamental questions about the nature of matter itself."[10] In fact, the x ray forced a transposition of the language of the Enlightenment from a figurative to a literal sphere. The metaphors of vision that inform so much of Enlightenment thinking were thrust beyond their figurative limits. The absolute radiance unleashed by the x ray now absorbed the subject, enveloped it in a searing light. The Enlightenment subject had become the focus of its own penetrating look, susceptible to the "self-destructive" force that Horkheimer and Adorno identify at the heart of the movement.[11] One year before the atomic irradiation of Hiroshima and Nagasaki, they warned: "The fully enlightened earth *radiates* disaster triumphant."[12]

▶

Wilhelm Conrad Röntgen (1845–1923)

While experimenting with Crookes tubes and cathode rays in 1895, Röntgen noticed a curious fluorescent effect. A mysterious form of radiation had passed through solid objects, casting fluorescent light upon distant surfaces. Attempting to fix that fluorescence on a photographic plate, Röntgen inadvertently discovered a new type of ray that penetrated organic and inorganic matter, leaving a "shadow" of that object on the plate. The invisible electromagnetic ray, it would later be learned, consisted of a shorter wavelength (and thus a higher frequency) than visible light, which allowed it to penetrate and illuminate solid matter. Röntgen named the as-yet-unidentified rays "x."

From the outset, Röntgen linked the x ray to photography by fixing his discovery on photographic surfaces. Although Röntgen protested the association of the x ray with photographic media, claiming that the use of photography had only been "the means to the end," the fusion, or confusion, had already taken hold of the public imagination. X-ray images came to be seen as essentially photographic documents, indelibly marked by their relationship to the superficiality of photographs. They were at once images of a three-dimensional flatness. Among Röntgen's first published x-ray photographs is one of his wife Berthe's hand, which was taken in the final months of 1895, fifty years after his birth and fifty years before the atomic explosions in Japan. The image depicts Berthe's skeletal structure, the bones that constitute her hand, but also the wedding ring that hovers on the surface, lacerating it from the outside. The trace of exteriority that Berthe's ring imposes on the interior dimension revealed the uncanny nature of the new medium. In fact, the image of women's interiority, from Irma to Berthe, appears to have gained enormous currency around 1895. "The frequently published image of a woman's hand," writes Lisa Cartwright, "gained enormous popularity, becoming an icon of female sexuality and death."[13] Upon seeing her flesh thus transgressed, Berthe is said to have shuddered at the "vague premonition of death" it evoked.[14] The x ray's link to iconographies of death is made explicit by Henderson, who claims that Röntgen's discovery "triggered the most immediate and widespread reaction to any scientific discovery before the explosion of the first atomic bomb in 1945."[15] "The discovery of x rays," Henderson concludes, "produced a sense that the world had changed irrevocably."[16]

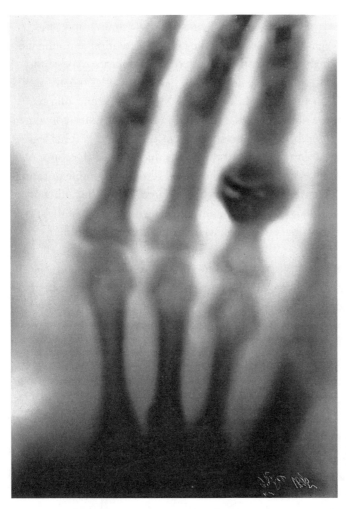

Berthe Röntgen's hand, 1895. Indices, inside and out.

Indeed Röntgen, the x ray, photographic media, and the atomic weapon circulate in a specular economy, bound—as are all *photographic* events—by the logic of anniversaries. By capturing unique moments in time, all photographs inscribe future anniversaries *yet to come*. The logic of anniversaries, like that of photographs, is always uncanny, phantasmatic, displaced: anniversaries comprise mnemic projections that never adhere, as it were, to the present moment. Anniversaries are forged by suturing one moment to another, one temporality to another—they are, therefore, allusive and allegorical by nature. In the case of 1895, the advent of radiographic imagery permeates by allusion the scientific and aesthetic discourses, establishing a kind of spectral episteme that revolves around the representation of interiority. Moreover, 1895 continues to haunt the anniversaries that precede and succeed it. The centennial of Röntgen's birth and the semicentennial of his discovery, Victor Bouillion has noted, coincide with the fiftieth anniversary of the advent of cinema and the annihilation of Hiroshima and Nagasaki.[17] Expanding the cycle of radiation and mnemic phenomena, one might add that the first successful daguerreotype of the sun was taken by Hippolyte Fizeau and J.-B. Léon Foucault on April 2, 1845, one week after the birth of Röntgen on March 27. From solar to atomic radiation, the anniversaries, measured in fifty-year units, converged most recently in 1995, bringing into sharp focus the thanatographic legacies of the twentieth century. Some of the events that marked the continuing dynamic of this anniversary included the global festivities commemorating the centennial of cinema, the controversy that erupted over the Smithsonian Institute's ill-fated *Enola Gay* exhibit, and the awarding of the Nobel Prize for physics to two scientists who had, as it were, exceeded the function of x-ray technology.[18]

The x ray situates the spectacle in its context as a living document even when it depicts, as it frequently does, an image of death or the deterioration of the body that leads to it. Almost immediately, the mimetic and consuming nature of the x ray became readily apparent. Shortly after the euphoria of Röntgen's discovery had begun to subside, a series of alarming symptoms began to appear on the bodies submitted to the x ray's probe. Sunburns, hair and nail loss, scaling of the skin, nausea, and an array of other pathogenic signs began to expose the destructive capacities of the x ray. Under the glow of the x ray, the body moved from a referent to a sign, from a figure to the primary site of inscription. X rays had turned the human body itself into a photographic surface, reproducing its function directly on the human skin. One might note, however, that the legacy of photography already contained a version of this phantasy with regard to the human body. Nadar recounts, for example, that Honoré de Balzac believed that the human essence comprised "a series of specters, infinitely superimposed layers of foliated film or skin *[pellicules]*."[19] According to Balzac, a layer of skin was removed and captured each time one posed before a camera. The x ray, then, appeared to have amplified the effects of an intrinsic *photophobia* already understood at work in photography.[20] The direct effects of radiation on the human surface would be reenacted exponentially fifty years later when the atomic explosions in Hiroshima and Nagasaki turned those cities, in the instant of a flash, into massive *cameras*; the victims grafted onto the geography by the radiation, *radiographed*.[21]

In a similar fashion, the x-ray sign assails the structure of visual signification: the referent of the x-ray photograph, for example, trembles between *what* is seen and the *process* by which it is seen. For the histories of optics, photography, and phenomenology, the impact of Röntgen's discovery of the x ray remains immeasurable. Michel Frizot writes: "The discovery of the x ray and its effects were to have a considerable impact on modern thought: It turned out that an invisible emanation could manifest itself on a photographic plate . . . and that one could visualize, with that invisibility, an internal reality of the body—also invisible—a type of 'interiority.'"[22] One hears in this description the resonances of Freud's dream. The convergence of psychology and photography, Frizot suggests, radically transformed the epistemology of the twentieth century, creating, in the process, an epistemology of the inside.

Although it has evolved primarily as a medical device and within the scientific institutions (Röntgen was a professor of physics at the University of Würzburg in Germany), the x ray has always maintained a precarious relation to the parasitical force of art. Because it cannot be perceived by the so-called naked eye, the x ray hovers in the interstice between science and art. At first, the x ray suggested a number of disciplinary uses: "In London a firm advertised in February 1896 the 'sale of x-ray proof underclothing,' and in the United States, Assemblyman Reed of Somerset County, New Jersey, introduced a bill into the state legislature prohibiting the use of x-ray opera glasses in the theaters."[23] The disciplines of trade and law thus surfaced in the interval between science and art. Still "others thought," notes Röntgen biographer Otto Glasser, "that with the x-rays base metals could be changed into gold, vivisection outmoded, temperance promoted by showing drunkards the steady deterioration of their systems, and the human soul photographed."[24] The x ray had become a fantastic repository, an extensive archive of unfulfilled wishes. In fact, the x ray's drive operates equally in the registers that span between science and art. The futurists— Duchamp, Kupka, Man Ray, and more recently filmmaker Barbara Hammer and artists Jean-Michel Basquiat, Gary Higgins, Alan Montgomery, and Ann Duncan Satterfield, among others—have deployed the x-ray image in their artwork, situating it at the thresholds of figure and fact.[25] And this is precisely the threat that all institutional apparatuses face: all scientific devices are susceptible to what is adamantly called "misuse." As both Martin Heidegger and Marshall McLuhan have argued in very different contexts, however, the concept of technological misuse—humanistic notions of good and bad uses of technology—cannot be maintained. All uses, they insist, are inscribed in the apparatus, actualized with each use of the instrument. Such is the nature of technology: it does not respond to the call of ethics, only to that of "bringing forth," of exposure. Technology is, in the psychoanalytic sense, "driven."[26]

The Greek term *techne,* according to Heidegger's reading of it, unites the functions of technology and art in an imaginary whole.[27] Science and art are confused, one might say, in the figure of the x ray. Indeed, when technological advances facilitate the appearance of previously unknown phenomena, they tend to take on the semblance of an artwork. The legacy of the atomic bomb, particularly its spectacular form, attests to this effect.

The Artefact

In 1946, one year after two atomic explosions incinerated Hiroshima and Nagasaki, Hungarian artist László Moholy-Nagy (1895–1946)—who also shares a birthday with the x ray—discussed the impact of x-ray technology on the practice of art. "In x-ray photos," he writes, "structure becomes transparency and transparency manifests structure. The x-ray pictures, to which the futurist has consistently referred, are among the outstanding space-time renderings on the static plane. They give simultaneously the inside and outside, the view of an opaque solid, its outline, but also its inner structure."[28] Moholy-Nagy's description of the use of x-ray technologies in art exceeds, however, that of a mere technique. The ability to expose simultaneously the inside and outside of a thing, to retain the object's surface even while probing its depths, describes a scientific phantasy as well as a scientific imperative.

Unlike the microscopes and telescopes that precede it, the x ray retains the dimension and shape of its object while rendering its inside. The imaginary x-ray document thus generates an impossible perspective. Figure and fact, an object's exterior and interior dimensions, are superimposed in the x ray, simultaneously evoking and complicating the metaphysics of topology in which the exterior signifies deceptive surfaces and appearances while the interior situates truths and essences, what Francis Bacon has called elsewhere "the brutality of fact."[29] The term *artefact* perhaps best describes the x-ray image, which is at once buried and revealed, invoking the archaeological aspect of its function. The x-ray image determines a kind of living remnant, a phantom subject. "Art" and "fact," fused together like the sign and referent of Roland Barthes's "Photograph," always arrive intact in the x ray as *artefact*.[30]

Moholy-Nagy's invocation of the x ray also contains a warning against the immediate consumption of images. X-ray images, he writes, "have to be studied to reveal their meaning; but once the student has learned their language, he will find them indispensable."[31] A type of exegesis is thus required, a kind of hermeneutics of the x-ray image that, not unlike dream analysis, extends, according to Moholy-Nagy, into the realm of language. X rays thus invoke an inherent grammatology. Indeed, the term *x ray,* especially its prefix, conjures a cultural semiology that includes pornography

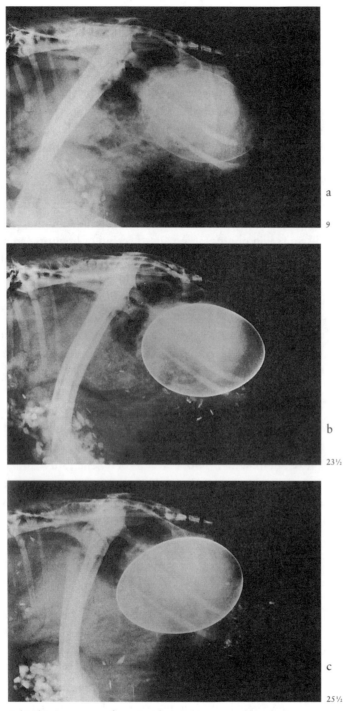

a

9

b

23½

c

25½

A birthing sequence from inside to out: x ray of hen laying
an egg (a) at 9 hours; (b) at 23½ hours; (c) at 25½ hours. Photo
by John A. Fairfax Fozzard (formerly of the Department of
Anatomy, University of Cambridge).

(adolescent notions of x-ray vision and "x"- and "triple x"- rated movies), medicine, algebra, and erasure.

A brief glance at the history of photography reveals that the rhetorical tension between nature (the signifier of the real) and the photographic referent has never been adequately resolved. From its inception, photography was endowed with a transcendental, scientific capacity even as it adopted the idiom of art. William Henry Fox Talbot, for example, spoke of photography as the "pencil of nature." The critical terminology that frames the photographic practice—"photogenic drawing" (Talbot) or "biogrammatology" (François Dagognet's characterization of Etienne-Jules Marey's project), for example—underscores the ambiguity between figure and fact in photography.[32] The blend of scientific and aesthetic terminology that informs the discourse on photography—itself a kind of linguistic emulsion—highlights another aspect of the photographic event: writing. As technological media, photography as well as film and video are marked by their ability to preserve the image, repeat it, and facilitate a contemplation of the external and internal worlds in a manner that invariably approaches what is called "reading." Records are, by definition, the traces of phenomena that remain in mnemic or historical archives. Accordingly, the x ray extended not only the limits of the empirical world and the human sensorium, but also the trajectory of photography: it extended the graphic reach of the apparatus into the invisible spectrum of light. The x ray unveiled a form of *exscriptive* writing. The result of that supplementation has required the spectator to function as an interpreter, a kind of cryptographic translator. Thus x-ray texts, despite their semblance of total penetration and absolute lucidity, require a form of mediation—they must read before they can be understood. In this light, the x ray can be seen as having reversed the trajectory of Enlightenment writing from inscription to *exscription*.

▶ _____

1895

A series of coincidences dictates the events of 1895, evoking Rémy Chauvin's notion of "the *aparallel evolution* of two beings that have absolutely nothing to do with each other."[33] In the case of 1895, however, the "aparallel evolution" involves more than two beings and seems to have been bound by a nascent episteme. On February 13 of the year that Röntgen published his discovery of the x ray, Louis Lumière patented the Cinématographe.[34] The Lumière brothers' first public screenings were held at the Grand Café in Paris on December 28, the *exact* date of Röntgen's publication. The Lumières, it is said, used a translucent screen that passed the image in reverse across to the other side. Thus spectators could pay more to sit on the side of the projector, and less to view the screenings from the other side. The contemporary configuration of the cinematic screen, which limits the viewing surface to one side, was a later development. In this sense, the original apparatus, with its transverse flow of light, more closely resembled the luminous economy of the x ray. The first film screen was itself a kind of porous tissue.

Other cinematic advances in 1895 included the introduction of R. W. Paul and Brit Acres's movie camera in March, the advent of the so-called Latham loop by Woodville Latham and his sons in April, and the debut of C. Francis Jenkins and Thomas Armat's Phantoscope in October.[35] In May 1895, Josef Breuer and Sigmund Freud published their *Studies on Hysteria,* after years of treating hysterics with hypnosis.[36] The "birth" of psychoanalysis in 1895 was followed by at least two significant afterbirths: the "dream of Irma's injection" in July and the birth of Anna, the last of Freud's children, in December. To overdetermine further the shape of 1895 — overdetermination being, among other things, a key feature of Freud's typology — Edison, according to Henderson, asserted confidently "that x rays would ultimately unveil the activity of the human brain."[37] Indeed, Cartwright and Brian Goldfarb have documented both Edison's and Louis Lumière's immediate explorations in x-ray imaging of the body and brain.[38] Brain, body, mind, and soul appear to orbit 1895 in a specular constellation that transgresses the liminal borders of each discrete function. Moholy-Nagy describes the sense of confusion that erupted between scientific developments and desire in the late nineteenth century:

> In the 19th century telescopic and microscopic "miracles," x-ray and infrared penetrations were substituted for fantasy and emotional longing. These phenomena, motion and speed, electricity and wireless, seemed to give food enough to the imagination without introducing subconscious automatism. Photography was the golden key opening the door to the wonders of the external universe to everyone. The astonishing records of this period were *objective* representations, though they went in some cases beyond the observation capacity of our eyes as in the high speed, micro-macro, x-ray, infrared and similar types of photography. This was the period of "realism" in photography.[39]

For Moholy-Nagy, photography represents the visualization of desire in the nineteenth century. It locates the topology of the unconscious prior to the advent of psychoanalysis, serving as the sign for an unconscious yet to be named.

Three phenomenologies of the "inside" thus appeared in 1895 — the x ray, cinema, and psychoanalysis, attempting to expose the anatomies of the body, motion, and the psyche, respectively. These three technologies not only altered the status of the referent or document of interiority, they also changed the terms by which such interiorities were viewed. They changed the structure of visual perception, shifting the terms of vision from the optical to phenomenal register. Moreover, the x ray, cinema, and psychoanalysis appear to be inextricably fused to one another, appropriating each other's features, functions, and rhetorical modes. The capacity to see through the surface of the object, to penetrate its screen, thus emerged in 1895 as the unconscious of the Enlightenment "look."

Walter Benjamin seized upon the proximity of photography to psychoanalysis, as did Jean-Martin Charcot, Albert Londe, and Freud before him, finding in these two probes two passages toward the discovery of the unconscious. "Evidently," writes Benjamin in a famous passage from the "The Work of Art in the Age of Mechanical Reproduction (1935–36)," "a different nature opens itself to the camera than to the naked eye—if only because an *unconsciously penetrated space* is substituted for a space consciously explored by man. . . . The camera introduces us to unconscious optics as does psychoanalysis to unconscious impulses."[40] In Benjamin's language, the movement from photography to the unconscious develops from the logic of penetration.[41]

▶────────────────────────────────────

Seventeen Years Earlier

Another, earlier, coincidence punctuates the history of interiority as a photographic phenomenon. It began in 1878, when Etienne-Jules Marey (1830-1904) encountered Eadweard James Muybridge (1830–1904) in the December 14, 1878, issue of *La Nature,* which had published Muybridge's pictures of horses in motion. The two EJMs eventually met in Paris on November 26, 1881.[42] Of the two, Muybridge first lacerated the apparently seamless flow of everyday life by dissecting its suturing mechanism, animal locomotion. By extracting the components of movement from perception, Muybridge transformed the experience of movement itself. Muybridge's static serial photographs (he also animated and projected his work using a zoopraxinoscope) suggest the presence of movement from which the images are torn. The minute instants effect a cinematic tension that is nonetheless invisible in film. They are like special effects or stills from a film that is yet to occur. Like Bergsonian fragments, Muybridge's stills point to a duration they cannot reproduce. In 1925, Germaine Dulac, lamenting the loss of pure cinema to excess narrativity, called for a return to a kind of Muybridgesque notion of film. "Cinema," she writes, "by decomposing movement, *makes us see,* analytically . . . the psychology of movement."[43] Dulac's complex idiom, which synthesizes metaphors of corporeality, psychology, and perception, reflects the profound dilemma that cinema seems to pose with regard to the rhetoric of interiority. For Dulac, cinema offers the possibility of decomposing the movement of things and revealing, in the process, its psychology, what she calls elsewhere its "soul." The purpose of the medium, she insists, is to facilitate a phenomenology of the imperceptible. "If machines decompose movement and set out to explore the realm of the infinitely small in nature, it is in order to visually reveal to us the beauties and charms that our eye, a feeble lens, does not perceive."[44] In a similar vein, Benjamin regards the advent of "close-up" and "slow-motion" effects in film, aspects that are already evident throughout Muybridge's precinematic corpus, as a means not only of enhancing perception but of conceiving new phenomena. He writes:

> With the close-up, space expands; with slow motion, movement is extended. The enlargement of a snapshot does not simply render more precise what in any case was visible, though unclear: it reveals entirely new structural formations of the subject. So, too, slow motion not only presents familiar qualities of movement but reveals in them entirely unknown ones.[45]

Inside familiar movements, Benjamin concludes, the cinema reveals new and unknown movements, new subjects of motion. Muybridge can be seen as having discovered the temporality of such movements before the advent of cinema. At once precinematic and anticinematic, Muybridge's studies deconstruct the foundations of cinema as well as its subject prior to their invention.

Marey's work toward the advent of cinema began with biology and acoustics, with the attempt to transcribe (record) and translate (make legible) the movements and sounds of life autographically, that is, without the intervention of sensation.[46] As Dagognet has shown, Marey invented virtual languages, a fantastic semiotics, that flowed directly from the living body. "Marey's brilliance," Dagognet writes, "lay in the discovery of how to make recordings without recourse to the human hand or eye. Nature had to testify to itself, to translate itself through the inflection of curves and subtle trajectories that were truly representative."[47] Photography, then, seemed like an appropriate destination for Marey's pursuit of the "trace": "Nature's own expression, without screen, echo or interference."[48] In his experiments with chronophotography, Marey sought to capture movement on a single photographic plate.

At stake in chronophotography was the attempt to record duration, to replicate the movement of an empirical object through time. In order to accomplish this, however, Marey needed to maintain the object in space, to sustain the world in which that object moved. The desire to investigate things in their natural environment or context lies at the source of all documentary activity. It is a desire that links the document to the animal body, documentary work to life. Against the conventions of vivisection, for example, which terminated the animal's life in order to assess the parts that sustained its movement, Marey's "biogrammatology" required the continued existence of movement, of life in the body that it explored. In this sense, Marey's project can be seen as radically antiscientific at the same time that it participated, without question, in the scientific praxis. It can be understood both structurally and figuratively within the epistemic glow of x-ray pictures. In the end, both Muybridge and Marey can be interpreted as key figures in the pre-*techne* of the x ray.[49] Their work marks the beginnings of cinema perhaps, but also the property of a "decomposing look" that cinema shares with the x ray.

▶

Toward the Surface

What separates Muybridge's and Marey's work from cinema is, perhaps, not so much the quality of motion as the texture of surfaces. Chrono-photography lacks the sheer superficiality of cinema. In this regard, cinema more closely resembles the tactile superimposition of subject and object, inside and outside found on the surface of the x ray. It is a surface, moreover, that is constantly collapsing, leaving intact only the trace of a surface that no longer limits anything. It is an empty surface that has become, in the idiomatic sense, superficial. Of the empty surface, Deleuze writes: "As there is no surface, the inside and outside, the container and the contained, no longer have a precise limit; they plunge into a universal depth or turn in the circle of a present which gets more contracted as it is filled."[50] Deleuze's description closely resembles Freud's economy of the unconscious.

In 1915, Freud enumerated the essential features of the unconscious: "*exemption from mutual contradiction,* primary motility [mobility] of cathexis, *timelessness,* and *substitution of psychic for external reality.*"[51] The screen on which the chaos of the unconscious is projected appears in the form of the system *Pcs,* the surface of the psyche. "Unconscious processes," Freud writes, "can only be observed by us under the conditions of dreaming and of neurosis."[52] As if in response to Freud's provocation, Bertram Lewin introduced the notion of the "dream screen" in 1946.[53] The "empty surface" facilitates, according to Lewin, the perception of otherwise imperceptible psychic phenomena. Jean-Louis Baudry explains the function of Lewin's psychic surface from the vantage of cinema:

The screen, which can appear by itself, like a white surface, is not exclusively a representation, a content—in which case it would not be necessary to privilege it among other elements of the dream content; but rather, it would present itself in all dreams as the indispensable support for the projection of images.[54]

Dulac also describes cinema, the seventh art of the "screen," as "depth rendered perceptible"—that is, projected onto the surface.[55] From this perspective, Irma's mouth, and indeed the whole of her interiority—with its white patches—can be seen as a kind of dream screen or surface. Freud had projected an image of the dream screen onto Irma's body; he had rendered her phantom body a screen. Freud was, perhaps, dreaming of dreams.
And in so doing, he may have inadvertently dreamed not only of a future psychoanalysis, but of cinema and the x ray as well. For the structures that bind the three phenomenologies of the inside always return to the site of a fragile surface; skin resurfaced as screens, screens as metonymies of skin. "The human skin of things," writes Antonin Artaud, "the epidermis of

Hiroshima, 1945; an icon of invisibility. U.S. Air Force photo.

reality: this is the primary raw material of cinema."[56] Tracing the genealogy of the dream screen, Lewin likens it to the surface of the mother's body, retained by the dreamer as a mnemic trace. The French term *pellicule* already carries this fusion of film and skin, photographic and corporeal surface. Here, the convergence of the screen with skin brings the constellation back to the x ray.

The surface of the x ray opens onto an impossible topography, a space that cannot be occupied by either the subject or object, or rather, a space in which the subject and object are dissolved into a phantasmatic hybrid or emulsion—an *atopos*. Indeed, the project of the Enlightenment was, perhaps, always to move toward this surface, always to search for that locus in which the subject would be annihilated by the glare of a sublime radiance. The figure that sutures Irma's body to the irradiation of Hiroshima and Nagasaki, acts that can be seen as ultimate violations of the human surface, may be found in the indelible mark of the x-ray photograph. The x ray may be the exemplary figure that binds the twentieth century to the legacy of Western science and art, the surfeit image of an Enlightenment sensibility. As Deleuze has concluded, "On these surfaces the entire logic of sense is located."[57]

♦ ————————————————————————————————————

NOTES

The first version of this essay was delivered at "Visible Evidence II: Strategies and Practices in Documentary Film and Video" in Los Angeles in 1994. I am grateful to Jane Gaines and Michael Renov for their rigorous critique of the manuscript. An earlier version of the text was published in *Qui Parle* 9, no. 2 (spring/summer 1996). I wish to thank the editors and readers at *Qui Parle* for their generous contributions to this essay.

1. In a letter from Sigmund Freud to Wilhelm Fliess, June 12, 1900, in Sigmund Freud, *The Complete Letters of Sigmund Freud to Wilhelm Fliess: 1887–1904,* ed. and trans. Jeffrey Moussaieff Masson (Cambridge: Harvard University Press, 1985), 417.

2. Sigmund Freud, *The Interpretation of Dreams,* in *The Standard Edition of the Complete Psychological Works of Sigmund Freud,* vol. 4, ed. and trans. James Strachey (London: Hogarth and the Institute of Psycho-Analysis, 1955), 107 (emphasis added).

3. Ibid.

4. In fact, Freud never found a satisfactory model for the activities of the psychic apparatus and actively criticized the demand for spatial or graphic figures for the psyche. In *Civilization and Its Discontents,* for example, Freud writes: "The fact remains that only in the mind is such a preservation of all the earlier stages alongside the final form possible, and that we are not in a position to represent this phenomenon in pictorial terms." In *The Standard Edition of the Complete Psychological Works of Sigmund Freud,* vol. 21, ed. and trans. James Strachey (London: Hogarth and the Institute of Psycho-Analysis, 1955), 71. The one exception may be the Mystic Writing-Pad or Wunderblock. See Sigmund Freud, "A Note upon the 'Mystic Writing-Pad,'" in *The Standard Edition,* vol. 19, 227–31.

5. Jacques Lacan, "The Dream of Irma's Injection," in *The Seminar of Jacques Lacan, Book II: The Ego in Freud's Theory and in the Technique of Psychoanalysis, 1954–1955,* ed. Jacques-Alain Miller, trans. Sylvana Tomaselli (New York: Norton, 1988), 154–55.

6. Ibid., 170.

7. Ernst Cassirer, *The Philosophy of the Enlightenment,* trans. Fritz C. A. Koelln and James P. Pettegrove (Princeton, N.J.: Princeton University Press, 1951).

8. Max Horkheimer and Theodor Adorno, *Dialectic of Enlightenment*, trans. John Cumming (New York: Continuum, 1944), 6.

9. Gilles Deleuze, *The Logic of Sense*, ed. Constantin V. Boundas, trans. Mark Lester with Charles Stivale (New York: Columbia University Press, 1990), 87.

10. Linda Dalrymple Henderson, "X Rays and the Quest for Invisible Reality in the Art of Kupka, Duchamp, and the Cubists," *Art Journal* 47, no. 4 (winter 1988): 324. See also Linda Dalrymple Henderson, "A Note on Francis Picabia, Radiometers, and X Rays in 1913," *Art Bulletin* 71, no. 1 (March 1989); W. Robert Nitske, *The Life of Wilhelm Conrad Röntgen, Discoverer of the X Ray* (Tucson: University of Arizona Press, 1971).

11. Of such radical turns in the economy of the gaze, Lacan offers the ecstatic utterance: "I am photo-graphed." Jacques Lacan, *The Four Fundamental Concepts of Psycho-Analysis*, ed. Jacques-Alain Miller, trans. Alan Sheridan (New York: Norton, 1977), 106.

12. Horkheimer and Adorno, *Dialectic of Enlightenment*, 3 (emphasis added).

13. Lisa Cartwright, "Women, X-Rays, and the Public Culture of Prophylactic Imaging," *Camera Obscura* 29 (May 1992): 30. A revised version of Cartwright's essay appears in her remarkable study of medical imagery, *Screening the Body: Tracing Medicine's Visual Culture* (Minneapolis: University of Minnesota Press, 1995). Operating simultaneously in the fields of film history, medical rhetoric and culture, and feminist theory and criticism, Cartwright's rigorous text situates the x ray at the crossroads of twentieth century arts and sciences. She writes: "The X ray is the pivotal site of investigation for this book's exploration of medicine's technological/visual knowledge, desire, and power. It is also the most conflicted site, embodying multiple paradigms of visuality and multiple political agendas" (108).

14. Otto Glasser, *Wilhelm Conrad Röntgen* (Springfield, Ill.: Charles C. Thomas, 1934), 81. "Many people," according to Glasser, "reacted strongly to the ghost pictures. The editor of the *Grazer Tageblatt* had a roentgen picture taken of his head and upon seeing the picture 'absolutely refused to show it to anybody but a scientist. He had not closed an eye since he saw his own death's head'" (81). Of Freud's dream image of Irma, Lacan adds: "The phenomenology of the dream of Irma's injection . . . leads to the apparition of the terrifying anxiety-provoking image, to this real Medusa's head, to the revelation of this something which properly speaking is unnameable, the back of the throat, the complex, unlocatable form, which also makes it into the primitive object *par excellence*, the abyss of the feminine organ from which all life emerges, this gulf of the mouth, in which everything is swallowed up, and no less the image of death in which everything comes to an end." "The Dream of Irma's Injection," 163–64.

15. Henderson, "X Rays," 324.

16. Ibid., 336.

17. Victor Bouillion, "War and Medicinema: The X-Ray and Irradiation in Various Theaters of Operation," in *Incorporations: Zone Six*, ed. Sanford Kwinter (New York: Zone, 1992), 253.

18. Concerning the partnership between the field of physics and x-ray technology during the twentieth century, the decision of the 1994 Nobel Prize committee may have signaled a critical moment. Among the recipients of the awards in science were two physicists, Clifford G. Shull and Bertram N. Brockhouse, who had, in the words of *New York Times* writer Malcolm W. Brown, succeeded in developing "neutron probes [that] gave scientists a set of tools more powerful than X-rays and other forms of radiation used for exploring the atomic structure of matter." Malcolm W. Brown, "American Awarded Nobel Prize in Chemistry," *New York Times*, October 13, 1994, natl. ed., A9. Ironically, then, x rays may have been superseded, even rendered obsolete, on the eve of the centennial of their discovery. Röntgen was himself the recipient of the first Nobel Prize for science in 1901.

19. Nadar, *Nadar: Dessins et Écrits*, vol. 2 (Paris: Arthur Hubschmid, 1979), 978 (my translation). "Donc selon Balzac, chaque corps dans la nature se trouve composé de séries de spectres, en couches superposées à l'infini, foliacées en pellicules infinitésimales, dans tous les sens où l'optique perçoit ce corps.

"L'homme à jamais ne pouvant créer,— c'est à dire d'une apparition, de l'impalpable, constituer une chose solide, ou de *rien* faire une *chose*,—chaque opération Daguerrienne venait donc surprendre, détachait et retenait en se l'appliquant une des couches du corps objecté."

20. A version of this phobia also existed in Meiji Japan (1868–1912). "During this time," writes Rika Sakuma, "numerous superstitions were associated with photography, including the beliefs that 'posing for a photograph drained one's shadow,' 'posing for a second shortened one's life,' and 'when three subjects posed for a photograph, the one in the middle would die.'" Rika Sakuma, "Shashin to josei—atarashii shikaku media no toujou to 'miru/mirareru' jibun no shutsugen [Photography and women: the advent of new visual media and the creation of a self that looks/is looked at]," in *Nihon joseishi saikou* [Redefining Japanese women's history], 6 vols., ed. Akiko Okuda (Tokyo: Fujihara Shoten,

1995), vol. 5, *Onna to otoko no jikuu: se-megiau onna to otoko* [The timespace of women and men: the confrontation of women and men], 200 (my translation). In an interesting aside to the photo-iconography of hands and the image of Berthe Röntgen's, many Japanese women at that time feared having their hands photographed. Small hands were considered a sign of feminine beauty and, according to Sakuma, these women believed not only that their hands looked bigger in photographs, but that the photographic process actually made their hands swell (228).

21. See Akira Mizuta Lippit, "Photographing Nagasaki: From Fact to *Artefact*," in *Nagasaki Journey: The Photographs of Yosuke Yamahata, August 10, 1945*, ed. Rupert Jenkins (San Francisco: Pomegranate, 1995), 25–29.

22. Michel Frizot, "L'Œil absolu: Les formes de l'invisible," in *Nouvelle Histoire de la Photographie*, ed. Michel Frizot (Paris: Bordas, 1994), 281 (my translation). "La découverte des rayons X et de leurs effets allait avoir une action considérable sur la pensée moderne: il était en effet avéré qu'une émanation tout à fait invisible pouvait se manifester sur une plaque photographique . . . et qu'en outre on pouvait visualiser avec cet invisible une réalité interne des corps, elle aussi invisible, une sorte d'«intériorité»."

23. Glasser, *William Conrad Röntgen*, 82.

24. Ibid., 83.

25. See Akira Mizuta Lippit, "The X-Ray Files: Alien-ated Bodies in Contemporary Art," *Afterimage* 22, no. 5 (December 1994): 6–9.

26. According to the Lacanian distinction between demand and drive, the former operates with the structures of subjectivity and desire; it is unconscious. The latter, however, originates in a place beyond the subject, traversing that subject always from the outside. A crisis in perception (false perceptions, hallucinations), Lacan argues, often precipitates the appearance of a drive. In such cases, the "so-called refusal to perceive produces a hole and there then appears in reality a drive that has been rejected by the subject." Jacques Lacan, *The Seminar of Jacques Lacan: The Psychoses 1955–1956*, vol. 3, ed. Jacques-Alain Miller, trans. Russell Grigg (New York: Norton, 1993), 293.

27. Martin Heidegger, "The Origin of the Work of Art," trans. Albert Hofstadter, in *Poetry, Language, Thought* (New York: Harper & Row, 1971), 15–87.

28. László Moholy-Nagy, *Vision in Motion* (Chicago: Paul Theobald, 1947), 252.

29. See David Sylvester, *The Brutality of Fact: Interviews with Francis Bacon* (Oxford: Thames & Hudson, 1987). Of the photograph, Bacon, who was heavily influenced by radiographic images, states: "I think it's the slight remove from fact, which returns me onto the fact more violently" (30).

30. Roland Barthes, *Camera Lucida: Reflections on Photography*, trans. Richard Howard (New York: Hill & Wang, 1981). Barthes writes: "It is as if the Photograph always carries its referent with itself, both affected by the same amorous or funereal immobility, at the very heart of the moving world. . . . The Photograph belongs to that class of laminated objects whose leaves cannot be separated without destroying them both" (5–6).

31. Moholy-Nagy, *Vision in Motion*, 252.

32. François Dagognet, *Etienne-Jules Marey: A Passion for the Trace*, trans. Robert Galeta with Jeanine Herman (New York: Zone, 1992).

33. Rémy Chauvin, *Entretiens sur la sexualité*, ed. Max Aron, Robert Courrier, and Etienne Wolff (Paris: Plon, 1969), 205.

34. Wilhelm Conrad Röntgen, "On a New Kind of Rays (Preliminary Communication)," in Glasser, *Wilhelm Conrad Röntgen*, 41–52. The article was reprinted in the *Annual Report of the Smithsonian Institution* in 1897.

35. Thomas Alva Edison's "Kinetoscope" and "Vitascope" exhibitions straddled 1895, taking place in 1894 and 1896, respectively.

36. Josef Breuer and Sigmund Freud, *Studies on Hysteria*, in *The Standard Edition of the Complete Psychological Works of Sigmund Freud*, vol. 2, ed. and trans. James Strachey (London: Hogarth and the Institute of Psycho-Analysis, 1955).

37. Henderson, "X Rays," 325.

38. Lisa Cartwright and Brian Goldfarb, "Radiography, Cinematography and the Decline of the Lens," in *Incorporations: Zone Six*, ed. Sanford Kwinter (New York: Zone, 1992), 190–201.

39. Moholy-Nagy, *Vision in Motion*, 210. See, in this connection, Thomas Mann, *The Magic Mountain*, trans. H. T. Lowe-Porter (New York: Alfred A. Knopf, 1951).

40. Walter Benjamin, "The Work of Art in the Age of Mechanical Reproduction (1935–36)," in *Illuminations*, ed. Hannah Arendt, trans. Harry Zohn (New York: Schocken, 1968), 236–37 (emphasis added).

41. Addendum to 1895: Albert de Rochas published in 1895 his collection of spectral and psychic images, *L'Exteriorisation de la sensibilité: Étude experimentale et historique* in Paris. Also in 1895, Hippolyte Baraduc began work on psychic photography— accomplished by inducing the subject to excrete "psycho-odo-fluidiques," which were then captured on the photographic plate. His *L'Âme humaine, ses mouvements, ses lumières et l'iconographie de l'invisible* appeared the following year (Paris: G. Carré, 1896). Baraduc, a gynecologist, believed that the human soul emitted a "subtle force" *(force subtile)* perceptible only to the camera.

Again, in an almost compulsive fashion, the specter of women's interiority is summoned to provide a figure for the representation of the invisible. Of the phenomenon of spirit photography that erupted in the late nineteenth century, Tom Gunning writes: "The medium herself became a sort of camera, her spiritual negativity bodying forth a positive image, as the human body behaves like an uncanny photomat, dispensing images from its orifices." Tom Gunning, "Phantom Images and Modern Manifestations: Spirit Photography, Magic Theater, Trick Films, and Photography's Uncanny," in *Fugitive Images: From Photography to Video*, ed. Patrice Petro (Bloomington: Indiana University Press, 1995), 58.

42. The coincidence between these two precinematic figures exceeds chronophotography and the dates of their births and deaths: both had tampered with their names, one altering the sequence (from Jules-Etienne to Etienne-Jules Marey), the other its spelling (from Edward Muggeridge to Eadweard Muybridge). The name as a transcription, an intended signifier of the real, living person, here takes on an interesting function in the hands of the two anatomists of movement, time, and sequence. It was as if the two technicians, under the sway of an irresistible magnetic force, had sought to modulate their work and vital statistics.

43. Germaine Dulac, "Visual and Anti-visual Films," in *The Avant-Garde Film: A Reader of Theory and Criticism*," ed. P. Adams Sitney, trans. Robert Lamberton (New York: Anthology Film Archives, 1987), 32.

44. Ibid.

45. Benjamin, "The Work of Art," 236.

46. See Michel Frizot, *La Chronophotographie* (Beaune: Ministère de la Culture, 1984); and Marta Braun, *Picturing Time: The Work of Etienne-Jules Marey (1830–1904)* (Chicago: The University of Chicago Press, 1992).

47. Dagognet, *Etienne-Jules Marey*, 30.

48. Ibid., 63.

49. Dagognet goes further: "What Marey produced was more than radiography, which showed the striking and baroque image of a skeleton beneath the living creature. He revealed structures that were buried yet mobile: a construction full of springs." Ibid., 132.

50. Deleuze, *Logic of Sense*, 87.

51. Sigmund Freud, "The Unconscious," in *The Standard Edition of the Complete Psychological Works of Sigmund Freud*, vol. 14, ed. and trans. James Strachey (London: Hogarth and the Institute of Psycho-Analysis, 1955), 187.

52. Ibid.

53. Bertram Lewin, "Sleep, the Mouth and the Dream Screen," *Psychoanalytic Quarterly* 15 (1946): 419–43.

54. Jean-Louis Baudry, "The Apparatus: Metapsychological Approaches to the Impression of Reality in Cinema," in *Narrative, Apparatus, Ideology: A Film Theory Reader*, ed. Philip Rosen, trans. Jean Andrews and Bertrand Augst (New York: Columbia University Press, 1986), 310.

55. Dulac, "Visual and Anti-visual Films," 34.

56. Antonin Artaud, "Cinema and Reality," in *Antonin Artaud: Selected Writings*, ed. Susan Sontag, trans. Helen Weaver (New York: Farrar, Straus & Giroux, 1976), 151.

57. Deleuze, *Logic of Sense*, 93.

JANE M. GAINES

[**4**] *Political Mimesis*
_____

> The first thing to remember is that there is, or rather should
> be, no cinema other than agit-cinema.
> :: Sergei Eisenstein, "The Montage of Film Attractions," 1924

▶
_____

Did Documentary Films Ever Produce Social Change?

In *Claiming the Real,* the first theoretically informed history of the documentary film in the English-speaking world, Brian Winston tells us what
we have suspected all along: John Grierson's famous definition of the new
mode was seriously flawed from the start.[1] Recently, the ambiguities in this
concept have begun to intrigue scholars, some of whom began to organize
a series of conferences in the mid-1990s that took up the question of what
makes one work of film and video a "documentary" and another not a
"documentary." Would there have been a need for these conferences if the
pioneers had been more precise? Why did it take scholars so long to see the
obvious (to which Winston finally draws our attention)—that the "creative
treatment of actuality" describes fiction as well as nonfiction film?[2]

From the ambiguity in the term *documentary,* I want to turn to another aspect of the tradition that the pioneer fathers left vague. What, over
the years since Grierson's 1929 definition, has produced and maintained
the theoretical connection between documentary film and social action or
social change? Winston demonstrates that the goal of the Griersonians, who
were essentially British civil servants, was to produce promotional pieces
for the government. The result was a carefully constructed and totally in-
offensive public relations vehicle. The legacy of *Drifters* (1929), *Night Mail*
(1936), and *Housing Problems* (1936) is today's "balanced" television
documentary, the form that scrupulously avoids taking stands. And just as

today's "balanced" television documentary is viewed in living rooms far from the front lines of political upheaval, the Grierson-produced films were never really shown in the context of social struggles. In contrast with today's television documentary, however, the Grierson films could not even claim social "influence" by virtue of having been widely *seen,* given that they received such limited exhibition.[3] Winston goes on to remind us that it is not only the early British documentaries, the forerunners, that, compared with fiction films, were seen by relatively small audiences. Few of the classic documentaries have ever had mass audiences. With the exception of some unusual films that enjoyed limited success as feature releases in the United States (*Harlan County, U.S.A.,* 1976; *The Atomic Cafe,* 1982; *Roger and Me,* 1989), the films in the documentary canon have not been box-office blockbusters. Actually, most scholars know this. But given this knowledge, why has the myth of sweeping social change remained attached to the documentary film both inside and outside the academy?

An earlier study to which Brian Winston refers drew my attention to this question. As Winston recounts the study, in 1995, Kirwin Cox of the National Film Board of Canada was asked to produce a list of "the 10 documentaries that changed the world" for the Centennial of Film celebration. The forty-eight scholars and filmmakers polled had difficulty thinking of films that had actually "changed" the world. In the end, they settled for films that had had some local "influence" for want of examples associated with cataclysmic change.[4] Inspired by this exercise, I decided to take my own poll. Much smaller and more informal, my sample consisted of some friends in film studies and people I know who work in distribution at Third World Newsreel and California Newsreel. This knowledgeable group also had trouble with the question, which they thought would have been better phrased, What films *should* have caused social change? Although they could list documentary films that moved them personally, they could not be certain that these films had actually changed anything for anyone. As I anticipated, they argued that it was only in connection with moments or movements that films could be expected to make a contribution to social change, and that in and of themselves, they had no power to affect political situations. More important, my sample group confirmed the existence of a mythology on the Left, telling me that many of us want to think that documentary film has a legacy of social change. We not only hope for social transformation in our lifetime, but we hope that independently produced documentary film and video will have something to do with this upheaval. Tom Waugh cleverly captures this sense in his introduction to *"Show Us Life,"* which he titles, "Why Documentary Filmmakers Keep Trying to Change the World, or Why People Changing the World Keep Making Documentaries."[5]

Waugh's emphasis on "trying to change" is useful because it conceives of social change as an effort, an almost utopian goal rather than an instrumental project. He offers the term "committed documentary," a concept that by foregrounding political allegiance neatly sidesteps the thorny problem of social consequences.[6] When we actually look at the history of this mode of intervention, this mode of engagement, we see very few examples of films that have even been viewed widely let alone have sparked anything resembling a chain of social reactions. Most curious of all, given that the Grierson model (carried over into the United States in the Pare Lorentz tradition of *The River,* 1937, and *The Plow That Broke the Plains,* 1936) is so undeniably apolitical, how is it that this model came to be associated at all with later film movements that claimed to have radical political agendas? Here I think that Winston is right to locate the U.S. women's movement films in the tradition of New Day's *Union Maids* (1976) as the aesthetic heirs of the Griersonian "problem moment" film, as he calls it.[7] If nothing else, the comparison reminds us of how *Union Maids* cautiously avoided dealing with the role of the American Communist Party in U.S. labor history.

But Winston's alignment of the U.S. women's movement films with the Grierson tradition also runs the risk of de-emphasizing the public policy agenda of the Griersonians, a state mandate that was significantly different from the goals of the independent Left, the engine behind New Day Film's production of *Union Maids.* Perhaps we need to do more to assert the differences in the conditions of production of the films that end up so often under the same vague banner of "social change." Most curious is how, given Grierson's job with the British government, the films he produced have been associated with radicalism at all. Winston suggests half facetiously that *Drifters* won its radical reputation because it once shared a double bill with Eisenstein's *The Battleship Potemkin* (1925), which was for a time banned in Britain.[8] The record shows, however, that Grierson eschewed the Russians—was disinterested in Vertov and was not particularly deferential to Eisenstein. Basil Wright once said of Grierson that he "never used the word revolution."[9] Although Grierson and the National Film Board of Canada as well as Pare Lorentz and the Farm Security Association may have a foundational relationship to social activism in the textbook version of documentary film history, most of us would be more inclined to look to the United States histories of Nykino and the Film and Photo League in the 1930s, and Newsreel in the 1960s in the United States for examples of films that "shook things up" politically.[10] Invariably, however, the search for social relevance leads us to Joris Ivens and Henri Storck's *Borinage* (1933), a film that ranked high in my informal poll. Considering the way the film was used as an organizing tool among Belgian Communist groups, it would seem to be a model of Tom Waugh's "committed documentary." But further, *Borinage* resulted in improved housing conditions among the miners it featured, and is thus perhaps one of the origins of the social change mythos. Significantly, the film also pioneered a look. A milestone in the history of political aesthetics, *Borinage,* Grierson later told Ivens, had influenced the cinematic style British documentary makers used to shoot slum conditions.[11]

Borinage also has the requisite socialist credentials, a political badge that many other documentaries made in the West cannot claim. Ivens began to shoot just after a visit to the Soviet Union, and it is well documented that the filmmakers as well as the workers featured in the film were engaged in a revolutionary struggle as part of the international Communist movement. Thus, in addition, *Borinage* raises the question of what it meant to import revolutionary politics from the Soviet Union and introduce them into Western economic and historical circumstances. Further, it also raises the question of changed and changing historical contexts and the difference between using revolutionary film to reeducate or resolidify solidarity among the converted and using film to initiate and convert. We might recall here that Dziga Vertov and Sergei Eisenstein were primarily doing the former and not the latter, and that none of the Soviet works that came to epitomize revolutionary film were shot in the heat of revolutionary overthrow, even though they have come to carry this connotation.

As we know, a wide range of filmmaking schools, often connected to political moments, have drawn from the Soviets, from Godard in his Dziga Vertov period to the feminist avant-garde of the 1970s.[12] The debt to the Soviets in film and video production as well as film and television studies is great and includes everything from theoretical principles of filmmaking to the image of workers to ideological analysis. However, when we think of "social change" in the contemporary sense, we may not immediately think of the Soviets, and this may be due, in part, to the way the Griersonian tradition mediates the relationship to the Soviets in the English-speaking world as well as to the way Robert Flaherty has eclipsed Dziga Vertov, as discussed in the introduction to this collection. Paralleling these developments in documentary film history, in Western political theory, "social change" has been decoupled from "revolution," disconnected in such a way that we are led to see revolution as an unrealizable extreme as opposed to a daily possibility. C. L. R. James, seeing such a possibility in the 1981 Brixton riot, helped to reconnect everyday events with social transformation when he declared of the totally spontaneous eruption, "That is revolution."[13] And if there is any doubt about the connection between changing conditions and the revolutionary moment, there is always the authority of Marx: "The coincidence of the changing of circumstances and of human activity or self-changing can be conceived and rationally understood only as *revolutionary practice*."[14]

Since the 1970s, a great deal of theoretical work as well as filmmaking practice on the Left has been devoted to developing a revolutionary aesthetics—a combative form that poses the right questions in the intellectual struggle against capitalism. But with all of this work, we still know too little about the radical film and the politicized body of its spectator. We are hampered, of course, by the empirical questions: What do we count as change? How do we know what effects the film has produced? How do we determine where consciousness leaves off and action begins?

Eisenstein, never one to be deterred by the need for empirical evidence, forged ahead with a theory of what it is that the film actually *does* to the body of the politicized spectator, while maintaining his close observation of the physical reactions of audiences to his films, closely noting applause and laughter. A recent return to the important essays on the "montage of attractions" in theater and film has also given us the chance to reconsider Eisenstein's fascination with the possibilities of the "agitational spectacle." This is the fascination that led him to consider the powers of "primitive" imitative practices.[15] The instrumentality of Eisenstein's theory is well-known. It is a theory that would go so far as to "calculate" the spectator, proposing a precise calibration of the film in relation to desired emotional response, often in terms of blows and shocks to the psyche.[16] But always softening Eisenstein's didacticism, which at times can sound rigid and authoritarian, is his emphasis on sensuality. This sensuality that tempers Eisenstein's driving intellectuality is less well known in his thought, perhaps because it never seems to have found its way into the work of his closest contemporary admirers following in the Godardian-Brechtian tradition. Sometimes, these references to sensuality sound like a carryover from Marx, for whom even the commodity was a "sensuous thing," and for whom idealism was at fault for not knowing sensuousness.[17] Putting the sensuous back into the theory of political aesthetics would require significant reconceptualization. In Eisenstein's theory of social change and cinema, the bodily senses *lead* the spectator, whose involvement is not strictly intellectual—politics is not exclusively a matter of the head but can also be a matter of the heart. Relevant here, I think, is Jacques Aumont's observation that in Eisenstein's critical vocabulary, "attraction" was supplanted by "pathos."[18] Was this a move from the importance of sensuality to the importance of extreme feeling?

With all that Eisenstein has to say about the spectator, it is interesting that in the new work on spectatorship, particularly from within feminist film theory, there has been no move to reconsider his insights into the "production" of the audience.[19] The easy explanation for this would be the incompatibility between the unabashed behaviorism of the Soviets and the more or less psychoanalytic approach of contemporary feminist film theory. And against the fullness of the psychoanalytic account, the Soviets *do* sound hopelessly mechanistic at times; the vocabulary of reflexes and stimuli in Eisenstein often smacks of the empiricism of contemporary "media effects" research.[20] Nevertheless, particularly since psychoanalysis does so little to help us with political action, we are returned to Eisenstein, who satisfies our interest in what it is that the body is *made to do* by the political film. To restate the problem, I am concerned with the question of what it might be that *moves* viewers to want to act, that moves them to do something instead of nothing in relation to the political situation illustrated on the screen. I raise an almost unanswerable question, I know. It is un-answerable because it is too large, requiring the intellectual resources of a range of fields, but also unanswerable because of the many empirical traps in the problematic. (What constitutes action? How do we measure that action? What are the signs of political consciousness?) Finally, the question of political action is unanswerable without exact knowledge of the political conditions in the world of the audience. In our approach to this question we are required to artificially put on hold the question of the political situation — the agitational climate within which a committed documentary is received, knowing that separating out the determinations in any multiply determined historical moment also has its drawbacks as an exercise.

I should be clear that what we are considering is also somewhat of a fantasy (and contemporary critical theory has something in common with fantasy, remaining as it does in the realm of the unactualized). This fantasy is based on some powerful documentary mythologies that have become intertwined with actual historical events. For instance, the idea of the audi-ence that is collectively *moved* to get up out of their theater seats and take some kind of group action on behalf of a political cause is part of the mix of documentary lore and documentary reality (somewhat like the stories of filmmakers shot at in the process of filming politically volatile events).[21] There is at least one example of spontaneous audience activism on record. The radical newsletter *Rat* reports the reaction to a screening of newsreel films at the State University of New York, Buffalo, in 1969: "At the end of the second film, with no discussion, five hundred members of the audience arose and made their way to the University ROTC building. They pro-ceeded to smash windows, tear up furniture and destroy machines until the office was a total wreck; and then they burned the remaining paper and flammable parts of the structure to charcoal."[22] An isolated incident yet part of the history and mythology of documentary, it is this kind of spontaneous reaction, sign of the politicized body, that I want to discuss in relation to what might be called *political mimesis*.

▶

Political Mimesis

Political mimesis begins with the body. Actualized, it is about a relationship between bodies in two locations—on the screen and in the audience—and it is the starting point for the consideration of what the one body makes the other do.[23] Inspired by Linda Williams's discussion of three genres that "make the body do things"(horror makes you scream, melodrama makes you cry, and porn makes you "come"), the concept of political mimesis addresses what it is that the committed documentary wants us to do. Although we might not want to make a case for the radical documentary as a body genre, we still need to think the body in relation to films that make audience members want to kick and yell, films that make them want to do something *because of the conditions in the world of the audience*. And what we want to retain from the body genre is this powerful mirroring effect. Body genres, as Williams defines them, feature a sensationalized on-screen body and "produce" on the bodies of spectators an "almost involuntary mimicry of emotion or sensation of the body on screen."[24] Our question will be one of the degree to which radical documentaries "produce" a similar "almost involuntary" imitation in sympathetic audiences. More than seventy years after Eisenstein's theories of the mechanical production of the spectator, we return to the idea that the "machine produces the body," but with the difference that all of the intervening and mediating factors are now givens. Whereas once it would have been theoretically unsophisticated to say that machines produced bodily effects, now to say that the "machine produces the body" is to say that machine discourse is powerful enough to bring entities into being.[25]

There has been little or no discussion of the sensationalized body in radical documentary films, perhaps because one tends to think of sense and body in terms of sexuality, and the committed documentary has always been seriously asexual. Appropriately, if one were to undertake an inventory of sensual documentaries, it would need to begin with Eisenstein's *Strike* (1924), which I am treating as an honorary documentary following Bill Nichols's new work on the film.[26] And I am not thinking of the sensual scenes of the male workers bathing, I am thinking of scenes of rioting, images of bodies clashing, of bodies moving as a mass. These are images of

From *Columbia Revolt* (1968). Courtesy of Third World Newsreel.

sensuous struggle, images exhilarating to politicized viewers, who would interpret them as action against a common enemy, an enemy that assumes a variety of guises—a racist state, capitalist management, a bigoted group.

These images of sensuous struggle might be understood as functioning generically in such documentaries and semidocumentaries as *In the Year of the Pig* (1969), *Word Is Out* (1977), *The Battle of Chile* (1979), *Berkeley in the Sixties* (1990), the Film and Photo League's *Bonus March* (1932), Newsreel's *Columbia Revolt* (1968), Black Audio Collective's *Handsworth Songs* (1986), Sankofa's *Territories* (1988), and New Day's *Union Maids* (1976) and *Seeing Red* (1984). The makers have chosen to show these images because, of course, they represent historical events, they stand for actuality. But the makers also use images of bodies in struggle *because they want audiences to carry on that same struggle,* even if carrying it on means fighting back in physical ways that exceed restrained public demonstrations of protest. The whole rationale behind documenting political battles on film, as opposed to producing written records, is to make struggle visceral, to go beyond the abstractly intellectual to produce a bodily swelling. Perhaps the most easily understood example of the bodily effects I am talking about are the effects produced by popular music, often rhythmically reinforced through editing patterns, or what Eisenstein calls the "emotive vibration" in montage.[27] The point of using Woody Guthrie *(Union Maids)* and Joan Baez *(Territories)* singing traditional solidarity ballads on documentary sound tracks is to reach audiences at the juncture of the physiological and the psychological and to use musical associations to "produce" (to use Williams's term again) not just affiliation but action. Although new studies of the music track in film have given us a more comprehensive approach to the question of image and affect, we are only just beginning to think about music and the rhetoric of documentary (for more on which see Neil Lerner's essay on Virgil Thomson's score for *The River* in chapter 5 of this collection).[28]

What I am calling *political mimicry* has to do with the production of affect in and through the conventionalized imagery of struggle: bloodied bodies, marching throngs, angry police. But clearly such imagery will have no resonance without politics, the politics that has been theorized as consciousness, in Marxism as class consciousness, the prototype for politicized consciousness in antiracist and feminist as well as gay and lesbian struggles. The dilemma here is that whereas we would never want to suggest that the process of developing class consciousness is involuntary or imitative, we need to concede that in the thrall of group song, in the heat of battle, in bodily strain and physical resistance, certainly, there could sometimes be an aspect of the involuntary, an aspect that "kicks in" on top of politicized consciousness.

The reason for using films instead of leaflets and pamphlets in the context of organizing is that films often make their appeal through the senses to the senses, circumventing the intellect. The reason for using the documentary to advance political goals is that its aesthetic of similarity establishes a continuity between the world of the screen and the world of the audience, where the ideal viewer is poised to intervene in the world that so closely resembles the one represented on screen. Yes, this is like saying that documentary depends upon the success of this famous illusion, and perhaps in this new period of reconsideration we can rethink the politics of illusionism. Further, documentary realism stands as stirring testimony or evidence of what has gone before. Its evidentiary status makes its appeal in the form of what I have called the "pathos of fact": this happened; people died for this cause; others are suffering; many took to the streets; this innocent victim can be saved if only something is done.[29] Probably this concept of documentary pathos is illustrated most easily with reference to films such as Christine Choy and Renee Tajima's *Who Killed Vincent Chin?* (1988), Isaac Julien's *Who Killed Colin Roach?* (1983), or Errol Morris's *The Thin Blue Line* (1988), films that document cases of social injustice that they then use as an argument for justice in the future. In such films, aesthetic realism works to align the viewer emotionally with a struggle that continues beyond the frame and into his or her real historical present. But isn't any consideration of pathos in the documentary, then, always on the verge of turning into a defense of realism? Much of the challenge of the new work on documentary has to do with finding a way to be both a champion of the critique of realism and a defender of the uses of realism. What I am asking for is the kind of political case for using realism that women's movement documentary makers have never made in defense of their own work, a situation that Alexandra Juhasz notes and moves to rectify in her essay in this collection (see chapter 10). To date, however, there is still no adequately theorized defense of the use of documentary realism in the politically committed film.

It is precisely because of the legacy of the problem of realism—more specifically, because of the general concern about the automatic ideological complicity of the aesthetic—that I want to start instead with the concept of mimesis, to see whether it can be rehabilitated for a theory of media activism. What I want to account for is the fact that radical filmmakers have historically used mimesis not only in the interests of consciousness change but also in the service of making activists more active—of making them more *like* the moving bodies on the screen. But mimesis has its discredited side in mimicry, a side that carries connotations of naive realism, mindless imitation, mechanical copying, and even animality. This phenomenon is like what Todd Boyd calls "monkey see, monkey do," which, after the final scenes of Spike Lee's *Do the Right Thing,* might be called the "Mookie effect."[30] Certainly the media concern that urban youth would imitate the character Mookie's act of arson or start a riot that *looked just like* the brawl that breaks out at the end of the film suggests the potential problem with a theory of mimesis that could conceivably play into right-wing fears about the "effects of violence," the alleged consequences of images that appear on the screen.

▶ ━━

Sympathetic Magic

In his *Mimesis and Alterity,* anthropologist Michael Taussig begins to recover the concept of mimesis and to restore its reputation as a "way of knowing," a project that is not likely to meet with automatic success.[31] Any argument for mimesis as a form of knowledge will meet with resistance in the First World, especially because the concept has long been associated with not-knowing, or "only imitating," reproducing without adding anything, and learning by means of the body without the engagement of the mind. However, as Taussig argues, that mimesis is a body-first way of knowing should be to its credit and not its detriment. There are things that the body "knows" that the mind does not, he would say. Still, our Enlightenment assumptions make us dubious. According to Taussig, what is best understood in South American indigenous culture as "sympathetic magic" has a legacy of interacting with the world that privileges nature over culture. Where the implications for media theory arise, however, is in the way sympathetic magic confers special powers on the image or copy, powers that come to have their influence over the real-world original. As Taussig puts it, the representation takes on the "power of the represented"—it is empowered by that which it represents.[32] Long associated in the First World with primitivism, mimesis would seem to have little to do with modern mechanical technologies, but Taussig insists on a carryover, even a "rebirth" of the ancient powers. The ritual practice in which an effigy has powers over the natural world is revisited in the miraculous reconstitutive powers of mimetic technologies. From the point of view of documentary film, however, the power that has the most resonance is the power of sympathetic magic to "manipulate reality by means of its image."[33] Eisenstein, as I have noted, was drawn to this very possibility of primitive mimesis, which he saw as nothing more than the use of imagery to achieve "mastery" over the physical world, a magical power based on one form echoing another rather than on repetitions of detail.[34]

A contemporary version of sympathetic magic would have to do with the power to produce compelling similarities—*in* one's body (through imitation) as well as through mimetic machines. It is really that the mimetic powers of the body are extended to the machine, which we already knew had a prosthetic function. Thus we need to think of recording and displaying machines as storing, recalling, and retrieving images or functioning rather like the body of a gifted mime. Not surprisingly, sympathetic magic acknowledges that screen images and "life" images will eternally mimic one another. But most important for radical documentary, a notion of sympathetic magic allows us to deal with the wish that images could change the world, that bodies on the screen could have their concrete connection with bodies in social space, whether those screen bodies are seen as performing the ideal or enacting the taboo. Finally, the notion of the world and the wide screen as having a "sympathetic" relationship, the one with the other, takes us out of the realm of any mechanical, behavioral connection and into the realm of unpredictability, opening up the possibility of miraculous transformation.[35]

The mimetic faculty has its production as well as its reception side. On the production side is the capacity for minority groups and cultures to "image back," to represent their own faces and bodies—the faces and bodies of peasants, of indigenous peoples, of racial Others, of working women—and to show them against a backdrop of the historical conflicts within which they lost or triumphed. To represent mimetically the brutalities historically perpetrated against ordinary people in the name of profit in an attempt to change conditions is to "manipulate reality by means of its image," to use imitation to influence present and future events magically. Certainly such a use of mimesis describes radical theater. But motion pictures and video have an even greater capacity to manipulate mimetically. Here there is a going beyond the mimetic powers of the body to engage the projective powers of mimetic technologies, but also a utilization of the machines of repetition, which have the capacity to throw up their imitations again and again and again. One might ask if these powers are not available to all producers who would seek to influence by means of mechanical and electronic technologies, including television advertisers, network newscasters, and Hollywood moguls. The difference is just this: the documentary film that uses realism for political ends has a special power over the world of which it is a copy because it *derives its power from that same world.* (The copy derives its power from the original.) The radical film derives its power (magically) from the political events that it depicts. What I am proposing is another way of formulating the power of documentary "truth" claims, a way that helps us around the problems of indexicality and overinvestment in "the real," issues discussed elsewhere in this collection.

If this is the production side, what is the reception side of the mimetic faculty? Here we come back to the question of what film realism "makes the body do." Can the motion picture apparatus produce "revolutionary effects" on the bodies of viewers just like that? And is it the rousing film or is it the *world* of the film that makes viewers want to do something—to shout, to kick, to scream—to loot? Yes, I said "to loot," because this would seem to raise the question of the things that the Rodney King video footage "made" sympathetic bodies do in retaliation against the police brutality witnessed by the video camera, represented on the tape. For our purposes, let's consider the way that the footage of the Los Angeles police beating Rodney King was reused in *The Nation Erupts,* a videotape produced by the collective Not Channel Zero and broadcast via Deep Dish TV's cable satellite soon after the April 29, 1992, trial verdict and consequent riots. The work of Not Channel Zero, as Deirdre Boyle tells us, is part of an important return to guerrilla video tactics, a move in which the 1960s video portapak is superceded by the 1980s camcorder. And furthermore, Boyle claims the Rodney King amateur footage as part of this same tradition, illustrating as it does "video's potential to be a tool, a weapon, a witness in the hands of ordinary people."[36] Here, also, the Rodney King footage is an example par excellence of the powers of mimesis, a use of the documentary image elevated to the status of icon by virtue of its connection to an original event. The representation acquires the power of the represented— so much so that it seems that it is the representation that *makes* people do things. It seems that the footage of police brutally beating a black man *made* disaffected African Americans and Asians in South-Central Los Angeles riot and loot, when it was actually the *world* of the footage—the world within which police conduct humiliating strip searches on young black men—that *made* people riot.

Not Channel Zero's tape acknowledges the mimetic power of the Rodney King imagery by reusing the original beating footage along with video imagery of the riots, news coverage, and interviews with black residents of the South-Central Los Angeles community. And it is this use of documentary imagery that attempts to change reality "by means of its image." Similar imagery characterizes Matthew McDaniels's *Birth of a Nation: 4*29*1992,* a video documentary on the riots shot from within the community.[37] In both instances, the loose montage structure is perhaps less aesthetically potent than the featured documentary footage, and it is as though the videomakers are deferring to the power of the images themselves—images of burning buildings and families looting grocery and dry goods stores. These documentary sections are important because something happened before the camera, and what happened invests the tapes with their ritual significance. Using the documentary footage of the Los Angeles riots to "image back," these guerrilla videomakers are also using the mimetic potentialities of the footage as a means of extending the community of resisters. In such cases, to say, "This happened" is to also say, "This happened because this was done to us. We will do this again if it happens to us again and it will look just like this." In other words, committed documentary may invoke Frantz Fanon's "colonial mirror."[38] Looking at insurrection through the colonial mirror, we are face-to-face with the question of revolutionary violence, but Fanon's theorization gives us as a structure of crimes answering crimes, a historical pattern not of random retaliation but of eerie repetitions and symmetrical returns. In Fanon, the black man's violence is in answer to the violence that originates with the white settler.

Thus the question of "images of violence" always needs to be politically interrogated. We must ask, Whose violence? There is a way in which the videotapes produced by African Americans and Latinos in the aftermath of the L.A. riots of 1992 answer the conservative fear of the "effects"

From *Birth of a Nation: 4/29/92.*

of violence in the media, always a deathly fear of mimesis. It is as though these makers are saying, "Images *do* incite acts of violence, and we want these images to do just that." Not surprisingly, the question of revolutionary violence has had an uneasy position in documentary studies, perhaps because of a certain queasiness about acts of violence. But we can't very well advocate media activism and decry screen "violence" in the same breath. The great tradition of social change documentary has been a commitment to representing injustice, to showing without flinching how some groups have treated other groups—to show beating, screaming, and shooting with full knowledge that Others somewhere will fight back, perhaps as a consequence of having seen these images. It is, of course, also a question of how far from the protected middle-class screening room this struggle will take place. At a conference panel discussion about the Rodney King tape soon after the events of April 1992, Michele Wallace remarked that there is always something disturbing to her about the way white people talk about violence. Mainstream violence discourse is unable to imagine revolutionary situations within which brutal reprisals are necessary. Its reduction of all acts to a generic violence denies the specificity of people's struggles and cancels the validity of their claims.

And finally, because white violence discourse understands all violent acts as irrational, it is unable to comprehend the rationality of social outbreak, particularly outbreak that is the product of an accumulation of oppressive conditions. Fanon goes so far as to stress the function of violence in the social education of colonized peoples. For the theorist of African revolution, violence is an exercise in political analysis: "Violence alone, violence committed by the people, violence organized and educated by its leaders, makes it possible for the masses to understand social truths and gives the key to them."[39] Here, violence is theorized as a discourse and a strategy, but also a kind of bodily analysis whereby the people come to grasp the situation through action. This action then becomes a pattern that gives itself to be read on a large scale. As some commentators on the Los Angeles riot pointed out, for instance, the looting and burning in the aftermath of the Rodney King verdict could be seen not only as the speech of the voiceless but as an "immanent critique" of mainstream politics.[40]

Historically, moving pictures and television have been submitted to a similar criticism—seen as mindless and unable to deliver political analysis and critique. Part of the challenge for a committed documentary like Not Channel Zero's *The Nation Erupts*, then, is to "image back" in such a way that the structure of the colonial mirror itself becomes visible. In the case of the Los Angeles riot, that historically significant urban uprising was not produced by the seen but by the unseen—the unseen silent depression and its economic stranglehold on a community. *The Nation Erupts* attempts to represent this complex mirror by means of a combination of signs very much in the style of Godard, interrupting the documentary fragments with didactic intertitles: "Looting is the natural response to the society of abundance." On "NCZ's Top 11 Reasons to Loot or Riot," number one is "Racism," while lower down on the list is "If you can't beat'em, join'em"—a parody of David Letterman, part of a mix of styles and tones that ranges from the dead serious to the humorous. Not Channel Zero even includes in-depth political lessons, connecting the 1992 L.A. riots to revolutionary moments in U.S. history by means of graphics over the images: 1863, Irish Draft Riot; 1917, East St. Louis; 1919, Chicago; 1935, Harlem Riot; 1943, Detroit Riot; 1963, Watts; 1967, Newark and Detroit; 1973, Wounded Knee. In other words, the analytic limitations of mimesis are a creative opportunity, a challenge to fill out the history of people's oppression *on top of* the immediate realism of the video footage.

But given political activism as a goal of the Not Channel Zero collective, what are the elements in the tape that could conceivably move audiences to *do something*? As I have been arguing, it may take more than a highly charged image to produce the desired bodily swelling, a physiological response as well as the enlargement of the body politic, the ranks. Not Channel Zero supplements the images of burning, looting, marching, and speaking out with a multilayered track including the politicized sound of Ice-T's "Cop Killer," Public Enemy's "Hazy Shade Criminal," and John Coltrane's "My Favorite Things." Again, I want to call attention to what has been unacknowledged about the work of many film- and videomakers who have produced intentionally incendiary documentary art. What has been unacknowledged is the use of elements on either the image track or the sound track that make a visceral impact, that may have a strong connotative resonance for particular communities.

Here, the use of black popular music in *The Nation Erupts* affirms existing music communities, assuming an overlap between rap music fans and politically disaffected African Americans. But the crucial question to ask about Not Channel Zero's work is whether it owes more to MTV than to the documentary tradition we have been examining. This is an extremely significant question for us as we undertake the reinvention of documentary film and video, for it is only by virtue of the use of documentary footage and its ambitious political goals that *The Nation Erupts* can be made to fit into this discussion of documentary tradition. New guerrilla video needs to be put higher on the agenda for future discussions of the political aesthetics of documentary.

What is it about the use of realism as a device that makes an impact on politicized audiences? First, although we would want to concede the pathos of the indexical (the "tragically, *this happened*" effect), it is important to remember that in the radical film the documentary image seldom appears entirely "naked," that is, entirely without aesthetic supplements. Certainly the conventionalized imagery of the radical documentary draws deeply on a mimetic aesthetic—sync sound images of workers marching, historical footage of peoples' struggles (with "real person" voice-overs), illustrated narration of the struggle, and music cues referencing the period. And it is where documentary has been subjected to aesthetic supplements that it exceeds what Bill Nichols calls the "discourses of sobriety," which seem to me to always describe the Griersonians.[41]

This is to say that although such films as *Union Maids* may have a cautious Griersonian "problem moment" structure, they can also make visceral appeals that work to rouse audiences despite this didactic structure. An even better example would be George Stoney's recent *Uprising of '34,* which goes beyond other films in this tradition (*With Babies and Banners,* 1977; *The Wobblies,* 1979; *The Life and Times of Rosie the Riveter,* 1980) in its creative uses of mimesis. Stoney supplements the sober discourses of traditional documentary with sections best described as a kind of celebratory mimesis in a film recollecting a failed strike among cotton workers in the American South during the Depression. The film opens with the kind of tour de force cutting one has seldom seen in the classical documentary, constrained as it has been by codes of cinematic transparency. What a thrill for Leftists old and new—a film with a radical political message and visceral pleasure to boot!

There are moments in *Uprising of '34* that could be understood as having the potential to produce political mimesis, by which I mean a use of mimesis that assumes a mimetic faculty on the part of its audience—the ability to "body back," to carry on the same struggle. Clearly, the decision of filmmakers to make and exhibitors to screen a documentary is a decision to use an image copy of the world to influence that world. But where the documentary project most resembles the sympathetic magic that Taussig describes is in its intent that the mimetic image will have its influence upon historical events in the world, upon the world of which it is a copy. And here is where the Griersonian pioneers may turn in their graves—this idea of documentary as having the capacity to produce political mimesis assumes a faculty on the part of its audience that is only narrowly analytic. It assumes a capacity to respond to and to engage in sensuous struggle, in the visceral pleasure of political mimesis.

▶————————————————————————————

Conclusion

I have raised many more questions than I have answered in this essay—testimony, perhaps, to the overwhelming need for more theoretical work on the question of activism and aesthetics. The generational, class, and race differences between the ideal audiences of *The Nation Erupts* and *Uprising of '34*, to give only one example, present a challenge for any theorization of political struggle. What is the difference between the romanticization of violence in U.S. labor history and the romanticization of violence in the contemporary urban scene? Why are acts of violence videotaped and photographed for the historical record? Is violence a key indicator of political consciousness because of its spectacular aspect? Are there other visible signs of struggle and solidarity as important but less spectacular? Significantly missing from this preliminary consideration is a discussion of the viewing subject who has the potential to exercise the mimetic faculty. Manthia Diawara, in his discussion of the images of conflict between West Indian youth and British police in Isaac Julien's *Territories*, offers a starting point for considering the continuity between bodies on the screen and bodies in the street. Drawing on Frantz Fanon, Diawara urges an understanding of violence as having the capacity to "suture" or "bind" together the future subjects of a new nation: "There we have it: violence is a system or a machine, or, yet, a narrative, of which the individual desires to be a part in order to participate in the (re)construction of the nation."[42] But although the West Indian subjects on the street may be sutured together by their collective resistance to the police, what is the cause that binds together the spectators of the film about that resistance? What is the significance, if any, of the reception of political documentaries in the absence of a struggle?

NOTES

Thanks to Miriam von Lier for the tape of *Borinage,* and to Brian Winston and Michael Renov for crucial historical input. Cornelius Moore, Ada Griffin, Tom Waugh, and George Stoney gave great answers in response to my poll.

1. Brian Winston, *Claiming the Real: The Griersonian Documentary and Its Legitimations* (London: British Film Institute, 1995). The other work that has served as the standard text for several decades has been Eric Barnouw's *Documentary: A History of the Non-Fiction Film* (New York: Oxford University Press, 1974).
2. See Winston, *Claiming the Real,* chap. 3.
3. Ibid., 61–62.
4. Ibid., 256 n. 42.
5. Thomas Waugh, "Why Documentary Filmmakers Keep Trying to Change the World, or Why People Changing the World Keep Making Documentaries," in *"Show Us Life": Toward a History and Aesthetics of Committed Documentary,* ed. Thomas Waugh, (Metuchen, N.J.: Scarecrow, 1984), xi–xxvii.
6. Ibid., xiii.
7. Winston, *Claiming the Real,* 256.
8. Ibid., 37. For more on the international reception of *Potemkin,* see Kristin Thompson, "Eisenstein's Early Films Abroad," in *Eisenstein Rediscovered,* ed. Ian Christie and Richard Taylor (London: Routledge, 1993).
9. Quoted in Winston, *Claiming the Real,* 60. This is not to say that Grierson was not influenced by Soviet formal style. Winston describes how the producer came to know *Potemkin* in detail when he prepared the titles for U.S. distribution (48).
10. For histories of the Film and Photo League and Nykino Films, see Russell Campbell, *Cinema Strikes Back: Radical Filmmaking in the United States 1930–1942* (Ann Arbor, Mich.: UMI Research, 1982); William Alexander, *Film on the Left: American Documentary Film from 1931 to 1942* (Princeton, N.J.: Princeton University Press, 1981). For the history of Newsreel, see Bill Nichols, *"Newsreel": Documentary Filmmaking on the American Left* (Salem, N.H.: Ayer, 1980); Michael Renov, "Early Newsreel: The Construction of a Political Imaginary for the New Left," *Afterimage* 14, no. 7 (1985): 12–15; Michael Renov, "Newsreel: Old and New—Towards an Historical Profile," *Film Quarterly* 41, no. 1 (1987): 20–33.
11. Joris Ivens, *The Camera and I* (New York: International, 1969).
12. It is also useful to remember that the Latin American revolutionary filmmakers, al-though solidly Marxist, were not necessarily followers of Eisenstein and the Soviet school of filmmaking, and it is well-known that the Latin American point of aesthetic reference was Italian Neorealism. Godard, however, was influential to a degree. See Tomas Gutierrez Alea, "Beyond the Reflection of Reality," interview in *Cinema and Social Change in Latin America: Conversations with Filmmakers,* ed. Julianne Burton (Austin: University of Texas Press, 1986).
13. C. L. R. James, *Cultural Correspondence* 2 (winter 1983): 21.
14. Karl Marx, "Theses on Feuerbach," in *The German Ideology,* ed. C. J. Arthur (New York: International, 1970), 121.
15. Sergei Eisenstein, "The Montage of Film Attractions," in *Selected Works,* vol. 1, *(1922–34),* ed. and trans. Richard Taylor (Bloomington: Indiana University Press, 1988), 49.
16. See ibid., 39, as well as Sergei Eisenstein, "The Montage of Attractions," in *Selected Works,* vol. 1, *(1922–34),* ed. and trans. Richard Taylor (Bloomington: Indiana University Press, 1988), 34.
17. Karl Marx, *Capital,* vol. 1 (New York: Vintage, 1977) 105; Marx, "Theses on Feuerbach," 121.
18. Jacques Aumont, *Montage Eisenstein,* trans. Lee Hildreth, Constance Penley, and Andrew Ross (Bloomington: Indiana University Press, 1987), 48. See also my discussion of pathos in Eisenstein in "The Melos in Marxist Theory," in *The Hidden Foundation,* ed. David James and Rick Berg (Minneapolis: University of Minnesota Press, 1995).
19. The most comprehensive overview of developments can be found in Judith Mayne, *Cinema Spectatorship* (London: Routledge, 1993). See also the influential "Spectatrix" issue of *Camera Obscura* 20–21 (1989), ed. Janet Bergstrom and Mary Ann Doane.
20. For more on "reflexology" in Eisenstein, see Aumont, *Montage Eisenstein,* 45–46.
21. There is the case of the National Film Board of Canada cameraman who was shot by a suspicious mountaineer during a film shoot in the Appalachians in the 1960s. Hostile shooting at the crew on the site of the picket line is recorded on film in *Harlan County, U.S.A.,* and also recorded on film is the death of the cameraman in *The Battle of Chile* whose camera still runs after he has fallen.
22. Quoted in Renov, "Early Newsreel," 14.
23. For an extremely provocative theorization of the "film's body," see Vivian Sobchack, *The Address of the Eye* (Princeton, N.J.: Princeton University Press, 1992), 219–48. It is not, however, the body of the film that I am dealing with; rather, it is the representation of bodies

that in documentary stand in for real historical people.

24. Linda Williams, "Film Bodies: Gender, Genre,
Excess," *Film Quarterly* 44, no. 4 (summer
1991): 4; this essay has been reprinted in
Film Genre Reader II, ed. Barry Grant (Austin:
University of Texas Press, 1995).

25. To a degree, this is the subject of Jonathan
Crary's *Techniques of the Observer* (Cambridge: MIT Press, 1995).

26. Bill Nichols, *Blurred Boundaries: Questions
of Meaning in Contemporary Culture*
(Bloomington: Indiana University Press,
1994), chap. 6.

27. Sergei Eisenstein, "Methods of Montage,"
in *Film Form*, ed. and trans. Jay Leyda (New
York: Harcourt, Brace & World, 1949), 80.

28. Good starting places for the consideration
of music and documentary affect would be
Claudia Gorbman, *Unheard Melodies:
Narrative Film Music* (Bloomington: Indiana
University Press, 1987); Rick Altman, ed.,
Sound Theory, Sound Practice (New York:
Routledge, 1992); and Michael Chion, *Audio-
Vision* (New York: Columbia University Press,
1994).

29. Jane M. Gaines, "The Romance of Social
Change: Documentary and the American
South," paper delivered at Visible Evidence
II, University of Southern California, August
1994.

30. Todd Boyd, "Put Some Brothers on the Wall:
Rap, Rock, and the Visual Empowerment of
African American Culture," in *Multicultural
Media in the Classroom*, ed. Diane Carson
and Lester Friedman (Champaign-Urbana:
University of Illinois Press, forthcoming).

31. Michael Taussig, *Mimesis and Alterity: A
Particular History of the Senses* (New York:
Routledge, 1993). The reference to resem-
blance and similitude as a "way of knowing"
in the sixteenth century is found in Michel
Foucault, *The Order of Things* (New York:
Random House, 1973).

32. Taussig, *Mimesis and Alterity,* xviii.

33. Ibid., 57.

34. Sergei Eisenstein, "Imitation as Mastery,"
in *Eisenstein Rediscovered,* ed. Ian Christie
and Richard Taylor (London: Routledge,
1993), 66–71; see also Mikhail Yampolsky,
"The Essential Bone Structure: Mimesis in
Eisenstein," also in *Eisenstein Rediscovered,*
177–88.

35. Taussig admits that there is some mysticism
in this, but here he has been influenced as
well by Walter Benjamin's curious mysticism.
The relevant text is "The Mimetic Faculty," in
Illuminations, trans. Edmund Jephcott and
Kingsley Shorter (London: Verso, 1985).

36. Deirdre Boyle, *Subject to Change: Guerrilla
Television Revisited* (New York: Oxford
University Press, 1997), 206.

37. Matthew McDaniels started his videotape
while, like other Angelenos, he watched the
televised verdicts in the trial of the police officers accused of beating Rodney King. To
the images he shot off the television screen,
he added the footage he shot in the streets,
and later on he "looted" a new Super VHS
camera, which noticeably helped the image
quality. See Dream Hampton, "Birth of a
Nation," *Vibe,* October 1993.

38. Frantz Fanon, *The Wretched of the Earth,*
trans. Constance Farrington (New York:
Grove Weidenfeld, 1963), 13.

39. Ibid., 148.

40. Michael Omi and Howard Winant, "The Los
Angeles 'Race Riot' and Contemporary U.S.
Politics," in *Reading Rodney King/Reading
Urban Uprising,* ed. Robert Gooding-
Williams (London: Routledge, 1993).

41. Bill Nichols, *Representing Reality: Issues and
Concepts in Documentary* (Bloomington:
Indiana University Press, 1991).

42. Manthia Diawara, "Black British Cinema:
Spectatorship and Identity Formation in
Territories." Public Culture 3, no. 2 (fall 1990):
41–42.

NEIL LERNER

[5] *Damming Virgil Thomson's Music for*
The River

Most analytic discussions surrounding film privilege the eye; questions concerning the role of the ear and its effects on shaping perceptions are traditionally ignored. Despite, and even because of, its marginalized status, music mediates and manipulates any cinematic discourses where it is present. Although it has become a topos in film music literature to lament the dearth of film music scholarship,[1] studies integrating a close reading of a film *and* its accompanying musical sound track remain quite rare. Textbooks, anthologies, and course syllabi all do little more than acknowledge music's presence, the more sophisticated ones perhaps systematizing it as either diegetic or nondiegetic, but almost never do they delve into the kinds of musical issues addressed by musicologists or music theorists, questions that, because of the nature of the filmic text, play absolutely crucial roles in the way a film is read. It is all the more striking, then, that in documentary film studies, a field committed to uncovering hidden or obscured agendas and ideologies, music is almost categorically muted, even when it plays a significant part in determining a film's rhetorical effectiveness (at least in the documentary's early history).

In writing about his first film, Pare Lorentz calls *The Plow That Broke the Plains* a "documentary musical picture," and the same designation seems equally appropriate for his next film, *The River,* released in 1937 and again with the support of the Roosevelt administration.[2] Both films featured landmark musical scores by the American modernist composer Virgil Thomson; both are exceptional and remarkable examples of how music can be closely coordinated within a film. Thomson found his second collaboration with Lorentz to be a more difficult assignment than writing the music for *The Plow*: "Floods, though murderous to land and houses, are not at all dramatic to observe. A film explaining how they come about and how they can be controlled by dams demands a far more complex composition, if one wants to make it powerful, than the blowing away of our dry high-lying West."[3] Lorentz, whose first career ambition was to become a music critic, was well aware of the integral role music plays in shaping perceptions of a film. Understanding music's conventionally secondary status in relation to that of the image, he notes that, "properly handled, music should be knit into a film so that the audience is no more aware of it than it is of the dimmed house lights or the actors' grease-paint."[4] Lorentz articulates one of the central principles of the then-nascent classical Hollywood film score, a principle identified as "inaudibility" by Claudia Gorbman in her important study of narrative film music. By "inaudibility," Gorbman means that "music is not meant to be heard consciously. As such it should subordinate itself to dialogue, to visuals—i.e., to the primary vehicles of the narrative."[5] Yet just because this paradoxically "unheard" music may not be noticed at the forefront of consciousness, this does not mean we should ignore its presence when explicating a film, be it Hollywood narrative or government documentary. If we are to examine the ideological and rhetorical practices employed in *The River,* we need a close analysis of the sound, including tightly organized sounds such as Virgil Thomson's musical score.

The metaphor of a dam can serve as a way of describing the process of explicating the music in *The River.* In certain ways, film music behaves not unlike a river; its mere presence, threaded throughout the cinematic narrative, creates a sense of flow and directionality. It acts as an agent of manipulation and change within the discourse of the film. And its raw power to alter the perceived visual landscape drastically has caused it to be subjected to a number of artificial constraints and conventions. An attempt to interpret, and thus control, film music involves the harnessing of forces that normally travel freely, if not passively, across the audience's consciousness; if engineered properly, this harnessing generates interpretive energy.

The dam serves as an especially appropriate metaphor for discussing the music in *The River,* a film whose argument centers not only on literal rivers and dams but also on the channeling and controlling of broad public opinions. The film employs a familiar documentary paradigm: an initial situation is described (the natural beauty and economic value of the Mississippi region), a problem is revealed (the misuse of the land has led to soil erosion and flooding), and finally a solution is recommended (a variety of government agencies, specifically the Farm Security Administration, the Civilian Conservation Corps, and the Tennessee Valley Authority, can repair this broken world).[6] The voice-over narration by Lorentz—which James Joyce called "the most beautiful prose I have heard in ten years"[7]—

moves, as Brian Winston notes, from an impersonal distance to a collective "we" and "us" to a "you" that is involved with the solution.[8] Through this rhetorical strategy, *The River* seeks sympathy for the political administration then in power, and it uses both visual and audible signifiers to manipulate. Lorentz encourages further identification by mentioning river names across the country and by showing maps of the United States, suggesting a problem owned by the nation as a whole. Despite these efforts to address the entire American population, the music contains a significant subtext that excludes certain segments of the "us" in question.

In their well-known introductory film textbook, David Bordwell and Kristin Thompson describe Thomson's music for *The River* as "distinctly American" in style, a type of music that could, by implication, appeal to nationalistic sensibilities extending beyond the American South as a region.[9] The notion of a distinctly American musical style, however, raises a number of questions. First, it seems to be assumed that we are discussing only the highbrow, concert-hall end of the musical culture from the 1930s. Although Thomson's score definitely has an American flavor and character insofar as it carries many of the stylistic features that we associate with some of the most commonly performed concert-hall music of that time (and George Gershwin's and Aaron Copland's music from this time has remained as some of the strongest models for a generic "American" sound),[10] it is still only one rather American music found in that decade. During the 1930s a number of composers sought to create a uniquely American voice, but by the end of the decade the entire musical landscape was awash in a flood of European immigrants who came to the United States representing many kinds of musical modernism, thus complicating even further the establishment and definition of an American nationalistic musical idiom. Thomson's music certainly should strike many ears as broadly American in its sound, but it can be described in far more precise terms, specifically, as an orchestral music utilizing nineteenth-century Protestant hymn tunes and folk tunes potentially familiar to inhabitants of the Mississippi regions where those tunes were most known.

Only a small proportion of Thomson's score for *The River* consists of originally composed music; most of Thomson's melodies are taken from hymns, folk songs, and popular tunes with which he had become familiar through a study of the region's music.[11] Thomson had earlier demonstrated facility with hymn and folk material in his *Symphony on a Hymn Tune* (1926–28), the last movement of which Thomson offered to Lorentz to accompany the last half reel of the film.[12] In addition to the fourth movement of the *Symphony,* which appears essentially unaltered, the beginning of the third movement also appears in the film score.[13] In its proportion of original versus borrowed material, *The River* score differs somewhat from Thomson's earlier film score for *The Plow That Broke the Plains,* in which Thomson employs a hymn melody ("Old Hundred") and several cowboy songs (such as "I Ride an Old Paint" and "Git Along Little Dogies") at key moments in the film, but the bulk of the score consists of originally composed music.

Several of the hymn melodies selected by Thomson for *The River* came from *The Southern Harmony and Musical Companion,* compiled by "Singin' Billy" Walker in 1835, and Benjamin Franklin White and E. J. King's *Sacred Harp* (first printed in 1844), two of the South's most important and influential early shape-note tune books.[14] These hymns were commonly referred to as "white spirituals."[15] The musical notation of these hymnals was designed to allow those with little or no formal training in reading music to do so; it replaced the standard European notation with various shapes (triangles, squares, circles) designating solfege syllables (see the illustration of the shape-note version of the hymn "Mississippi" from *The Southern Harmony*). It is significant that (the well-educated) Thomson attempted to establish an American (as opposed to European) sound by using these early American hymns, because these hymns had already been at the center of even earlier debates regarding the nature of what constitutes

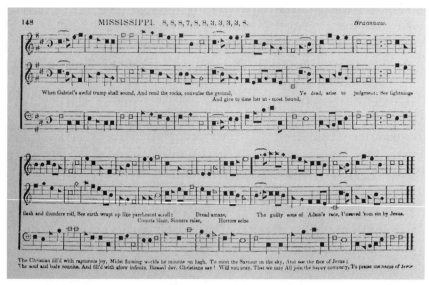

"Mississippi," from *The Southern Harmony & Musical Companion* (1854). The middle staff of this music, notated in shape notes, contains the melody that Thomson borrowed for *The River.* Reprinted from Glenn C. Wilcox, *The Southern Harmony & Musical Companion,* copyright 1987 by the University Press of Kentucky, reprinted by permission of the publishers.

American music: Lowell Mason's sweeping reforms of religious music in the first half of the nineteenth century. Mason favored European musical models and worked to rid American churches and schools of fuging tunes and shape notes, something he achieved for the most part in New England and the mid-Atlantic regions, although the frontier areas of the time (basically anything from Appalachia to the West) continued to use shape notes (and still do in isolated pockets).[16] Thomson's choice of shape-note hymns, then, while linked geographically and historically with the region addressed within the film, is also politically charged as a potentially anti-European gesture.

The religious music Thomson uses as a launching point for his film score comes from a source identifiable in terms of race (white), class (generally lower), and religion (Protestant). Because both tune books were widely circulated throughout the South, these hymns were potentially familiar to certain listeners in the Mississippi region. The words sung to these melodies reflect a specific set of religious values, one that does not speak either for or to all American citizens. This music, and the entire "documentary musical picture" that relies so heavily upon it for its effectiveness as a form of persuasive, manipulative media, thus speaks most persuasively to a particular religious group, those white Protestants familiar with the hymn melodies and cognizant of the words normally sung with them. Although the score is completely instrumental—we never hear a vocalist or choral ensemble sing any of the words to the hymn tunes or folk melodies—the words would very possibly sound through to the appropriately educated audience member (i.e., Protestant), forming an important subtext to the musical and cinematic discourse.

Although the images on the screen may present a seemingly objective and authoritative discourse surrounding a natural disaster and its possible causes and solutions, the subtext of the music and its textual references suggest an unquestionably Christian narrative. The music accompanying the opening credits of *The River* uses melodic material from the hymn "Foundation" (also known as "Sincerity"), the text of which opens with "How firm a foundation, ye saints of the Lord, / Is laid for your faith in his excellent word." A later verse of the same hymn, just as possibly evoked by the melody as the first verse, employs a metaphor that is germane to this film and its images of flooding:

> When through the deep waters I call thee to go,
> The rivers of water shall not overflow;
> For I will be with thee thy troubles to bless
> And sanctify to thee thy deepest distress.

At first glance, it appears Thomson selected his melodies solely for their titular connections. To write music for a film discussing redemption after flooding, why not find melodies whose texts talk about redemption after flooding? Since the earliest days of accompanying films with music, it has been common to borrow musical melodies with textual references to the visuals.[17] A cowboy on a horse appears—for instance, to borrow an example from *The Plow*—and we hear "Git Along Little Dogies," the audible sign paralleling the visual.[18]

Curiously, Thomson has repeatedly denied that the hymn and folk tunes he borrowed were taken for their textual connotations. In program notes for a performance of the concert suite arrangement of the music from *The River*, Thomson says that "the ironical appropriateness of these titles [of the tunes] need not be taken to mean that they have been chosen for their topical references. Quite the contrary. It is simply that tunes which have an expressive or characteristic quality usually end by getting themselves words of the same character."[19] Perhaps Thomson wanted to avoid the charges of merely choosing tunes solely for textual purposes, of resorting to synchronous scoring. Notice, however, that he qualifies his explanation of the titles' ironic appropriateness with the phrase "need not be taken," suggesting (with a wink?) that they still might very well be taken as ironically appropriate.

In standard fictional films, the opening musical cues perform important narrative functions, such as the establishment of genre and mood.[20] For the listener acquainted with the melody and words of "Foundation" ("How firm a foundation . . ."), the melody dominating the opening cue of the film score, one initial message is clear: faith in Christ offers relief from misery. As the (unheard words of the) music alludes to the divine agency of Jesus, the opening credits mention the Farm Security Administration, a government agency also—like Jesus—charged with providing relief to the masses. Rather significantly, the same music, with the same implied words, returns for the closing scene, providing in the musical recapitulation a sense of formal closure; musical expressions of Christian faith frame the film in both formal and ideological ways.

Thomson and Lorentz use other musical conventions familiar to fiction films in their documentary musical picture, such as the repeated association of a musical motive with a certain image (the leitmotiv derived from Wagnerian opera). An original monophonic theme appears at four different times in *The River* (at approximately :35, 7:50, 12:40, and 26:20 into the film); each occurrence accompanies visual images of natural scenes, usually long pans and tilts of mountains, trees, and clouds. This "mountain theme" in its first form consists of a five-note pitch collection

Example 1. Diatonic version of the mountain theme from *The River*. Copyright 1958 by Virgil Thomson. All rights for the world exclusively controlled by Southern Music Publishing Co., Inc. Reprinted by permission.

(D-E-G-A-B) that gives it a folklike sound (folk melodies are often pentatonic; see example 1). Thomson's choice of a single-lined texture here reinforces the primacy and solitude of "nature" in its pure and altered states, from lush and majestic (underscored with consonance) to barren and abused (accompanied by dissonant rewritings of the consonant original).

The initial statement of the melody is diatonic, but Thomson alters it to achieve different effects, as when he chromaticizes the motive in its third appearance (see example 2). In chromaticism, the octave is divided into more, smaller intervals than in diatonic divisions, allowing for more color, melodically and harmonically. Contrasting consonant diatonicism with dissonant chromaticism creates a stark opposition, the first sounding stable and at rest, the second unstable and in need of resolution. The direction of the intervallic leaps stays the same, but the sizes of the leaps change (e.g., a leap up of an octave becomes a leap up of a major seventh, the second sounding far more unstable and jarring than the familiar, comfortable octave). Thomson and Lorentz establish the following parallel visual and musical dichotomies:

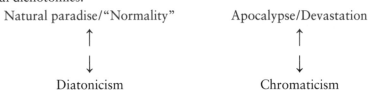

Natural paradise/"Normality"	Apocalypse/Devastation
↑	↑
↓	↓
Diatonicism	Chromaticism

The third iteration of the mountain theme serves as a transition into the flood montage; the chromatic melody that remains after Thomson changes his octaves and perfect fourths into major sevenths and tritones supplies tension and signals impending doom, doom that follows in the form of the extended flood montage sequence. Thomson achieves a similar effect earlier in the film by gradually chromaticizing the trumpet fanfare accompanying Robert E. Lee's vertically scrolling letter of surrender. (In fact, when Lee's name appeared on the screen at *The River*'s world premiere in New Orleans, the audience stood up and cheered, although probably not out of excitement at the recognition of heightened chromatic instability.)[21]

Thomson moves away from religious melodies in his music written for the scenes illustrating industrial growth and the subsequent misuse of the river. For the sequences showing commerce along the Mississippi—

French horn   English horn

(transposed to C)

Example 2. Chromatic version of the mountain theme from *The River*. Copyright 1958 by Virgil Thomson. All rights for the world exclusively controlled by Southern Music Publishing Co., Inc. Reprinted by permission.

commerce represented metonymically as cotton fields and steamboats— Thomson uses the melody from "Rose of Alabama," a popular minstrel song from the nineteenth century. Just as significant as the use of this tune is Thomson's instrumentation at this point in the score. Until "Rose of Alabama" occurs, the instrumentation consists of typical (European) symphonic brass, woodwinds, strings, and percussion. With "Rose of Alabama," however, Thomson introduces the sound of a banjo into his timbral palette, a slightly transgressive act in the context of the symphonic tradition (the introduction of a lowbrow instrument into the citadel of musical highbrow culture, the symphony orchestra). Thomson made use of an orchestrator for his score to *The River,* Henry Brant, a young Canadian composer who had served in the same capacity in *The Plow That Broke the Plains.* Using an orchestrator was, and is, a common practice in Hollywood scoring, the orchestrator's presence reflecting Hollywood's assembly-line approach to creating a product and the extreme deadlines under which most film composers work. When orchestrators are used, it is sometimes hard to know who chose what instrument in specific passages. Brant, however, takes no "credit for any special features of the orchestral sound" in his orchestration for Thomson:

> Some 60, 50 and 40 years back, when I worked as an orchestrator to Aaron Copland, Virgil Thomson, Marc Blitzstein, William Schuman, George Antheil, Douglas Moore and Alex North, my sole aim was to carry out the orchestral ideas of the composer and to prepare the score in battle-ready order, for performance or recording. All these composers consulted me, on occasion, on matters of timbre and balance.[22]

Besides drawing attention because of its piquant, plucked twang, the banjo's presence raises important questions about the relationship of instruments and politics. Roland Barthes has written that "every musical instrument, from the lute to the saxophone, implies an ideology."[23] The links between instruments and specific cultural traditions are strong; instruments participate in the signification of any number of identities. Lorentz was intuitively aware of these relationships. In his instructions to Thomson for the composition of the score for *The Plow That Broke the Plains,* he wrote,

"If the instrument of the herder was the guitar, the banjo certainly was the music brought from the South and the highlands by the homesteader, along with the accordion brought by the Norwegians into the Northwest, the fiddle, of course, being the instrument of the devil wherever it appeared."[24] The associations Lorentz mentioned delineate many of the stereotypical uses of these instruments in Hollywood film scores, revealing his keen sensitivity to music's functional capabilities. The modern banjo is a nineteenth-century commercial adaptation of an instrument brought to North America by African slaves. When the instrument sought respectability in polite middle-class parlors after the Civil War, an effort was made to rewrite the banjo's history and deny its association with African culture.[25] The banjo's appropriation by middle-class white parlors has not diluted any of its potency as a symbol of southern culture, a culture still haunted by divisions of race, class, and religion.[26] The banjo's presence, characteristically non-diegetic and thus not linked to any visual images of the performer's race or body, can, if nothing else, serve as a reminder of the South's history of racial division and of white culture's attempts to master and control African culture.

Reminders of racial discord in *The River* do not end with the use of the banjo. In planning the energetic log sequence, Lorentz advised Thomson that the music should evoke "minstrel show numbers":

> This entire sequence should be a trumpet and trombone extravaganza. That is, it should sound like those nigger bands that used to play outside the theatres before the minstrel show started: almost a circus band, but with the river-negro-Spanish-water-heat-drunken-careless-carefree-Mississippi motif which we should establish as the feeling of the river.[27]

Some of Thomson's music followed Lorentz's instructions, but some of it did not. His music for the log sequence includes quick-paced arrangements of popular songs like "Hot Time in the Old Town Tonight" as we watch log after log shoot through the water. The implied sexual tension present in the text of this song causes these images to be (at least potentially) bizarrely erotic, the ejaculatory stream of the logs coursing into the water establishing a connection between the uncontrolled consumption of natural resources and masculine sexual fulfillment.

The music accompanying the steel mill scenes, however, runs contrary to Lorentz's dictates for the sound of a minstrel band. This music is neither "careless" nor "carefree," but full of dissonant tone clusters (in the eight measures in example 3, Thomson employs nine of the twelve available pitches), cacophonous parallel tritones, and the harsh grinding sound of a ratchet, suggesting that the images accompanying it are somehow ominous

Ratchet begins here

Example 3. Steel Mill Music from *The River.* Copyright 1958 by Virgil Thomson. All rights for the world exclusively controlled by Southern Music Publishing Co., Inc. Reprinted by permission.

and evil. The image of the steel mill is here meant to represent one of the villains of the film, and the music acts accordingly, providing a synchronous musical track that criticizes the growth of industry linked with the river. If the steel mill were meant to be viewed in a positive light, which is not the case in this film's argument, then this music would be in a contrapuntal relationship to the visual track (this use of the term *contrapuntal* coming from Eisenstein, Pudovkin, and Alexandrov in their famous "Statement").

Among other titles, the interval of the tritone has been called *diabolus in musica,* its characteristic dissonance carefully monitored and controlled throughout much of the history of Western music. The presence of the devil—signified by the use of melodic and harmonic tritones—juxtaposed alongside several secular tunes reinforces the sense that, at least in terms of musical symbolism, we are in the midst of a fallen, postlapsarian world of sin. To extend this narrative further would bring us to a climactic, apocalyptic event. The music accompanying the flood sequence is based on the hymn "Mississippi" from *The Southern Harmony,* and its lyrics describe the expected apocalyptic nightmare:

> When Gabriel's awful trump shall sound,
> And rend the rocks, convulse the ground,
> And give to time her utmost bound,
> Ye dead, arise to judgment;
> See lightnings flash and thunder roll,
> See earth wrapt up like parchment scroll;
> Comets blaze, sinners raise,
> Dread amaze, horrors seize
> The guilty sons of Adam's race,
> Unsaved from sin by Jesus.

Thomson's treatment of this musical material blends synergistically with the imagery; as the flood on the image track builds up from dripping icicles to an overpowering deluge, the music grows from a single line stating the hymn melody (the English horn over a timpani ostinato) into a thick polyphonic texture, finally culminating in the original harmonization of the hymn as found in the shape-note books. Visuals—long aerial shots of the bloated river—and music climax at this moment.

When conveying the sense of the aftermath of the flood, Thomson's music connotes the depths of despair by utilizing the familiar folk tune "Go Tell Aunt Rhody," a melody whose words already contain a sad tale: the old gray goose is dead.[28] Lorentz shows several shots of washed-out land and barren trees, complete with buzzards circling above. Thomson creates an even darker mood by applying an increasing number of distortions to the "Aunt Rhody" melody: first, it is placed in a minor mode while the oboe and English horn play it (it is normally major); then, the tune switches between minor and major while in the French horns; and finally the bassoon and bass clarinet play a rhythmically augmented version of the tune in parallel tritones. This last gasp of satanic dissonance yields to a music of redemption, a progression made even more obvious in the concert suite version of this music (in the suite, the music progresses immediately from the dissonated "Go Tell Aunt Rhody" material to the redemptive hymn music; in the film, there are moments of silence and then voice-over narration without musical underscoring between these two sections). As the film moves on to show the rebuilding efforts of the FSA, CCC, and TVA, the music continues with consonant harmonizations of the hymns "Yes, Jesus Loves Me," "There's Not a Friend Like the Lowly Jesus," and "My Shepherd Will Supply My Need." Once again, divine and governmental agencies occupy different levels of the same narrative, both of which find subtle support through the ever-flowing musical score.

Thomson's music for *The River* supplies a specifically southern dimension to the film and its argument. Reanalyzing this famous documentary with our ears as well as our eyes exposes a religious subtext that alters our understanding of the film, the ways it works, and how certain audiences may have understood it (at the exclusion of others). Although it was first screened only to southern audiences, *The River* was intended for national distribution, which it eventually got through the assistance of Paramount Pictures.[29] Discovering traces of racial friction and southern fundamentalism in a southern documentary is not especially surprising, but does discovering these traces in the music of a southern documentary not cause us to reconsider the damming metaphor as a pun as well?

♦──

NOTES

1. Roy M. Prendergast indulges in the trope by titling his book *Film Music: A Neglected Art: A Critical Study of Music in Films* (New York: New York University Press, 1977; 2d ed., New York: W. W. Norton, 1992). Caryl Flinn questions the "neglected" status of film music in

her introduction to *Strains of Utopia: Gender, Nostalgia, and Hollywood Film Music* (Princeton, N.J.: Princeton University Press, 1992). Royal Brown ends the first paragraph of his introduction to *Overtones and Undertones: Reading Film Music* (Los Angeles: University of California Press, 1994) by writing that "music by and large remains one of the two most 'invisible' contributing arts to the cinema. The other is montage" (1). James Buhler and David Neumeyer address this question in their review of Flinn's book and Kathryn Kalinak's *Settling the Score: Music and the Classical Hollywood Film,* in the *Journal of the American Musicological Society* 47, no. 2 (summer 1994): 381–85, posing an alternative question: "What has enabled both musicology and film studies to feel secure in treating the existence of film music as irrelevant?" (382).

2. Pare Lorentz, *Movies 1927 to 1941: Lorentz on Film* (New York: Hopkinson & Blake, 1975), 135. See Robert L. Snyder, *Pare Lorentz and the Documentary Film* (Reno: University of Nevada Press, 1994), 50–78; this volume was originally published under the same title by the University of Oklahoma Press in 1968. In 1937, the Resettlement Administration, which had been responsible for the production of *The Plow That Broke the Plains,* became a part of the U.S. Department of Agriculture and was renamed the Farm Security Administration. The story of the Tennessee Valley Authority was told to the American public in book form by its chairman, David Lilienthal, in *TVA: Democracy on the March* (New York: Harper & Brothers, 1944), a section of which was reprinted in the Office of War Information's *U.S.A.* 2, no. 4 (February 1945): 1–7. *U.S.A.* was intended solely for distribution abroad, and it was not to be viewed by Americans overseas; rather, it was part of the Office of War Information's efforts to disseminate information about American policies around the world.

3. Virgil Thomson, *Virgil Thomson* (New York: Alfred A. Knopf, 1966), 270.

4. Lorentz, *Movies 1927 to 1941,* 87.

5. Claudia Gorbman, *Unheard Melodies: Narrative Film Music* (Bloomington: Indiana University Press, 1987), 73.

6. Bill Nichols, *Representing Reality: Issues and Concepts in Documentary* (Bloomington: Indiana University Press, 1991), 18. The issues involved in the creation of federally funded dams included the myriad concerns arising from the creation of electrical power, which would position the federal government in competition with private utilities; the use of that power to create nitrates for fertilizer or for the manufacture of explosives; flood control; reforestation and afforestation; the attraction of industry through the lure of cheap power; and the relocation of farmers from flooded lands to less productive areas in the hills. In short, it was a project that would have massive political, economic, and ecological repercussions for the entire region. For a brief overview of the concerns facing Roosevelt in the creation and implementation of the Tennessee Valley Authority, see Raymond Moley, *The First New Deal* (New York: Harcourt, Brace & World, 1966), 323–34.

7. Quoted in W. L. White, "Pare Lorentz," *Scribner's* 105, no. 1 (January 1939): 10.

8. Brian Winston, *Claiming the Real* (London: British Film Institute, 1995), 71–72.

9. David Bordwell and Kristin Thompson, *Film Art: An Introduction,* 4th ed. (New York: McGraw-Hill, 1993), 115.

10. For example, short snippets of Gershwin's *Rhapsody in Blue* (1924) and Copland's ballet music (e.g., *Appalachian Spring,* 1943–44), or close imitations thereof, are frequently used by television advertisers to sell products meant to resonate as explicitly American (such as airline travel and luxury sedans).

11. Claudia Widgery's dissertation, "The Kinetic and Temporal Interaction of Music and Film: Three Documentaries of 1930s America" (University of Maryland, 1990), contains an exhaustive study of the primary sources for Thomson's score for *The River* (see chap. two, "Temporal Perspective in *The River,*" 174–255). She identifies in her Appendix B.2 (404–7) the following hymn tunes in the film score: "How Firm a Foundation," "My Shepherd Will Supply My Need" (also known as "Resignation"), "What Solemn Sound the Ear Invades (also known as "Mount Vernon"), "When Gabriel's Awful Trump Shall Sound" (also known as "Mississippi"), "Savior, Visit Thy Plantation," "Yes, Jesus Loves Me," and "There's Not a Friend Like the Lowly Jesus." The popular songs Widgery identifies are "Rose of Alabama," an obscure version of "Carry Me Back to Old Virginny," "Hot Time in the Old Town Tonight," and "Captain Kidd."

12. Thomson, *Virgil Thomson,* 273. Thomson said Lorentz gave him no cue sheets for the last reel, and only asked for a five-minute finale. It is apparently a coincidence that some of the same hymn tunes quoted in the *Symphony* (such as "How Firm a Foundation") had also been quoted in the score for *The River.* The connections between the *Symphony* and *The River* have been mentioned by Thomson and later writers, and I identify a melodic similarity between one of the *Symphony*'s motifs and a repeated melody in the score for *The Plow That Broke the Plains* in chapter 3 of my dissertation, "The Classical Documentary Score in American Films of Persuasion: Contexts and Case Studies, 1936–1945" (Duke University, 1997).

13. Widgery, "The Kinetic and Temporal Interaction," 200.
14. William Walker, comp., *The Southern Harmony and Musical Companion*, ed. Glenn C. Wilcox (Lexington: University Press of Kentucky, 1987 [1835]); Benjamin Franklin White and E. J. King, *Sacred Harp* (Breman, Ga: Sacred Harp, 1991 [1844]).
15. See George Pullen Jackson, *White Spirituals in the Southern Uplands* (Chapel Hill: University of North Carolina Press, 1933).
16. See Gilbert Chase, *America's Music: From the Pilgrims to the Present* (New York: McGraw-Hill, 1955), 149–63; and H. Wiley Hitchcock, *Music in the United States: A Historical Introduction*, 3d ed. (Englewood Cliffs, N.J.: Prentice Hall, 1988), 64–68.
17. *Textual* here refers to the actual words normally sung with the melody. Two important sources on the history of the early musical accompaniment of films are Gillian Anderson's "A Warming Flame: The Musical Presentation of Silent Films," in *Music for Silent Films, 1894–1929: A Guide* (Washington, D.C.: Library of Congress, 1988); and Martin Miller Marks's *Music and the Silent Film: Contexts and Case Studies, 1895–1924* (New York: Oxford University Press, 1997).
18. One of the chief complaints music critics have had about film composers has been their overreliance on synchronous, instead of contrapuntal, scoring. Eisenstein, Pudovkin, and Alexandrov call for "only a contrapuntal use of sound in relation to the visual montage piece" to "afford a new potentiality of montage development and perfection." Sergei Eisenstein, V. I. Pudovkin, and Grigory Alexandrov, "A Statement," in Sergei Eisenstein, *Film Form*, ed. and trans. Jay Leyda (New York: Harcourt, Brace & World, 1949), 258. For a further definition of the term *counterpoint* as discussed in film—as opposed to its use in music as a designation of note-against-note writing—see Kristin Thompson, "Early Sound Counterpoint," *Yale French Studies* 60 (1980): 115–40.
19. Quoted in Kathleen Hoover and John Cage,

Virgil Thomson: His Life and Music (New York: Thomas Yoseloff, 1959), 180–81. Thomson made similar claims in a December 8, 1986, interview with Claudia Widgery; see "The Kinetic and Temporal Interaction," 204–5.
20. For more on the narrative functions of beginning and ending music, see Gorbman, *Unheard Melodies*, 82.
21. See Snyder, *Pare Lorentz*, 64.
22. Henry Brant, letter to the author, August 16, 1995.
23. Roland Barthes, "Loving Schumann," in *The Responsibility of Forms: Critical Essays on Music, Art, and Representation*, trans. Richard Howard (Los Angeles: University of California Press, 1985), 293.
24. From a twelve-page typed document that contains Lorentz's preliminary timings and scene explanations, part of the Virgil Thomson papers held at the Yale Music Library (ms. 29, box 51, folder 542), 4.
25. See Karen Linn, "The 'Elevation' of the Banjo in the Late Nineteenth Century," in *That Half-Barbaric Twang: The Banjo in American Popular Culture* (Chicago: University of Illinois Press, 1991), 5–39.
26. Consider the significant diegetic placement of banjos and banjo music in John Boorman's *Deliverance* (1972), another film about an encounter with a southern river. In this case, the timbre and characteristic folk repertoire of the banjo becomes a symbol for presumably incestuous cross-breeding and poverty (the mute banjo boy appears to be a product of both).
27. From an eight-page document at the Yale Music Library titled "Musical Notes: The River" (ms. 29, box 17, folder 3), 7. Quoted in Widgery, "The Kinetic and Temporal Interaction," 208.
28. Hitchcock points out that the melody of this song was a resecularization of the folk hymn "Hallelujah" from John Wyeth's *Repository of Sacred Music, Part Second*, 2d ed. (1820); see *Music in the United States*, 103–4.
29. See Snyder, *Pare Lorentz*, 64–78.

NANCY LUTKEHAUS AND
JENNY COOL

[**6**] *Paradigms Lost and Found:*
The "Crisis of Representation"
and Visual Anthropology

The "paradigms lost" of our title refers to the "crisis of representation" that beset anthropology and other fields in the humanities during the 1980s. This postmodern, postcolonial, postfeminist erosion of paradigmatic authority posed significant challenges to anthropology—a discipline grounded in the Enlightenment project of rationality and objectivity and intimately bound up in the history of Western imperialism. Beginning with the critiques of Dell Hymes, Edward Said, Johannes Fabian, Clifford Geertz, James Clifford, and George Marcus and Michael Fischer, anthropologists have been called to task for their unself-conscious production of cultural representations.[1] Descriptions and analyses written from observations and field notes—the very heart of ethnography—have come into serious question, epistemologically as well as politically. Criticism has been made of anthropologists' naive assertions of objectivity in the construction of their ethnographic representations. Even more pointedly, Said and others have suggested that through their inability, or refusal, to appreciate sufficiently the discipline's imperial legacy, anthropologists continue to "act to shut and block out the clamor of voices on the outside asking for their claims about empire and domination to be considered."[2] The implications of this statement are several: that, on the one hand, anthropologists have systematically misrepresented social reality by presenting images of homogeneous cultural "wholes"; that hegemonic relations of authority and representation have silenced alternative visions and voices in favor of those toward which anthropologists, for whatever personal, professional, or political reasons, are most disposed; and that the very act of representing others not only bears with it moral responsibility, but, more sinisterly, is a form of domination.

Anthropologists, however, have not remained silent in the face of these attacks on the discipline. The most extreme response to the crisis of representation has been the stance that anthropology as a social practice in general and ethnographic film as a particular extension of it are colonialist enterprises that have no place in a postcolonial world. Those who take this view would put an end to anthropology's cross-cultural tradition, arguing that the most valid cultural representations are those made by indigenous ethnographers (or image makers) working *in* and *on* their own cultures.[3] Although we are sympathetic to the reasons underlying this view, we argue that it represents an unnecessary abandonment of anthropology's cross-cultural aims.[4] Far from heralding the end of anthropology, in this essay we show that the crisis of representation has given rise to both written and filmic ethnographies that incorporate critiques of Enlightenment thinking while still maintaining the moral, social, and epistemological validity of cultural representations made by "outsiders."

We begin with the premise that written and visual representations of culture have long shared a dialectical relationship of interaction and impact, each affecting the other, but seldom overtly referencing this inter-relationship. Moreover, we assert that this cross-fertilization has played, and can continue to play, an important role in the revitalization and trans-formation of the creation of cross-cultural representations. In presenting a brief overview of the "new ethnography" (the experiments in anthropological writing catalyzed by the critique of the so-called realist representations characteristic of traditional ethnography), we also describe examples of their counterparts in ethnographic film—what might be called, in homage to ethnographic filmmaker Jean Rouch and his influence on French fictional film, "a new wave" of ethnographic film. The new ethnographies we refer to have not only influenced recent ethnographic films, but they in turn bear evidence of the impact of cinema in general, and ethnographic film to a lesser extent, on the writing of ethnography.[5]

The majority of the films and videos we discuss in this chapter are the products of filmmakers and anthropologists associated with the Center for Visual Anthropology (CVA) at the University of Southern California. This is no mere coincidence, as both of us are or have been associated with the center.[6] Nor is it simply a matter of self-promotion; rather, we feel that it is important to be able to write about the relationship between ethnography and ethnographic film from the perspective not only of film critics, but as practitioners of both anthropology and filmmaking. Both of us are trained as professional ethnographers, and we have both made ethnographic films. Lutkehaus, in her capacity as professor of visual anthropology at the CVA, has been involved in aspects of the production (i.e., research, filming, editing) of most of the films described in this essay. However, by limiting the films discussed here to those produced at the Center for Visual Anthropology, we do not mean to imply that these are the only ethnographic films and videos produced recently that reflect the changes in ethnographic film that we describe. More specifically, our decision to limit the range of films discussed reflects our desire to document a historical movement in the development of ethnographic film and visual anthropology that began at the University of Southern California during the late 1970s as the result of the intellectual and aesthetic influence of anthropologist Barbara Myerhoff and ethnographic filmmaker Timothy Asch, two of the founding forces behind the creation of the Center for Visual Anthropology.[7] Through the examples of their own films, several of which we mention below, as well as their interest in developing an institutional space for the production and analysis of visual anthropology, Myerhoff and Asch helped to create the Center for Visual Anthropology as a site of experimentation and the rethinking of the genre of ethnographic film.

After a brief discussion of the dialectical relationship between written ethnography and ethnographic film, we describe two recent trends in ethnographic film that we interpret as a response to the crisis of representation in anthropology: first, the trend toward indigenous and autobiographical films, and second, the trend toward global/transnational films. Although at first glance these two trends appear almost to be diametrically opposed, we suggest that they are united by the common denominator that each involves a new relationship to the subject of ethnographic film. Finally, we present a detailed discussion of Jenny Cool's video *Home Economics* (1993) as one example of an ethnographic film that preserves the cross-cultural tradition, yet also successfully negotiates the epistemological and political minefield of contemporary anthropology.

▶───────────────────────────────────

The Dialectical Relationship between Ethnography and Ethnographic Film

New ethnographies are characterized by a rejection of the anthropological paradigm that posited the omnipotent authority of the ethnographic observer vis-à-vis his or her distanced object of observation. Although these ethnographies take a number of different forms, they share in a self-conscious effort to portray the socially constructed nature of ethnographic knowledge. They also attempt to portray new subjects of ethnographic investigation, such as contemporary Western society itself. And they share the assumption that ethnography can serve to enable intelligent dialogue across ethnic, class, and cultural lines, among individuals different from one another, but who nonetheless can benefit from attempts to convey their differences.

Some of the earliest examples of experimental ethnography focused precisely on the dialogical nature of ethnographic inquiry. Books such as Vincent Crapanzano's *Tuhami* and Kevin Dwyer's *Moroccan Dialogues* attempted to reproduce the dialogical relationship between ethnographer and informant(s) as part of their literary exposition.[8] These representations aimed not only to present the socially constructed nature of ethnographic knowledge, but also to present consciously the ethnographer and his or her "subjects" as specific individuals encountering one another within specific social contexts. Thus, in contrast to the disguised and distant voice of the narrator/anthropologist in traditional realist ethnographies, dialogical ethnographies sought to represent distinct voices engaged in conversation. (One might include yet a third work based on research in Morocco, Paul Rabinow's *Reflections on Fieldwork in Morocco*, as transitional, bridging the gap between the genre of fictionalized or disguised fieldwork narratives exemplified by Laura Bohannan's pseudonymous classic *Return to Laughter* and the "new ethnographies" that integrate the anthropologist as actor within the ethnography itself.)[9]

This practice of representing the ethnographer as a particular individual—rather than an omnipotent, authorial voice whose identity is disguised—has been referred to as "reflexivity."[10] Other reflexive texts include Jean-Paul Dumont's *The Headman and I*, Paul Friedrich's *The Princes of Naranja*, Tanya Luhrmann's *Persuasions of the Witch's Craft*, and Kamala Visweswaran's *Fictions of Feminist Ethnography*.[11] Visweswaran's book also represents another trend within anthropology—the overt development of new agents of investigation, such as anthropologists of mixed cultural heritage using their own cultural bifurcation as a means of empathy in their exploration of other cultural worlds.[12]

Through their very praxis, prompted in part by the development in the late 1960s of portable synchronous sound, ethnographic filmmakers experimented even earlier than ethnographic authors with this issue of voice. Thus, for example, in their African trilogy *Turkana Conversations*, shot in Kenya in 1973–74, David and Judith MacDougall allowed the recorded conversation to give dramatic shape and tension to their ethnographic films. In contrast to these films that sometimes have the quality of eavesdropping on other people's conversations, Jean Rouch, the French ethnographic filmmaker, working almost twenty years before, collaborated with his West African informants in producing innovative films such as *Les Maîtres Fous* (1955), *Moi, Un Noir* (1957), and *Jaguar* (1967). In these films Rouch lets his subjects speak for themselves, while his own voice is not an omniscient, anonymous narrator, but that of a distinct individual, the ethnographer/filmmaker. Even more experimental was Rouch's decision, as in *Jaguar*, to film semifictional sequences created by his collaborators. These films were also innovative in that they dealt with then nontraditional ethnographic subjects such as migration, urbanization, and indigenous responses to colonialism in West Africa. Both Rouch, with his cinema verité, and the MacDougalls practiced a form of "participatory cinema" in which the camera was acknowledged, indeed encouraged, to provoke action and responses in a manner we can now identify as a precursor to the notion of reflexivity in written ethnography; in both instances the presence of the ethnographer and/or camera is acknowledged as a significant participant in the event or interaction represented.[13]

Also focusing on the issue of voice, in the late 1960s Tim Asch began to shift his thinking about narration in his films. Like the MacDougalls, he thought that the filmmaker could present a "truer" representation of filmic subjects if they were allowed to speak for themselves on-screen without the presence of a narrator or voice-over. This shift also allowed for a shift in the content of his films, from a focus on observable behavior to a foregrounding of voice as a means of conveying cultural interpretation and indigenous meaning.[14] Asch and Myerhoff also produced early examples of ethnographic films that employed reflexivity to portray the process and personal dynamics through which ethnographic knowledge is obtained. These include Asch and Chagnon's *The Ax Fight* (1975), Barbara Myerhoff and Lynne Littman's Academy-Award-winning documentary *Number Our Days* (1977) as well as their *In Her Own Time* (1985), and *Jero on Jero: "A Balinese Trance Séance" Observed* (1984) by Patsy and Timothy Asch, produced in conjunction with anthropologist Linda Connor.

The Ax Fight is a precursor to these other films. Unlike their explicit portrayal of the anthropologist in dialogue with ethnographic subjects, in *The Ax Fight* we are made privy only to Asch's voice, as cameraman, in conversation with the anthropologist Napoleon Chagnon. We do, however, hear Chagnon's speculation about the behavior we have witnessed on-screen. His explanation, which later proves to have been incorrect, provides the overall framework for the film: the discovery of how anthropological explanation is constructed through the process of fieldwork and analysis.

In subsequent films such as *Number Our Days*, the anthropologist plays an on-camera role. We see Barbara Myerhoff interacting with the subjects of her film—the elderly men and women who congregate at a Jewish community center in Venice, California—and hear her reflect upon her initial interest in these individuals. The product of ongoing ethnographic research, *Number Our Days* was not shot strictly as cinema verité, but was filmed after Myerhoff had been working for some time with the people at the Aliyah Community Center and thus knew which individuals she wanted to focus on in the film. Nevertheless, through Myerhoff's inter-action with people such as Shmuel, a former tailor, and Rebekah, who had once been a seamstress and still loved to dress up in fanciful hats, we hear the dialogue the anthropologist engaged in with her informants and see their sometimes emotional responses to her questions.

In the film *In Her Own Time,* the concept of reflexivity and the nature of ethnographic inquiry is carried a dramatic step further. Here, in Myerhoff's last film, the anthropologist's increasingly deteriorating health—her ultimately unsuccessful fight against cancer—becomes the focus of her in-vestigation into the beliefs and practices of a community of Hasidic Jews who live in the Fairfax district of Los Angeles. Through their efforts to help her in her struggle with her illness, we gain insight into the world of the Hasidim and their religious practices, as well as the meaning of spiritu-ality in their lives and their belief in its power to help others. Part of the dramatic tension in this film lies in the ambiguity between Myerhoff's roles as distanced ethnographic observer and earnestly engaged participant. The anthropologist becomes as much the subject of this film as the Hasidim she is studying.[15]

In contrast, *Jero on Jero: "A Balinese Trance Séance" Observed* offers the viewer an opportunity to observe the anthropological subject— a Balinese woman named Jero who is a skilled masseuse and healer—view and comment on her own previously filmed performance documented in *A Balinese Trance Séance.* In *Jero on Jero* we see Jero watching herself on film and observe her responses to seeing herself possessed as she conducts a séance in which she converses with the dead relatives of her clients. We also hear the dialogue she carries on with the anthropologist, Linda Connor, who poses questions to her as Jero watches the film on a small monitor.[16] The presentation of these multiple levels of reflexivity—of Jero witnessing her own performance, of the anthropologist questioning her informant— allows skeptical Western viewers the opportunity to evaluate this post-performance discussion of Jero's previous behavior.

Besides dialogism and reflexivity, the new ethnography has been char-acterized by a conscious focus on the narrative structure of ethnography as a genre. Sometimes referred to as "the literary turn" in anthropology and other social sciences, this focus on ethnographic representation qua literary production has led scholars such as Marcus and Cushman, Marcus and Fischer, Clifford, Fabian, Geertz, and Strathern to look at the ethnographies of earlier anthropologists—Malinowski, Benedict, Frazer, Lévi-Strauss— and to analyze their narrative and rhetorical strategies.[17]

Anthropologists' self-conscious reflection on narrative structure has parallels in recent ethnographic films. Works such as Sylvia Sensiper's

Films Are Dreams That Wander in the Light of Day (1989) and Wilton Martinez's *Viewing Cultures* (1991) series challenge our naive assumptions about the objectivity of ethnographic representations through their visual investigation of the sources and impact of cross-cultural images. Sensiper's video, for example, explores Hollywood's portrayal of Tibet as Shangri-La in classic films such as *Lost Horizons* in order to demonstrate the impacts such stereotypical representations have had on ethnographic films. Bringing herself into the picture—literally and figuratively—she also discusses the effects of these romanticized images on her own interest in Tibetan culture and their contrast with the political and social reality of contemporary Tibet. Creating an even more complexly dialogic film, Sensiper includes the representation of her friendship with a Tibetan refugee whom she accompanies on his return to his homeland for the first time since his departure as a child in the late 1950s. Through his words, we also learn the "native's" point of view, hear his thoughts in anticipation of his return to his homeland, view his reunion with his family, and are privy to his post hoc ruminations about the visit. The juxtaposition of the two perspectives, Sensiper's and the refugee's, as well as the video's "before-and-after" narrative structure provide an additional layer of irony and hindsight to the simplistic images and hopes presented at the beginning of the video.

Striking even closer to home, Martinez's series *Viewing Cultures* probes the academic world of teaching anthropology with film and attempts to represent aspects of the processes of film production, circulation (the use of ethnographic film by professors), and reception (students' responses to a variety of ethnographic films).[18] One of the only studies to document the reception of ethnographic film, and the only one to present such evidence visually, *Viewing Cultures* presents a complex message about the social process of film spectatorship as well as an analysis of genres of ethnographic film. Both Sensiper's and Martinez's films force us to reflect upon the social factors that contribute to visual stereotypes of the idyllic and exotic Other in ethnographic and documentary film, as well as the effects of these stereotypes on viewers.

▶ ───────────────────────────────

Montage in Ethnographic Writing and Ethnographic Film

Returning to the topic of written ethnography, although anthropological theory may have been influenced by postmodern discourse, Marcus reminds us that as textual strategies, these self-conscious experimental moves away from realist representation in the writing of ethnography are merely modernist in the classic literary sense.[19] Referring to the historical development of the modernist style, and following the literary critic Keith Cohen, who has written about the historical relation of film to modern fiction,[20] Marcus argues that there is a strong cinematic basis to the contemporary experiments in ethnographic writing. Both Marcus and Cohen consider the cinematic technique of montage—the physical juxtaposition of images in the editing of film—to have had primary influence in creating the transformations identified with classic literary modernism and, by extension, according to Marcus, with the new ethnography.

Montage provides a technique that allows a break with existing rhetorical conventions and narrative modes that in turn allows for the problematizing of the construction of space, temporality, and perspective or voice in ethnography. For example, Marcus points out that not only does Taussig's ethnography *Colonialism, Shamanism, and the Wild Man* explicitly draw upon the concept of montage to analyze shamanic performances, but aspects of Taussig's verbal representation of these performances also assume the effects of montage. By calling attention through the use of verbal montage to the essentially oral conventions and techniques of other cultures, ethnographers such as Taussig are better able to give voice to the qualities of oral genres of communication in performance.[21]

Whereas mundane montage provides the building blocks of narrative structure in film, intellectual montage—as distinguished by Eisenstein and exemplified in his films—has been used less creatively by ethnographic filmmakers. Its primary function—for example, in films such as John Marshall's *N!ai: The Story of a !Kung Woman* (1979)—has been to provide flashbacks to earlier events, either prior to the ethnographic present of the film or within the film itself.[22] More recently, however, ethnographic filmmakers have begun to break with the time-space convention of realist film practice to experiment consciously with montage as a means of conveying specific ideas; for example, to represent visually concepts such as memory, identity, and class differences. In their short film *Pepino Mango Nance* (1995), Bann Roy and Gillian Goslinga effectively use intellectual montage to portray the unequal relationship between a young urban male Chicano composer living in a loft in downtown Los Angeles and the illegal Latin American immigrant women fruit vendors whose street chants have provided inspiration for his avant-garde music. The juxtaposition of images eliminates the need for any narration to spell out the contrast in lifestyles, the gap of class differences that separate them, and allows the viewer to muse upon the irony of their uneasy—and unequal—relationship.

In another, lengthier example, in the film *Bui Doi* (Life of dust) (1993), about a group of teenage Vietnamese gang members in Orange County, California, filmmakers Ahrin Mishan and Nicholas Rothenberg use montage as a means of exploring aspects of identity and memory. Undoubtedly influenced by Trinh T. Minh-ha's striking use of found footage in her documentary film *Surname Viet Given Name Nam* (1989), and unable to film in Vietnam themselves or gain access to any earlier footage of the youths' childhoods there, Mishan and Rothenberg used stock footage of the Vietnamese countryside and newsreel images of the war in combination with voice-over reminiscences by the gang members in order to provide dreamlike flashbacks to their former lives in Vietnam. These sequences are interspersed with actual footage of the gang members' everyday lives together. The mundane activities of eating, sleeping, and horsing around are eerily juxtaposed with images of the gang members casually fondling guns and striking macho poses with them. These images—as well as the youths' comments about the violent acts they perform to support their independent lifestyle—reverberate ironically with their statements that their life is "just like a movie." To what extent has the camera provoked their posturing? To what extent is it merely capturing on film an accurate projection of their own self-images? While far removed from the realist conventions of traditional ethnographic/documentary film—yet evocative of Rouch's earlier work—the stylized black-and-white format of *Bui Doi* evokes a sense of lost innocence, the poignancy and quiet desperation of alienation, and the thrill of crime and violence that infuses the communal life of the surrogate "family" the gang members have created for themselves.

▶————————————————————————

New Ethnographic Subjects

In addition to experimentation with narrative structure, new ethnography also has been characterized by a shift in subject matter. Rather than the so-called exotic or primitive Other, contemporary ethnographers have increasingly turned to the study of their own society, or aspects of it, thereby "bringing anthropology home." Thus Tanya Luhrmann's *Persuasions of the Witch's Craft* looks at the phenomenon of contemporary witchcraft among the middle class in England; Faye Ginsburg, Emily Martin, Rayna Rapp, and Marilyn Strathern have explored the gender and class dynamics of the pro-choice/anti-abortion movements, the female body, and new reproductive technologies in Euro-American societies; Sharon Traweek, Bruno LaTour, and Paul Rabinow have studied the culture of theoretical physicists, research scientists, and biotechnology, respectively; and George Marcus has turned an ethnographic eye on the lives and fortunes of American dynastic families and the institutions they beget.[23]

In a similar manner, ethnographic film has also been shifting its traditional focus away from the foreign and exotic toward the familiar and near. Both of Myerhoff's films, *Number Our Days* and *In Her Own Time,* are early examples of an anthropologist's attempt to study her own culture. Although her previous work had fit the traditional cross-cultural model— she had studied the religious pilgrimages of the Huichol Indians in northern Mexico[24]—Myerhoff later turned her ethnographic gaze toward the elderly Jews of Venice Beach, California, partly out of a desire to know something more about the lives of these old people because, as she remarks in *Number Our Days,* she would someday be "a little old Jewish lady" herself.[25]

Although not all new ethnographic films that focus on American culture have turned so personally toward exploration of the ethnographer's own ethnic identity, ethnographic filmmakers have focused with increasing frequency on segments of their own society and on social classes other than those of the ethnic subcultures, deviants, or underprivileged that have characterized more traditional sociological and ethnographic films.

In *Gang Cops* (1989), for example, Toby Fleming and Daniel Marks follow a special unit of the Los Angeles Sheriff's Department as they patrol the turf of gang members in South-Central L.A. In traditional ethnographic fashion, for more than a year Fleming and Marks were participant observers, accompanying the officers on their patrols, hanging out with them during off-hours and in their barracks, attending their public appearances as spokesmen for law and order, to present a compelling and insightful portrait of the symbiotic relationships among cops, gang members, and neighborhood residents.

In yet another portrait of middle-class Americans—ironically titled *Natives* (1993)—Jessie Lerner and Scott Sterling focus their camera on the activities of participants in the Light Up the Border movement in San Diego, allowing audiences not only to see the protesters' picket lines, but also to hear the point of view of these staunchly conservative, predominantly white Americans who see it as their patriotic duty to keep illegal aliens from entering the United States from Mexico. Although there is no voice-over narration that comments on the opinions and activities of the individuals shown, the odd camera angles sometimes used to shoot the interviews, the expressionistic use of sound in repeated sequences showing close-ups of a border fence in the process of being locked, and the use of intellectual montage serve to create the film's distinct point of view.

More recently, Gillian Goslinga, curious about the human dimensions of the new reproductive technologies, used a video camera to record and analyze the social dynamics of the relationship between a gestational surrogate and the biological parents of the infant she was carrying in *The Baby the Stork Brought Home* (1997). We watch as the pregnancy unfolds, witness the birth of the baby girl, and see the bitter disappointment of the surrogate as she is left alone, feeling like "a breed cow," after the parents—no longer wanting to acknowledge the surrogate's role in the birth process—have achieved their goal: a healthy baby girl. Aside from the documentary value of the film, which allows us to get to know both sets of partners in the relationship—the surrogate and her husband and the biological parents—over a nine-month period, *The Baby the Stork Brought Home* is enriched by a companion thesis that analyzes surrogacy as a new form of social and kinship relationship, questions traditional feminist critiques of surrogacy and motherhood, and probes the class dynamics of the new reproductive technologies.[26]

▶ ───

Subjects: Two New Trends in Ethnographic Film

In addition to these examples of changes in the traditional subject matter of ethnographic films—epitomized in the past by either the portrayal of exotic and/or visually resplendent rituals or the exact opposite, the lengthy recording of prosaic, everyday activities—the homeward turn in ethnographic writing is paralleled in visual anthropology by two other seemingly unrelated, but paradoxically kindred, trends. The first is found in the production and analysis of indigenous media and "autobiographical" films, the second in explorations of the signifying practices and transnational nature of postmodern consumer society. We will first briefly characterize these trends, then identify the source of their kinship in their radically altered conception of the relationship between ethnographer and subject. Finally, we explore the impact of this changed relationship on the practice of ethnographic filmmaking with a detailed discussion of the video *Home Economics*.

■ ───

The First Trend

The fact that indigenous filmmakers from the Amazon to the Arctic and Aboriginal Australia have begun to produce their own filmic representations of their cultures has not only created a new corpus of visual representations, it has generated new subject matter for anthropologists and documentarians to explore. Thus, on the one hand, an increasing number of films and videos are made by indigenous filmmakers, working either independently or in collaboration with outside anthropologists.[27] On the other hand, just as an increasing number of studies by anthropologists, and other media scholars, aim to document and analyze the cultural products and social organization of indigenous media production,[28] there is also a new genre of ethnographic film and video that documents indigenous film- and videomakers' use of filmic images as a political and cultural tool. Thus we have films such as *Kayapo: Out of the Forest* (1987), by the American anthropologist Terence Turner, made in conjunction with British TV, and *Taking Aim* (1992), by Brazilian ethnographic filmmaker Monica Frota, that document the use the Kayapo Indians have made of video images in their struggle against outside encroachment in the Amazon.[29]

The inverse of this trend to put the camera into the hands of the proverbial non-Western Other—whose focus is often social in character, looking at group experience rather than that of the subjective individual— is the production of autobiographical films and videos that make the Self the focus of the camera. Michael Renov has recently explored this burgeoning genre of new ethnographic "life history" films (see chapter 7, this volume). Both developments, as different forms of self-representation, alter the social distance between the observer and observed by conflating it. Work produced under the rubric of ethnographic film that fits this category includes SoYun Roe's *My Husband's Families* (1994) and Ju-hua Wu's *Worlds Incomplete: From Nation to Person* (1997). A step removed from a purely autobiographical voice, yet clearly still speaking from the filmmaker's own experiences, in the video *My Husband's Families* recently married Korean American visual anthropologist SoYun Roe uses her camera to allow the multiple members of her new husband's two families of origin—one the Swiss-German/Italian family in which he was raised through adoption, the other his Korean birth family—to speak about the meaning of kinship and family. In order to do so, the video moves from Europe to the United States and then to Korea. Ultimately, this exploration of cross-cultural adoption is not only a comment on the nature of the postmodern family, but also a means for the filmmaker to explore the complexity of her husband's personal background and her relationships to the individuals who make up her new, extensive set of in-laws.[30]

In *Worlds Incomplete: From Nation to Person,* Ju-hua Wu uses video footage of her Chinese father in Taiwan and China in combination with personal narrative in the form of a voice-over commentary that reflects upon her transnational identity, her feelings of filial betrayal evoked by her marriage to an American, and her father's return to China to visit his home village forty-six years later—only to find it submerged beneath a lake that was created by a dam. Her commentary questions the nature of identity and the roles that the cultural construction of the nation and national identity play in the determination of personal identity. Wu creates a personal narrative that transcends the simplistic formula of "one can only know oneself" as an ethnographic subject to probe personal memories and kinship relation in order to understand more fully the complexity of the relationship between personal and political identities.[31]

■───

The Second Trend

Less well-known is the second trend in ethnographic film that has responded to Marcus and Fischer's clarion call for a postmodern ethnography, one that in the manner of such theorists as Jameson, Harvey, and Baudrillard explores contemporary societies through the crossing of national boundaries and covers the vast global culture of consumerism and transnational identities.[32] Recent examples of this type of film that break out of the insular time-space frame of traditional ethnographies and ethnographic films that remain bound to a single community, locale, or event include *Transnational Fiesta: 1992* (1993) by anthropologist Paul Gelles and Peruvian filmmaker/anthropologist Wilton Martinez, *A Chief in Two Worlds* (1993) by Micah van der Ryn, *For Here or To-Go?* (1997) by Bann Roy, and *In and Out of Africa* (1992) by anthropologist Christopher Steiner and ethnographic filmmakers Ilisa Barbash and Lucien Taylor.

Transnational Fiesta: 1992 follows a group of Peruvian immigrants currently living in Washington, D.C., as they return to their former home, the Andean village of Cabanaconde, to sponsor an annual fiesta in honor of the village's patron saint. Afterward, we return with the Peruvian sponsors—and, in some cases, their American spouses—to their homes in Washington, D.C. We see them at their daily jobs, learn of why they left Peru, and listen as they discuss their reasons for continuing to return to Peru and to sponsor the village ritual. In seeing the same individuals first in their home village in Peru and then in their suburban houses in Washington, D.C., not only do we hear them talk about their multiple identities as Peruvian villagers and American immigrants, we are also privy to the social and cultural contexts, experiences, and relationships that produce these identities. In a second example of this genre, *A Chief in Two Worlds*, working-class Samoans in Los Angeles parlay their wages into chiefly titles that assure them access to land back in Samoa. In this case prestige—in the form of chiefly status—can be acquired only in Samoa, in exchange for goods and money more easily acquired by wage earners in Hawaii, the mainland United States, and New Zealand. Finally, in *For Here or To-Go?* filmmaker Roy, himself from India, focuses on the story of Amitabh, an

Indian graduate student studying architecture in Los Angeles. The film cuts back and forth between interviews with Amitabh in L.A. and with his father, girlfriend, colleagues, and mentor in India. Through the juxtaposition of these various dialogues, we gain insight into the complex set of issues concerning home and identity that many foreign students face when they are given the opportunity to study abroad. As Amitabh says, "The F1 [student visa] becomes the beginning of a new way of life for many," but not without conflicts over where one's loyalties and heart lie and how one creates a bicultural identity.

Whereas it is people who cross national boundaries in *Transnational Fiesta: 1992, A Chief in Two Worlds,* and *For Here or To-Go?* it is objects (and people) that travel between different worlds in *In and Out of Africa.* The video moves between Côte d'Ivoire and the United States, visually exploring the creation and transformation of value in cultural artifacts as so-called indigenous art moves from its source of production and distribution in Côte d'Ivoire to its circulation in the art markets of New York and Los Angeles.[33] Here objects are transformed by their location in different social contexts, their fluctuating value dependent upon the particular set of social relations in which they are embedded. The video documents the activities and attitudes of the traders who facilitate the transport of the objects from one cultural milieu to another, for they are the middlemen who, through their knowledge of the different social contexts, profit from the fluctuating values of the different spheres of exchange. All four of the videos discussed here as examples of the second trend focus on an inherently anthropological topic—exchange and the creation of value—with a decidedly postmodern twist: the visual representation of transnational forms of consumption and the circulation of goods and people.

Although the first trend discussed above, a turn toward self-representation, stands in contrast to the second, which looks at global social processes and phenomena, the two share certain views on the relationship between filmmaker and filmed, certain views about the *connectedness* of groups on either side of the screen.[34] Both recognize the political, situated nature of representation, and both posit a more intimate relationship between knower and known than is assumed in the Enlightenment scheme. Both genres recognize, and here we crib from Geertz, that "one of the major assumptions upon which anthropological . . . [work] rested until only yesterday, that its subjects and its audience were not only separable but morally disconnected, that the first were to be described but not addressed, the second informed but not implicated has fairly well dissolved."[35]

The indigenous, autobiographical, and reflexive works of the first trend tend to handle this dissolution by asserting an identity of subject and author, whereas those of the second handle it in a more typically anthropological way. They engage in research and representation across lines of cultural difference, not in an effort to produce totalizing depictions of "how the [fill in the blank] live," but in an attempt to *enable conversation* across those lines. Such attempts, moreover, rest on the conviction that because difference proliferates—even as the world's peoples are drawn ever more tightly into each other's affairs and into the vast transnational processes of postmodernity—working toward mutual understanding and the construction of some common ground is a valid anthropological endeavor. Here the connection between author and subject takes the form not of a given identity, but of an affinity that must be constructed during the fieldwork and filmmaking process.

▶

Home Economics

Researched and produced between 1990 and 1994 at the Center for Visual Anthropology, Jenny Cool's video *Home Economics* draws on both the critical insights of "new ethnography" and the legacy of the "new wave" in ethnographic film that was passed to a generation of visual anthropologists trained at the center that Myerhoff and Asch helped to found in the late 1970s. Though its choice of subject and approach to representing that subject in film are clearly informed by the "crisis of representation," *Home Economics* looks at the ideal of home ownership in suburban Los Angeles County and makes a quintessentially anthropological argument—it seeks to show the logic and validity of a particular way of life, that of petit bourgeois, suburban home owners, and it turns this showing into a critique of contemporary American society. As Marcus and Fischer have argued, this two-step process of critiquing the Self via a detour through the Other has been a mainstay of anthropological writing from the outset.[36]

Subtitled *A Documentary of Suburbia, Home Economics,* like a number of recent ethnographic works discussed in this essay, deliberately eschews the exotic, spectacular otherness of classical anthropology in favor of the domestic and the everyday.[37] Anthropologist/filmmaker Cool and the video's three subjects are all white American women deeply concerned with the social costs of the American Dream of home ownership. Yet the film is neither autobiographical nor the work of an indigenous suburbanite— the identities shared by author and subject are divided and crosscut by class difference and by the division between expert and lay inherent in any attempt at anthropological representation. Like the films discussed above that explore the transnational circulation of goods and people, *Home*

A homeward turn in anthropology, *Home Economics* (1994) bursts the bubble of the suburban American Dream.

Economics recognizes the multiple, fluid, and overlapping identities of the postmodern subject. Cool's video negotiates the multifarious relationships of otherness and connectedness between anthropologist/filmmaker and informants/subjects in two important ways, which we discuss in detail below because they represent Cool's strategy for responding to postmodernist critiques of anthropology without abandoning that discipline's cross-cultural mission.

■————————————————————————————————————

Subjects Addressed, Not Described

Home Economics contains no voice-over narration, but consists of "real-time takes" (i.e., single runs of the camera uninterrupted by cutaways) in which the video's three subjects give lengthy responses to Cool's short prompts and questions. Shot in the subjects' kitchens, living rooms, and backyards and recorded with a camera carefully set up on a tripod and left to run unattended for long periods of time, the interview portions of *Home Economics* take on the tone of "kitchen conversations" rather than interviews proper. These dialogue sections run from two and a half to five minutes in length and are connected by much shorter montage sequences of the surrounding landscape that alternately illustrate and comment upon each woman's words. Although Cool's preoccupation with the meaning and value of home ownership conveys an implicit critique of consumerism in late-twentieth-century America (as the video's title ironically signals), her filmmaking technique serves to foreground her subjects' experiences as home owners, to reveal the meanings that home ownership holds for them, and to present their perceptions of the logic and contradictions of their lives and social relations.[38]

This avoidance of voice-over narration and the impulse to present subjects who speak for themselves in real time have a long history in documentary and ethnographic filmmaking that begins in 1960 with the development of portable synchronous sound.[39] As Erik Barnouw has written in his history of the nonfiction film:

> The documentarist's conquest of synchronized sound decisively influenced the makers of ethnographic films. . . . Such works as *Tidikawa and Friends* (1971), made among the Bedamini of New Guinea by Jef and Su Doring; *Last of the Cuiva* (1971), made by Brian Moser in eastern Colombia; *Kula* (1971), made by Yasuko Ichioka among the Trobriand islanders of the Western Pacific; and *To Live With Herds* (1973), made in northern Uganda by David MacDougall, gave audiences—whether the language was understood or not—a sense of immersion in the societies they portrayed. . . .
>
> Synchronized sound affected editing style. The silent film editing tradition, under which footage was fragmented and then reassembled, creating "film

Subjects addressed: intimate portraits from suburbia. *Home Economics* (1994).

time," began to lose its feasibility and value. With speech, "real time" reasserted itself. . . . This resulted in long films depicting long rituals, as in [Roger] Sandall's *Gunabibi* (1971), made in Australia; sometimes in short episodic films such as *Dedeheiwa Weeds His Garden* (1971) and *Dedeheiwa Washes His Children* (1971), and numerous others of the same sort made by Napoleon Chagnon and Timothy Asch among the Yanomamo Indians of southern Venezuela.[40]

Cool's technique in *Home Economics* of presenting long, uninterrupted shots of speaking subjects owes as much to the films the MacDougalls and the Asches made during the 1970s and 1980s as it does to the dialogical mode of textual production characteristic of "new ethnography." *Home Economics*'s rhetorical power as ethnography and as social documentary draws heavily on the persuasive power of its subjects, its characters, and on the immersive sense of "being there" that the video constructs. Yet it moves beyond observational cinema to situate the anthropologist/filmmaker within the video and to acknowledge the authored nature of the representations it presents.

■───────────────────────────────────────

Authorship Acknowledged

Influenced by the cinema verité of Rouch, by the MacDougalls' "participatory cinema," and by the reflexivity practiced by Myerhoff, Asch, and their students at the CVA, *Home Economics* openly acknowledges its own constructed nature. Cool appears on camera several times, and when she is not in the shot, either her voice is heard asking questions from just outside the frame or her presence there is indicated by her subjects' gestures. In *Home Economics* Cool acknowledges her authorship but does not present herself as a subject in the text, in the manner of more intensely reflexive films and writings. Instead, the video's quiet reflexivity and straightforward narrative structure serve to remind the audience that *Home Economics* is presenting an ethnographic argument. As Cool explains:

> Making *Home Economics,* I tried to close the strange distance between expert and lay person, representor and represented, by talking to—rather than watching—my informants; and by taking their words—not as raw data—but as the interpretations and insights of reasoning social actors who might well have something to teach me about the world I sought to represent. In keeping with ethnographic tradition, I looked upon my informants' discourse as expressing a specific cultural logic and worked to demonstrate its rationality. . . . In *Home Economics* I do not claim to be telling my informants' stories, rather I give them room and time to emerge as expert witnesses whose thoughts and experiences corroborate, but also enlarge, my own story about the nature of the society in which we live together.[41]

Kitchen conversations and relaxed reflexivity: the "key witness," center, talks to the anthropologist/filmmaker, at right. *Home Economics* (1994).

In addition to reflexivity, *Home Economics* uses montage sequences to break free of the real-time dialogue and create an overarching "film time." Cool edits her subject's interviews so that they present a clear narrative arc. The ideals and expectations driving the American Dream of suburban home ownership, built up in the first half of *Home Economics,* are eroded in the second half by stories of "latchkey kids," stressful commutes, racism, and social atomization that reveal the deep human costs of suburbanization. Cool's rhetorical aim in acknowledging her authorship and craft was to avoid creating a documentary that might be read in observational or realist terms as "a slice of life." By representing the anthropologist/filmmaker as a voice in dialogue with—but distinct from and *external to*—the film's subjects, *Home Economics* creates a place from which to advance its anthropological critique, namely, that home ownership in contemporary, suburban America is often achieved at the expense of the very values a home is said to represent.

Reviewed in *Variety* as "a pure use of the documentary format and a model of how to evoke the general from the particular," *Home Economics* consciously works to negotiate between the particularities of its subjects' testimony and the generalities of its author's argument, and thus to incorporate each informant's voice—as the voice of an active, rational social agent—into the anthropologist's interpretive narrative.[42] In this way, Cool responds to critiques of Enlightenment modes of representation while still maintaining the moral, social, and epistemological validity of cultural representations made by "outsiders."

▶──────────────────────────────────

Conclusion

Recently, visual anthropologist Jay Ruby sounded an alarm. "To survive," he asserts, "ethnographic film must find a new relationship to its subject, perhaps find a new subject, and abandon its slavish attachment to the realist conventions of the documentary and broadcast journalism."[43] We have argued here that in some arenas this is exactly what has been going on within ethnographic film: new subjects have been found (from middle-class white Americans in suburbia to art dealers in Manhattan and surrogate mothers at high-tech fertility clinics), and new relationships of mutuality and interconnection have been developed between filmmaker and subject.

While acknowledging that these new conceptions of the relationship between ethnographer and subject owe much to critiques of the traditional anthropological paradigm, we have also suggested that the sort of recognition about ordinary human actors that Cool and others have emphasized in their films has actually been central to the ethnographic paradigm since it emerged in anthropology.[44] From Evans-Pritchard's classic explanation of Zande witchcraft as natural philosophy to Lévi-Strauss's resplendent account of the science of the concrete, anthropologists have long sought to demonstrate the existence and validity of "other" cultural logics.[45] It is this sense of human agency, this apperception of a certain empirical quality among all humans, be they expert or lay, tribesmen or citizens, that the filmmakers of the second trend we have described work to evoke. What makes it empirical rather than ethical is that its apperception does not rest on assumed identity but on evidence and insight gathered in the fieldwork and filmmaking process.

We have also suggested that the relationship between ethnographic film and written ethnography has not simply been one-way, nor have the changes in ethnographic film simply been derivative, mere applications of insights from written to filmic representations. Although many of the recent ethnographic films we have described have indeed been influenced by the self-conscious critique of written representations of culture, creating new subject matter and new relationships between ethnographers and their subjects, ethnographic filmmakers foreshadowed and experimented with some of the same issues of representation—in particular those concerned with dialogism, reflexivity, and narrative structure—that later came under scrutiny by critics of the realist conventions of written ethnography.

Rather than abandoning anthropology—whether textual or visual—in the wake of the crisis of representation, we argue that critiques of Enlightenment ways of knowing and representing can provide a new understanding of the relationship between ethnographers and their subjects. This new understanding should, in turn, serve to deepen and extend the most valuable aspects of the ethnographic enterprise: our knowledge of ourselves and of others.

◆————————————————————————————————

NOTES

We would like to thank Michael Renov for his initial encouragement of this project and Patsy Asch for her critical reading and comments on an earlier version of the manuscript. We dedicate this essay to the memory of Timothy Asch and his legacy as a pioneer in the field of visual anthropology.

1. Dell Hymes, *Reinventing Anthropology* (New York: Vintage, 1974); Edward Said, *Orientalism* (New York: Pantheon, 1978); Edward Said, "Representing the Colonized: Anthropology's Interlocutors," *Critical Inquiry* 15 (1989): 205–25; Johannes Fabian, *Time and the Other: How Anthropology Makes Its Object* (New York: Columbia University Press, 1983); Clifford Geertz, *Works and Lives: The Anthropologist as Author* (Stanford, Calif.: Stanford University Press, 1988); James Clifford, *The Predicament of Culture: Twentieth-Century Ethnography, Literature, and Art* (Cambridge: Harvard University Press, 1988); James Clifford and George E. Marcus, eds., *Writing Culture: The Poetics and Politics of Ethnography* (Berkeley: University of California Press, 1986); George E. Marcus and Michael M. J. Fischer, *Anthropology as Cultural Critique: An Experimental Moment in the Human Sciences* (Chicago: University of Chicago Press, 1986).
2. Said, *Orientalism*, 219.
3. For example, visual anthropologist Jay Ruby's comments from the first Visible Evidence conference in 1993 are representative of a less extreme version of this position. Although Ruby sees three possible roles the visual ethnographer can play now that "the natives speak for themselves," he is skeptical of the first two—ethnographers as facilitators and cultural brokers for indigenous media makers or collaborators with them—and thus finds the third alternative—the filmic exploration of the ethnog-

rapher's own culture—ultimately to be the most viable. Jay Ruby, "The Moral Burden of Authorship in Ethnographic Film," *Visual Anthropology Review* 11, no. 2 (1995): 77–82. For a provocative critique of indigenous media as a panacea for ethnographic film, see Rachel Moore, "Marketing Alterity," in *Visualizing Theory*, ed. Lucien Taylor (New York: Routledge, 1994), 126–39.
4. For a similar point of view specifically with regard to ethnographic film, see Terence Turner, "Representation, Collaboration and Mediation in Contemporary Ethnographic and Indigenous Media," *Visual Anthropology Review* 11, no. 2 (1995): 102–6.
5. See George E. Marcus, "The Modernist Sensibility in Recent Ethnographic Writing and the Cinematic Metaphor of Montage," in *Fields of Vision: Essays in Film Studies, Visual Anthropology, and Photography*, ed. Leslie Devereaux and Roger Hillman (Berkeley: University of California Press, 1995), 35–55.
6. Nancy Lutkehaus is currently codirector of the Center for Visual Anthropology as well as associate professor in the Department of Anthropology at the University of Southern California. Cool is a graduate of the center's master's degree program in visual anthropology.
7. Myerhoff died in 1984 and Asch in 1994.
8. Vincent Crapanzano, *Tuhami: Portrait of a Moroccan* (Chicago: University of Chicago Press, 1980); Kevin Dwyer, *Moroccan Dialogues* (Baltimore: Johns Hopkins University Press, 1982).
9. Paul Rabinow, *Reflections on Fieldwork in Morocco* (Chicago: University of Chicago Press, 1977); Elenore Smith Bowen [Laura Bohannan], *Return to Laughter* (New York: Harper & Row, 1954).
10. Jay Ruby, ed., *A Crack in the Mirror: Reflexive Perspectives in Anthropology*

(Philadelphia: University of Pennsylvania Press, 1982).

11. Jean-Paul Dumont, *The Headman and I* (Austin: University of Texas Press, 1978); Paul Friedrich, *The Princes of Naranja: An Essay in Anthropological Historical Method* (Austin: University of Texas Press, 1986); Tanya Luhrmann, *Persuasions of the Witch's Craft: Ritual Magic in Contemporary England* (Cambridge: Harvard University Press, 1989); Kamala Visweswaran, *Fictions of Feminist Ethnography* (Minneapolis: University of Minnesota Press, 1994).

12. See also Lila Abu-Lughod, "Writing against Culture," in *Recapturing Anthropology,* ed. Richard Fox (Santa Fe, N.M.: School of American Research Press, 1991), 140; Lila Abu-Lughod, *Writing Women's Worlds: Bedouin Stories* (Berkeley: University of California Press, 1993); Ruth Behar, *Translated Woman: Crossing the Border with Esperanza's Story* (Boston: Beacon, 1993).

13. See David MacDougall, "Beyond Observational Cinema," and Jean Rouch, "The Camera and Man," both in *Principles of Visual Anthropology,* ed. Paul Hockings (Chicago: Aldine, 1975). Rouch's best-known work outside of anthropology is probably *Chronicle of a Summer* (1960), filmed in Paris during the period of the Algerian War. Not only did Rouch's work influence documentary filmmakers, his cinematic style—which came to be known as cinema verité—was of crucial influence on the Parisian "New Wave" feature filmmakers of the 1960s, who had in turn been influenced by aspects of modernist fiction.

14. Patsy Asch, personal communication, May 1995.

15. For further discussion of Myerhoff and her films, see Gelya Frank, "The Ethnographic Films of Barbara G. Myerhoff: Anthropology, Feminism, and the Politics of Jewish Identity," in *Women Writing Culture,* ed. Ruth Behar and Deborah A. Gordon (Berkeley: University of California Press, 1995), 207–32; Riv-Ellen Prell, "The Double Frame of Life History in the Work of Barbara Myerhoff," in *Interpreting Women's Lives: Feminist Theory and Personal Narratives,* ed. Personal Narratives Group (Bloomington: Indiana University Press, 1989), 241–58.

16. See Patsy Asch and Linda Connor, "An Exploration of Double-Voicing in Film," *Visual Anthropology Review* 10, no. 2 (1994): 14–28.

17. George E. Marcus and Dick Cushman, "Ethnographies as Texts," *Annual Review of Anthropology* 11 (1982): 25–69; Marcus and Fischer, *Anthropology as Cultural Critique;* Clifford, *The Predicament of Culture;* Fabian, *Time and the Other;* Geertz, *Works and Lives;* Marilyn Strathern, "Out of Context: The Persuasive Fictions of Anthropology,"

Current Anthropology 28, no. 3 (1987): 251–81.

18. See Nancy Lutkehaus and Wilton Martinez, "The Visual Translation of Culture" (unpublished report to the Spencer Foundation, 1990); Wilton Martinez, "Who Constructs Anthropological Knowledge: Toward a Theory of Ethnographic Film Spectatorship," in *Film as Ethnography,* ed. Peter Ian Crawford and David Turton (Manchester: Manchester University Press, 1992), 131–61.

19. Marcus, "The Modernist Sensibility," 40.

20. Keith Cohen, *Film and Fiction: The Dynamics of Exchange* (New Haven, Conn.: Yale University Press, 1979).

21. Marcus, "The Modernist Sensibility," 47; Michael Taussig, *Colonialism, Shamanism, and the Wild Man: A Study in Terror and Healing* (Chicago: University of Chicago Press, 1987).

22. Jean Rouch's use of montage is more complex. For example, in *Les Maîtres Fous* he also uses montage didactically to illustrate a relationship between the ritual participants' practice of cracking an egg on the symbolic head of the colonial governor and the plume on the hat of the actual governor.

23. Luhrmann, *Persuasions of the Witch's Craft;* Faye Ginsburg, *Contested Lives: The Abortion Debate in an American Community* (Berkeley: University of California Press, 1989); Emily Martin, *The Woman in the Body* (Boston: Beacon, 1987); Rayna Rapp, "Constructing Amniocentesis: Maternal and Medical Discourses," in *Uncertain Terms: Negotiating Gender in American Culture,* ed. Faye Ginsburg and Anna Tsing (Boston: Beacon, 1990), 28–42; Marilyn Strathern, *Reproducing the Future: Essays on Anthropology, Kinship and the New Reproductive Technologies* (New York: Routledge, 1992); Sharon Traweek, *Beamtimes and Lifetimes* (Cambridge: Harvard University Press, 1989); Bruno LaTour, *The Pasteurization of France* (Cambridge: Harvard University Press, 1989); Paul Rabinow, *Making PCR: A Story of Biotechnology* (Chicago: University of Chicago Press, 1996); George E. Marcus, ed., *Elites: Ethnographic Issues* (Albuquerque: University of New Mexico Press, 1983); George E. Marcus, with Peter Dobkin Hall, *Lives in Trust: The Fortunes of Dynastic Families in Late Twentieth-Century America* (Boulder, Colo.: Westview, 1992).

24. Barbara Myerhoff, *Peyote Hunt: The Sacred Journey of the Huichol Indians* (Ithaca, N.Y.: Cornell University Press, 1974).

25. See also Barbara Myerhoff and Jay Ruby, "A Crack in the Mirror: Reflexive Perspectives in Anthropology," in *Remembered Lives: The Work of Ritual, Storytelling, and Growing Older,* ed. Barbara Myerhoff (Ann Arbor: University of Michigan Press, 1992). (This paper

appeared originally as the introduction to Ruby, *A Crack in the Mirror*.)

26. Like the other CVA-produced films mentioned thus far, Goslinga's film—while able to stand on its own as a visual text—is enhanced by the existence of a written text that describes the filmmaker's research, her involvement with her research subjects, and her anthropological interpretation of her research results. It is this dual product—a film/video and a written text to accompany it—that Tim Asch, in particular, has asserted is essential to ethnographic film. Timothy Asch, "Using Film in Teaching Anthropology: One Pedagogical Approach," in *Principles of Visual Anthropology*, ed. Paul Hockings (The Hague: Mouton, 1975), 385–420.

27. See Ginsburg's contribution to this volume (chapter 8). See also Pat Aufderheide, "The Video in the Villages Project: Videomaking with and by Brazilian Indians," *Visual Anthropology Review* 11, no. 2 (1995): 83–93; Sarah Elder, "Collaborative Filmmaking: An Open Space for Making Meaning, a Moral Ground for Ethnographic Film," *Visual Anthropology Review* 11, no. 2 (1995): 94–101; Jacqueline Urla, "Breaking All the Rules: An Interview with Frances Peters," *Visual Anthropology Review* 9, no. 2 (1993): 98–106.

28. See Aufderheide, "The Video in the Villages Project"; Faye Ginsburg, "Indigenous Media: Faustian Contract or Global Village?" in *Rereading Cultural Anthropology*, ed. George E. Marcus (Durham, N.C.: Duke University Press, 1992), 356–76; Debra Spitulnik, "Anthropology and Mass Media," *Annual Review of Anthropology* 22 (1993): 293–315.

29. Some of Vincent Carelli's material on the Kayapo also falls into this category as well. See Aufderheide, "The Video in the Villages Project"; Vincent Carelli, "Video in the Villages: Utilization of Video-tapes as an Instrument of Ethnic Affirmation among Brazilian Indian Groups," *Commission on Visual Anthropology Newsletter*, May 1988, 10–15.

30. For a detailed discussion of adoption and the postmodern family, see SoYun Roe, "My Husband's Families: Kinship in an International Korean Adoptive Superextended Family" (master's thesis, University of Southern California, 1994).

31. For a theoretical discussion of the relationship between the anthropology of the self and the nation-state, see Ju-hua Wu, "Worlds Incomplete: From Nation to Person" (master's thesis, University of Southern California, 1997).

32. Fredric Jameson, "Postmodernism, or the Cultural Logic of Late Capitalism," *New Left Review* 146 (July–August 1984): 53–92; David Harvey, *The Condition of Post-modernity: An Enquiry into the Origins of Cultural Change* (Oxford: Basil Blackwell, 1989); Jean Baudrillard, *For a Critique of the Political Economy of the Sign*, trans. Charles Levin (St. Louis, Mo.: Telos, 1981); Jean Baudrillard, *Jean Baudrillard: Selected Writings*, ed. Mark Poster (Cambridge: Polity, 1988).

33. Christopher B. Steiner, *African Art in Transit* (Cambridge: Cambridge University Press, 1994).

34. Given that the filmmaker Roy is himself a graduate student from India, his film *For Here or To-Go?* contains a submerged autobiographical theme—Amitabh is to a great extent his alter ego. Thus Roy's film bridges the two trends we discuss here.

35. Geertz, *Works and Lives*, 132.

36. Marcus and Fischer, *Anthropology as Cultural Critique*.

37. Cool's focus on everyday life reflects the impact of cultural studies and the work of contemporary theorists such as Bourdieu, de Certeau, and Jameson rather than the continuation of anthropology's traditional description of the quotidian practices of a particular culture transferred to a postmodern venue. See Pierre Bourdieu, *The Logic of Practice*, trans. Richard Nice (Stanford, Calif.: Stanford University Press, 1980); Pierre Bourdieu, *Distinction: A Critique of the Judgement of Taste*, trans. Richard Nice (Cambridge: Harvard University Press, 1984); Michel de Certeau, *The Practice of Everyday Life* (Berkeley: University of California Press, 1984); Jameson, "Postmodernism." For an analysis of the different dimensions of "the everyday" as a prominent ideological construct of academic writing about the social, see George E. Marcus, *Everything, Everywhere: The Effacement of the Scene of the Everyday* (Brasília: University of Brasília, 1993). Marcus suggests that there are three distinct discursive functions of the construct: as a site of moral order, as a site of resistance, and as a site of the experientially real and mundane (4). It is this last function that attracts Cool's attention, for she attributes everyday life with providing her informants with the experiential basis for moral insights.

38. As she describes in detail in her master's thesis, "The Experts of Everyday Life: Cultural Reproduction and Cultural Critique in the Antelope Valley" (University of Southern California, 1993), Cool ascribes to her subjects the status of "experts of everyday life" and finds them paradoxically to be simultaneously critical and perpetuating of dominant middle-class American ideologies. Cool's ethnographic data show that the requirements of home ownership, which her informants have wholeheartedly embraced, conflict with the very ideals of family and community that home is said to represent.

39. For further discussion of the crucial role

played by portable synchronous sound in observational cinema, direct cinema, and cinema verité, see Erik Barnouw, *Documentary: A History of the Non-fiction Film* (Oxford: Oxford University Press, 1974), 234–41.

40. Ibid., 251.

41. Jenny Cool, "Automatic Borders," unpublished research notes, 1994, n.p.

42. John P. McCarthy, "P.O.V. Home Economics," *Variety* (Los Angeles ed.), July 17–23, 1995, 28. *Home Economics* was broadcast nationally in the United States in July 1997, on the Public Broadcasting Service's independent documentary series *POV.*

43. Ruby, "The Moral Burden of Authorship," 77–78.

44. For a similar statement regarding ethnography, see Marcus and Fischer, *Anthropology as Cultural Critique,* 129.

45. E. E. Evans-Pritchard, *Witchcraft, Oracles and Magic among the Azande* (Oxford: Clarendon, 1976); Claude Lévi-Strauss, *The Savage Mind,* 2d ed. (Chicago: University of Chicago Press, 1966).

MICHAEL RENOV

[7] *Domestic Ethnography and the Construction of the "Other" Self*

If the West has produced anthropologists, it is because it was tormented by remorse.

:: Claude Lévi-Strauss, *Tristes Tropiques*, 1978

The ethnographic project has long been haunted by the legacy of its colonialist past. Over the past fifteen years, critiques have been launched from many quarters against the premises of participant observation, which James Clifford has described as "shorthand for a continuous tacking between the 'inside' and 'outside' of events," but which Johannes Fabian has understood more radically as a *disjunction* between experience and science, research and writing, and thus "a festering epistemological sore" in the discipline.[1] Peter Mason has traced the philosophical problem of alterity (and the necessary setting of boundaries between self and other) to the work of Emmanuel Levinas, for whom the construction of the alterity, the absolute exteriority of the other, is a function of Desire.[2] Mason notes Levinas's concern for understanding the other without recourse to the "violence of comprehension" whereby the other is reduced to self, deprived of the very alterity by which the other *is* other.[3]

Trinh T. Minh-ha has, rather more stringently, declared that anthropology's romance with the Other is "an outgrowth of a dualistic system of thought peculiar to the Occident (the 'onto-theology' which characterizes Western metaphysics)" in which difference becomes a tool of self-defense and conquest. Anthropological discourse, according to Trinh, produces "nothing other than the reconstruction and redistribution of a pretended order of things, the interpretation or even transformation of [information] given and frozen into monuments."[4] Most recently, Michael Taussig, returning brilliantly to the work of Walter Benjamin, has written of the mimetic faculty as the compulsion to become the Other through the magic of the signifier. "I call it the mimetic faculty, the nature that culture uses to create second nature, the faculty to copy, imitate, make models, explore difference, yield into and become Other."[5]

All of these critical perspectives converge around the problems entailed in representing the other. For some, it is representation itself that is the problem. Stephen A. Tyler has called for the practice of what he terms "post-modern ethnography" whereby the inherited mode of scientific rhetoric is jettisoned; "evocation" displaces representation. In Tyler's view, the ethnographic text, long treated as an "object," is more appropriately understood as a "meditative vehicle."[6] George E. Marcus has pointed to the essay form as practiced by Adorno—fragmentary, reflective, final judgment suspended—as a way out of the trap of realist convention. Formal experimentation, attention to the dialogical context of fieldwork, the incorporation of multiple authorial voices, a retreat from an illusory holism—all can contribute to "a particularly appropriate self-conscious posture," one "well suited to a time such as the present, when paradigms are in disarray, problems intractable, and phenomena only partly understood."[7]

So many replies to this crisis of ethnographic authority: calls for coevalness, evocation, fragmentation, magic, "understanding" shorn of the violence of comprehension, the unlearning of privilege, even silence.[8] My interest here is in work currently being made by independent film- and videomakers that suggests itself—at least to me—as yet another response to the ethnographic impasse. If indeed participant observation founders in its tacking between "inside" and "outside," a passage that restages the subject/object dichotomization installed in the post-Enlightenment West, the films and tapes that I term *domestic ethnography* play at the boundaries of inside and outside in a unique way. This work engages in the documentation of family members or, less literally, of people with whom the maker has maintained long-standing everyday relations and has thus achieved a level of casual intimacy. Because the lives of artist and subject are interlaced through communal or blood ties, the documentation of the one tends to implicate the other in complicated ways; indeed, consanguinity and co(i)mplication are domestic ethnography's defining features. By *co(i)mplication* I mean both complexity and the interpenetration of subject/object identities. To pursue the point yet further, one could say that domestic ethnography is a kind of supplementary autobiographical practice; it functions as a vehicle of self-examination, a means through which to construct self-knowledge through recourse to the familial other.

But domestic ethnography is more than simply another variant of autobiographical discourse given its explicitly outward gaze. Nominally, at least, this mode of documentation takes as its object the father, mother, grandparent, child, or sibling who is genetically linked to the authorial subject. Care must be taken in defining the particular relations that obtain between the domestic ethnographer and her subject. There is a peculiar sort of reciprocity (which might equally be termed self-interest) built into the construction of Other subjectivities in this para-ethnographic mode. There can be no pretense of objectivity for an investigation of a now-dead mother whose alcoholism has helped give rise to the eating disorder of the videomaker in Vanalyne Green's *Trick or Drink* (1984), just as there is little doubt that Kidlat Tahimik's eldest son (also named Kidlat), with whom the filmmaker travels and to whom he frequently addresses his insights and admonitions throughout *The Rainbow Diary* (1994), functions both as heir apparent and as autobiographical foil. Familial investigation in these recent films and tapes is, on one level, a kind of identity sleuthing in which family-bound figures—progenitors and progeny—are mined for clues to the artist's vocation, sensibility, or pathology. Domestic ethnographies tend to be highly charged investigations brimming with a curious brand of epistephilia, a brew of affection, resentment, even self-loathing. The point to stress is that for this mode of ethnography the Desire for the Other is, at every moment, embroiled with the question of self-knowledge; it is the all-too-familiar rather than the exotic that holds sway.

I do not wish to suggest, however, that domestic ethnography of the sort I am outlining is exclusively an exercise in self-inscription. Put another way, these works could be said to enact a kind of participant observation that illumines the familial other while simultaneously refracting a self-image; indeed, the domestic ethnographic subject exists only on condition of its constitutive relations with the maker. Here there is little sense of a tacking back and forth between insider and outsider positions, the ethnographic norm. For the domestic ethnographer, there is no fully outside position available. Blood ties effect linkages of shared memory, physical resemblance, temperament, and, of course, family-forged behavioral or attitudinal dysfunction toward which the artist—through her work—can fashion accommodation but no escape.

In a limited way, domestic ethnography occasions a kind of intersubjective reciprocity in which the representations of self and other are simultaneously if unequally at stake. This kind of work is all but indemnified against the charges often made against the pseudopositivism of the anthropologist, who treats the human subject as scientific datum or statistical proof, for the domestic ethnographer qua social scientist can never wholly elude her analytic scene. It has of course been argued that this is ever so and from several perspectives: Clifford Geertz has addressed the "signature issue," the ways in which the authorial voice necessarily enters into ethnographic discourse, echoing Hayden White's notion of the "tropic" dimension of scholarly discourse (the play of language) as "inexpungeable" from the human sciences.[9] For its part, psychoanalytic criticism assumes that authorial desire is figured in all texts, never more so than when the Other is the subject of representation. With domestic ethnography, authorial subjectivity is explicitly in question or on display. There exists a reciprocity between subject and object, a play of mutual determination, a condition of consubstantiality. The Desire (figurable as dread or longing) of the domestic ethnographer is for the Other self.

▶

Fathers and Daughters

Desire is always destabilizing and delirium inducing, and instability is particularly inscribed in discourses of domestic ethnography. Su Friedrich's remarkable *Sink or Swim* (1990) evokes the artist's family history through a succession of twenty-six titled segments, each beginning with a one-word chapter heading framed against black leader, one for each letter of the alphabet displayed in reverse order, beginning with "z" for "zygote" and the artist's conception. The sound track is composed of what seem to be memory fragments, voiced by a younger Friedrich surrogate, in relation to which the accompanying images (all of them black-and-white and asynchronous, some of them drawn from Friedrich family home-movie footage) seem at times illustrative, at times responsive to the previous narration, at times linked only through an associational logic. Despite the elliptical (though chronological) character of the narrated segments, the viewer is lured toward a thematically coherent reading of the text through the chapter titles, which function as a semic reservoir for the family romance: "virginity," "temptation," "seduction," "pedagogy," "kinship," "bigamy."

The film's textual coherence is uneven despite the fact that *Sink or Swim*'s narrative continuity remains more or less intact: the "zygote" section properly launches the film's autobiographical trajectory, and each fragment supports the "life story" trajectory. The sense of linearity is undermined by the thematic discontinuities among the lexia as well as by the frequently oblique character of the sound/image relations, but these tactics are altogether consistent with the dream logic of recovered memory. As the meaning of the piece gathers force, the film's focus increasingly becomes the identity-defining relations between the father (accomplished, demanding yet remote) and the artist/daughter. "Sink or swim" is the dictum that defines the father's philosophy of parenting; his is a world of maleness and action, aloof from the reactive feminine, which tends toward lamentation

This dreamlike image of the female bodybuilders from *Sink or Swim* accompanies a story about "temptation." Photo courtesy of Su Friedrich/Downstream Productions.

and numbing resentment. After the father's departure from home and family, Friedrich's mother spends her evenings weeping to obsessively played Schubert lieder while the filmmaker resorts to consulting her anthropologist father's academic tomes, vainly searching—long after the fact—for the emotions he refused to share with the family he was abandoning at the time of their writing.

By the film's close, Friedrich has assembled a cumulative portrait of a father whose once-unassailable authority has begun to unravel. Always the source of judgment, the father is now himself exposed to the collective appraisal of the film's audience, who, in one notable example, are led to intuit the father's sense of sexual rivalry toward his adolescent daughter's admirers during a trip to Mexico. The film is, in part, her delayed revenge for his having unceremoniously sent her home for her transgressions against his incestuous authority. Hers cannot be an outright victory, however. Recall that the defining characteristics of domestic ethnography are consanguinity and co(i)mplication. Even as *Sink or Swim* moves toward its conclusion and a sense of the artist's vindication through a willful act of historiographic revisionism, the final roundelay of acoustic elements and the double printing of the home-movie footage in the film's coda return us to the instability of the domestic ethnographic locus. Over home-movie

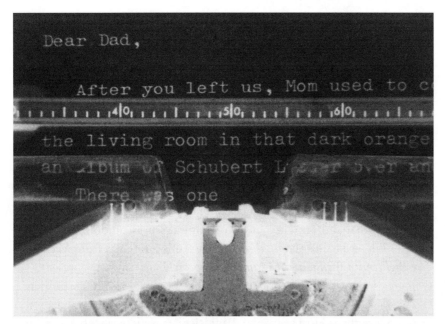

Dear Dad,

After you left us, Mom used to c

the living room in that dark orange

an album of Schubert L over an

There was one

From *Sink or Swim,* filmmaker Su Friedrich types the letter she'll never send to the father who abandoned her. Photo courtesy of Su Friedrich/Downstream Productions.

images of the artist as "the girl," clad in swimsuit, ready to sink or swim, Friedrich sings the "ABC Song" in a round of overlapping voices that rhyme with the ghostly doubling of the image. The final and fateful words of her song are, of course, "tell me what you think of me." Only on that concluding, deeply other-directed phrase do the discrepant voices and images coalesce.

But even as we gaze at the now-unified semblance of an achingly fragile young girl, we are filled with the knowledge that Friedrich can never entirely elude her father's grasp. Their histories are forever intertwined, their pathologies are enmeshed in one another's. Filmmaking as therapeutic discourse, like analysis, remains interminable, always unfinished. Equally germane to this discussion, the particularity of this instance of domestic ethnography—*Sink or Swim* as Su Friedrich's family history—is countervailed by the familiarity of the dynamic displayed. It is on this account that identification (more with dynamic than with character or situation) is engendered.

It is the depth and indelibility of familial attachment that makes the domestic subject such a special ethnographic case. And I would argue that *Sink or Swim* functions as a kind of ethnography—instructive and generalizable—for the way in which it exceeds the bounds of family portraiture. The film is structured by a series of generic elements that reinforce the universality of the subject matter: the use of the alphabet as structuring device, the elemental chapter headings, the constant use of the third person ("the girl," later "the woman") rather than first person, the generic home-movie images, the concluding childhood anthem. The specificity of the narration is sustained in tension with the universality of these elements, and through that tension domestic ethnography is forged.[10]

▶

Sharing Textual Authority

The growing attention being accorded indigenous media making at film festivals and conferences and in professional journals speaks to the desire to share textual authority in matters of cultural representation. The frontispiece of Edward Said's *Orientalism* contains this quotation from Marx's *The Eighteenth Brumaire of Louis Bonaparte*: "They cannot represent themselves; they must be represented."[11] The book goes on to perform an extended critique of the epistemological arrogance of such pronouncements. More than thirty years ago, Paul Ricouer could write about the dawning of a "universal world civilization" and the disorientation it would bring to the waning colonial enterprise: "When we discover that there are several cultures instead of just one and consequently at the time when we acknowledge the end of a sort of cultural monopoly, be it illusory or real, we are threatened with the destruction of our own discovery. Suddenly it becomes possible that there are just *others,* that we ourselves are an 'other' among others."[12] To that sense of aborted cultural monopolies must be added the tremendous growth of access to the representational tools. What once might have occasioned the bewilderment or disdain of social scientists—this vision of ethnography as a free-for-all—is now routinely reinforced by the camcorder documentation of police abuse in Compton or crumbling Giotto frescoes at Assisi. Given the explosive growth and curious coalescence of travel and surveillance technologies, representational authority no longer resides solely with the professional classes of scholars, journalists, and state functionaries.

In this context, I propose to consider a particular textual gesture, what amounts to a moment of authorial crisis occurring in certain of the domestic ethnographies. I am referring to moments at which the maker hands over the camera to his subject, at the subject's request, moments at which filial obligation outpaces directorial control. This sharing of textual authority is born not of egalitarianism nor of a penchant for the hyper-reflexive; instead, it is an outgrowth of the domestic ethnographer's intimate relations with her subject. When, in *Tomboychik* (1993), Sandi DuBowski's grandmother takes his video camera, then rolling, she intends only to "snap a picture" of her "adorable grandson." The camera is a mysterious toy to the erstwhile subject of the piece. We, on the other hand, know the game and strain to see a face already described in detail by the grandmother. *Tomboychik* is a search for the roots of DuBowski's sexual identity by way of the memories of his forebear—reminiscences of the grandmother's gender-blending childhood and of the mannish strength of her mother before her, who routinely lifted hundred-pound sacks of sugar unaided while making chocolate. The presumption may be that DuBowski's gayness can be explained genetically; the tape may also function as an unspoken reply to Nana's occasional references to a wished-for wedding and great-grandchildren.

DuBowski elicits memories of the young Nana's gendered identity. She had once been thought transgressive, a "boy/girl": she wore pants rather than dresses, fought like a boy, ran as fast and jumped as high as any of them. But Nana playfully turns the discussion—as well as the camera—to DuBowski himself. She can do this because she is Nana and because this is her dear grandson toward whom there can be no barriers. Such an exchange would not be possible with an "outsider," but this is "insider" discourse. If *Tomboychik* is ethnography, it is all but absent of the sort of description or explanation we associate with that mode of discourse. But the piece is about shopping for sexual identity in grandma's closet and about the performance of an intergenerational family masquerade (complete with wigs). The point I wish to stess is that the trope of the "shared camera," which effects an erosion of textual authority or directorial control, is endemic to domestic ethnography, one measure of the intersubjective reciprocity I have previously described.

The sharing of the apparatus with the subject packs a particular wallop in Mindy Faber's *Delirium* (1993), an essayistic investigation of her mother's madness and, more broadly, of the history of women and madness and of the link between depression and domesticity. Faber made the tape at the moment of her own motherhood, presumably to break the cycle of family horrors. We learn about the mother's symptoms, the threat she had posed to her children, as well as the mother's own memory of childhood abuse at the hands of her mother, through a series of intensely framed interview sequences. Faber's voice—pressing for details, unsatisfied by partial explanations—is never long absent from the sound track. We learn of the husband/father's paternalism, the mother's repeated institutionalizations and escapes, her suicide fantasies, her inability or unwillingness to recall her children's fright. These on-camera recitations, prompted and in dialogue with the videomaker, are interspersed with other registers of material: archival footage of madwomen, vignettes from Faber's imagined

Mother and daughter share textual authority in Mindy Faber's *Delirium*. Photos courtesy of Video Data Bank.

sitcom about her mother's middle-class doldrums, printed excerpts from the clinical diagnoses of hysteria as female malady, a discursus on the career of Jean Martin Charcot and his famous clinic at Salpêtrière, a music video-like performance sequence of a nude woman as a puppet controlled by and for the pleasure of men.

Near the end of the piece, as Faber—with intentionality but little aggressivity—presses her mother to remember the details of her abusive behavior toward the young Mindy, the mother says, "Here, give me the camera." Unprepared for the turnabout, the now-imaged videomaker struggles to hold her ground against her mother's version of their past. The authorial subject now objectified speaks to the camera at point-blank range about the terrors of returning from school to a Mom who threw pots and pans at her head. But equally terrifying is the sense of Faber's loss of control in the present tense interaction. As with Su Friedrich's treatise on her father but with greater empathy, Faber's task is, at least in part, a therapeutic one— a setting to rights of a painful family history in which the daughter has the last word. It is precisely this power to shape discourse that is temporarily ceded along with the camera. Of course, the footage need not have been included in the final tape. It is to Faber's credit that she recognized the sequence as consistent with her theme: the delirium-inducing potency of family-forged relations across lines of gender and generation. When the

videomaker recovers the camera, it is because she has her own idea for an ending for the tape: a staged scene in which the mother's revenge (a slow-motion stabbing of the father with a banana) is enacted from the point of view of the daughter, a primal scene of retribution.

Delirium offers striking illustration of domestic ethnography's potential to mine cultural memory with a level of intensity unavailable to outsiders. Afforded a depth of access to its subjects, domestic ethnography discloses secrets, performs masquerades of identity, and, temporarily at least, rearranges familial hierarchies. Its sleight of hand is the rendering public of private-sphere material, but not, I would argue, as spectacle.

▶

Families We Choose

Despite the attention given here to the biological family as the nexus within which identity is constructed, in which self-inscription and the representation of the familial other are reciprocally determined, it is important to note that our understanding of "the domestic" has undergone significant change in recent decades. In contrast to the family as ascribed or inherited, Kath Weston has drawn attention to an ascendent paradigm, namely, "families we choose." Weston's specific reference is to the emergence of gay and lesbian families and the reconfiguration of the inherited model they have enacted. "Chosen families do not directly oppose genealogical modes of reckoning kinship. Instead, they undercut procreation's status as a master term imagined to provide the template for all possible kinship relations."[13] Far from aligning themselves with the conservative rhetoric of "family endangerment," many commentators see the "chosen family" paradigm as pluralizing (rather than destroying) the received model of kinship structure: "The more recent forms of alternative life styles have now become part of the official fiber of society, because they are now being tolerated much more than in the past. In short, what we are witnessing is not a fragmentation of traditional family patterns, but, rather, the emergence of a pluralism in family ways."[14]

This pluralization of the familial is dramatically rendered in Thomas Allen Harris's recent tape *Vintage: Families of Value* (1995), in which the artist explores issues of influence and identity among three sets of African American gay siblings. Harris announces his interest in a tactics of pluralized family identities with the utmost directness; his voice-over, accompanied by black leader, precedes the first image:

> In 1990, I wanted to celebrate the intensity of my relationship with my brother Lyle. I was 28 years old and just beginning to explore feelings of ambivalence, fear and hope regarding my family. I recruited two other groups of siblings, members of my community who are also queer, to join me in taking a critical look at their own families. This film is a family album created over the course of five years.

It is a family album constructed through recourse to both heredity and choice, affirmed at every turn by the active participation of all three sets of siblings: Harris and his brother Lyle Ashton Harris; sisters Adrian Jones, Anita Jones, and Anni Cammett; and a brother-sister pair, Paul and Vanessa Eaddy. If domestic ethnography's defining features are consanguinity and co(i)mplication, *Vintage* pushes the latter term to new ends.

Harris rarely backs off from the heat of the relationships he shows us, least of all his own complex interaction with his brother, fellow artist Lyle Ashton Harris. But, in a manner consistent with the pluralization of the family model described above, *Vintage* chooses to focus on *queer siblings,* three groups of individuals each of which is linked internally by blood ties and, across the biological family groupings, by affinity. Although this is not the precise "families we choose" template discussed in the recent sociological literature (i.e., gay or lesbian couple plus adoptive child[ren]), the horizontalizing emphasis on multiple sets of queer siblings positions community alongside biological family grouping and introduces the element of choice. Harris's editing scheme establishes the mutuality of horizontal *and* vertical family investigation throughout the tape's seventy-two minutes. We are never allowed to settle in on any of the three family narratives; just as we become thoroughly engrossed in the hermeneutic tensions of one sibling set, we find ourselves elsewhere. Harris consistently reminds us of the resonances and overlappings of sexual fantasies, family secrets, and shifting alliances narrated and performed—within and across families. We thus see for ourselves the complex, multilayered character of sexual identities, for, while the siblings define themselves with, against, and through one another at the level of the biological family, they are also defined, at the level of the text, by a shared identification of queerness that links each to all.[15]

Moreover, all of the tape's participants share another sort of community affiliation: all are African American. Yet each challenges stereotypical gender roles recognizable within the black community: Thomas and Lyle celebrate their masculinity—baring sinewy bodies for the camera—yet identify with their mother; Vanessa Eaddy, not her brother Paul, talks of having idolized her father, tagging after him and his pals; Anni Cammett

Filmmaker Thomas Allen Harris with brother Lyle Ashton Harris, from *Vintage: Families of Value*. Photo courtesy of Thomas Allen Harris.

shares a passionate commitment to basketball and her young daughter. Yet it is to *Vintage*'s credit that neither "blackness" nor "queerness" is accorded primacy of influence in the work of identity formation. They are all queer, all black, but it is a queerness and a blackness that never ceases to mutate despite the "family resemblances." Difference and repetition, self and community, race and sexuality are experienced as interpenetrating categories, mutually determining (indeed undecidable) rather than contradictory or self-canceling.[16]

What we see and hear are three sets of siblings—mobile in their affinities, desires, and familial identifications—narrating their life stories, interrogating the discrepancies of family histories, questioning the hierarchies and psychosexual dependencies that formed each of them. This interrogation of the past, at times singular and introspective (here the expository mode is decidedly interactive, with Harris focusing his camera and attention on one or another sibling),[17] can also be undertaken sibling to sibling. In the latter instances, brothers or sisters exchange versions of their shared histories, at times firing questions at one another from behind the camera. At such times, the trope of shared textual authority discussed above comes into play, reminding us that the operation of the camera is also always a wielding of power. "Were you ashamed of the way I acted?" Vanessa Eaddy asks her brother Paul. Vanessa, though younger, had been out as a dyke while Paul was still closeting his sexuality. Pressing a momentary advantage, a camera-wielding Vanessa suggests that "Mommy is gonna want to talk to you!" The brother hesitates to reply, shifting uneasily beneath his sister's and the camera's gaze. He rises first to grab a cigarette then returns to his perch only to pop up again, demanding, in an attempt to regain control of the situation, that Vanessa "move the camera! Where's Thomas?" The younger, female sibling is now asking the questions of the elder brother, unsettling his inherited authority, overturning the hierarchies. In other sequences between them, it is also clear that Paul and Vanessa (two among eight siblings) are in fact quite close. Their relationship, like that of the other sibling sets, is intense, shifting, co(i)mplicated.

In all instances of domestic ethnography, the familial other helps to flesh out the very contours of the enunciating self, offering itself as a precursor, alter ego, double, instigator, spiritual guide, or perpetrator of trauma. Domestic ethnography entails but exceeds autobiography. In Thomas Allen Harris's tape, it is not just Harris who matters—it is also his brother Lyle as well as the other members of an aggressively extended family who perform a shared identity, that of black queer sibling. In so doing, they redefine the family as the crucible of identity and the locus of domestic ethnography.

Conclusion

What brings out the "ethnographic" in the domestic ethnography is the way in which the work calls attention to the dynamics of family life as the most fundamental (which is not to say universal) crucible of psychosexual identity. Universality is at odds with the historical, cultural, and psycho-social differences encountered in any examination of family structures, as exemplified by the variations apparent in three recent pieces. Domestic ethnography offers up the maker and her subject locked in a family embrace; indeed, as we have seen, subject/object positions are at times reversed. I have argued for domestic ethnography as an extension of autobiography, a pas de deux of self and other. It is discursively unstable. If it tells us about cultures and societies, as Fabian claims all ethnography must, it does so only in miniature. But by abandoning any pretense to authoritative or generalizable knowledge of the one for the other, domestic ethnography eludes the colonialist remorse to which Lévi-Strauss once referred.[18] Self and other encounter one another at home rather than in the village square, but the dynamics of social and sexual identity formation it rehearses leaves few of us unscathed.

NOTES

1. James Clifford, *The Predicament of Culture: Twentieth-Century Ethnography, Literature, and Art* (Cambridge: Harvard University Press, 1988), 34; Johannes Fabian, *Time and the Other: How Anthropology Makes Its Object* (New York: Columbia University Press, 1983), 33.

2. "Desire is desire for the absolutely other.... A desire without satisfaction which, precisely, *understands* the remoteness, the alterity, and the exteriority of the other. For Desire this alterity, non-adequate to the idea, has a meaning. It is understood as the alterity of the Other and of the Most-High." Emmanuel Levinas, *Totality and Infinity*, 2d ed., trans. A. Lingis (The Hague: Nijhoff, 1978), 34.

3. Peter Mason, *Deconstructing America: Representations of the Other* (London: Routledge, 1990), 2. The work of Levinas, called by Tzvetan Todorov "the philosopher of alterity," has helped to introduce an increasingly influential perspective in debates surrounding the ethical status of research in the social and human sciences. In a deeply radical gesture, Levinas has suggested that it is Reason itself that has functioned to "neutralize and encompass" the other, translating difference into its own terms in the insatiable pursuit of Knowledge. Emmanuel Levinas, *Totality and Infinity*, trans. Alphonso Lingis (The Hague: Martinus Nijhoff, 1961), 43. The Levinasian view does not so much undercut the potential for knowledge in cross-cultural research as relativize its value within a moral universe: "It is not a question of putting knowledge in doubt. The human being clearly allows himself to be treated as an object, and delivers himself to knowledge in the *truth* of perception and the light of the human sciences. But, treated exclusively as an object, man is also mistreated and misconstrued.... We are human before being learned, and remain so after having forgotten much." Emmanuel Levinas, *Outside the Subject*, trans. Michael B. Smith (Stanford, Calif: Stanford University Press, 1994), 2–3.

4. Trinh T. Minh-ha, "Difference: 'A Special Third World Women Issue,'" *Discourse* 8 (fall/winter 1986–87), 27, 14, 16.

5. Michael Taussig, *Mimesis and Alterity: A Particular History of the Senses* (New York: Routledge, 1993), xviii, xiii.

6. Stephen A. Tyler, "Post-modern Ethnography," in *Writing Culture: The Poetics and*

Politics of Ethnography, ed. James Clifford and George E. Marcus (Berkeley: University of California Press, 1986), 122–40.

7. George E. Marcus, "Ethnography in the Modern World System," in *Writing Culture: The Poetics and Politics of Ethnography,* ed. James Clifford and George E. Marcus (Berkeley: University of California Press, 1986), 190–93.

8. Historically, the notion of the "unlearning of privilege" recalls a notable response of feminist theorists to the lure of incrementally shared patriarchal authority and is currently echoed by the growing attention being given indigenous media making around the world. The work of certain progressive scholars becomes a "facilitation" of representation made by and for indigenous peoples.

9. See Clifford Geertz, *Works and Lives: The Anthropologist as Author* (Stanford, Calif.: Stanford University Press, 1988), 1-24; Hayden White, "Introduction: Tropology, Discourse, and the Modes of Human Consciousness," in *Tropics of Discourse: Essays in Cultural Criticism* (Baltimore: Johns Hopkins University Press, 1978), 1–3.

10. There remains a lacuna that the present commentary cannot adequately address and that pertains to the etiology of the artist's sexual orientation. Given Friedrich's public stance as a lesbian filmmaker, and given the film's inclusion of images alluding to Friedrich's sexuality (mostly water imagery—women showering together, Friedrich bathing alone), the matter of the father's role in the shaping of the daughter's sexual identity seems to be raised, but only indirectly. Such an elliptical treatment of the topic shrewdly sidesteps diagnostics while remaining consistent with the generally oblique approach to the construal of meaning adopted by the work.

11. Edward Said, *Orientalism* (New York: Pantheon, 1978).

12. Paul Ricouer, "Universal Civilization and National Cultures," in *History and Truth,* trans. Charles A. Kelbley (Evanston: Northwestern University Press, 1965), 278.

13. Kath Weston, "The Politics of Gay Families," in *Rethinking the Family: Some Feminist Questions,* rev. ed., ed. Barrie Thorne and Marilyn Yalom (Boston: Northeastern University Press, 1992), 137. One proviso is worth adding in this context. The phrase "families we choose" stresses volition, the conscious selection of new family groupings. Although it would be wrong to deny that gays and lesbians have indeed begun to "choose" to reinvent the family more aggressively and in greater numbers, it would be a mistake to focus a discussion of queerness and its interventions solely at the level of consciousness. Such a stance would miss the pertinence of

what Judith Butler has called "psychic excess," that which surpasses the domain of the conscious subject in the determination of sexuality. "This psychic excess is precisely what is being systematically denied by the notion of a volitional 'subject' who elects at will which gender and/or sexuality to be at any given time and place. . . . Sexuality may be said to exceed any definitive narrativization. . . . There are no direct expressive or causal lines between sex, gender, gender presentation, sexual practice, fantasy and sexuality. . . . Part of what constitutes sexuality is precisely that which does not appear and that which, to some degree, can never appear." Judith Butler, "Imitation and Gender Insubordination," in *Inside/Out: Lesbian Theories, Gay Theories,* ed. Diana Fuss (New York: Routledge, 1991), 24–25. All of which is to say that sexuality—gay or straight—eludes volition and the regime of the visible in a most fundamental way.

14. Tamara K. Hareven, "American Families in Transition: Historical Perspectives on Change," in *Family in Transition: Rethinking Marriage, Sexuality, Child Rearing and Family Organization,* 5th ed., ed. Arlene S. Skolnick and Jerome H. Skolnick (Boston: Little, Brown, 1986), 55.

15. The matter of sexualized identifications is a tremendously complex one, requiring more qualification than can be undertaken here. As Eve Kosofsky Sedgwick has argued, identifications can be consolidating as well as denegating, structured through a play of idealization and abjection. Sexual identifications can be identifications *with, as,* or *against.* Sedgwick elaborates on the sheer profusion of relations implicit in but one subset, *identifying with,* which she describes as potentially "fraught with intensities of incorporation, diminishment, inflation, threat, loss, reparation, and disavowal." Eve Kosofsky Sedgwick, *Epistemology of the Closet* (Berkeley: University of California Press, 1990), 61. To its credit, *Vintage: Families of Value* allows for the discussion and performance of an astonishing array of identificatory positions and intensities played out among its three sets of siblings. The tape, for the most part, steers clear of etiology, a search for queer sources, opting instead for an interactive, on-camera interrogation of family dynamics entailing parents, children, spouses, and lovers as well as siblings. If what emerges is a vision of pluralized queer sexualities in which even siblings are unique in their object choices, fantasies, and preferred practices, this can only be a contribution to the overthrow of the discursive rigidities in which queer subjectivity is still closeted.

16. I am purposely invoking the Derridean notion of undecidability with regard to the

determination of identity. Derived from the critical writing of Jacques Derrida, the deconstructive method of textual analysis challenges binary oppositions, first by acknowledging the often unspoken hierarchy through which one term controls the other (race over sexuality, sexuality over race), then by overthrowing that hierarchy and finally displacing it. Jacques Derrida, *Positions*, trans. Alan Bass (Chicago: University of Chicago Press, 1981), 41–43. In Derrida's work, apparently conflictual categories are often found to inhabit one another, resisting and disorganizing the binary in such a manner as to betray the boundaries of "inside" and "outside." This may well be the case for the queer black/ black queer subject as constructed within *Vintage: Families of Value*, in which blackness, queerness, birth order, and family relations play out unevenly though decisively.

17. The reference here is to Bill Nichols's discussion of the several modes of documentary exposition, among them the interactive mode, which "stresses images of testimony or verbal exchange. . . . Textual authority shifts toward the social actors recruited: their comments and responses provide a central part of the film's argument. Various forms of monologue and dialogue (real or apparent) predominate." Bill Nichols, *Representing Reality: Issues and Concepts in Documentary* (Bloomington: Indiana University Press, 1991), 44. In *Vintage*, Thomas Allen Harris does indeed delegate authority to his interlocutors, who have been quite literally recruited for that task; their experiences supplement his own.

18. Claude Lévi-Strauss, *Tristes Tropiques*, trans. John Weightman and Doreen Weightman (New York: Atheneum, 1978), 389.

FAYE GINSBURG

[8] The Parallax Effect: The Impact of Indigenous Media on Ethnographic Film

parallax: *(mf parallaxe fr. Gk. parallaxis, change, alternation . . .) 1. the apparent displacement of an object as seen from two different points.*
:: Webster's Third New International Unabridged Dictionary, 1976

Ethnographic film no longer occupies a singular niche. Other voices call to us in forms and modes that blur the boundaries and genres that represent distinctions between fiction and documentary, politics and culture, here and there. For those situated in the larger, nonspecialist audience outside of anthropology per se, these other voices often seem more incisive, informative, and engaging. . . . The voice of the traditional ethnographic filmmaker has become one voice among many. Dialogue, debate, and a fundamental reconceptualization of visual anthropology in light of these transformations is, quite simply, essential.
:: Bill Nichols, *Blurred Boundaries,* 1994

Where should the dividing line between insider and outsider stop? How should it be defined? By skin color (no blacks should make films on yellows)? By language (only Fulani can talk about Fulani, a Bassari is a foreigner here)? By nation (only Vietnamese can produce works on Vietnam)? . . . What about those with hyphenated identities and hybrid realities?
:: Trinh T. Minh-Ha, *When the Moon Waxes Red,* 1991

Fanon speaks of the necessary decision to accept "the reciprocal relativism of different cultures, once colonialism is excluded." Each group offers its own exotopy (according to Bakhtin), its own "excess seeing," hopefully coming not only

to "see" other groups, but also, through a salutary estrangement, to see how it is itself seen.
:: Ella Shohat and Robert Stam, *Unthinking Eurocentrism*, 1994

This essay is an effort to rethink the way we position ethnographic film at the end of the twentieth century, with special attention to the relationship of the genre to the burgeoning of work by filmmakers from communities that have, historically, been anthropology's objects, in particular the work of indigenous media makers. Because the assaults on indigenous people have been so severe, these current efforts to reassert their cultural and historical presence through a widely acccessible media form are particularly important for those engaged in the production of indigenous media; their self-consciousness about their work as a form of cultural production suggests a close parallel to the project of anthropology, yet one whose urgency is far greater than any academic agenda. Moreover, ethnographic film at the fin de siècle cannot pretend (anymore than can anthropology in general) that it occupies the same postion in the world it did even twenty-five years ago, as the only show in town, so to speak. The genre now exists amid a bewildering array of imagery from around the planet and within an equally complex range of technologies for its production and circulation. These new media forms present a kind of moral imperative to rethink the genre's project at the present moment. Additionally, the rich possibilities that this rethinking can offer in terms of epistemology, aesthetics, pedagogy, production, and research seem more than sufficient to justify the expanded framework I sketch here, and that others have elsewhere from slightly different perspectives.[1]

I am not in any way advocating that indigenous media should displace ethnographic film. Rather, I argue more positively for developing a framework that will allow us to think of the different but related projects of ethnographic film and indigenous media in relation to each other, to help expand and refine the broader project of representing, mediating, and understanding culture through a variety of media forms. To do so requires attending to both ethnographic and indigenous films as representations of culture *and* as objects that are themselves implicated in cultural processes. Although my research (and therefore my case) is based on my work with Australian Aboriginal and other indigenous media makers, my suggestions easily might be extended to work being done by media makers from diasporic communities and (so-called) Third World communities, although with careful attention to the historical and political differences inherent in these terms and the people and objects to which they point.[2]

Specifically, I am interested in how indigenous film and video can offer productive challenges to the assumptions of the genre of ethnographic film by (1) reframing questions about the representation of cultural differences to account for how they operate as forms of cultural production; (2) highlighting media making as a dimension of contemporary (and historical) social, cultural, and political processes; and (3) expanding the discursive framework of the field in order to bring a wider variety of subjects into conversation around questions raised by these media as they travel across boundaries of difference. Finally, and of most interest to this volume, this work demonstrates the necessity of acknowledging multiple points of view in the creation, distribution, and reception of screen representations of culture.

To capture the sense I have of the epistemologically positive impact that indigenous media might have on ethnographic film, I use the metaphor of the parallax effect. This term was originally invented to describe the phenomenon that occurs when a change in the position of the observer creates the illusion that an object has been displaced or moved. In astronomy, this effect is harnessed to gain a greater understanding of the position and nature of stars and planets in the cosmos. In optics, the small parallax created by the slightly different angles of vision of each eye is recognized as that which enables us to judge distances accurately and see in three dimensions. Drawing on a similar principle, one might understand indigenous media as arising from a historically new positioning of the observer behind the camera so that the object—the cinematic representation of culture—appears to look different than it does from the observational perspective of ethnographic film. Yet, by juxtaposing these different but related kinds of cinematic perspectives on culture, one can create a kind of parallax effect; if harnessed analytically, these "slightly different angles of vision" can offer a fuller comprehension of the complexity—the three-dimensionality, so to speak—of the social phenomenon we call culture and those media representations that self-consciously engage with it. It is my argument that resituating ethnographic film in relation to related practices such as indigenous media can help expand the field's possibilities and revive its contemporary interest and purpose beyond a narrowly defined field. The parallax created by the different perspectives in these media practices is one that is particularly important now as anthropology struggles to position itself in relation to contemporary critiques.

This notion of the parallax is not without precedent in the field of visual anthropology. Since the 1950s, Jean Rouch has sustained a commitment to and development of film as a vehicle for the creation of a "shared anthropology," not only in research and production, but in exhibition, through what he calls *regards compares* (or comparative perspectives).[3]

The name of this concept was first coined in 1978, when Rouch organized a series of conferences in Paris at the Musée de l'Homme devoted to a comparative study of film projects made with so-called tribal peoples, beginning with the Yanomamo.[4] The events brought together people from all over the world, including not only the expected anthropologists, filmmakers, television producers, and even video artists, but people from the societies being viewed who offered judgments on the works made about them. These events were an early effort to demonstrate how different agendas, as well as the culture, nationality, gender, and institutional location of producers, shaped the range of images produced about a single culture. The resulting *regards compares* brought about by the juxtaposing of the producers and subjects of these films to interrogate them jointly as representations is an early precedent for the current sense of the parallax effect that I am after: the object (the filmed image of a culture) appears to change in different films, depending on the position of the observer/filmmaker. When these different images are considered together, a more dialogical understanding results.

By expanding the context in which it is understood as a representational practice, a revised sense of ethnographic film—what I am calling the parallax effect—can offer an exemplary model for recent work in social theory that increasingly argues for more dialogical approaches that take into account the complex nature of ethnographic texts and the likelihood that "natives" might well be readers if not writers of ethnographies. In this more Derridian and textual view of the ethnographic process, ethnographies (whether books or films) are not so much engaged in constituting an anthropological object so much as they are "sites of meaning potential." This underscores the importance of taking into account not only the rethinking provoked by work such as indigenous media, but also the changing composition of *audiences* for these works. This is true even within the walls of the Western academy, as that universe has grown more diverse with increasing numbers of transnational and diasporic students. Indeed, as Ella Shohat and Bob Stam point out in their book *Unthinking Eurocentrism,* "Spectatorship is not sociologically compartmentalized; diverse communities can resonate together."[5]

In my own experience during the past decade of teaching ethnographic film to graduate students in New York City, my classes have become increasingly "multicultural." Seminars regularly include Native Americans, African Americans, recent immigrants from the Caribbean, Latin Americans, Asian Americans, Indonesians, Indians, Pakistanis, and Iranians, to name just a few. Many of these people are themselves media producers and sometimes find cultural versions of themselves objectified in the films we watch in class; they often bring sophisticated and sometimes unexpected perspectives to "classic" works. Discussions have ranged from a lively debate about why (unpredictably) the Native American students liked *Nanook of the North* to what difference it made to watch *N!ai: The Story of a !Kung Woman* from the subject position of a black female spectator. The responses of these students to films over the years have made it clear that the assumed spectators for most ethnographic films, until recently, have been white, middle-class, male, and straight.[6]

Audience research is not simply an exercise in how to be aware of the changing conditions of spectatorship. A number of indigenous filmmakers trace their inspiration to become filmmakers back to the experience of watching films in which they felt themselves objectified, stereotyped, or erased. For example, Australian Aboriginal filmmaker Frances Peters describes her film-viewing experiences in mainstream art schools as both alienating and clarifying.[7] The avant-garde films and European theory to which she was exposed seemed to deny her experiences and interests; in the end, that sense of erasure served as a kind of "conversion experience" that motivated her to make films expressive of *her* cultural and historical concerns.[8] In advocating for the importance of indigenous media to contemporary ethnographic understandings, I am not simply hoping to further "polyphonic possibilities" or account for our increasingly diverse audiences. Attending to the work and experience of people such as Frances Peters is part of a broader effort on the part of a number of contemporary anthropologists to reframe ethnographic research (as well as texts) according to the distinctive experiences of collective identity in the late twentieth century.[9] For example, in a groundbreaking article first published in a collection addressing how anthropologists might "work in the present," Arjun Appadurai introduces the neologism "ethnoscapes" to characterize the "changing social, territorial, and cultural reproduction of group identity."

> As groups migrate, regroup in new locations, reconstruct their histories, and reconfigure their ethnic "projects," the *ethno* in ethnography takes on a slippery, nonlocalized quality. . . . The landscapes of identity—the ethnoscapes—around the world are no longer familiar objects, insofar as groups are no longer tightly territorialized, spatially bounded, historically unselfconscious, or culturally homogeneous.[10]

> Anthropology can surely contribute its special purchase on lived experience to a wider, transdisciplinary study of global cultural processes. But to do this, anthropology must first come in from the cold and face the challenge of making a contribution to cultural studies without the benefit of its previous principal source of leverage—sightings of the savage.[11]

Appadurai's work represents a very influential and generative reformulation for contemporary anthropological work—reflected in the journal *Public Culture,* for example—but he also has been particularly interested in attending, analytically, to media. He argues that although imagination has always been expressed in songs, myths, rituals, dress, and performance, it has a peculiar new force today because of the circulation of new forms of media. Because of that, "more persons in more parts of the world consider a wider set of possible lives than they ever did before."[12]

> One of the principal shifts in the global cultural order, created by cinema, television, and VCR technology (and the ways in which they frame and energize other, older media), has to do with the role of the imagination in social life.[13]

> Some of these forms may start out as extremely global and end up as very local—radio would be an example—while others such as cinema, might have the obverse trajectory.[14]

In other words, Appadurai (and others) encourage ethnographic understanding of the relationship between shifts in the global cultural order and the ways in which daily social life is imagined. Such a framework is crucial to understanding indigenous media as a form of social action, as will be evident in my discussion below of several Australian cases. Before engaging in that analysis, however, I want to address how this work is seen in relation to the genre of ethnographic film.

▶

Genre Positions: Indigenous Media and Ethnographic Film

> Ethnographic film is in trouble. Not entirely due to what ethnographic filmmakers have done, or failed to do, but also because of the nature of the institutional discourse that continues to surround this mode of documentary representation. And not entirely due to either of these factors, but also because of the ground-breaking, convention-altering forms of self-representation by those who have traditionally been objects (and blind spots) of anthropological study: women/natives/others. For over ten years a significant body of work has been accumulating that comes from elsewhere, telling stories and representing experiences in different voices and different styles.[15]

The origins of what we have come to identify as ethnographic film were in the efforts of Western scholars, travelers, explorers, and filmmakers to record on film what they regarded as the supposedly "vanishing worlds" of people from non-Western, small-scale, kinship-based societies—that is, those who had been the initial objects of anthropology as it developed in the early twentieth century. However, it was only after World War II that ethnographic film took on definition and shape as a genre, particularly during the 1960s and 1970s, when efforts to "reinvent anthropology" kept pace with a variety of historical, intellectual, and political developments.[16] Briefly stated, these include movements for independence by colonized peoples, the radicalization of young scholars in the 1960s who began to question the purpose of their knowledge and its relevance to those they were studying, the replacing of positivist models of knowledge with more interpretive and politically self-conscious approaches, and a reconceptualization of "the native voice" as one that should be in more direct dialogue with anthropological interpretation. By the 1980s, this constellation of events precipitated what some have called "a crisis in representation" for the field that required new, experimental, and more dialogical strategies for transmitting anthropological understandings.[17]

It is, perhaps, a reflection of ethnographic film's position in the academy that little attention was paid to the fact that a number of central figures in ethnographic film already had responded to this "crisis" with moral, intellectual, and aesthetic creativity.[18] One of the few attempts to put the means of production and representation into hands of indigenous people was carried out by Sol Worth and John Adair in the 1960s. Their project, discussed in their 1972 book *Through Navajo Eyes,* taught filmmaking to young Navajo students without the conventions of Western production and editing, to see if their films would reflect a distinctively Navajo film worldview.[19] Although it was a short-lived project, it helped expand the classic paradigm of ethnographic film of "us" always filming "them." Still, the sense that the Navajo project was of interest only as a way to provide data for anthropologists on Navajo cognitive processes has come under criticism from "natives." Vietnamese filmmaker and critic Trinh T. Minh-ha, for example, identifies the Navajo project with the general field of visual anthropology and condemns them both as patronizing, "so that We can collect data on the indigenous ethnographic filmmaking process, and show Navajos through Navajo eyes to our folks in the field," allowing "white anthropology to further anthropologize Man."[20] On the other hand, Native American students in my classes have found this project and the films produced as part of it both compelling and valuable.[21]

In any case, Trinh's remarks were appropriate for the state of the field at the time that project was carried out, in the late 1960s and early 1970s. More pertinent now are questions about the changing circulation and exhibition of both ethnographic film and indigenous media and their categorizations, that is, the social spaces they have come to occupy. Since the late 1970s, ethnographic film has changed considerably,[22] and indigenous people increasingly have been producing their own images for their communities and for outsiders. In some cases, they have chosen to work with accomplished and sympathetic filmmakers and activists such as Vincent Carelli at the Centro de Trabalho Indigenista in São Paulo, Brazil, and Sarah Elder and Leonard Kamerling at the Alaska Native Heritage Project or with anthropologists such as Terry Turner, who initated the Kayapo Video Project.[23] Others have entered directly into film and video production themselves, for example, Hopi video artist and activist Victor Masayesva Jr. and Inuit producer/director Zacharias Kunuk.

The media work of indigenous people has been provoked by an increasing awareness on their part of the politically charged nature of media representations about them; this recognition has been spurred on by a range of developments, such as the not always welcome introduction of communications satellites that bring television reception to indigenous people living in remote areas. The desire to be in control of imagery made about them has been facilitated by the increasing availability of relatively inexpensive media technologies, such as portable video cameras and VCRs, as well as more complex communication forms that have been used to facilitate regional linkages, as in the development of compressed video through the Tanami Network in Central Australia.[24]

The enthusiasm with which these new forms have been embraced suggests the importance of these communication forms to contemporary indigenous concerns, expressive of a desire on the part of Aboriginal people to "talk back" on their own terms to those who might have presumed to speak for them. It seems that the interest in hearing "the native voice" is too often confined to those texts that are already inside the academic circle, providing "new and improved ways for institutionalized ethnographers to vex each other more precisely by involving 'others' more thoroughly in the process."[25] As Aboriginal activist and anthropologist Marcia Langton has observed in discussing the development of Aboriginal media:

> Aboriginal people have invented a theatre of politics in which self-representation has become a sophisticated device, creating their own theories or models of intercultural discourse such as land rights, self-determination, "White Australia has a black history" and so on.[26]

Moreover, she points out that different genres and academic social rules for production and circulation of work can sideline such alternative kinds of creative analysis made by Aboriginal activists, consigning indigenous media to a ghetto unless it follows the protocols of academic discourse.

> Some intellectuals even demand that the Native answer back in a refereed journal, say something about the French intellectuals, Jacques Derrida or Jean

Baudrillard, and speak from the hyperluxury of the first world with the reflective thoughts of a well-paid, well-fed, detached scholar.[27]

Indigenous media, because it can circumvent the more rigid hierarchies of print genres, can also provide a unique opportunity to bring these kinds of representations into a more equitable relationship with other kinds of discourse about media representation and production, despite the vast inequalities that nonetheless exist between the academy and what feminist theorist Nancy Fraser calls "subaltern counterpublics."[28] Indeed, this essay (and the idea of a parallax) is part of an effort to expand the well-policed boundaries of genres of textual production in ethnographic film.

With these developments in mind, I would like to consider the challenge that indigenous media poses to the assumptions on which ethnographic film has been based. One response to the presence of indigenous media production (in its broadest sense) is a concern with whether it renders ethnographic filmmaking obsolete.[29] In some formulations, only members of particular communities are considered entitled to represent these groups, thus reinscribing essentialism in the face of a growing recognition of the complexity and instability of identity.[30] Although such ideas seem patently out of date in relation to contemporary work in anthropology, they nonetheless undergird recent critiques by First World white academics of indigenous media practice as inherently corrupting and commodifying.[31] Similarly (and equally discouraging), Euro-American anthropologists have, on occasion, called into question whether indigenous peoples can authentically claim their identities if they are using cameras and making media about themselves. For example, some American anthropologists have responded critically to videos I have shown of traditional ceremonies made by Pitjantjatjara people of Central Australia as if they were documenting disappearing cultural practices; my colleagues could not comprehend a situation in which the camera was not a "cause" for the performance of the ceremony, as in this case, when the videotaping of ceremonies had been incorporated into an ongoing ritual practice to be replayed for further pleasure and valorization of the event. Clearly, there are also institutional structures that channel the circulation of work to certain kinds of spectators who bring a whole range of suppositions to the viewing event. As an example of a very different kind of setting for viewing indigenous work, the film *Box of Treasures* (1983), shown at the Umista Cultural Center, shows how contemporary Kwakwaka'wakw (formerly Kwakiutl) are utilizing a number of resources—including colonial photography—to facilitate cultural renewal.[32]

Given the inadequacies of arguments concerning singular positions of producers or audiences as bases for holding ethnographic and indigenous film apart, I want to explore further the possibilities for considering these practices within the same analytic frame. This is part of a more general and healthy revision of the field that comes out of a broad rethinking of cultural theory that takes into account the changing zeitgeist since the 1980s.[33] David MacDougall suggests the term "intertextual cinema" to draw attention to these changes as they apply to ethnographic film:

> Since 1896, ethnographic film-making has undergone a series of revolutions, introducing narrative, observational and participatory approaches. With each, a set of assumptions about the positioning of the film-maker and the audience has crumbled. Now it is the single identity of each of these that is under review. . . .
> . . . we are already seeing the changes in a new emphasis on authorship and specific cultural perspectives. . . . I think we will increasingly regard ethnographic films as meeting places of primary and secondary levels of representation, one cultural text seen through another . . . films which are produced by and belong equally to two cultures. . . .
> If we are in the midst of a new revolution, as I believe we are, it is one which is interested in multiple voices and which might be called an *intertextual cinema*.[34]

MacDougall's idea of intertextual cinema addresses concerns similar to those I am addressing with the concept of the parallax effect; we are both looking for a broader frame that can accommodate the changing world of media production within which ethnographic film is now situated. I would argue not only for intertextuality but also for an emphasis on the *social relations* constituted and reimagined in the production and circulation of media explicitly engaged in representing culture (for example, in groups such as the National Aboriginal and Islanders Media Association in Australia). This focus on the social reframes the Griersonian assumption regarding documentary practice that Jane Gaines addresses elsewhere in this collection—that viewing a documentary work will lead to enlightened action; in the case of indigenous media, the work is already part of a continuum of social action. For audiences watching work produced by people from another culture, there may be more than epistephilia at work—such viewing may summon up new sources of identification and engagement.[35] Arguing that identity is less something one has than something one does, Shohat and Stam write:

> The concept of crisscrossing identifications evokes the theoretical possibility and even the political necessity of sharing the critique of domination and the burden of representation. It even involves making representation less of a burden and more of a collective pleasure and responsibility.[36]

In terms of an *analytic* frame that we can use in thinking about this work, we need to attend more closely—even ethnographically—to the very activity of film/video production, as part of a social process engaged in the mediation of culture. In other words, rather than expecting documentary to motivate political action from its viewers who *are* in fact interested in learning from the films they watch, it is more fruitful to turn our attention to those who find media production to be part of a broader project of cultural resistance and transformation. This understanding builds on the insights of indigenous producers who clearly recognize their media work as a form of social action when they become the authors of representations about themselves. Describing this situation, Aboriginal activist, anthropologist, and producer Marcia Langton writes:

> The motivations behind Aboriginal community video production and television transmission can be seen as basic issues of self-determination, cultural maintenance, and the prevention of cultural disruption.
>
> . . . The strategies which indigenous Australians have employed to overcome the problems posed by the impact of television and video include: cultural and aesthetic interventions; control of incoming television signals; control of self-representation through local video production in local languages; refusal to permit outsiders to film; and negotiation of co-productions which guarantee certain conditions aimed at cultural maintenance.
>
> An expansion of experimental film- and videomaking is vital to allow Aboriginal people to make their own self-representations and to create culturally useful meaning.[37]

In other words, for Aboriginal producers and viewers, the value in creating and viewing media about their own lives derives from the very production and circulation of this work as forms that enable them to articulate and enhance their own histories, political concerns, and cultural practices. This is true for work that is viewed primarily in Aboriginal communities as well as for work that is explicitly intended for "white audiences" (although such categories are questionable, given that these media quickly and inevitably escape their original circuits).

In the case of indigenous work created explicitly for members of the dominant society, the intervention of Aboriginal views of Australian history, for example, is part of an ongoing struggle against the erasure of Aboriginal people that began with the colonial doctrine of *terra nullius*. This concept allowed British settlers to declare Australia "unoccupied," justifying the colonial appropriation of lands from Aboriginal peoples from the seventeenth century until the present, a hegemonic legacy that was challenged successfully only in the 1993 Mabo decision.[38] Under such circumstances, not unlike those faced by indigenous peoples in many other parts of the world, the very creation and viewing of work representing Aboriginal perspectives is a significant form of social action. An example of the mobilization of media to assert Aboriginal presence in Australian history, on a national scale, occurred with the approach of Australia's bicentenary celebrations in 1988. Protests over the lack of appropriate media representation for Aboriginal people became widespread, as activists drew attention to their view of the founding of a British colony on their shores by referring to it as "Invasion Day." The state television channel, the ABC, in response to such pressures, formed the Aboriginal Programs Unit. The first piece produced by the unit, *BabaKiueria,* directed by Don Featherstone, was created by a mixed ensemble of European and Aboriginal Australian actors and producers. This biting satire of the two-hundred-year legacy of racism in Australia entails a recasting of Australia's past as if the native population had been white Europeans and the colonists Aboriginal. This is signaled in a wonderful opening sequence depicting the primal colonial encounter in which the cultural positions are reversed. We see a peaceful gathering of white working-class people at a barbecue near the ocean; a young white boy chases his ball to the water's edge, where he spots a strange boat approaching. It lands, and several Aboriginal "colonists" dressed in military outfits come ashore and ask in slow and careful English, "What do you call this place?" The bewildered whites respond politely and incomprehendingly (and with an Australian accent), "Why it's a bah-be-q [barbecue] area." Oblivious to the obvious claims of the whites, the Aboriginal leader plants the Aboriginal flag on the site and announces, in an iconic enactment of the injustice of *terra nullius*: "BabaKieuria. A quaint native name. I like it." The title comes up over this apocryphal vision of the white workingman's paradise lost with the sound of clapsticks and Aboriginal chanting on the sound track.

The body of the piece is built around a parody of ethnographic inquiry and the journalistic pretension to knowledge, using the strategy of reversal to expose the multiple ways in which racist practices are naturalized through the ascendance of one culture's values over another. We are led through the inquiry by a young female Aboriginal investigative reporter (played by actress Michelle Torres) who opens with the statement, "I've always been fascinated by white people, but what do we really know about them?" Dressed in a tailored khaki-colored safari suit, she carries out a send-up of the vox pop sequence in which Aboriginals on the street and in shopping malls are asked what they think of white people; they explain that they've "never really met one" or that "they love their music but they can't dance," finally ending with an interview at the office of the "minister of White Affairs" (played by Aboriginal actor Bob Maza). Turning from his computer screen and peering over his half glasses, he pronounces in a voice heavy with euphemism, "They are a developing people." The reporter clearly won't settle so easily for bureaucratic racism, although the minister always remains as her interlocutor. Return visits to the minister's office are cut throughout the film in which the reporter asks him "hard" and supposedly sympathetic questions such as "Is it fair for us to expect white people to improve?"—questions that at first sound ridiculous but are close enough to popular stereotypes about Aborigines to also be chilling.

Standing outside a modest brick bungalow, the reporter creates the narrative of her journey into the heart of whiteness: "Five years ago, I decided to find out about these fascinating people. I came to live in this typical white ghetto with a typical white family." She walks into the house and seats herself in the living room, where the family—working father in coveralls, housewife/mother in shirtwaist and cardigan, older boy and younger girl—is arrayed awkwardly on the sofa, a large television set in the background. With her camera perched on her knees, the reporter addresses the viewer: "These are happy people, always ready to have their picture taken, living simple, uncomplicated lives." A photo of children at school shows them looking at a blackboard drawing of a mushroom cloud labeled "A-Bomb"; a visit to the family's grandmother in an isolated urban old-age high-rise covered with graffiti is prefaced by the reporter's explanation that the key to white society is the family. When the reporter returns to the bungalow, the girl is being removed by the BabaKieuria police. With the ominous sounds of a didjeridu and clapsticks in the background, the reporter turns to the viewer: "Parting with a loved one is never easy. I parted with my mother when she went on holiday." In a further indictment of the discursive space of television, she then turns to the parents and asks them if they want to say anything, reminding them that "anything you say will be broadcast and seen by a lot of black people."

BabaKiueria continues to surprise the viewer, looking at gambling as a form of prayer for good fortune and war veterans' parades as ancestor worship. The reversals turn deadly serious at the end, when the white family is dumped on a barren lot, removed from their home because the government needs their land as part of a new "resettlement policy." The son, angry and defiant, runs off, and as the parents are driven away in the back of a pickup truck, the reporter turns to the camera and confesses, "This was a very emotional experience for me. A real lump in the throat. As I watched them drive away, I felt myself missing them." Returning to the minister of White Affairs to ask what happened, she is told that this is an exciting opportunity, an "interesting new training scheme." Turning back to the viewers, she asks, "Do white people need to change their attitude toward us, or do we need to change it toward them?" The final ominous shot shows the television playing in the abandoned house, with the news announcing "another outbreak of white protest" as someone throws a rock through the window, breaking the glass in slow motion in the final sequence over which the credits roll.

BabaKieuria, along with other works such as *Ritual Clowns* and *Petit a Petit* or Manthia Diawara's *Rouch in Reverse* (1995), exemplifies an emerging subgenre of "reverse ethnographies" that either parody or in some other ways reverse the usual trajectory of power and knowledge in ethnographic/documentary inquiry. Although at first such works appear simply to be subverting ethnographic knowledge altogether, in certain ways they use humor to achieve the same kind of effect desired by those who make the forms they parody: to defamiliarize the everyday practices of our own society (including those of anthropologists and bureaucrats) in a way that offers a profound cultural critique of the ethnocentrism on which contemporary race and power relations are built. Inuit filmmaker Zacharias Kunuk explains how his "reverse anthropology" both borrows from and subverts the practices by which Inuit people have been categorized and studied. In a 1996 proposal for a project called "Qallunaat: Oral History as Inuit Anthropology," he writes:

> For 175 years, since the Parry expedition of 1822–23, Igloolik Inuit have been observed, examined, measured, and studied by other cultures. To our knowledge, this practice of "anthropology/ethnography" has been entirely a one-way street. *Qallunaat* [non-Inuit] study Inuit, but Inuit do not study *qallunaat.* This uneven exchange influences all levels of relations between the two cultures: political, economic, social, and so forth with *qallunaat* values and assumptions defining both cultures.

For several years Zacharias Kunuk has wanted to conduct a systematic study of *qallunaat* that might be called "reverse anthropology," examining the habits, values, social behaviors, political institutions, and multicultural differences among non-Inuit.[39] As these reverse ethnographies make clear, film and video can provide an especially important arena in which an Aboriginal past and present as well as social relations with the encompassing society can be playfully reimagined, a possibility more traditional indigenous forms cannot so easily accommodate.

Other indigenous productions are often directed toward what I call the mediation of ruptures of cultural knowledge, historical memory, and social relations between generations. For example, *Manyu Wana* (Just for fun) is a community-based Aboriginal children's program made at Yuendumu, a remote desert settlement of Warlpiri people living in the Northern Territory.

The project was initiated by Warlpiri elders who, along with schoolteachers, were concerned about the loss of traditional language and numerical skills that seemed to accompany the acquisition of English literacy. Aware of the lure of dominant television for their children, they decided to make a series of video programs that would help teach them to read in Warlpiri, with the participation of the children themselves and the help of a sympathetic local white filmmaker, David Batty. Resembling a combination of *Sesame Street* and home movies, the programs use considerable humor, sight gags, and modest special effects; for example, in one of the segments, a cardboard box "magically" turns into a truck. The programs comprise short segments improvised with children at Yuendumu; written Warlpiri words are superimposed along the bottom of the screen. Originally designed for local television in Warlpiri communities, for schools and for outstations, the tapes quickly escaped their original circuit. *Manyu Wana* has been shown on national television in Australia (on the SBS channel) and has charmed audiences at festivals and exhibitions in London, New York, and Montreal, despite the fact that it is entirely in Warlpiri. The series was funded by the National Aboriginal Languages Programme in Australia, along with Central Television, London, indexing the increasing combination of local and global interests in creating this kind of indigenous cultural imagery.

In other media productions, one can see how long-standing Aboriginal skills of collective self-production through narrative and ceremonial performance are engaged in innovative ways that are simultaneously indigenous and intercultural. *Coniston Story* (1984), one of the first tapes made at Yuendumu by Frances Jupurrurla Kelly and the Warlpiri Media Association with American researcher Eric Michaels, records an elder telling about "the Killing Time" in 1929, when one hundred Warlpiri men, women, and children gathered for a ritual were massacred by whites at Coniston Station, near their settlement, in retaliation for the killing of a white trapper. According to Michaels, this story "has come to function like an origin myth, explaining the presence and nature of Europeans and articulating the relations that arose between the two cultures. Which version of the story becomes 'official' would seem to matter greatly. . . . These are crucial historiographic issues."[40] When they began shooting the story, twenty-seven people turned up to make a film that featured only three people and required only two operators. Upon inquiring as to why so many people had come along, Michaels was told: "They're *kudungurlu* [ceremonial managers of the land]. They want to stay on the side for this story." In other words, video production was organized socially according to the same structures as the performance of religious ritual. These structures still had to be observed in the production of a video if it was to be "true"; the *kurdungurlu* were required to stand back and witness and instruct the *kirda* (owners of the land) on their performance.[41] Such mediations enable Aboriginal people to envision what the late Eric Michaels called a "cultural future," some "third path" along which possibilities can be imagined other than those offered by the nonchoices of assimilation or traditionalism, possibilities that might allow for something as basic as literacy in an Aboriginal language or an Australian nation in which an Aboriginal perspective on local and national history can be acknowledged.

The mediating qualities of this work point to the common (and perhaps most significant) characteristic that they share with much recent work in ethnographic film and documentary: an interest in the *processes* of identity construction, creating and asserting a position for the present that accounts for the inconsistencies, contradictions, and complex subject positions of contemporary cultural identification. They also bring important questions to the fore regarding the intersections of cultural difference and social inequalities, occasionally calling attention to the sometimes tragic lack of comprehension across cultural and social difference, as in, for example, Aboriginal feminist Tracey Moffatt's film *Night Cries* (1989), in which an aged, dying white woman and her middle-aged Aboriginal nurse daughter are unable either to recognize one another or to escape their historically determined relationships with each other.

▶─────────────────────────────────────

Conclusion

I would like to return to the metaphor of the parallax effect and the framework it can provide for ethnographic film and indigenous media. The common object of interest of these two practices—the representation of culture in film and video—has not been displaced because of the changed position of certain observers—in this case, the perspective of indigenous media makers. The media produced by these cultural activists helps to realign a long outdated paradigm of ethnographic film built on the assumption of culture as a stable and bounded object, and documentary representation as restricted to realist illusion. As we recognize such works as forms of social action, we are obliged to move away from comfortable and taken-for-granted narrative conventions that reify "culture" and "cultural difference." Instead, we—as producers, audiences, and ethnographers—are allowed to encounter the multiplicity of points of view through which culture is produced, contested, mediated, and reimagined. This shift is very much a part of what Terry Turner has recently articulated as historically emergent "praxis-oriented notions of culture as the realization of a collective human potential for self-production and transformation."[42]

Indigenous media not only opens up sociocultural questions regarding the production and circulation of media, but also shifts our attention to new possibilities for the expression and interrogation of questions of culture and its representations. Looking at how film and video are produced cross-culturally, we encounter a complex range of formal/narrative strategies for reflecting on subjective and objective conditions of identity formation as a means of "representing reality." As examples, I would cite the effective use of parodic juxtaposition and performance in a number of Native American films, such as *Ritual Clowns* (Masayesva, 1992), *Sun, Moon, and Feather* (Rosen and Miguel Sisters, 1989), and *Cowtipping* (Redroad, 1992); and the use of multilayered screen texts to explore the complex relations between generations and former homelands explored by Asian diasporic videomakers such as Richard Fung (*The Way to My Father's House,* 1992) and Rea Tajiri (*History and Memory,* 1991); and the use of dramatic reflexivity to consider the intersections of class, culture, subjectivity, historical iconography, and sexuality in works such as *Looking for Langston* (1993) and *The Attendant* (1994) by Black British filmmaker Isaac Julien.

To restate my case, I am arguing that the cinematic practice of ethnographic film should be seen as part of a continuum of practices engaged in representing culture, practices that are all enmeshed in wider social, cultural, and political processes in which cross-cultural "looking" must be understood within relations of inequality. Shohat and Stam, in making a similar kind of argument in their work on multiculturalism and the media, have called the process "mutual and reciprocal relativization," which they define as

> the idea that the diverse cultures placed in play should come to perceive the limitations of their own social and cultural perspective. The point is not to embrace the other perspective completely but at least to recognize it, acknowledge it, take it into account, be ready to be transformed by it. . . .
>
> At the same time, historical configurations of power and knowledge generate a clear asymmetry within this relativization. The powerful are not accustomed to being relativized. . . . It is therefore not merely a question of communicating across borders but of discerning the forces which generate the borders in the first place. Multiculturalism has to recognize not only difference but even bitter, irreconcilable difference.[43]

With the development of indigenous media (as well as work from other communities that historically have not had power, including the power to represent themselves) the possible positions of authorship in ethnographic film and video expand, and we are more able to "see" the multiple ways cultural realities are understood and experienced. These works, when they are considered along with ethnographic film, produce an illuminating (if slightly disorienting) parallax effect. Thus indigenous media not only provides important new arenas of cultural production, it also re-situates ethnographic film as a cinematic mediation of culture by calling attention to the presence of other perspectives as well. It is my argument that this revision of the genre of ethnographic film is necessary if the field is to keep in step with changing understandings of culture and cultural representation, both in the academy and, more important, in the world. In my view, this is not a revolution for the genre, but the logical next step for a field that has been shifting slowly over the past twenty years toward more dialogical, reflexive, and imaginative modes and away from the monologic, observational, and privileged Western gaze stereotypically associated with the field.

NOTES

This essay is based on a presentation at the 1993 Visible Evidence conference, and an earlier version appeared in *Visual Anthropology Review* 11, no. 2 (1995): 64–76. I would like to thank a number of people who helped make this chapter possible, including Nancy Lutkehaus, Fred Myers, Bill Nichols, Jay Ruby, and Terry Turner for extremely helpful comments on early drafts, and Jane Gaines and Michael Renov for suggestions on the version that appears in this collection. Fieldwork on which this work is based could not have been done without the help of Fred Myers in 1988 and Francoise Dussart in 1992 in the logistics and languages of Aboriginal research in the field and out; I am deeply grateful to both of them. In addition, I want to thank the following people in Australia who shared their time and insights with me in 1988, 1989, 1992, and 1994: Philip Batty, Annette Hamilton, Freda Glynn, Francis Jupurrurla Kelly, Ned Lander, Marcia Langton, Mary Laughren, Michael Leigh, Judith and David MacDougall, Michael Niblett, Rachel Perkins, Frances Peters, Nick Peterson, Tim Rowse, David Sandy, Peter Toyne, and Neil Turner. For research support, I am grateful to the Research Challenge Fund of New York University (1988) and the John Simon Guggenheim Foundation (1991–92). I would also like to thank fellows and colleagues at the Center for Media, Culture, and History for their insights and feedback.

1. Eric Michaels, *The Aboriginal Invention of Television in Central Australia: 1982–1986* (Canberra: Australian Institute of Aboriginal Studies, 1986); Eric Michaels, "For a Cultural Future," in *Bad Aboriginal Art: Tradition, Media, and Technological Horizons* (Minneapolis: University of Minnesota Press, 1994), 99–126; Bill Nichols, *Blurred Boundaries: Questions of Meaning in Contemporary Culture* (New York: Routledge, 1994); Harald Prins, "Indigenous Advocacy in the Electronic Domain: Documentary Film and Human Rights" (paper presented at the Ninety-third Annual Meeting of the American Anthropological Association, Washington, D.C., 1994); Lorna Roth, "Northern Voices and Mediating Structures: Their Emergence and Development of First People's Television Broadcasting in the Canadian North" (Ph.D. diss., Concordia University, 1994); Terence Turner, "Visual Media, Cultural Politics, and Anthropological Practice: Some Implications of Recent Uses of Film and Video among the Kayapo of Brazil," *Commission on Visual Anthropology Newsletter*, spring 1990, 8–13; Terence Turner, "Defiant Images: The Kayapo Appropriation of Video," *Anthropology Today* 8, no. 6 (1992): 5–16.

2. In their book *Unthinking Eurocentrism: Multiculturalism and the Media* (New York: Routledge, 1994), Shohat and Stam write: "The concept of the 'Third World' also elides the presence of a 'Fourth World' existing within all of the other worlds; to wit, those peoples

variously called 'indigenous,' 'tribe,' or 'first nations'; in sum, the still-residing descendants of the original inhabitants of territories subsequently taken over or circumscribed by alien conquest or settlement. As many as 3,000 native nations, representing some 250 million people, according to some estimates function within the 200 states that assert sovereignty over them" (32).

3. Rouch has been subject to some criticism over the years from African intellectuals and filmmakers—most recently for his nostalgia for the past. Nonetheless, his works constitute early important efforts to create cultural dialogue and critique through the juxtapositioning of commentaries of Europeans and Africans, accommodating not only diverse views but also multiple formal strategies.

4. Jen Sloan, "Compared Views of the Yanomamo," *Film Library Quarterly* 12, no. 1 (1979): 20–22.

5. Shohat and Stam, *Unthinking Eurocentrism*, 351.

6. More systematic interrogation of the relationship of ethnographic films to other kinds of audiences is long overdue, and would be a welcome extension of the recent excellent research on ethnographic film spectatorship by Wilton Martinez and others. See Wilton Martinez, "Who Constructs Anthropological Knowledge? Toward a Theory of Ethnographic Film Spectatorship," in *Film as Ethnography*, ed. P. Crawford and D. Turton (Manchester: University of Manchester Press, 1993), 131–63.

7. See Jacqueline Urla, "Breaking All the Rules: An Interview with Frances Peters," *Visual Anthropology Review* 9, no. 2 (fall 1993): 98–106.

8. Frances Peters, personal communication, at the Center for Media, Culture, and History, March 1995.

9. For discussion of new trends in the field, I recommend the journals *Cultural Anthropology* and *Public Culture*. Richard Fox's edited collection *Recapturing Anthropology: Working in the Present* (Santa Fe, N.M.: School of American Research Press, 1991) provides a useful overview as well.

10. Arjun Appadurai, "Global Ethnoscapes: Notes and Queries for a Transnational Anthropology," in Fox, *Recapturing Anthropology*, 197.

11. Ibid., 209.

12. Ibid., 197.

13. Ibid., 198.

14. Ibid., 207.

15. Nichols, *Blurred Boundaries*, 63.

16. Dell Hymes, "The Use of Anthropology: Critical, Political, Personal," in *Reinventing Anthropology*, ed. Dell Hymes (New York: Vintage, 1969), 3–81.

17. George E. Marcus and Michael M. J. Fischer, *Anthropology as Cultural Critique: An Experi-*

mental Moment in the Human Sciences (Chicago: University of Chicago Press, 1986).

18. For example, questions of epistemology, ethics, and the position of the native interlocutor were being addressed as early as the 1950s by ethnographic filmmaker Jean Rouch, in works such as *Les Maîtres Fous* (1955) and *Chronicle of a Summer* (1960). Visual anthropologists such as Jay Ruby also articulated arguments in print advocating a critical reflexivity in ethnographic film, and, in an important shift toward the current paradigm in 1975, David MacDougall called for more participatory methods of production and styles of representation. Jay Ruby, "Exposing Yourself: Reflexivity, Anthropology, and Film," *Semiotica* 30, nos. 1–2 (1980): 153–79; David MacDougall, "Beyond Observational Cinema," in *Principles of Visual Anthropology*, ed. Paul Hockings (Chicago: Aldine, 1975), 109–24. Beginning in the mid-1970s, David and Judith MacDougall, John Marshall, Gary Kildea, Barbara Myerhoff, and Jorge Preloran, and later filmmakers such as Sarah Elder, were developing collaborative and/or highly reflexive film projects that subverted the purely observational style that had initially characterized the field. In the hands of Rouch, such methods also challenged the prevailing scientific realism of the time through "ethno-fiction" projects. In films like *Jaguar* (1967) and *Petit à Petit* (1969), the imaginative re-creation of contested cultural and political realities provided rich alternative possibilities for native self-representation, foreshadowing indigenous media in terms of both production and style.

19. Sol Worth and John Adair, *Through Navajo Eyes* (Bloomington: Indiana University Press, 1972).

20. Trinh T. Minh-ha, *When the Moon Waxes Red: Representation, Gender, and Cultural Politics* (New York: Routledge, 1991), 72.

21. See Richard Chalfen's introduction to the second edition of *Through Navajo Eyes* (Albuquerque: University of New Mexico Press, 1996) for a helpful summary of the arguments as well as valuable background material to the project.

22. See note 18.

23. Pat Aufderheide, "The Video in the Villages Project: Videomaking with and by Brazilian Indians," *Visual Anthropology Review* 11, no. 2 (1995): 83–93; Sarah Elder, "Collaborative Filmmaking: An Open Space for Making Meaning, a Moral Ground for Ethnographic Film," *Visual Anthropology Review* 11, no. 2 (1995): 94–101; Terry Turner, "Defiant Images: The Kayapo Appropriation of Video," *Anthropology Today* 8, no. 6 (1992): 5–16.

24. Faye Ginsburg, "Aboriginal Media and the Australian Imaginary," in "Screening Politics

in a World of Nations" special issue, ed. Lila Abu-Lughod, *Public Culture* 5, no. 3 (1993): 557–78.

25. Nichols, *Blurred Boundaries*, 84.

26. Marcia Langton, *Well, I Heard It on the Radio and Saw It on the Television* (Sydney: Australian Film Commission, 1993), 83.

27. Ibid., 84.

28. Nancy Fraser, "Rethinking the Public Sphere: A Contribution to the Critique of Actually Existing Democracy," in *The Phantom Public Sphere*, ed. Bruce Robbins (Minneapolis: University of Minnesota Press, 1993).

29. The making of images by anyone, whether by "outsiders" or "insiders," is problematic when ethical and social rules have been violated in the process and the grounds for the filmmaker's presence unacknowledged. Conversely, the fact that one is an "insider" does not guarantee an untroubled relationship with one's subject, as is dramatically clear in Navajo filmmaker Arlene Bowman's problematic encounter with her traditional grandmother in her film *Navajo Talking Pictures* (1991).

30. Underlying these responses, of course, is a profoundly static and reified understanding of culture. The very notion of "we" and "they" as separate is built on the trope of the noble savage living in a traditional, bounded world, for whom all knowledge, objects, and values originating elsewhere are polluting of some reified notion of culture and innocence. This approach, of course, erroneously places cultural others outside of normal (and universal) social processes of historical and cultural change, as Johannes Fabian clarifies so eloquently in *Time and the Other: How Anthropology Makes Its Object* (New York: Columbia University Press, 1985).

31. James Faris, "Anthropological Transparency, Film, Representation and Politics," in *Film as Ethnography*, ed. P. Crawford and D. Turton (Manchester: University of Manchester Press, 1992), 171–82.

32. Rosalind Morris, *New Worlds from Fragments: Film, Ethnography, and Representations of Northwest Coast Cultures* (Boulder, Colo.: Westview, 1994), 113.

33. For example, in an essay on this topic, Terence Turner makes a compelling argu-

ment for rethinking our understanding of culture in a way that clarifies how practices like indigenous media are linked to broader struggles for political rights: "From the critical vantage point of a conception of culture as empowerment to collective action, self-production, and struggle, the presently constituted forms of *multiculturalism* may be seen as embryonic expressions of the revolutionary principle that the protection and fostering of the human capacity for culture is a general human right and, as such, a legitimate goal of politically organized society." Terence Turner, "Anthropology and Multiculturalism: What Is Anthropology That Multiculturalists Should Be Mindful of It?" *Cultural Anthropology* 8, no. 4 (1993): 428.

34. David MacDougall, "Complicities of Style," in *Film as Ethnography*, ed. P. Crawford and D. Turton (Manchester: University of Manchester Press, 1992), 92.

35. In an ironic critique of that Griersonian premise, film theorist Bill Nichols argues that documentary consumption is indeed built on the viewers' pleasure in knowing that draws on our social imagination and cultural identity, what he calls "epistephilia" (as a parallel to the erotically based scopophilia in theories of narrative film spectatorship); epistephilia, he argues, creates a paradoxical aesthetic that produces "less a disposition to engage directly with the world than to engage with more documentary." Nichols, *Blurred Boundaries*, 180.

36. Shohat and Stam, *Unthinking Eurocentrism*, 346.

37. Langton, *Well, I Heard It on the Radio*, 85.

38. Noel Pearson, "Mabo: From Remnant Title to Social Justice" (lecture delivered at the University of Sydney, Centre for Peace and Conflict Studies, 1994).

39. Zacharias Kunuk, "Qallunaat: Oral History as Inuit Anthropology" (unpublished proposal, Tariagsuk Video Centre, 1996), n.p.

40. Michaels, *For a Cultural Future*, 40–41.

41. Langton, *Well, I Heard It on the Radio*, 64–65.

42. Turner, "Anthropology and Multiculturalism," 427.

43. Shohat and Stam, *Unthinking Eurocentrism*, 359.

LINDA WILLIAMS

[**9**] *The Ethics of Intervention:*
Dennis O'Rourke's
The Good Woman of Bangkok

Some time ago, I heard on National Public Radio of the death by suicide of
Kevin Carter, a photographer whose photo of a starving African girl stalked
by a vulture once won a Pulitzer Prize. After taking the photo Carter is said
to have scared away the vulture, sat down under a tree, and cried.[1] Like
many other stories of supposedly objective observers of human tragedy,
this one poses the question of what we might call the ethics of intervention:
in forms such as journalism, documentary photography, and documentary
film, where value has traditionally been placed on a noninterventional, objective observation of reality, when should a journalist or documentarian
cease to occupy the neutral position of observer to intervene in the lives
of his or her subjects? Should Carter have frightened away the vulture—in
which case his photo would not have been so likely to grab the attention
that won him the Pulitzer? What is the ethically appropriate response of
a documentarian faced with human misery? What is the documentarian's
commitment to the truth of a situation as weighed against his or her subjective entanglement within it? What, indeed, is documentary truth?

I wish to pursue these and other difficult questions through a discussion of an even more complicated case: Dennis O'Rourke's 1991 documentary film, *The Good Woman of Bangkok.* I am interested in this film about
a Thai prostitute hired by the filmmaker to be his lover and the subject of
his film because its ethical dilemma both fascinates and provokes me. When
I first saw the film at the Berlin Film Festival, I was sufficiently provoked
to reproach O'Rourke in person with what appeared to be his gross abuse
of his subject, smoothed over, so I thought, by his gift to her of a rice farm
designed to "save" her from the sex trade. On further reflection, however,
I have come to value the film's challenge to my too-quick and certain judgments. Clearly a man who makes a film about a prostitute by becoming her
client makes himself vulnerable to feminist wrath, but I will argue that that

very vulnerability is also what makes this film so challenging to conventional documentary ethics. In the following I hope to pursue the question of the ethics of documentary intervention through an analysis of O'Rourke's film. But first, I want to explore more about what it means to intervene in the life of a film subject.

In *Representing Reality*, film critic Bill Nichols notes that the shift from a more conventional expository and observational mode of documentary to a "witness-centered voice of testimony" leads away from arguments about the world to arguments about the ethics of the filmmakers' interactions with witnesses: What do they disclose about the filmmaker and what do they disclose about his or her subject?[2] In an essay to which Nichols refers, Vivian Sobchack describes a range of possible reactions a film viewer might have toward the extreme instance of a real person in a film faced with danger or death. Building on Sobchack's notion of ethical reaction, Nichols has developed a taxonomy of what he calls documentary "gazes"—different implied ethical stances taken by the camera/filmmaker toward the events filmed. Sobchack and Nichols can be seen to distinguish six such types of "gazes," beginning with the least involvement with the film or video subject and proceeding to the most: (1) the *clinical or professional gaze,* committed to objective reportage and thus to refraining from any kind of intervention in the situation; (2) the *accidental gaze,* which just happens to catch an important action, as in Zapruder's home movie of the assassination of JFK, or George Holliday's videotape of the Rodney King beating; (3) the *helpless gaze,* registering an involuntary passivity, as when a filmmaker records a situation in which intervention is desirable but impossible; (4) the *endangered gaze,* showing the cameraperson's own personal risk, as in the famous moment in *The Battle of Chile* when a cameraman "shoots" a gunman who literally shoots him back, the very jostling of the camera registering the bullet's effect until the camera stops running and the screen goes black; (5) the *humane gaze* (Sobchack's term), when the film registers an extended subjective response to the moment or process of death; and finally (6) the *interventional gaze,* assumed when the film abandons the distance between filmmaker and subject, placing the filmmaker on the same plane of historical contingency as its subject. Nichols explains that this intervention is usually on behalf of someone who is more immediately endangered than the cameraperson, as when filmmakers take their place alongside struggling strikers in *Harlan County, U.S.A.* or *Medium Cool.*[3]

Though I do not propose to apply this taxonomy of gazes directly to the ethical questions raised by O'Rourke's film—it would be simplistic, for example, to say that the interventional gaze is the most ethical and the clinical gaze the least—the terms introduced here may nevertheless prove useful. They may help us to consider, for example, the complex ethical questions raised by new forms of documentary practice that seem to have abandoned the traditional respect for objectivity and distance and call for greater degrees of intervention in the lives of subjects in contexts fraught with sexual, racial, and postcolonial dynamics of power.

Dennis O'Rourke's film observes Yaowalak Chonchanakun (called Aoi) as she shuttles back and forth between the bars where she attracts customers to the hotels where she sexually services those customers. It also follows her as she moves back and forth between the raucous, bustling night city of Bangkok, where she makes her money, to the slow, daytime country village where she spends that money on the support of her mother and young son. The story of Aoi's life is told through three markedly different forms of interview with film subjects, each of which can be seen to resemble one of Nichols and Sobchack's gazes.

The first way of filming corresponds more or less to Sobchack's notion of the clinical or professional gaze. It consists of respectfully distanced, objective interviews with Aoi's aunt, who is shown seated on the ground outdoors in the quiet Thai village that is Aoi's home. Although these country scenes offer a strong contrast to the raucous activity of Bangkok nightlife contained in other sections of the film, O'Rourke does not idealize the country over the city. What we see in the country is simply an entirely different set of life rhythms diametrically opposed, through the film's editing, to the constant bustle (and hustle) of Bangkok.

Seated on the ground, leisurely chewing something that looks like chewing tobacco, "Auntie" slowly tells how Aoi's husband left her when she was pregnant, how Aoi became saddled with a debt incurred by her father, how her family lost their land to pay the debt, and how she finally had no choice but to go work as a prostitute in Bangkok. Segments of O'Rourke's interviews with the aunt are interspersed throughout the film and constitute its most conventional, objective, and ethnographic thread.

In marked contrast to these objective, sustained interviews is a series of much more spontaneous interviews in raucous Bangkok bars with Anglo-American, Australian, and European men dancing and drinking with Thai prostitutes. In these male-dominated nocturnal bars, where the drunken customers must yell in order to be "heard" by the camera, we witness a display of unbridled misogyny rendered accessible to our gaze, we soon come to understand, by the filmmaker's own participation in it. Although we never see O'Rourke in the image, it becomes clear from the men's reactions to this camera's different gaze, that the filmmaker is received by them not as an objective, clinical observer, but as a fellow reveler who happens to hold a camera; he enjoys the same white male privilege as the other men in the bars. This complicit gaze of "one of the boys" elicits a masculine braggadocio and misogyny that a more professional-clinical interview would preclude. One American boasts to O'Rourke's camera that he has bought seven women in one day; another claims that, unlike American women, who are "fucking bitches," these women are "the top of the line," not only because their "bodies [are] the best" but because they "have the right attitude"—they will fold your clothes and give you "a shower, a massage and a blow job" all in one session.

Particularly revealing is a half-shouted interview in a noisy bar with a drunken group of O'Rourke's fellow Australians. These men claim to feel sorry for the women and comfort themselves that the money they pay them will help the next generation of women to get an education and extricate themselves from a life of exploitation. Of course, such sympathy rings hollow, because we can plainly see that their pleasure depends upon the continued exploitation of these uneducated, subservient Thai women. This interview ends when the youngest and most embarrassed of the Australians lamely adds, "Hopefully the Thai women won't have to do this for too long."

Sobchack and Nichols have no precise category for this kind of "gaze," although Nichols does note that "an ethic of irresponsibility," in which a filmmaker participates in, rather than opposes, a morally deplorable act, is a possible flip side to the responsibility of intervention. The hypothetical case he cites is a camera gaze that actively sides with the agency of death, as in the filming of lethal medical experiments in Nazi concentration camps or even the filming of the hanged body of William Higgins, American hostage in Lebanon.[4] Nichols seems to presume, then, that it is the nature of the interactive mode of documentary either to be activist and oppositional (that is, to intervene responsibly in potentially harmful events) or to be complicit (that is, to participate irresponsibly in situations and actions that should be opposed rather than recorded).

On the face of it, then, what we might call O'Rourke's *complicit participation* with the drunken johns places the filmmaker on the same level as these morally suspect subjects. This "participatory gaze" makes no effort to prevent activities that abuse and objectify women—in fact, it encourages them, egging the men on. Compounding the offense to feminist sensibilities, the very next scene, continuing the film's general depiction of the Bangkok bar scene, shows a Thai woman on a stage pulling a string of razor blades out of her vagina and another who writes a greeting to a Japanese customer, "Nice to see you Japan," with a pen inserted into her vagina.

As if to emphasize his complicity with these First World male exploiters of Third World sex workers, O'Rourke offers an explanatory scroll toward the beginning of the film in which he speaks of himself in the third person:

> The filmmaker was 43 and his marriage had ended.
> He was trying to understand how love could be so banal and also so profound.
> He came to Bangkok the mecca for western men with fantasies of exotic sex and love without pain.
> He would meet a Thai prostitute and make a film about that.
> He seemed no different than the other 5,000 men who crowded the bars every night.
> It was three in the morning when she finished dancing and sat with him.
> She said her name was Aoi—that it meant sugar cane or sweet. . . .
> The pimp came over and said: "only 500 baht or 20 dollars—keep her until the afternoon—do anything you like—OK?"
> He paid and was her customer; she became the subject of his film.
> They stayed at a cheap hotel in the red-light district.
> Filming and video recording took place there.

Thus the making of O'Rourke's film hinges upon the literal procurement of its subject. This third-person "filmmaker" participates in the institution of prostitution in order to make the film. "He paid and was her customer; she became the subject of his film." The interaction with a prostitute in her capacity *as prostitute* is thus crucial to the film. And it is this participation that raises a range of complex ethical issues that go to the heart of questions about the contemporary documentary's intervention in the realities it films. It asks, in effect, Can a First World filmmaker's inherently exploitative gaze at a Third World sex worker reveal anything of value, and of "truth," about this subject? Can a filmmaker who freely portrays himself as a man who buys the sexual favors of a woman do anything "good" for this "good woman"? The answer depends partly on how we read the film's climactic moment of attempted intervention into Aoi's life.

The interviews with Aoi that eventually culminate in the filmmaker's gesture of intervention in her life constitute yet a third type of gaze at his subject. They take place in the the strange "intimacy" and isolation of a hotel room in a red-light district of Bangkok, where Aoi and O'Rourke lived together as prostitute and client. Unlike the clinical-professional interviews with the aunt, which keep a respectful distance, or the raucous slap-dash participatory cinema verité of the interviews with the men in the bars, these interviews are self-consciously orchestrated and tightly framed. They frequently press too close to their subject, who is sensitive to the invasion. Aoi is often seated near a mirror, and frequently her image is doubled in its reflection. Her speech to the camera (and thus to O'Rourke, who operates both camera and sound throughout the film) alternates between extremely factual accounts of the economics of her life, such as her efforts to pay her dead father's debts or her trips home each time she has saved two hundred dollars, and extremely emotional accounts of her hatred of men, beginning with the account of the husband who deserted her and continuing through her relations with clients and pimps who treat her badly. Speaking sometimes in Thai, sometimes in broken English, she painfully tells of how Thai men taunt her when they see her on the street with unattractive foreign customers. It becomes apparent that she feels a kind of sexual shame to be seen with Western men before fellow Thais. She clearly condemns the patriarchal system that holds her in such thrall, and she astutely includes her relationship with O'Rourke as part of that system.

Woven throughout the film, these segments of Aoi responding to O'Rourke's questions eventually build to a kind of crescendo of self-loathing, at the peak of which the filmmaker will finally intervene. Aoi suddenly speaks of love—a topic that has not been raised before. Seated before her reflection in a mirror—a mirror that pointedly does not reflect the filmmaker—Aoi says, "I don't know what love is. . . . No people can love me. I don't have anything good, only bad. Who can love me? They think they know me. I know me. I cannot give."

It is in response to this despairing statement that we hear O'Rourke's voice for the first time making his dramatic gesture of intervention. Speaking slowly and dispassionately, he says, "Okay. I'm going to buy this rice farm for you and I want you to stop working. It's time you started caring about yourself." When Aoi repeats that she doesn't care about herself, O'Rourke seems to set a condition for giving her the rice farm: "I will do this for you but only if you go home. . . . This life you are leading will kill you. It's not like before. Many women are dying of AIDS." Aoi then indicates that she *might* stop working, but O'Rourke insists that she promise. At this point Aoi balks: "If you want to help me that's fine. But don't expect anything from me. There are some things that I can't do. I'm sorry. Don't help me if you want something in return. I don't want to talk now."

At this point in the film O'Rourke seems to choose to intervene in his subject's life. He effectively attempts to end her career as a prostitute—the career that interested him in her in the first place—in order to "save" her from its occupational hazards. The promise of the rice farm is thus an extreme example of Nichols's (and Sobchack's) interventional mode. Seeing that AIDS poses a danger to her life, and wishing to effect a permanent change in that life, the filmmaker-john seems to do the "right" thing: he gives her the financial means to end her career as a prostitute. Yet in this same scene Aoi vehemently refuses to accept the condition that she cease to prostitute herself. A scroll at the end of the film informs us, in what may be a crucial shift to the first person from the film's initial third-person reference to "the filmmaker":

> I bought a rice farm for Aoi and I left Thailand.
>   A year later I came back but she was not there.
>   I found her working in Bangkok in a sleazy massage parlor called "The Happy House."
>   I asked her why and she said, "It is my fate."

In the end, despite the filmmaker's good intentions, the interventional gaze reverts to another one of Sobchack's and Nichols's gazes: the helpless involuntary passivity that can only register the facts of what it is powerless to change. Thus the grand gesture of documentary intervention fails: O'Rourke does not succeed, at least as far as the film lets us know, in altering Aoi's "fate." In a statement made earlier in the film, Aoi can be seen to explain this resistance, at least partially:

> You say you understand me. But I don't quite believe you. You are the sky and I am the ground. I'm just rotten garbage. You pulled me out of the rubbish heap only because you wanted to make this film. I think everything you do and say to me is to manipulate me for your film. Even if you promised to buy me a rice farm it's not much compared to your film. I'm sure you'll get much more for your film.

Aoi seems to understand perfectly the nature of the bargain O'Rourke wants to strike with her. In this situation, just as in her profession, she performs for pay. Though her filmic performance is not of sex—in fact, it is a kind of antisex in its repeated expressions of a vehement hatred of men— she recognizes the parallel—that the film consists of a man buying some aspect of her behavior. As in the relation of prostitution, the power inequity between client and whore remains the same. But unlike the male fantasy of the whore waiting to be rescued from "the life," Aoi does not want to be rescued; she wants to be well paid. Indeed, she criticizes the arrogance of the participant-interventionist who would flatter himself that he can rescue her from "her fate."[5]

It is worth noting—though I admit I do not know how much prominence this note should receive—that although the offer of the rice farm was genuine (that is, O'Rourke really did make the offer and did in fact buy Aoi the farm), it is also a fictional construct. O'Rourke had already given Aoi the rice farm up front, at the beginning, before any substantive shooting had begun. Although the film's fiction is that O'Rourke uses the farm as an inducement to Aoi to quit prostitution, in fact, the payment had already been made. O'Rourke thus portrays himself as more of a stereotypical john than he actually was.[6] In other words, the attempted intervention in Aoi's life as a prostitute *is* true, but what is not true is the way it is represented in the film. Here, then, is a documentary "truth" that is highly scripted. Because of such manipulation of his subject matter, O'Rourke prefers to call his work "documentary fiction."

I do not think, however, that such a designation should be construed as a nihilistic despair at the impossibility of attaining any truth in documentary. For if, as Errol Morris once put it, "truth isn't guaranteed," documentaries (even fictional ones) nevertheless seek some, highly relative, contingent, nonguaranteed, forms of truth, otherwise they would simply be fictions. In calling his film a documentary fiction, it would seem that O'Rourke attempts to overcome the simple dichotomization between truth and fiction, to suggest that there is no a priori, self-evident truth to be "captured" by the camera, but that there are multifaceted, receding horizons of "truth" that can be constructed within a multivocal (multigazing) form.[7]

It is through the combination of these very different observational, participatory, and interventional approaches to his subject that O'Rourke's film gets at the "truth" of this Bangkok prostitute's life—a truth that can be had only through these sticky relations. It is precisely because this truth is so compromised and so refracted through multiple points of view— including that of the johns—that it cuts through all previous conventions of the representation of prostitutes. One of these conventions is the well-known feminist representation of prostitution as an institution of pure female victimization. This knee-jerk feminist reaction was much in evidence in the reviews of O'Rourke's film and, indeed, in my own initial response.[8] However, I want to argue that because the filmmaker makes himself vulnerable to feminist condemnation, the film opens itself up to a level of ethical questioning that is quite exceptional in documentary film, and that such questioning should not be dismissed out of hand by feminist, or any other, viewers.

Take, for example, the line from the scroll that appears early in the film: "He seemed no different than the other 5,000 men who crowded the bars every night." Is O'Rourke saying this only so that we will eventually see him as different when he offers Aoi the rice farm? Or does he mean for us to see that he is, basically, no different? Certainly he is no different in that he buys a woman; sexually and cinematographically he enjoys what he pays for. As if to prove his prurience, he even throws in a scene that portrays his camera's gaze as sexually intrusive and that portrays Aoi's resistance to this gaze. A half-naked Aoi lies on her stomach on the bed trying to sleep, ignoring the invasion of O'Rourke's camera. She deftly uses her feet to pull the sheet up over the naked parts of her body, all the while facing away from the camera, never giving it the satisfaction of acknowledging its look at her. Excruciating as this blatant male gaze is, the obvious feminist con-demnation invited by such a scene misses the more complex ways in which the whole film explores the dynamics of power within an inherently unequal relationship, for at the same time O'Rourke's camera attempts to capture Aoi's naked vulnerability, it also captures (or precipitates, or directs?) her defiance of its intrusion. Had O'Rourke not risked the abuse of his power by staging its voyeuristic gaze—had he stuck, for example, to the respect-fully distanced ethnographic interview—he would not also have elicited Aoi's verbal and visual resistance to his intrusion.

Perhaps the best way to characterize the ethics of O'Rourke's relation to his subject would be to say that, like the Brecht play to which his title alludes, this relation acknowledges that there can be no morally pure posi-tion, no truly "good" person. O'Rourke is *not* different from these other men even if he does, like the good woman of Setzuan, *try* to behave more ethically. Yet, at the same time, it is his very willingness to risk the kind of relation that is so vulnerable to feminist critique that makes this film such an exceptionally acute and honest exploration of the prostitute-john rela-tionship rather than a pat condemnation.

In a fascinating survey of sociological studies of prostitution, Lynn Sharon Chancer shows the limits of the numerous sociological studies of the "pros" and "cons" of prostitution conducted by external observers. Despite a theoretical awareness that patriarchal culture continuously en-gages in historically variable forms of the "traffic in women"—whether this traffic is in wives or whores—Chancer argues that feminists have been very reluctant to study the specifics of prostitution. Moreover, most of the studies conducted have lacked any focus on the male customers who make the business possible. Chancer insists that prostitution needs to be defined, from the outset, as an interaction between two parties.[9] Although O'Rourke is no sociologist, and certainly could not be described as a femi-nist, as an astute observer of the complexities of power in a postcolonial, postmodern era, he has produced a document about prostitution that goes to the relational heart of the roles played out within this institution. This is possible because, rather than standing outside looking in at the prostitute and her world, O'Rourke has taken up a partly real, partly fictionalized position internal to that relation. He recognizes that there is no neutral, ob-jective view; he is implicated in truth *and* in fiction.

As feminists, some of us may not like the fact that the relations he en-gages in are not equal. But as long as there exists a male "traffic in women" in both legal and extralegal forms, there can be no easy ethics of the male sexual relation to women, whether as wives, lovers, or prostitutes. The only alternative to engaging in representations within such an "imperialist" imbalance of power would be to avoid picturing the prostitute altogether, or, as one critic of O'Rourke puts it, to insist on the necessity of a "dialogical form of filmic representation" in which the prostitute presumably speaks on equal terms with the filmmaker-john.[10] But such a solution presumes a relation of false equality. I would argue instead that O'Rourke's effort to be ethical within an unequal situation—which is, after all, the situation that most men and woman inhabit in the real world—poses the deeper and more important question of the ethical relation of filmmaker-john to client. This seems to me to be the real interest of his film. It is not that O'Rourke "saves" Aoi and shows himself a good documentarian, but that he does not and cannot "save" her, and yet in the process of trying he generates resistances by Aoi, both to his prurience and to his rescue, resistances that grant her more integrity and autonomy as a man-hating, self-supporting whore than she would have had as a "saved" good woman.

Consider, for example, the contrast with Bonnie Klein's 1982 documentary about the sex industry, *Not a Love Story*. Klein's film is made in a spirit of sisterly equality with its main "native informant"—a stripper named Linda Lee Tracy—who becomes a kind of collaborator in the making of the film. Like O'Rourke, the filmmaker attempts to intervene in and prevent the sale-of-sex career of the film's subject, who, after learning about the degradations of the sex industry, appears to quit the business. Unlike O'Rourke, Klein seems to succeed in her attempt to dissuade this sex worker from participation in "the life." In the course of the film, Tracy is educated by the filmmaker to see the ways women's bodies are exploited by the sex industry. She ultimately becomes almost as good an antiporn campaigner as she was a stripper. She even submits to a pornographic photography session in order to be able to reflect during the session on the degradation of being a sex object. This degradation then appears to provide the impetus for Tracy to renounce the life of a sex worker and to achieve a "happy" feminist ending in which she is freed from the need to perform sexually for men.[11]

Klein's film would thus seem to be a successful intervention in the sex career of its subject, but I would submit that it is for this very reason a less honest and less ethical film than O'Rourke's. Whereas O'Rourke's purchase of his subject is made overt in his ongoing negotiation with her, Klein's purchase of Tracy is covert. Hidden under the pretense of a sisterly, "dialogic" equality that entirely ignores the class differences between the antipornography filmmaker and the antipornography feminists and the stripper is the fact that Tracy is still performing, still trying to please the customer, now a feminist instead of a john. Whether Tracy was ever paid for her role in the film I do not know. Presumably such remuneration would not have been ethical in the eyes of the filmmaker, whose goal was to convince Tracy to stop selling her sexual performances. However, anyone who has seen this documentary will attest that the strength of the film lies in Tracy's sexual performances, whether as enthusiastic sex worker, reformed and hesitant pornographic model, or anti–sex work crusader. In becoming the star of the film, she is, in effect, remunerated by the possibility of pleasing a much bigger audience than she ever reached in the strip clubs.

Both films probe the sex industry—its women performers and its male customers. Each film intervenes to dissuade its representative sex worker/native informant from further pursuing her trade. Both films offer the substitute occupation of a new kind of performance in an anti–sex work drama of the films themselves. Thus Linda Lee Tracy, a very good stripper with a comic flair, transforms herself, under the interventional influence of on-camera director Bonnie Klein, into a beset female victim and antiporn campaigner. In contrast, Aoi, Bangkok prostitute and successful whore (having landed the client of a lifetime in O'Rourke), *refuses* to transform herself into a respectable rice farmer—at least during the course of the film.

Interestingly, both films' attempts to rescue their sex workers are also forms of seduction. Bonnie Klein seduces Linda Lee into a feminism that will presumably save her from the degradation of further selling her sexual performances to men; Dennis O'Rourke attempts to seduce Aoi into a more monogamous relationship with himself and a rice farm. The flaw in both seduction-rescues is that rather than freeing the sexual performers they seek to rescue, they only submit them to a different regime of performance: instead of the performance of pleasure, they now produce performances of degradation. Linda Lee as subject of Bonnie Klein's film submits herself to a pornographic photography session *in order to report on the degradation she feels*. Aoi submits herself to other male customers in the course of the film in order to confess later to O'Rourke's camera how she loathes the "old, ugly, filthy and obscene" men she must service.

I would argue, however, that the ethical superiority of O'Rourke's film, along with its greater richness as both document and fiction, lies in its recognition of the fantasy of rescue and its class, race, and gender bases. A film does not need to be a successful intervention in the lives of its subjects, the way say Errol Morris succeeds in *The Thin Blue Line,* to be ethically successful. Morris's film is a remarkable case of a successful intervention, actually clearing the film's primary subject of a murder charge. But a film does not have to be about an ethical person to have ethical value. Rather, O'Rourke's film illustrates that ethical acts are entirely compromised. Just as Bertolt Brecht shows in *The Good Woman of Setzuan* (1943—the play from which O'Rourke partly borrows his title) that acts of private charity will never change a rotten system, so O'Rourke shows that his own acts of private charity are useless.[12] Yet just as Brecht's cynicism about moral goodness produces a highly ethical play about a prostitute who cannot transcend her ethical situation, so O'Rourke's cynicism produces a highly ethical documentary fiction about a prostitute who cannot transcend hers.

Thus, although there may be some reason to be morally suspicious of this filmmaker whose efforts to understand the profundity and banality of love lead him to hire a prostitute, it is this very entanglement with the power differential that informs all pursuits of heterosexual pleasure that makes *The Good Woman of Bangkok* such an ethically challenging film. Because O'Rourke is so incautious as to seek an impossible truth about "love" from a prostitute, because he sets himself up so grandly to fail, his film actually succeeds—not as a clear-cut intervention in the fate of his subject, but as a rich mix of clinical, participatory, interventional, and helpless gazes at the complexity of the relations between First and Third World, between female object and male customer.

There is no easy ethical position once a filmmaker decides to become entangled with the life circumstances of the subjects he or she portrays. If we come back, for example, to the dilemma of the photographer faced with the starving child and the vulture, we can now see that the issue is not simply whether to intervene, it is how to intervene without so radically altering the original situation that one is no longer true to it. Faced with the reality of a starving girl stalked by a vulture, photographer Kevin Carter settled on the imperfect solution of taking the picture, then shooing away the vulture, and then sitting down to cry. Whether he was crying over the suffering of the starving girl, his own impotence to change the basic conditions of her suffering, or the realization that he too was a kind of vulture feeding off her misfortune, his particular ethical dilemma presumed an either/or choice between intervening (and spoiling the truth of the girl's endangerment upon which the photograph is based) and not intervening (and thus becoming a kind of participant in her abuse).

O'Rourke's solution is to put his participation in the abuse of his subject up front *and* to intervene in it as well. He thus opens up a range of intermediate possibilities between Carter's don't-intervene-and-get-the-picture/intervene-and-don't-get-it dilemma. O'Rourke's purchase of the rice farm at the beginning of his relationship with Aoi and then acting out the fiction of proffering it in the end is one solution to what we might call the vulture problem. In effect, it allows him to depict Aoi's vulnerability to vultures without leaving her entirely their victim. And it allows him to acknowledge his own complicity with vultures without completely being one.

Documentary filmmakers, even fictional ones, have a responsibility to the truth of the situations they represent. If vultures are part of that truth, then they need to be in the picture. In the end, neither O'Rourke's participation in the institution of prostitution nor his intervention in Aoi's practice of the profession represents the whole truth. There is no whole truth because there is no objective place to stand from which to see it. There is no perfect ethical solution to the question of documentary intervention, but *The Good Woman of Bangkok* suggests that once a more interventional mode of filmmaking is embraced, there are all sorts of messy relativities.

◆──

NOTES

This essay is a slightly revised version of "The Ethics of Documentary Intervention: Dennis O'Rourke's *The Good Woman of Bangkok*," which appeared in *The Filmmaker and the Prostitute: Dennis O'Rourke's* The Good Woman of Bangkok, edited by Chris Berry, Annette Hamilton, and Laleen Jayamanne (Sydney: Power Publications, 1997). Special thanks to John Powers for conversation, the loan of a tape, and honest criticism. Thanks also to Tom Gunning for helping me to think through the fictional aspects of O'Rourke's intervention, and to Michael Renov and Jane Gaines for timely prodding and fine editing.

1. National Public Radio report by Scott Simon, July 23, 1994.
2. Bill Nichols, *Representing Reality: Issues and Concepts in Documentary* (Bloomington: Indiana University Press, 1991), 48, 44–45.
3. Ibid., 86–87; Vivian Sobchack, "Inscribing Ethical Space: Ten Propositions on Death, Representation, and Documentary," *Quarterly Review of Film Studies* 9, no. 4 (1984): 283–300.
4. Nichols, *Representing Reality*, 85–86.
5. In a special issue of *Social Text* on sex workers, a female escort named "Barbara" complains about this male fantasy of rescuing the prostitute: "The worst are the ones who want to rescue you. They are totally, totally, totally dangerous. They are the ones who are liable to flip. They see you as someone who needs saving. . . . And when you say you don't want to be rescued, that seems to trigger something in their brains: 'Right, I'll go for you then.' Their fantasy is that they're going to rescue you from your life of drudgery, and thereafter you'll be eternally grateful to them and will kiss their feet when they walk through the door." "Barbara," "It's a Pleasure Doing Business with You," *Social Text* 37 (winter 1993): 12–13.
6. According to O'Rourke, this bargain was for-

mally struck between Aoi and O'Rourke in the presence of a nongovernment women's aid organization specializing in support for sex workers. Aoi did not give up prostitution, also according to O'Rourke, because her mother rightly perceived that if she had found one gullible foreigner to buy her a farm she could probably find another. Dennis O'Rourke, "A Rejoinder to 'Conceiving the Post-Colonial Everyday: An Interrogation of *The Good Woman of Bangkok*,'" *Visual Anthropology Review* 9, no. 2 (1993): 116. See also Dennis O'Rourke, "Afterword," in *The Filmmaker and the Prostitute: Dennis O'Rourke's* The Good Woman of Bangkok, ed. Chris Berry, Annette Hamilton, and Laleen Jayamanne (Sydney: Power, 1997), 217.

7. In an article on Morris's film, I argue that the self-reflexive and interactive tendencies of what might be called the postmodern documentary need not be seen as a sign of nihilistic abandonment of a quest to represent truth. Rather, it seems to me that some of the more intrusive, interactive, and self-reflexive modes of documentary have sometimes, paradoxically, led to remarkably ethical interventions in the very reality that documentary records. Morris's *The Thin Blue Line* (1988) is a case in point. Morris saved Randall Adams from death row through his manipulative explorations of the past leading to the near confession of David Harris, the man who committed the crime for which Adams had been convicted. In this essay I am interested in pursuing the ethical questions raised by a much less successful, and much less ethically clear, form of intervention, yet one that nonetheless does intervene. Linda Williams, "Mirrors without Memories: Truth, History, and the New Documentary," *Film Quarterly* 46 (spring 1993): 9–21.

8. See, for example, the reviews of the film collected in Chris Berry, Annette Hamilton, and Laleen Jayamanne, eds., *The Filmmaker and*

the Prostitute: Dennis O'Rourke's The Good Woman of Bangkok (Sydney: Power, 1997).

9. Lynn Sharon Chancer, "Prostitution, Feminist Theory, and Ambivalence: Notes from the Sociological Underground," Social Text 37 (winter 1993): 151.

10. Martina Rieker, "Narrating the Post-colonial Everyday: An Interrogation of The Good Woman of Bangkok," Visual Anthropology Review 9, no. 1 (1993): 122.

11. For more discussion of this film, see the excellent commentary by B. Ruby Rich, "AntiPorn: Soft Issue, Hard World," Village Voice, July 20, 1982, 1, 16–18, 30 (reprinted in Films for Women, ed. Charlotte Brunsdon [London: British Film Institute, 1986]). See also E. Ann Kaplan, "Pornography and/as Representation," Enclitic 9 (1983): 8–19.

12. When acts of private charity fail, Brecht's good woman creates a masculine alter ego, Shui Ta, who conducts her more ruthless business deals and who enables the good Shen Te to go on existing.

ALEXANDRA JUHASZ

[10] *They Said We Were Trying to Show Reality—All I Want to Show Is My Video: The Politics of the Realist Feminist Documentary*

▶

A Demonstration of Contradictions 1

The scene opens on a gray steel door, which itself then opens to reveal a middle-aged black woman: "Hi, I'm Marie and I'm HIV-positive. Welcome to my home. I'd like to show you what has and has not changed here since my diagnosis. Welcome, and come in." The camera follows Marie on an intimate tour of her apartment. For ten minutes of barely edited footage, she moves from room to room, talking about eating with her family, cleaning the toilet, and not necessarily sleeping by herself in her double bed. In "real time," she recounts to the camera her experiences and offers advice: "Once I dropped AZT on the floor, and my granddaughter said, 'Here it is, Mommy.' Then I knew I had to be more careful."
::   description of a scene from Women's AIDS Video Enterprise, *We Care: A Video for Care Providers of People Affected by AIDS*, 1990

Any revolutionary strategy must challenge the depiction of reality; it is not enough to discuss the oppression of women within the text of the film; the language of the cinema/the depiction of reality must also be interrogated, so that a break between ideology and text is effected.
::   Claire Johnston, "Women's Cinema as Counter Cinema," 1973

▶

The Legacy of Misreading Realist, Feminist Documentaries

In formulating a notion of a feminist "counter-cinema" that would counter not only the stereotypes but also the very language of patriarchy, the British feminists rejected the cinema verité practices of the first generation of feminist documentary films.

:: Mary Ann Doane, Patricia Mellencamp, and Linda Williams, "Feminist Film Criticism: An Introduction," 1984

The women's movement of the early 1970s was enmeshed in a politics of representation. This inspired an unprecedented deluge of feminist films, the majority of which were documentaries.[1] In perhaps the only significant and coherent body of feminist film theory about documentary—the so-called feminist realist debates[2]—feminist scholars of this period used what Doane, Mellencamp, and Williams refer to in the quote above as the "rejection" of the "cinema verité practices of the first generation of feminist documentary films" as the foundation for the critical discourse-based theory that would become Feminist Film Theory as we know it today.[3] This has meant that as a feminist scholar of the media in the 1980s and 1990s, I have been instructed to believe that *realism* and *identification*—which are claimed to be axiomatic of talking-heads, cinema verité, or realist documentary—are not sophisticated, or even legitimate, formal strategies. And then correspondingly, feminist documentary films and videos that use such strategies (like my own *We Care*, cited above) are *bad*, or at least naive, feminist projects. E. Ann Kaplan, in a chapter concerning the feminist-realist debates, concisely describes the position taken up by feminist film theorists in the 1970s and beyond: "Realism as a style is unable to change consciousness because it does not depart from the forms that embody the old consciousness."[4] Realism masks the production of meaning; identification affirms the coherence and power of the individual. "So what actually happens then," writes Eileen McGarry in an early contribution to the debates, "is that those relationships already coded within the dominant ideology enter into the film unquestioned by the aesthetic of realism."[5] Instead, Kaplan concludes, feminists need to make and view films that do four things: focus on the cinematic apparatus as a signifying practice, refuse to construct a fixed spectator, deny pleasure, and mix the codes of documentary and fiction.[6]

For the majority of feminist film critics in the late 1970s and the 1980s, such pronouncements engendered a turn toward analysis of feminist avant-garde filmmaking and a concurrent erasure of more conventional political documentary practice. This inspired a theoretical and practical legacy that is the subject of this essay: the legacy of a large and important body of feminist film work that has been inadequately theorized and undertheorized, and the same-time canonization and institutionalization of films that represent only one side of the "feminist realist debates." Perhaps the most disturbing consequence of this legacy is the loss of many of the documentaries that didn't quite make the list. Due to the insidious economic relationship between film scholarship and alternative film distribution, many of these films are lost for reevaluation because only twenty years later they are very difficult, if not impossible, to find.

Manohla Dargis begins her review of the Whitney Museum's 1992 program of 1970s feminist documentaries, "From Object to Subject: Documents and Documentaries from the Women's Movement," by contemplating her lack of exposure to this body of film work. Dargis and I, both products of NYU graduate cinema studies in the 1980s, saw a great deal of Rainer, Potter, Ackerman, and Mulvey in our classes. But I didn't see realist feminist documentaries until I began teaching my own courses in women's documentary. However, when I tried to rent *Self-Health,* a film featured in Julia Lesage's 1978 "The Political Aesthetics of the Feminist Documentary Film," the feminist distribution companies that had carried it were no longer in business, and the film could not be found. Lesage writes that the film shows women learning how to give themselves vaginal self-exams, breast exams, and vaginal bimanual exams, and then talking together about their "feelings about and experiences with their bodies and their sexuality."[7] In our present climate, where women are reinventing the feminist wheel to fight yet again for our rights to health care and reproductive freedom, it is critical for feminist educators in film and other fields to see and show these realist accounts of how women approached similar political work less than a generation ago. Meanwhile, without these films to guide us, women are continuing to produce films and videos surprisingly similar in form, tone, and content to those realist documentaries of the women's movement of the early 1970s.[8]

Equally frustrating is my feminist theoretical indoctrination, which was dedicated almost solely to the critique of realism and the endorsement of formalism. Although research for the writing of this project has led me to many articles from the period that argued against the move toward formalism, critical theory, and the avant-garde at the expense of the political work coming out of the women's movement, I was not *taught* this intervention in college or graduate school (perhaps because very few of these articles have been anthologized in textbooks of feminist film theory).[9] This results in an unsettling experience: when I attempt to view, teach, or make political documentary I find that I am unequipped (at least if I use standardized feminist film theory as my guide) to evaluate or understand the past and ongoing reliance upon "realist" representation by feminists, AIDS activists, and the like, even as we "know better." When I view 1970s (and 1980s and 1990s) realist, talking-heads documentaries by feminists and other dis-

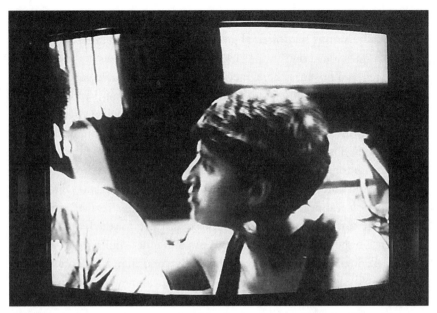

Alex Juhasz, from *We Care: A Video for Care Providers of People Affected by AIDS,* WAVE, 1990.

enfranchised producers, and, perhaps more significantly, as I make video with groups of political women, I am struck by two things: how often political producers are drawn to realist strategies and then, in contradiction, how often such work is evaluated by academics in an overly critical and sometimes simplified manner.

Where many critics have seen "naive realism," I see and make videos that utilize a variety of "realist" techniques with a variety of effects, only one of which is the dreaded psychoanalytic grip of "identification." Yet it seems that some early feminist film theory—which has since become a kind of received wisdom—utilized relatively direct translations of Marxist concerns about "realism" and "bourgeois ideology" and psychoanalytic concerns about "identification" and the "individual" to analyze a body of political work without carefully interrogating how these terms, when applied to political documentaries, are themselves dependent upon a variety of extratextual conditions, including intentionality, viewing context, economics, power, and politics. Take "realism," for example. Are the effects of the "realism" of the narrative Hollywood film identical to those of the "realism" of a cinema verité documentary? We make and view such films in noticeably different contexts and with strikingly diverse intentions. How is "realism" used and interpreted in either PBS-style documentaries or activist videos that quote, parody, and deconstruct this style (often within the same videos)? How are many of the accepted codes of "realism" dependent upon access to funds, equipment, "professional" formats, and the conventional ideological positions that often align with power and capital?

Such questions point to the largely overgeneralized ways the term *realism* (as well as a host of others, including *documentary, cinema verité, identification, political film,* and *feminism*) is used in feminist film criticism toward the valuable work of making sense of the ideological effects of the filmic apparatus. Although such work has been immensely important, it has also often obscured the *distinctions* allowed by the always unique extra-textual conditions that define the production, reception, and form of non-industrial film and video, especially when film and video is motivated primarily by political urgency. If, in fact, it is true that the "realist" style of much of the early feminist documentaries confirmed for the feminist viewer some sense of herself as a unified subject in a manner similar to how this is enacted through identification with the Hollywood film, how do we figure into this analysis that at this time this was a radical, new, and politicized reinterpretation of that very female subjectivity, one that mobilized vast numbers of women into action for the first time?

In the service of creating a feminist, formalist film theory, some articles were written, later to become an orthodoxy, that did not adequately describe the documentary films that they critiqued, or the experience of making or viewing politically engaged films.[10] Feminist film theory was founded upon a misreading of two integral features of feminist realist documentary: that there are usually *multiple* film styles and theoretical assumptions in any given "realist" film and, more important, that realism and identification are used as viable theoretical strategies toward political ends within these films. Thus, for the sake of this essay, I will define *realism* and *identification* in ways that are indebted to, but necessarily more complicated than, how these terms have been used by many feminist film theorists in the past twenty-five years. I think my definitions point to the way I am both molded and frustrated by feminist film theory in the face of directly political representational work.

By *political documentary,* I refer to any film or video that espouses an explicit opinion or position whose articulation contributes toward some manner of change. A great deal of political documentary uses realist form to do this work. By *realist form,* I refer to any of a number of always-changing conventions that signify for the maker and/or the spectator a condition, experience, or issue found in the "real world" or in the "real experience" of a person or group of people within the world. A variety of realist forms can be used within any particular film and video, and often their play against each other serves as an (intentional or unintentional) critique of the use or legitimacy of mimetic style. "Realism" can function in any of a number of ways, including, but not limited to, the confirmation, perpetuation, and reflection of bourgeois, patriarchal reality. It can testify to alternative, marginal, subversive, or illegal realities; it can critique the notion of reality. To portray the world with a realistic film style is not necessarily to imply that one believes that the "reality" portrayed is fixed, stable, complete, or unbiased, although it probably means that one has an opinion about what this reality means, what it feels like, how it functions, or how it might change. To see a representation of something that occurred in the real world is not necessarily to confuse that image with reality. In fact, politically motivated realist documentaries usually take great pains to show that theirs is a politicized, opinionated vision of some reality. In the same vein, I use *identification* to refer to the unconscious psychoanalytic processes that are the function of viewing any film or video text, many of which confirm our sense of ourselves as gendered, unified individuals. Yet I also acknowledge the many *conscious* forms of identification, misidentification, and refusal of identification that occur when individuals view political films or videos (which are rarely the mass forms of media—Hollywood film, broadcast television—upon which so much of our theory is based, but are, more likely, organizing tools of grassroots or activist organizations).

As a feminist, AIDS activist, media scholar, and videomaker, I am disturbed that the theory I respect and use is so often at odds with the media I make and watch. In this essay I attempt to reconcile the contradictions

Aida Matta and her son, Miguel, from *We Care: A Video for Care Providers of People Affected by AIDS*, WAVE, 1990.

between my practical experience as teacher, maker, spectator, and scholar of political documentary by women and the critical and theoretical knowledge I have amassed in my academic work. Must I feel embarrassed, stupid, or apologetic for liking and using these formal strategies? Why did many of the intelligent, highly educated, political women who invented feminist film theory simplify, and then disown, these complex films? I will argue that this did not occur as some evil, poststructuralist, feminist conspiracy, but rather as the result of particular economic, intellectual, historical, personal, and political motivations, including the translation of high French theory into English and the need to legitimate and authorize the highly suspect work of feminist interpretation and the deeply troubling fact of feminist scholars in the academy. In the service of such understandable ends, feminist film critics misread or simplified a body of film practice to make other legitimate points, loosely applied sets of terms from a variety of disciplines to a political documentary practice founded upon other schools of political theory, and thus most certainly used an inadequate theoretical lens to interpret what such films actually *do* accomplish.

Thus in this essay I attempt to retrieve 1970s realist feminist documentaries from their devalued position in feminist film history by looking more closely at what these films did accomplish and by using other theoretical grids, beyond feminist film theory, to do so. This is not to suggest that the antirealist position is without any warrant whatsoever. Nor is it to posit that we haven't learned from this critique. For, in fact, many current feminist documentaries about AIDS use "realist" styles in highly self-conscious, even self-critical, ways (although some do not) that are indebted to the feminist theoretical legacy of the past fifteen years. Yet even as I hope to note the "deconstructive" uses of realist style, I will continue to emphasize that more conventional uses of these forms are not without importance, sophistication, or effect.

In fact, I am arguing several (sometimes contradictory) positions about the use of realist style in the service of feminist political film- or videomaking. First, I am arguing that a careful look at the formal strategies of many of the feminist "realist" documentaries of the 1970s, 1980s, and 1990s will allow us to see what many earlier critics missed: that there is contradiction, antirealism, and many realisms within specific "realist" texts. But second, I am arguing that even the most "naively realist" moments within such films can function in ways more viable than many critiques of realism have allowed for. And third, the reason for this is the political efficacy of realism: the power to convince, document, move to anger and action and the ability to take control of identity and identification within systems of representation so as to move toward personal and collective action.

ALEXANDRA JUHASZ

So, even as the problems with realist form that have been identified by anti-realist critics remain valid, I believe that when makers and viewers are moved to use film or video as part of a political project the benefits are often evaluated as strategically more important than the limits of such form.

This in turn serves my more selfish ends of understanding and affirming recent political documentary work by feminists (including myself), specifically the vast numbers of alternative AIDS videos by women, which continue to rely upon "realist" strategies to accomplish their political goals of ending or altering the course of the AIDS crisis for the real women and men who daily suffer because of it. Although I understand how the feminist documentaries of the early women's movement and those of the second decade of the AIDS epidemic remain distinct in their intended audiences, formats, and understandings of political action and representational politics, I am most interested in their shared reliance upon realist strategy, even as a decade of critical theory advises against it. In this essay, I first look at realist political documentaries from the 1970s and then conclude with a discussion of my own AIDS video production. This work represents my attempt to understand both what the antirealist position missed and how it also contributed to a critical vocabulary that has pushed many makers and viewers of realist documentaries in the 1990s toward a more noticeably self-aware theoretical/political practice.

▶ ──

A Demonstration of Contradictions 2

"Hi, I'm Cathy Elaine Davies, a patient here at Woodhull Hospital. I'd like to inform you on safer sex." A young black woman faces the camera with a blackboard behind her. She draws a picture of a woman's vulva, highlighting the vaginal opening and the clitoris ("the man in the boat"). She then cuts a condom open and places the sheet of latex over her drawing. "I'm sure you wouldn't want anything to happen to yourself, or the person you're with. That's why you must always use one of these: a dental dam."
::   description of a scene from VIP Video Group, *HIV TV,* 1991

The sort of direct mode of address in both films [Janie's Janie and Joyce at 34] encourages us to relate to the images of Joyce and Janie as "real" women, as if we could know them. Yet, in fact, both figures are constructed in the film processes of camera, lighting, sound, editing. They can have no other ontological existence for the spectator than that of representation. . . . Underlying all of the above is the key notion of the

*unified self which characterizes pre-semiological thought. Both
Joyce and Janie, as subjects, are seen in the autobiographical
mode, as having essences that have persisted through time
and that reveal growth through individual change outside of
influence from social structures, economic relations, or psychoanalytical laws.*
:: E. Ann Kaplan, "The Realist Debate in the Feminist Film," 1983

A Little Feminist Film History

*The unity, discovery, energy, and brave we're-here-to-stay
spirit of the early days underwent a definite shift in 1975, mid-
decade. . . . Overall, there is a growing acceptance of feminist
film as an area of study rather than as a field of action. And
this may pull feminist film work away from its early political
commitment, encompassing a wide social setting; away from
issues of life that go beyond form; away from the combatative
(as an analysis of and weapon against patriarchal capitalism)
into the merely representational.*
:: B. Ruby Rich, "In the Name of Feminist Film Criticism," 1978

Although I do not wish to simplify the specific conditions of the writing of
early feminist film theory by a diverse group of women, there do seem to

How HIV is transmitted, from *We Care: A Video for Care Providers of People
Affected by AIDS*, WAVE, 1990.

be certain historical, political, and theoretical imperatives that may explain their shared simplification of feminist documentaries. Feminist film theory was born out of a unique historical and intellectual conjuncture during which women began to gain a foothold in the U.S. academy, while the newly translated to English theories of the mostly male French poststructuralists, semiologists, and psychoanalysts were also gaining a foothold there. Meanwhile, work by feminist critics from Britain and France that focused on this theory was itself providing a legitimating discourse for American scholars. Thus, before Kaplan critiques *Janie's Janie,* she devotes six pages to "the theoretical sources for such arguments," schematically citing the work of Lévi-Strauss, Lacan, Metz, Barthes, Kristeva, and Althusser.[11] In their introductory chapter to a 1984 collection of foundational essays on feminist film theory, Doane, Mellencamp, and Williams look back thirteen years to construct a brief teleological history of feminism and film. They describe a transition from "film festivals which were an integral part of the activism and consciousness-raising of the women's movement" to "the introduction of new critical theories and methodologies of semiology and psychoanalysis by British feminists; and finally, the rise of feminist film criticism as an academic field that has already begun to produce a generation of feminist film scholars."[12] They are quick to bemoan a "loss of activism," but they treat this as a natural progression rather than as the result of strategic professional and political choices. Laura Mulvey explains: "In terms of my own history, I sometimes feel that the excitement, novelty and sheer difficulty of semiotic and psychoanalytic theory overwhelmed other political concerns and commitments."[13]

Beyond the "excitement, novelty, and sheer difficulty" of the new theories under investigation at this time, a critique of "other political concerns and commitments" was often waged by academic feminists who began to find the women's movement to be essentialist and in other ways simple.[14] The word *naive* regularly accompanied the critique of feminist documentaries that recorded real women talking about their lives and issues in real time. *Naive* means "If they knew better, they wouldn't do this." The "they" here are most often producers of color, poor people, less educated people, some women; "they" use realism naively. The critique of "their" work has often come from well-educated, upper-middle-class scholars, often women, who usually identify themselves as political. Dargis wonders:

> Why does it seem like the criticism lobbed at documentaries such as those on tap at the Whitney was not only too harsh, but suspiciously self-interested? Could it be that once these messy, activist, and earnest works were banished to the dustbin, attention would be paid to the sort of filmmaking that neatly mirrored the same concerns of a certain emerging, academic feminism?[15]

There is absolutely nothing *naive* about rejecting films that do not replicate a theoretical position:

> Earlier US feminist documentaries—*Growing Up Female, Janie's Janie, The Woman's Film,* and *Antonia, Portrait of a Woman*—had aimed at creating more truthful, unstereotyped images of women in their particular social, racial and class contexts. . . .Yet the British feminists criticized them on the basis of their acceptance of realistic documentary modes of representation associated with patriarchy. This theoretical work was also buttressed by a growing number of feminist avant-garde films which explicitly dealt with issues of representation, language, voyeurism, desire and the image—e.g. *Riddles of the Sphinx,* and more recently, *Thriller* and *Sigmund Freud's Dora.*[16]

Well before, during, and after the creation of a feminist avant-garde film tradition in the 1970s, there was a long and rich tradition of a "naive," window-on-the-world type of political documentary production that includes much of the work of the Third Cinema, the identity film and video movements of women, people of color, and gays in the 1970s, and a good deal of current ethnographic media production. Importantly, much of this so-called realist film and video practice is and was theoretically informed in the traditional, academic, sense—not at all naive. For example, theories of de- and postcolonialism, and much current writing about identity politics, support the complexity of utilizing realist codes toward the construction of identities in cultures where some individuals and communities continue to be invisible, voiceless, and misrepresented for political ends.

Thus my intent in this essay is not so much to challenge the theory upon which the antirealist critique was built (I am trained in, and use, this theory), nor am I contesting the practical efficacy of gaining positions within primarily male institutions by using the master's tools with and against him (I owe my academic position to this legacy). Rather, I am attempting to find what was lost along the way. Most certainly, subtle and supportive critical attention was denied an immensely important body of film by women, largely, I think, because one theoretical grid was held up against a body of film work that was itself based upon another set of theoretical principals. Kaplan, Johnston, McGarry, et al. did not invent the realist critique that they applied to feminist documentaries (although they certainly improved it by integrating gender into the mix);[17] rather, they privileged this discourse over another contemporaneous constellation of theories, those of the second-wave American women's movement, for example. B. Ruby Rich delineates what was actually a split in feminist film theory during its formative period: the American, "so-called sociological, approach" and the "originally British, so-called theoretical, approach." Against the now institutionalized voices of theorists like Johnston, Pam

Cook, and Mulvey she cites another feminist theoretical tradition embodied in the work of American feminist theorists such as Adrienne Rich and Mary Daly.[18]

Using "sociological" theory as one's guide, many of the naively realist documentaries of the 1970s take on a sophistication and self-awareness typically denied to them. For example, *Janie's Janie* (1970–71), the subject of a great deal of academic feminist realism-bashing, actually utilizes a range of documentary techniques, some more "realist" than others. The film documents the coming into consciousness of a working-class, single mother, who by film's end has joined a group for welfare mothers fighting for better education for poor children and child care for working mothers. It is true that a direct-cinema camera documents images of Janie at home in grainy and shaky black-and-white: the camera sloppily zooms to catch her making sandwiches or cleaning the living room. We are allowed to see, as it "really" happens, her housework, the demands of her children, her poverty. However, a good many of the images of Janie's "real" life in her busy and loud household capture her being *interviewed,* which is nothing like her real life (and nothing like the "verité" style claimed to define this film). As she takes care of her "real" tasks at home, she also answers questions about the pain she experienced when she lived with her husband and before that with her father, and about how she fought and beat the electric company when it tried to turn off her service. Distinct from these two sorts of sequences are the dramatically lit, direct-address statements that she makes about her life while sitting alone in her kitchen. Meanwhile, midway through the film an arty sequence occurs that metaphorically depicts Janie's growth into a feminist consciousness. Staged images of Janie looking into a mirror and washing dishes (shot from outside the house through a grimy window) are set, proto-MTV style, to folksy women's music. Later the camera follows Janie to a political meeting, and then out into the world, as she informs us in a voice-over about the many issues for which she, and other women, still need to fight.

The filmmakers use a range of documentary techniques to record specific tensions within, and interpretations of, Janie's identity and reality. Yet this is not so much to convince the audience that Janie is a real woman ("the direct mode of address . . . encourages us to relate to the images of Joyce and Janie as 'real' women, as if we could know them")[19] as to make what was at the time a current and radical political argument concerning women's self-discovery as a route toward feminist *collective identity* and political action. In 1970, Barbara Susan wrote about consciousness-raising as a radical political theory:

Consciousness raising is a way of forming a political analysis on information we can trust is true. That information is our experience. It is difficult to understand how our oppression is political (organized) unless we first remove it from the area of personal problems. Unless we talk to each other about and see how many of our problems are shared by other people, we won't be able to see how problems are rooted in politics.[20]

Coming directly out of this political philosophy, *Janie's Janie* makes use of the camera in a manner similar to the structure of a consciousness-raising group: by articulating and sharing in public her personal history and experience *on film,* she works to construct a political critique regarding the status of all women. This is marked formally by the transition from Janie's single, isolated image recorded alone in the domestic sphere to her communal political action in the outside world: a move discussed and performed by many women in and out of representation during this period. For example, Lynn O'Conner writes about women's experiences in consciousness-raising, "She begins to understand that the process of consciousness-raising is in fact a process that probably has no end, that she may now understand the need for collective revolutionary solutions, but her own consciousness is still on the move and she knows not where it will end."[21] Only after speaking *to the camera* about her past, her relationships with men, her lack of job training, and the racism that was bred in her by her family, school, and neighborhood does Janie recognize her need to interact with other poor women with needs similar to her own, regardless of their race.

"It was an act of previously unarticulated knowledge," Julia Lesage wrote in 1978 about the feminist documentary film of the 1970s, "of seeing that knowledge as political (i.e. as a way of beginning to change power relations), and of understanding the power of this knowledge was that it was arrived at collectively."[22] The making of this film provides the forum for Janie's "previously unarticulated knowledge"; it propels Janie's individual experience into the realm of the collective. The film does not document Janie's fixed and unproblematic identity so much as it documents Janie's identity-in-process, her coming into a politicized identity, the making of one political woman through the focus upon identity allowed by cinematic realism. So intent were some film theorists upon inventing a new, more liberatory, filmic language that it seems the cinematic realism of consciousness-raising—a term that loosely encompasses the variety of formal techniques used in *Janie's Janie* and films like it—blinded them to what else occurred in the film (its class- and gender-based analysis, its critique of the fixed identity of the isolated housewife). Thus Kaplan can argue that simply because Janie is depicted in a realist "autobiographical mode," she is necessarily seen in the manner of all realist films—having an essence that

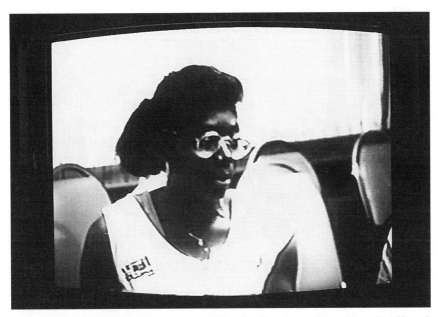

Glenda Smith-Hasty, from *We Care: A Video for Care Providers of People Affected by AIDS*, WAVE, 1990.

has "persisted through time and whose personal growth or change is autonomous, outside the influence of social structure, economic relations, or
psychoanalytical law"[23]—even as Janie articulates a politicized critique in
these self-same talking-head interviews.

The reliance upon talking-head style of many early feminist documentaries has also inspired a great deal of harsh criticism. Yet, in retrospect,
Amy Taubin insists that a primary lesson of 1970s documentaries is that
"the way to insure marginalized people a place in history is to record their
stories on film."[24] Realist codes and talking-head conventions are most
typically used to do the political work of entering new opinions, new subjectivities, or newly understood identities into public discourse. Thus *It
Happens to Us* (1972) compiles testimony of women who have had abortions by utilizing primarily a talking-head interview technique. We see
women addressing an interviewer or the camera and telling out loud their
gruesome, undocumented, private experiences with illegal abortions. The
interviews of a diverse group of women are edited thematically. Although
the individual stories of the women are compelling and unique, the power
of the film is not in its conventional realist function of confirming these
women's realities or identities as fixed or complete—in inspiring identification with individual women—but in its documentation of the reality of a
collective, gendered oppression. Words that have rarely been said by women
out loud form a revisionist history that unifies *a range of positions* as one

potential for a shared feminist identity and the political action that this collective articulation of oppression will inspire.

Similarly, films like *Healthcaring: From Our End of the Speculum* (1976) and *Birth Film* (1972) enter "private" images of women's bodies into the public domain: we see a close-up of a mother giving a gynecological exam to her daughter; we see a close-up of a woman's vagina as she gives birth to a child. The female genitals are shot in such extreme close-up that we lose sight of the "real" woman attached to them. Instead, these images provide visual evidence toward the contemporaneous political critique of the health care system and the social construction of women's sexuality. In an article written in 1971 about the politics of women's sexuality, Alix Shulman explains:

> Now that women, the only real experts on female sexuality, are beginning to talk together and share notes, they are discovering their experiences are remarkably similar and that they are not freaks. In the process of exposing the myths and lies, women are discovering that it is not they who have individual sex problems: it is society that has one great big political problem.[25]

According to Taubin, 1970s feminist documentaries are defined by "a realpolitik rather than the politics of representation."[26] But this realpolitik *is* based upon a politics of representation, although not one directly indebted to semiotics or psychoanalysis. Rather, feminist realist documentaries focus attention on the *condition of constructing collective identity through representation.* A large number of these documentaries include self-referential footage that records the delight and power felt by women learning to use film and audio equipment. In *The Woman's Film* (1971), images of women with cameras and Nagra sound recorders accompany the voices of women in a consciousness-raising group who are discussing the importance of women's taking control of technology. As with the political strategy of consciousness-raising, these films attempt to confirm not the stability or unity of identity, but rather its flexibility and the potential political power of individuals connecting through systems of discourse that allow for the recognition of the relatedness of their identities and thus the possibility for collective action.

Thus what may seem to be an irreconcilable split between competing feminist theories founded upon either second-wave feminist consciousness-raising (as evidenced in much of the period's documentary film production) or adaptations of ideological analysis (as evidenced in the feminist film critique of these films) is instead a more subtle contradiction in beliefs about the political efficacy of reality and identity. Both of these schools of feminist film theory and practice agree that the identities that are created for

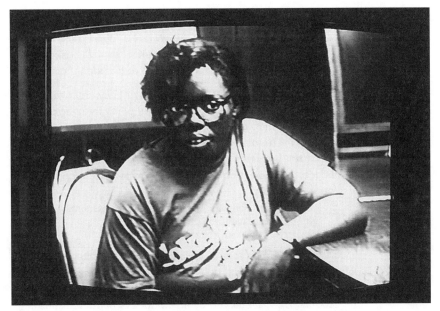

Sharon Penceal, from *We Care: A Video for Care Providers of People Affected by AIDS,* WAVE, 1990.

women by bourgeois, patriarchal ideology are dangerous and oppressive. They also share the belief that neither identity nor reality is essential or fixed; rather, both are constructed by patriarchal culture. Yet academic feminists of the period seemed to argue that a dismantling of identity is the viable response to these conditions, and most feminist documentarians utilized the strategic reconstruction of identity as their first step. "Any revolutionary strategy must challenge the depiction of reality," writes Johnston.[27] I agree, and I suggest that realist images of women discussing their lived experience constitute one such strategy with which to initiate this challenge.

▶──────────────────────────────────

A Demonstration of Contradictions 3

During the spring semester of 1992, I taught a course at Swarthmore College called "Women and Documentary." The final class of a section devoted to women's documentary practice in the 1970s focused upon the talking-head history film. We viewed Union Maids, *having read a great deal of contemporaneous feminist film theory in the preceding weeks. As we discussed why feminists had criticized these less than formally innovative films, two comments seemed particularly demonstrative of the sentiment in the classroom. One student explained that whenever she found herself liking the film, getting wrapped up in the words or struggles of the women speaking on the screen, she would think of me so as to remember why I would say this wasn't a "good" film. After viewing* Union Maids, *another student sheepishly asked, "Remind me why we're not supposed to like identification?"*

The psychoanalytically informed film criticism following Mulvey's original attack on the visual pleasure of narrative cinema is still marked by a suspicion of any kind of feminine role model, heroine or image of identification. . . . "Identification" itself has been seen as a cultural process complicit with the reproduction of dominant culture by reinforcing patriarchal forms of identity.

:: Jackie Stacey, "Feminine Fascinations: Forms of Identification in Star-Audience Relations," 1991

Discussing Union Maids, *my students say that they enjoy hearing smart, brave, political women recounting their lives. Feminist film theory be damned, young feminists need role models. They are moved by the images of beautiful, smart, political, and articulate women on the TV screen. Realism-schmealism; we are almost entirely denied this privilege in our culture. In a review of a Whitney Museum series highlighting the documentaries of the women's movement, Manohla Dargis and Amy Taubin have a similar reaction: "After a decade of Phil and Oprah and Sally, it was startling to hear and see women give witness, but not in the degraded language of talk TV."*

▶

Making Identity in Alternative AIDS Media By Women

It seems useful at this point to make a general distinction between the use of talking heads to represent some official and authoritative position, and the use of talking heads of people who are telling their own stories.

:: Barbara Halpern Martineau, "Talking about Our Lives and Experiences: Some Thoughts about Feminism, Documentary and 'Talking Heads,'" 1984

As she critiques realist documentaries, Claire Johnston claims that "it is idealist mystification to believe that 'truth' can be captured by the camera."[28] The mystification seems misplaced here: it is an elitist mystification to believe that nonacademics believe that "truth" is the only thing captured by cameras. In my work producing alternative AIDS videos with collectives of individuals who are affected by the crisis (working-class, minority women from Brooklyn for *We Care*, poor HIV-positive men and women from

Brooklyn for *HIV TV,* privileged college undergraduates for *Safer and Sexier: A College Student's Guide to Safer Sex*), I have seen again and again that activist videomakers are doing something quite different from capturing truth with their camcorders. AIDS documentaries that focus upon the real words and experiences of real women attempt to make with video *a better vision* of those individuals' reality as well as to contribute toward a better reality for the intended viewer.[29] Political women need to make and watch videos to hear and see themselves speak—a condition unavailable for many of them in the "real" world. Women in AIDS videos such as *We Care* and *HIV TV* aren't experts in the "real" world; Marie and Cathy don't get the time and privilege to define themselves publicly in the "real" world; they don't communicate effortlessly across divisions of class, race, and geography. Thus a large number of alternative tapes about AIDS by women document, celebrate, and affirm, in the dreaded "autobiographical mode," the words and experiences of the makers and those who then identify with them: "Hi, I'm Marie, welcome to my home." "I'm Cathy Elaine Davies. I'm a patient here at Woodhull. I'd like to inform you on safe sex." While Kaplan worries that we will be duped by the "unified self which characterizes pre-semiological thought," those of us making feminist documentaries are deciding the best way to be ourselves *for the camera,* for the scene, for the particular video with its particular purposes. We ask questions like "Should I sound familiar, or like an expert?" "Did I say that right?" "Could you shoot that again?"

In feminist documentaries such as *Union Maids, Janie's Janie, We Care,* and *HIV TV,* codes of realism *are* used, and identification *is* intended to occur among maker, subject, and viewer. Yet, even as a woman speaks as herself on camera, or even as a viewer identifies with her, these makers, subjects, and spectators are perfectly aware of the videotape mediating between the women watching in the world and the women represented to them through discourse. If you've ever shot a video or been interviewed, you know that using a camera is not an innocent act. You become aware of the power there; you become aware of how the camera affects an interaction. The videotape left over after an event or a moment simply isn't that moment—it is not as complete, not as rich, not as thorough as your real experience. It is something else—something powerful, too, something like a video. If you've ever edited you know this with an irrefutable certainty, as you move an image of a moment next to an image of another moment that wasn't next to it in reality, as you pull a good sentence out of a muddled paragraph, as you make yourself more articulate by dropping the "ums" and "ands." You've *made* something there. If what you've shot is a person, perhaps yourself, then you *know,* no naïveté here, that the act of making a

Carmen and Willy, from *We Care: A Video for Care Providers of People Affected by AIDS*, WAVE, 1990.

video is a work of self-production. By working with and through forms of representation like video, we make identity and meaning. This is precisely what the feminist realist debate said we *did not* know. But how could one not recognize that it is the self-conscious telling of oneself and one's ideas, to a camera and through an editing machine, that makes the self that one becomes on video? It is a privilege, as a woman, and as a political woman, and as a culturally disenfranchised woman, to get to do this: we are so rarely allowed to work on and then present ourselves as we hope to be seen.

To make images of little-represented identities is just that: to make *images*. The point is not that by shooting a video you lock yourself, your identity, into one place, but rather that you work on it, that you are self-consciously aware that there needs to be an identity there. A steady shot of a woman does not necessarily fix her with an essential identity, especially if she is discussing (or depicting) in front of the camera her own ambiguity about her identity. Because so much of feminist and other "identity" video movements are specifically about *constructing* our own identities in a society that has usually done this for minorities, much of the "realist" footage in minority-produced productions ends up recording people reflexively discussing the meaning, reinterpretation, and importance of their own identity.

If the construction of identity is so clear to the women who make political documentary, is it equally evident to those who watch it? If the work of film production highlights the act of identity construction for the maker, is this readily available to the viewer? Does the powerful draw and pleasure of identification, as defined by feminist film theory, deplete the realist image of its self-aware identity production? Certainly we "identify" with the aspects of women's experiences that sound and look like our own, but we also emulate traits and experiences that are different from our own, and we discard the stuff we don't like or don't understand. In a recent article about women's fascination with female stars, Jackie Stacey attempts to expand the earlier, psychoanalytic, feminist theoretical understandings of identification so that she can understand a range of processes described by female fans about their relations to the stars.[30] She found that women's recollections about their favorite stars invariably brought forth discussion of a variety of processes of identification, only some of these filling the rigid feminist, psychoanalytic mold.[31]

The work of defining who we are in relation to AIDS is encouraged by realist images of real women. Our identity in relation to AIDS is not stable and final, so we produce new and useful identities in relation to what we see on the screen. We appreciate that these women on tape tell us facts we need to know, while at the same time modeling images of proud, powerful, and dedicated black, HIV-positive women. Because the women who watch and make political documentary share beliefs, feminist positions, or a political agenda, viewers use their identification with women on the screen as do women in consciousness-raising groups: not to form a complete sense of self, but to cross through individual identity so as to unify a collective, ideological agenda.

Thus I believe that the worry that many feminist film critics communicated in the realist debates that in such films "the filmic processes leave us with no work to do, so that we sit passively and receive the message" is shortsighted.[32] First, it is condescending to the feminist spectator, who has a real stake in interpreting and evaluating the rare representations of her beliefs and "identity"; it is not only feminist film scholars who question and challenge representation. And there are many formal and thematic elements within even a realist, talking-head video that refer to the act of representation, that call attention to video as video, that remind the viewer that realist representation is not necessarily transparent. Direct address is one such element. When Marie talks to us, she calls attention to the power of the video camera: it lets her show her house to people who will never be there, it lets her pass information beyond the spaces and places she travels in her life as an AIDS educator. Voices off-screen talking to the talking head (for example, when a group member off-camera prompts Cathy with the words "dental dam") remind the viewer that there is a space on the

Sharon Penceal, from *We Care: A Video for Care Providers of People Affected by AIDS*, WAVE, 1990.

other side of the camera. The comfort that resonates between subject and maker in many AIDS videos is palpable to the viewer. It reminds us that there is a process and interaction involved in taping: Marie lets this camera into her home—that must be someone she likes or knows behind the camera; Cathy is acting comfortably, even in relation to articulating these difficult and personal topics.

Johnston's projection that "a cinema of non-intervention . . . promotes a passive subjectivity at the expense of analysis" also overgeneralizes filmic spectatorship, as if all viewing situations are the same.[33] Recent ethnographic approaches to spectatorship have stressed that we view *in context*. For instance, viewers of alternative, political films do not watch them as they would Hollywood films, even when the forms of the films are similar, because the screening of such films usually occurs in intimate gatherings where discussion subsequently focuses response. Somehow, in the flurry to disavow the talking head, realism, and identification in the service of understanding and critiquing mechanisms of signification, feminist scholars stopped thinking critically about the complex and intelligent ways that many people watch and make realist film and video. Stacey finds that female spectators describe multiple and complex processes of identification:

> The research also challenges the assumption that identification is necessarily problematic because it offers the spectator the illusory pleasure of unified subjectivity. The identifications represented in these letters speak as much about

partial recognitions and fragmented replications as they do about the mis-recognition of a unified subjectivity in an ego ideal on the screen.[34]

Finally, the feminist realist debate missed the most critical point of all: the impact and power of these films and videos comes more from their *use* than from their *form*. These films are first, but not merely, forms of political action.

They said we were trying to show reality. All I want to show is my video. The theoretically sophisticated directors of the Third Cinema voiced a similar defense for the production of reality-based films for the political movements of the underdeveloped. Film theorist and maker Fernando Birri writes: "By testifying critically to this reality, to this sub-reality, to this misery, cinema refuses it. It rejects it. It denounces, judges, criticizes and deconstructs it."[35] Birri's simultaneous use of "reality" and "deconstructs" points to an understanding of real-world conditions that are formed in, but are not reducible to, discourse. Gledhill, after questioning "reality" and "realism" for most of her article about developments in feminist film theory, concedes that when one considers feminist documentaries as *political* tools, the theory itself must change as well: "If a radical ideology, such as feminism, is to be defined as a means of providing a framework for political action, one must finally put one's finger on the scales, enter some kind of realist epistemology."[36]

This tension between theory and practice seems most tense for theorists. People making political art are more than capable of simultaneously understanding that while reality is constructed through discourse, it is also lived in ways that need to change for many individuals. James Meyer recognizes how this tension is resolved in AIDS activist art. In his article "AIDS and Postmodernism," he argues that both postmodern and realist techniques are used as a "double strategy," "at once critical and presentational" in activist AIDS video production.[37] Producers of alternative AIDS video need to root their activist position in the claim of a strategic identity shared by others (caregivers; black, gay, male people with AIDS; members of ACT UP) while at the same time working toward representing or building a society more flexible in how it uses identity to label and control people. Thus Meyer identifies a strange blend of "avant-gardist criticality versus essentialist instrumentality" in AIDS activist art production.[38]

The recent writings of feminist, ethnic, and gay cultural theorists invoke a similar understanding of identity: it is always constructed, it is neither fixed nor essential, but it needs to be present nevertheless. Cornel West suggests that although postmodern theory has made central the concerns of difference and otherness, there has been little focus on how considerations

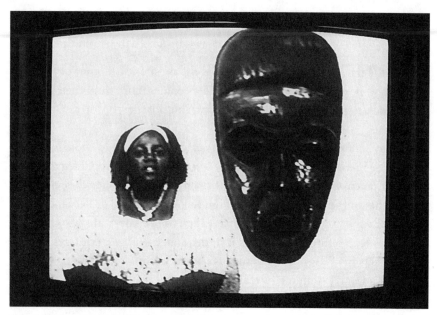

Marcia Edwards, from *We Care: A Video for Care Providers of People Affected by AIDS,* WAVE, 1990.

of the nonessential nature of identity can itself be used politically.[39] People who are oppressed because of their identities, essential or culturally constructed, do not have the luxury of celebrating the end of identity. However, they do have the power first to define for themselves and then to unify around identities that are ever adaptable and contextually useful. bell hooks invokes this position when she discusses "radical postmodernism," which "would need to consider the implications of a critique of identity for oppressed groups":

> We return to "identity" and "culture" for relocation, linked to political practice—identity that is not informed by a narrow cultural nationalism masking continued fascination with the power of the white hegemonic order. Instead identity is evoked as a stage in a process wherein one constructs radical black subjectivity.[40]

The making and watching of alternative AIDS video provides a space in culture where political women with limited access to cultural production can partake in "radical postmodernism." Using video, women affected by AIDS can begin to invent, articulate, and debate who they are, what they know, what they could be. For the women in the AIDS community, the political instance of access to media production allows us to speak our needs, define our agenda, counter irresponsible depictions of our lives, and recognize our similarities and differences. Cathy, who was a sex worker and is a recovering IV drug user, who lives in Woodhull Hospital in Brooklyn and is

HIV-positive, gets the authority of being treated as an expert. Marie, an HIV-positive, middle-aged black woman, is allowed the affirmation of the camera and the TV screen, as she takes her image to workshops and conferences. The spectator gets the rare pleasure and privilege of seeing ideas, communities, and information that are rarely represented. There is pride to be gained from making a work that is important and useful to others. There is pleasure to be gained from seeing and being oneself. These are some of the many real prides and pleasures allowed by realism and identification when utilized as feminist strategies within politically motivated documentaries.

I have highlighted here several critics who refer to cultural production as at once directly political and theoretically complex. Too much criticism has needed to sever these agendas that many of us find perfectly compatible: the attempt to represent in order to contribute toward change in real-world, lived conditions and at the same time offer a critique of the notion of the unified, gendered, classed, raced subject who can be unproblematically represented and oppressed within that "reality." Although I would not want to suggest that all political documentary struggles within both of these realms with equal skill, self-awareness, or energy, I am trying to suggest that feminist realist documentary—especially that motivated by political struggles focused upon the consequences of identity and community in a bigoted society—will position itself, in both form and content, in some relation to reality. And more often than not, this position is one of criticality, theoretical sophistication, and practical efficacy.

◆—————————————————————————————

NOTES

1. The Whitney Museum showed twenty-six of these feminist documentaries in its January 1992 program "From Object to Subject: Documents and Documentaries from the Women's Movement." The program included *Three Lives* (Women's Liberation Cinema Company, 1970), *The Woman's Film* (Woman's Caucus of San Francisco Newsreel, 1971), *Women's Lib* (People's Video Theater, 1970), *The Politics of Intimacy* (Julie Guftason, 1972–73), *Another Look* (Women's Video News Service, 1972), *The Fifth Street Women's Building Film* (Janus Lurie, 1971), *Healthcaring: From Our End of the Speculum* (Denise Bostrom and Jane Warrenbrand, 1976), *It Happens to Us* (Amalie Rothschild, 1972), *Birth Film* (Susan Kleckner, 1972), *Growing Up Female* (Julia Reichert and James Klein, 1971), *Fifty Wonderful Years* (Optic Nerve, 1973), *Nun and Deviant* (Nancy Angelo and Candace Compton, 1976), *Makeout* (New York Newsreel, 1972), *Not a Pretty Picture* (Martha Coolidge, 1975), *Nana, Mom and Me* (Amalie Rothschild, 1974), *Ama l'uomo tuo* (Cara de Vito, 1974), *Daughter Rite* (Michelle Citron, 1978), *The Emerging Woman* (Women's Film Project, 1974), *Antonia: Portrait of the Woman* (Judy Collins and Jill Godmilow, 1974), *Union Maids* (Julia Reichert, James Klein, and Miles Mogulescu, 1975), *Janie's Janie* (Geri Ashur and Peter Barton, 1970–71), *Harriet* (Nancy Cain, 1973), *Chris and Bernie* (Deborah Shaffer and Bonnie Friedman, 1975), *In the Best Interests of the Children* (Iris Film Collective, 1977), *Dyketactics* (Barbara Hammer, 1974), and *The Amazon Festival* (Santa Cruz Women's Media Collective, 1973–77). See Lucinda Furlong, "From Object to Subject," program notes, Whitney Museum of Modern Art, 1992.

More films are listed in Julia Lesage's "The Political Aesthetics of the Feminist Documentary Film," *Quarterly Review of Film Studies* 3, no. 4 (fall 1978), including *Three Lives* (Kate Millett), *Joyce at 34* (Joyce Chopra), *Woman to Woman* (Donna Deitch), *The Flashettes* (Bonnie Friedman), *Parthenogenesis* (Michelle Citron), *Like a Rose* (Tomato Productions), *We're Alive* (California Institute for Women Video), *Self-Health* (San Francisco Women's Health Collective), *Taking Our Bodies Back* (Margaret Lazarus, Renner Wunderlich, and Joan Fink), and *The Chicago Maternity Center Story* (Kartmquin Films). Most of these films are very difficult, if not impossible, to find. They were often distributed by the makers, and the distributors that handled many of these films are long out of business.

2. E. Ann Kaplan entitled the chapter on women's documentary in her book *Women and Film: Both Sides of the Camera* (New York: Methuen, 1983) "The Realist Debate in the Feminist Film: A Historical Overview of the Theories and Strategies in Realism and the Avant-Garde Theory Film (1971–81)."

3. I've capitalized *Feminist Film Theory* here to help signify the highly canonical nature of what is in fact, a very recent and only small subset of a much larger and more contradictory body of critical writing. Throughout this essay, I refer to the few authors and texts that have been much anthologized as *feminist film theory*, even as I am aware that the tradition of feminist writing on film is more diverse than this body of selected texts would demonstrate. Just so, the writings from one "side" of this "debate" have been more broadly circulated; the writings that participate in the antirealist side of this "debate" include Christine Gledhill, "Recent Developments in Feminist Film Criticism," *Quarterly Review of Film Studies* 3, no. 4 (fall 1978): 458–93; Claire Johnston, "Women's Cinema as Counter Cinema," in *Movies and Methods*, vol. 1, ed. Bill Nichols (Berkeley: University of California Press, 1976) (this appeared originally in *Notes on Women's Cinema*, ed. Claire Johnston [London: Society for Education in Film and Television, 1973]); Kaplan, "The Realist Debate" (this chapter is revised and expanded in the article "Theories and Strategies of the Feminist Documentary," in *New Challenges for Documentary*, ed. Alan Rosenthal [Berkeley: University of California Press, 1988], 78–102); Eileen McGarry, "Documentary, Realism, and Women's Cinema," *Women and Film* 2, no. 7 (1975): 50–57.

4. Kaplan, "The Realist Debate," 131.

5. McGarry, "Documentary, Realism," 53.

6. Kaplan, "The Realist Debate," 138.

7. Lesage, "The Political Aesthetics," 510.

8. The video work of Repro-Vision, a feminist collective devoted to documenting the recent upsurge of reproductive rights activism, either consciously or unconsciously quotes many of the techniques and subject matter of 1970s feminist documentaries. For instance, the group is currently in production on a tape about feminist self-health.

9. Some of these articles that contest the antirealist position include Julia Lesage, "The Political Aesthetics"; Barbara Halpern Martineau, "Talking about Our Lives and Experiences: Some Thoughts about Feminism, Documentary and 'Talking Heads,'" in *"Show Us Life": Toward a History and Aesthetics of Committed Documentary*, ed. Thomas Waugh (Metuchen, N.J.: Scarecrow, 1984); B. Ruby Rich, "The Crisis of Naming in Feminist Film Criticism," *Jump Cut* 19 (1979); Christine Gledhill, "Whose Choice? Teaching Films about Abortion," *Screen Education* 24 (autumn 1977); and Lesley Stern, "Feminism and Cinema-Exchanges," *Screen* 20, no. 3–4 (1979–80).

10. Several of the articles that participate in the "debate" conclude by suggesting that practice rooted in political struggle must have some connection to the "real." For instance, Kaplan writes, "But if we want to create art that will bring about change in the quality of people's daily lives in the social formation, we need a theory that takes account of the level now usually referred to scornfully as 'naively materialistic.'" "The Realist Debate," 134. Similarly, Gledhill suggests, "If a radical ideology, such as feminism, is to be defined as a means of providing a framework for political action, one must finally put one's finger on the scales, enter some kind of realist epistemology." (Christine Gledhill, "Developments in Feminist Film Criticism," in *Re-Vision: Essays in Feminist Film Criticism*, ed. Mary Ann Doane, Patricia Mellencamp, and Linda Williams (Frederick, Md.: University Publications of America and American Film Institute, 1984), 41. However, these realist forests were somehow missed for the semiotic trees. The legacy of these articles centers on their criticism of realist practices.

11. Kaplan, "Theories and Strategies," 79–80.

12. Mary Ann Doane, Patricia Mellencamp, and Linda Williams, "Feminist Film Criticism: An Introduction," in *Re-Vision: Essays in Feminist Film Criticism*, ed. Mary Ann Doane, Patricia Mellencamp, and Linda Williams (Frederick, Md.: University Publications of America and American Film Institute, 1984), 4.

13. Laura Mulvey, *Visual and Other Pleasures* (Bloomington: University of Indiana Press, 1989), xii.

14. See, for example, *Camera Obscura* 3–4 (1979). "Chronology," written by the Camera Obscura Collective in this issue, documents the Collective's intellectual history, from the

founding of the first feminist film journal, *Women and Film*, in 1973 to the present in 1979. The Collective explains that its intellectual shifts dealigned it from "radical feminism, the major tendency among American feminists at the time," because most American feminists were against "theoretical work," meaning the writings of Marx and Freud.

15. In Manohla Dargis and Amy Taubin, "Double Take," *Village Voice*, January 21, 1992, 56.

16. Doane, et al., "Feminist Film Criticism," 7–8.

17. Stuart Hall writes: "Is it true that ideologies work exclusively by their forms? This position depends on an anti-realist aesthetic—a fashionable position in debates about ideology in the early 1970s. . . . It represented at the time a certain justified 'formalist' reaction to the over-preoccupation with 'content' and 'realism' on the traditional left. But it was and is open to very serious criticism. For one thing it was founded on a rather loony and quite ahistorical view of the narrative and presentation forms in television. They were said *all* to belong to the same type of 'realism'—*the* realism of *the* realist text, was the phrase—which, apparently, was introduced in the fourteenth century and had persisted, more or less, right up to *Man Alive*." Stuart Hall, "The Whites of Their Eyes," in *The Media Reader*, ed. Manuel Alvarado and John Thompson (London: British Film Institute, 1990), 21.

18. B. Ruby Rich, "In the Name of Feminist Film Theory," in *Movies and Methods*, vol. 2, ed. Bill Nichols (Berkeley: University of California Press, 1985), 349–50.

19. Kaplan, "Theories and Strategies," 87.

20. Barbara Susan, "About My Consciousness Raising," in *Voices from Women's Liberation*, ed. Leslie Tanner (New York: Signet, 1970), 242.

21. Lynn O'Conner, "Defining Reality," in *The Small Group* (pamphlet), quoted in Charlotte Bunch-Weeks, "A Broom of One's Own: Notes on the Women's Liberation Program," in *The New Women*, ed. Joanne Cooke, Charlotte Bunch-Weeks, and Robin Morgan (Greenwich, Conn.: Fawcett, 1970), 189–90.

22. Lesage, "The Political Aesthetics," 515.

23. Kaplan, "Theories and Strategies," 87.

24. In Dargis and Taubin, "Double Take," 56.

25. Alix Shulman, "Organs and Orgasms," in *Woman in Sexist Society*, ed. Vivian Gornick and Barbara Moran (New York: Basic Books, 1971), 301.

26. In Dargis and Taubin, "Double Take," 56.

27. Johnston, "Women's Cinema," 215.

28. Ibid., 214.

29. A similar project is seen in the Soviet constructivist documentaries of Esther Shub and Dziga Vertov. See Annette Michelson, ed., *Kino-Eye: The Writings of Dziga Vertov* (Berkeley: University of California Press, 1984); Vlada Petric, "Esther Shub: Cinema Is My Life," *Quarterly Review of Film Studies* 3, no. 4 (fall 1978): 430–56.

30. Interestingly, such feminist reinterpretations of earlier film theory have been focused for at least the past ten years on the "women's film" and other popular texts. As scholars try to understand how women can watch mainstream cinema and television without being duped and without being considered stupid, they have had to expand and alter feminist interpretations of identification and negotiation. Perhaps because of a profession-wide disappearance of studies of both documentary and the avant-garde, this feminist critique has remained almost entirely in the domain of mainstream culture.

31. Jackie Stacey, "Feminine Fascinations: Forms of Identification in Star-Audience Relations," in *Stardom: Industry of Desire*, ed. Christine Gledhill (London: Routledge, 1991), 160.

32. Kaplan, "The Realist Debate," 127.

33. Johnston, "Women's Cinema," 214.

34. Stacey, "Feminine Fascinations," 160.

35. Fernando Birri, "Cinema and Underdevelopment," in *Twenty-five Years of New Latin American Cinema*, ed. Michael Chanan (Bloomington: Indiana University Press, 1983), 12.

36. Gledhill, "Whose Choice?" 389.

37. James Meyer, "AIDS and Postmodernism," *Arts Magazine*, April 1992, 65.

38. Ibid.

39. Cornel West, "Black Culture and Postmodernism," in *Remaking History*, ed. Barbara Kruger and Phil Mariani (Seattle: Bay, 1989), 92.

40. bell hooks, *Yearning: Race, Gender, and Cultural Politics* (Boston: South End, 1990), 27, 20.

EITHNE JOHNSON

[11] *Loving Yourself: The Specular Scene in Sexual Self-Help Advice for Women*

Sexual self-help advice is issued both by professional clinicians with academic credentials, such as research sexologists, sex therapists, and counseling psychologists, and by community-based "sexperts," including Susie Bright (who coined the term), Betty Dodson, and Carol Queen.[1] In the late 1960s and early 1970s, both clinicians and community-based sexperts claimed that women experienced much lower rates of masturbation and orgasm than men; hence the sexual self-help discourse for women has been organized around the "problem" of achieving orgasm, especially through masturbation. According to sexological research, only the female body has a structure—the clitoris—devoted solely to sexual pleasure; moreover, such research, influenced by feminist ideas, has asserted that, when compared with the male body, the female body's orgasmic productivity is theoretically more reliable and steady across the life span. Thus, in sexual self-help advice, the woman's relationship with her body is figured as both more problematic and more potentially erotic than the man's relationship with his body.[2] Shaped by the political intent of second-wave feminism as well as the commercial intent of consumerism, sexual self-help advice privileges the woman's primary relationship with herself; she is responsible for her own sexual pleasure. Addressing women in her video *SelfLoving,* Betty Dodson says, "Masturbation is the ongoing love affair that each of us has with ourselves throughout our lifetime."[3] However, although both professional clinicians and community-based sexperts situate female sexual agency within a narrative of self-love, they envision different resolutions.[4] The former normatively concludes that a woman finds her greatest sexual fulfillment in heterosexual coupling; the latter resists the romantic tradition, privileging sexual autonomy—"the ongoing love affair"—without foreclosing on potential partnerships, whether lesbian, bisexual, or heterosexual.

The significance of the mirror to this female self-love story cannot be underestimated. As articulated in sexual self-help advice for women, becoming orgasmic is an inherently specular process, one that begins ideally with catoptric self-representation. In the early 1970s, both clinicians and community-based feminist health educators promoted the use of the mirror for genital inspection. Since then, this self-representation practice has been widely popularized across advice literatures, yet little scholarly attention has been paid to it or to its elaboration in sexual self-help videos.[5] In sexual self-help advice, the mise-en-scène for female masturbation typically includes a mirror, flowers and floral prints, incense, candles, and music. The woman seeking sexual self-improvement is encouraged to imagine herself as both the performer and the director of her orgasmic performances. Dodson makes this process most explicit: in her chapter "Making Love Alone," exercises 7 and 8 are titled "Setting the Stage" and "Lights, Camera, Action."[6] More important, Dodson describes her epiphany through the specular scene: "One night I watched myself masturbating with the magnifying side of a makeup mirror. It was a fabulous sight, like watching an erotic movie on a miniature screen."[7] To see oneself as a sexual performer reflected in a mirror—a picture literally in motion—initiates the process of making love to one's own body. With its exercises and techniques, sexual self-help advice for women must be understood as a performative process for eroticizing the female body, especially for women's visual pleasure. How is it that female self-loving came to be signified through this specular scene? And how do video productions by professional clinicians and community-based sexperts differ in this regard, even as both seek to encourage women to love themselves?

▶───

The Specular Scene of Female Self-Seduction

In order to address these questions, the specular scene of self-seduction must be understood as an intertext for signifying practices that serve to distinguish between the professional clinician's discourse and the community-based sexpert's advice. In *Screening the Body,* Lisa Cartwright provides such an argument for the film motion study: "Its greatest importance is its function as an intertext between popular and professional representations of the body as the site of human life and subjectivity."[8] She maintains that a fascination in physiological processes—tracking life through the body—has motivated various kinds of scientific imaging, from early motion studies to neurological films to microscopy to radiography. Moreover, she concludes, "The pleasures of 'distanced' analytic viewing . . . are not peculiar to the genre of motion study but have pervaded the popular cinema and

other institutions."[9] Similarly, a scientific interest in sexual physiology—
tracking sex through the body, especially the female body—has motivated
both clinical and popular imaging, particularly in the postwar period. As
Linda Williams, Lisa Cartwright, and Giuliana Bruno all have argued, an
anatomic-analytic signifying practice produces the body in an objective,
mechanistic manner organized around breaking that body down into component parts.[10] For example, laboratory sexology's approach to imaging
the body results in a flattening of the body's dimensionality (Cartwright)
and an analytic "dissection" of the genital structures (Bruno).[11] Such
renderings—focusing on skin flushes, nipple reactions, vaginal expansion
and lubrication, and so on—are neither easily accessible nor self-evident
to popular audiences. Therefore, as an intertext produced through both the
therapeutic clinic and the community-based health clinic or sex workshop,
the act of catoptric self-representation functions as a technology of sex-
gender that may be appropriated to different conceptions of female sexuality.[12] Indeed, I will argue that this specular scene has been articulated by
professional sex instruction in a dramatic-analytic mode and by community-
based sexperts in an autobiographic-holistic mode. The purpose of these
categories is to explore the major boundaries, though clearly they have been
permeable due to the social connections among clinicians and community-
based sexperts. For example, one of the most popular self-help authors,
Lonnie Barbach, turned her clinic-based work with preorgasmic women's
groups into a doctoral dissertation (1974) and a best-selling sexual advice
book, *For Yourself* (1975).[13] In their respective ways, both clinicians and
sexperts have elaborated signifying practices for female genital display and
masturbation—the sexual performances that are supposed to follow from
the specular scene of female self-representation.[14]

Considered in the abstract, genital display and masturbation are significant to a wide range of productions, from popular porn movies and
professional sexual self-help tapes to other sexually explicit productions,
such as experimental films and health care documentaries. However, the
signifying practices for female genital display and female masturbation can
be radically different. I suggest that professional sex instruction videos and
community-based sexpert videos differ not only because of the different social contexts that produce them, but because of the countertactics sexperts
have developed through feminist activism. For this reason, I will argue that
the sexperts' articulation of the specular technology has resulted in two
counteraesthetic signifying practices: genital portraiture and masturbation
demonstration. These counteraesthetic signifying practices can be traced
to diverse sexually explicit films, which, though they cannot be subsumed
under any single genre, are stylistically distinct from both popular pornog-

raphy and professional sex instruction. Thus it is necessary to trace these counteraesthetic signifying practices through earlier films, including feminist health care documentaries, women's experimental films, and female masturbation films produced by the National Sex Forum (now the Institute for the Advanced Study of Human Sexuality). These productions emerged from countercultural contexts that were politically intended as feminist and/or woman-identified: health care activism, community-based sex education, and body-image art practices by and for women. Given the fact that professional clinicians and community-based sex educators crossed paths at the National Sex Forum, its films can also be studied as prototypes for the professional sex instruction video.

To understand genital portraiture and masturbation demonstration as countering other forms of genital display and female masturbation, it is necessary to consider the intent of feminist countertactics. Feminists have not only formed alternative health care techniques, they have deployed counteraesthetics to both pornographic and clinical imaging. In the abstract, the aim of the specular scene of female self-seduction is to shatter "negative" body images in order to liberate women to produce "positive" images of their bodies. However, the professional sexual self-help discourse encourages women to compare what they see in the mirror to anatomic illustrations, as if clinical knowledge itself were sufficiently "positive." By contrast, community-based sexperts have been sensitized to feminist critiques of both clinical and pornographic imagery. For them, "positive" images may derive from such imagery, but they are more likely to result from women-identified sexual knowledges and erotic aesthetics. Instead of calling for the destruction of a male-identified visual pleasure, as feminist film theory has, this specular counteraesthetics, however undertheorized, has sought to produce erotic visual pleasure for women. Like the avant-garde signifying practices lauded by some feminist film theorists, a specular counteraesthetics is socially as well as personally reflexive: it refers the individual woman to community-based sexpertise, which questions clinical and popular conceptions of the female body, sexuality, and gender identity. Moreover, this specular counteraesthetics can be traced back to the reflexive mise-en-scène of collective self-examinations. Out of such reflexivity has emerged genital portraiture and masturbation demonstration.

By understanding the specular scene of self-seduction as the intertext for the sexual self-help discourse and community-based advice for women, we are able to revise our understanding of the counteraesthetics in films that film theorists dismissed for their "bourgeois realism," as in health care documentaries, or overlooked, as in female masturbation films produced by the National Sex Forum. By acknowledging this counteraesthetic impulse across diverse films and videos, we can better theorize the cultural significance of genital shots and sexual performances in a variety of productions. Because it is made for the mass market in a popular format, the professional sex instruction video, I will argue, has elaborated a voyeuristic specular scene through a dramatic-analytic mode. In the manner of the film motion study or the popular science documentary, the professional sex instruction video uses anatomic-analytic shots to exhibit visual documentation of sexual physiology. However, this type of analytic exhibitionism is very different from the reflexive exhibitionism implied by the counteraesthetic signifying practices of genital portraiture and masturbation demonstration evident in the sexpert video. Thus I will argue that the sexpert video has elaborated an exhibitionistic specular scene through an autobiographic-holistic mode.

▶

Anatomy Lessons and Genital Portraiture

In the late 1960s and early 1970s, feminist self-care advocates began to encourage women to inspect their genitals on a regular basis with mirror, speculum, and flashlight, the same tools used in clinical gynecology. That the mirror should play an important role in the construction of a female gaze directed at the genitals underscores two points: (1) it was easy for women to use this specular technology, and (2) the mirror was already implicated in the production of feminine identity. Indeed, this specular scene offers what Teresa de Lauretis has defined as a "technology of gender": "The construction of gender is both the product and the process of both representation and self-representation."[15] Theorizing female agency in mirror gazing, Jenijoy La Belle asserts, "Since the mirror image is both self and other, it becomes possible to conceive of a relationship with the glass having a degree of intimacy more intense than any relationship a woman can have with a lover."[16] Her argument about the significance of mirror gazing in women's literature makes sense for understanding the specular scene of self-seduction as a self-representational, autobiographic performativity. If we follow Judith Butler's theory of corporeal performativity—that "the body is not merely matter but a continual and incessant *materializing* of possibilities"—then it is possible to argue that genital display can become a form of autoerotic foreplay.[17] In the feminist-inspired sexual self-help discourse, the catoptric act of genital self-examination sets the stage for styling and activating the vulva as desiring subject and desirable object. However, by distinguishing between the professional clinician's dramatic-analytic mode and the sexpert's amateur autobiographic-holistic mode, we can see how this specular scene has been elaborated either to inscribe genital display within the narrative of the "heterosexual social contract" or to produce genital portraiture at the "'local' level of resistances, in subjectivity and self-representation."[18]

Although the exact "origins" for the specular scene are not clear, it was popularized in the early 1970s by both community-based sex educators and clinical sex therapists. In 1972, Dr. Joseph LoPiccolo and W. Charles Lobitz published a paper describing their "unique" masturbation treatment program for women with "orgasmic dysfunction."[19] "In step 1, the client is told that she is 'out of touch' with her own body, that indeed she has never really known her own body nor learned to appreciate the beauty of her sexual organs."[20] Subsequently, clinicians have encouraged women to use mirrors to examine their genitals in order to bridge what Masters and Johnson identify as the "spectator" problem: feeling alienated from one's own body during sexual arousal.[21] As Masters and Johnson hypothesize, "It seems more accurate to consider female orgasmic response as an *acceptance* of naturally occurring stimuli that have been given erotic significance by an individual sexual system than to depict it as a learned response."[22] Conceiving of the sexually dysfunctional female as a spectator alienated from her naturally sensual body, clinicians have formulated therapeutic techniques that train the woman to give "erotic significance" to sensations. According to the professional sexual self-help discourse, female orgasmic productivity can best be improved through sequential, programmatic exercises: bathing, mirror gazing, practicing "sensate focus," working out the pelvic muscles, simulating orgasm, masturbating to orgasm, and finally making love with the male partner. In particular, catoptric self-examination is supposed to enable the woman to break free of the presumed constraints of alienated spectatorship inhibiting her ability to perform sexually. By comparing what she sees in the mirror with clinical diagrams, the client is supposed to develop a new awareness and acceptance of the "beauty" of her genitals in terms of their anatomic normality.[23]

Based on sexological research and clinical practice, professional sex instruction videos specialize in helping the implied couple bring their sexual cycles into correspondence for mutual pleasure.[24] Although both the professional sex instruction video and the community-based sexpert video organize female sexuality around the specular scene, they do so in different ways. Raymond Williams's distinction between the "market-professional" and "artisanal" modes of production helps clarify the social relations that determine the respective signifying practices in sexual self-help videos.[25] Dominating the sexual self-help market, the professional sex instruction video is a standardized product, with programmatic techniques, professional clinicians, and paid actors.[26] In the format of the popular science documentary, the clinician-narrator assumes an objective role, signaling scientific authority. Given that professional clinicians appear as authoritative "social actors," these videos are modeled on the popular science documentary, with its conventions of "talking heads" and voice-over narration.[27] Conforming to an industrial mode of production, these videos feature actors who play couples, rather than playing themselves as "social actors."[28] In a dramatic, "representational" style of acting, as if unaware of the camera, the actors enact sexual performances that are programmatically broken down into components of the larger narrative of heterosexual coupling.[29]

In four professional video segments chosen for study—*Advanced Sexual Techniques Vol. 2* (1992), *Better Orgasms* (1992), *The Female Orgasm* (1992), and *Becoming Orgasmic* (1993)—sexual improvement for the woman begins with the specular scene of self-seduction. Each segment features an actress who uses a hand mirror to gaze at her genitals. As she strokes the various areas, a voice-over commentary identifies the parts in technical terms. In this way, the female genitals are introduced through the dramatic-analytic discourse of the sex clinic. At the same time, these "domestic" examination sequences are typically staged in a romantic mise-en-scène: dimmed lights, bouquets on bedside tables, and floral bedspreads. Throughout these sequences, shots alternate between the actress looking at the mirror and the genital display reflected in the mirror. As "representational" performances, these examination scenes avoid the self-consciousness evident in amateur-artisanal productions in which exhibitionism for oneself, but also for female onlookers, is a particular kind of visual pleasure. By privileging what David James defines as a voyeuristic psychic economy, this dramatic-analytic signifying practice stages the specular scene of genital self-examination solely for the viewer's (rather than the performer's) visual curiosity.[30] Indeed, the professional sex instruction and sexpert videos can be differentiated along the same lines as can professional and amateur pornographic videos. As James argues, "The different economies correspond to different psychological states: the voyeurism of pornography depends on concealed observation, while [in the amateur porn videos] the performers' self-consciousness allows them the pleasures of exhibitionism, of seeing themselves reflected back by the monitor or by the more extended gaze of the tape's social distribution."[31] In the professional sex instruction video, as in the professional porn video, the actors' own visual and sensual pleasures are not at stake to the same degree as in the autobiographic-holistic mode (as will be explained below). Made for the heterosexual mass market, this specular scene of genital self-examination is voyeuristic, dramatic, and analytic.

Whereas clinicians conceive of genital self-examination as a step toward improved heterosexuality, sexperts and health care advocates have theorized genital self-examination within a feminist community-based understanding of "body education."[32] Through their alternative health care manuals and live presentations, feminist self-care advocates have focused especially on cervical self-examination. By staging and shooting mirror reflections of posed cervixes, feminist documentaries have explored the exhibitionistic practice of cervical self-representation. As discussed separately by Julia Lesage, Patricia Erens, and E. Ann Kaplan, feminist documentaries on women's health care and sexuality, including *Self-Health* (San Francisco Women's Health Collective, 1974), *Taking Our Bodies Back* (Lazarus, Wunderlich, and Fink, 1974), and *Healthcaring: From Our End of the Speculum* (Bostrom and Warrenbrand, 1976), emerged for educational and political uses in the early 1970s.[33] These and other feminist documentaries have been criticized for many reasons, especially for failing to provide, in Claire Johnston's terms, a challenge to the "language of the cinema," or a political strategy against medical discourses and institutions.[34] For example, critics Stephen Grosz and Bruce McAuley argue against what they take to be the "realist" effect of the signifying practice in these documentaries: "The implication is that through *seeing* (one's cervix) comes knowledge and through knowledge comes control. The pitfall of this approach lies in its acceptance of a neutral gaze—a force which illuminates unambiguously."[35] Describing a specular scene in *Self-Health,* they write, "The fact that the cervix shown is abnormal goes virtually unnoticed and raises the important issues of how these women are going to use the observations of self-examination."[36]

Although it is important to critique both medical and holistic epistemologies and their diagnostic implications, I want to take issue with Grosz and McAuley's dismissal of this specular scene on the grounds of a naively "neutral gaze." Whereas avant-garde signifying practices lauded by some critics reveal the camera/gaze to the viewer, sometimes through mirror reflections, these documentaries reveal the specular scene as a means for female body-image production. As a reflexive act of self-representation, the specular performance begins with a demonstration of the use of a hand mirror to gaze at the genitals, then the sharing of that view with other women. Julia Lesage describes the sequence in *Self-Health* in which a group of women practice self-examination and present themselves for viewing:

> A mixture of voices exclaims and comments on what [the women] see, especially on the variety and uniqueness of the genitalia. This sequence is a first in narrative cinema in the way it presents women's sexuality. It decolonizes women's sexuality. Women occupy the whole space of the frame as subjects in a collective act of mutual, tangible self-exploration.[37]

Lesage speaks to the feeling of transgression that this experience conveys for the women as "social actors."[38] Clearly, Grosz and McAuley fail to pick up on this, as when they argue that knowledge about anatomy and physiology is vital for women, yet "the importance of this [specular] activity is less clear."[39] They should qualify their point by admitting that its "importance" is obscure to them. Connected to their respective communities, these health care documentaries, like later sexpert videos, are produced through an "artisanal" mode. Such productions feature "social actors" who can "'be themselves' before a camera in an emotionally revealing manner."[40] Framed within an autobiographic-holistic mode, this specular scene signifies a counterpractice to the anatomic-analytic gaze: the effect is one of focusing an undisciplined glance into an aesthetically appreciative gaze (which may not result in the correct clinical diagnosis) at anatomical parts that traditionally had been observed by a medically trained, male-identified gaze designed for diagnosis. The cervical shot is offered to the practitioner and her audience within the film, inviting the film's spectator in at both levels. Rather than operate in the scientifically analytic mode to be objective in order to isolate this part of the body, this signifying practice works to integrate the interior and exterior genitals into a synthetically unified body image, one that can be shared among amateurs.[41]

Indeed, this specular scene of cervical self-examination offers more than a clinical display of female genitals; it articulates a practice of genital portraiture. The voluntary exhibition of one's cervix for an intended female viewer—in an alternative health care context within the films and in the wider distribution circuit of community-based sex education—must be seen as a strategy for making that cervical self-portrait personally and socially meaningful to women. Thus this autobiographic-holistic specular scene shares with amateur-experimental filmmaking a psychic economy of exhibitionism rather than the voyeurism of classical cinema or professional pornography.[42] To extend this analysis, cervical portraiture constructs a shot-reverse shot strategy in which the genitals appear to "return the look" to the women gathered around within the film and in the ideal screening space of the community sex education event.[43]

In the counteranalytic and counterpornographic spirit of negating the (male) visual pleasure associated with either the anatomic display or the pornographic "beaver," these feminist documentaries focus on the hidden space of the vagina and cervix. Similarly, Anne Severson's *Near the Big Chakra* (1972) offers a radically counterpornographic signifying practice of genital display.[44] This film features extreme close-up shots of different vulvas presented to the camera by anonymous volunteers of varying ages and races. According to Scott MacDonald, the film subverts the "tradition of transforming female bodies into lifeless, 'erotic' icons" and avoids "romanticizing" the female body—vulvas of all ages are shown, pubic hair does not appear to be styled, tampon strings and body fluids are occasionally evident.[45] The film has been described as shocking to its audiences. For this reason, it might be useful to compare its imagery to Cartwright's description of the "primitive" physiological motion study: such films "both amuse and repel precisely because they represent subjects attempting to escape normative bodily conventions (for example, visual beauty and recognizability)."[46] Although *Near the Big Chakra* offers genital displays that conform to the "natural" body styles championed by some feminists, the antiaesthetic style of this film has not been popularized either in professional sex instruction videos or in community-based sexpert videos.

In fact, the counterpornographic and counteranalytic tendencies of both this film and cervical portraiture are also antierotic, avoiding the issue of female sexual pleasure and the cultural significance of the clitoris. However, other countercultural productions have eroticized the vulva and clitoris through genital portraiture. As it has been articulated through lesbian iconography and Dodson's productions, genital portraiture emphasizes the "beauty" of the vulva and clitoris by displaying them in aesthetically pleasing, even romanticized ways. Barbara Hammer's early experimental films, both erotic and autobiographic, feature genital portraiture in direct close-up to extreme close-up shots, usually in long takes. *Women I Love* (1976) and *Multiple Orgasms* (1977) superimpose floral and landscape shots over genital shots, including masturbatory self-portraiture. In *Women I Love*, one sequence even comments on the antierotic sterility of the genital self-exam by explicitly aestheticizing the speculum: a daffodil is inserted in it, perhaps also recalling the antiwar gesture of flowers in gun barrels. Regarding floral iconography in lesbian films, Richard Dyer notes, "Vaginal imagery in cultural feminist work looks both head on at female genitals and sees them as beautiful."[47] This beauty is invoked through the frequent use of flowers, vegetables, and landscape shots to symbolize the vulva or to associate it with nature. Although this "natural iconography" may be rooted in "cultural feminism," as Dyer suggests, its broad appeal to women should not be simply dismissed as sexist or politically incorrect.[48] Indeed, it can also be regarded as both counteranalytic and counterpornographic: such visual "beauty" contests the clinic's abstract anatomic exhibits as well as the pornographic "principle of *maximum visibility*."[49]

As a gay critic, Dyer maintains that "lesbian use of such imagery insisted on its sexual—rather than its procreative—significance, and such imagery is even more significant for lesbian sexuality than for hetero."[50] Although this assessment may be valid, in fact genital portraiture emerged during a time when nonprocreative and clitoral-based sex practices were widely popularized across the United States.[51] That emphasis on sex without procreativity has also been fostered by community-based sexperts who draw on the same romantic-natural aesthetic categories for genital portraiture. As the "Mother of Masturbation," Betty Dodson claims to have introduced "'cunt consciousness' to feminism" with her explicit drawings and her 1973 NOW slide show titled "Creating an Esthetic of Female Genitals."[52] Recalling the preparations for the photographs, in which her models composed their pubic areas, looked at each other's genitals, and used mirrors to see their own, Dodson writes, "I saw styles emerging like a Baroque Cunt, then a Danish Modern, a Gothic type, a Classical Cunt, and many Valentine Cunts."[53] By associating self-styled vulvas with aesthetic categories, Dodson seeks to make the genitals personally meaningful through portraiture in comparison to the pornographic "split beaver" and the analytic-clinical genital display.[54]

Through her "BodySex Workshop," Dodson has developed a feminist model for sexual consciousness-raising designed around an autobiographic-holistic specular scene.[55] In 1991, Dodson released *SelfLoving: Video Portrait of a Women's Sexuality Seminar,* which was shot in her home to share with viewers the workshop process, including genital portraiture. As each naked participant styles her vulva—with Dodson's enthusiastic help—then gazes at its reflection in a small mirror, the other participants look directly at her and appraise her exhibit. For the viewer, the camera presents extreme close-up shots of each presentationally exhibited genital portrait. As in *Near the Big Chakra,* these vulvas fill the screen for several seconds, but with the added pleasure of the women's self-conscious participation in this autoerotic process.[56] When, for example, a self-identified grandmother shows her vulva to the group, Dodson draws on romantic and feminine metaphors of "flower" and "shell" to give affirmational meaning to this fifty-year-old woman's genitals.[57] In this way, the video challenges visual conventions for representing only youthful female bodies as sexy. Similarly, Dorrie Lane's "Wondrous Vulva Puppet," in *How to Find Your Goddess Spot* (1993), transforms the female genitals through fantasy sculpture into something aesthetically pleasing for an implied female gaze.[58] Lane's choice of rich fabrics and lush colors for the puppet provides an alternative to analytic representations in clinical diagrams.

Like Dodson's tape, sexpert videos are created through an "artisanal"— literally domestic at times—mode of production.[59] Rather than feature performances by professional actors, these productions are committed to exhibiting female sexual pleasure as performed by "social actors" known for their community-based work, including Dodson, Debi Sundahl, Annie

Sprinkle, Dorrie Lane, and Shannon Bell. Instead of acting in the "representational" style, as if the camera were not present, these sexperts perform in the "presentational" style, described by Waugh as the "convention of performing an awareness of the camera rather than a nonawareness, of presenting oneself explicitly for the camera."[60] In the feminist-activist tradition of community-based leadership, these sexperts might be defined as amateurs in the best sense; they make an art of self-loving, demonstrating genital display and masturbation with their own bodies. Some of the countertactics in sexpert videos, such as Lane's puppet act, may strike audiences as silly or funny. For example, Dodson's *SelfLoving* may carry the autobiographic-holistic signifying practice of genital portraiture too far when she treats her own clitoris as a ventriloquist's puppet, manipulating it in an extreme close-up shot and introducing it as "Clitty Ann" in a high-pitched voice. At the same time, such absurd gestures may speak to the feeling of corporeal alienation and disunity reportedly experienced by women and around which both the sexual self-help discourse and community-based advice are organized.

▶ ───

Masturbation Demonstration

With beautification as the first step in sexual self-help advice for women, the next step is masturbation. Based on their laboratory research, Masters and Johnson popularized the idea that women achieve the most intense orgasms through "autostimulation."[61] Thus it is no surprise that female masturbation figures prominently in sexual self-help advice for women. Both clinicians and community-based sexperts have seized the opportunity to translate this scientific knowledge—formulated through laboratory observation and recording devices—into popular terms, whether for mass markets or for various communities. The exercises elaborated by the sexual self-help discourse—originally formulated for the anorgasmic woman—have been duly incorporated into the heterosexual romance of the professional sex instruction video. In comparison with professional clinicians, sexperts extol the benefits of more eclectic "how-to" instructions. For example, Dodson and Sprinkle claim that Eastern practices of meditation and yoga lead not only to better orgasms, but also to holistic self-improvement. Instead of emphasizing the achievement of orgasm with a partner (male or female), sexperts adhere more strictly to the idea that masturbation for its own sake is crucial to female health and well-being. As the intertext for scientific and popular imaging about female sexuality, the specular scene organizes an autoerotic performativity that can logically lead the practitioner to self-pleasuring (once known medically as self-abuse). Whereas Masters and Johnson withheld their laboratory-based imagery from the public, the signifying practices for both the professional sex instruction video and the community-based sexpert video can be traced to prototypes for the dramatic-analytic and autobiographic-holistic modes. In their heterogeneity, sexpert videos are more likely to show traces of reflexive counteraesthetic signifying practices—women controlling specular technologies (camera or mirror) and contesting dominant conventions through self-consciously presentational performances.[62] Indeed, such videos are organized around the sexpert who exhibitionistically demonstrates masturbation rather than solely narrating its performance as does the professional clinician, who takes a distanced, analytic perspective to masturbation instruction. Of particular note is the significance to sexperts of feminist health center–based conceptions of the female clitoral structure—and its capacity to ejaculate.

As female self-pleasuring techniques were formulated by clinicians and community-based sex educators in the early 1970s, the film prototype for teaching masturbation emerged in a progressive, educational context.[63] Under the auspices of the National Sex Forum in San Francisco, Ted McIlvenna produced and Laird Sutton directed several films about female masturbation, including *Susan* (1971), *Handvoice* (1971), *Shirley* (1972), *Margo* (1972), and *Joy in Her Pleasure* (1973).[64] Seen retrospectively, these films anticipate the development of the professional sex instruction video, with its programmatic narrative of sexual exercises. For example, in *Handvoice,* the woman explores her body with oil, a technique promoted by Masters and Johnson; *Shirley* begins with a shower sequence to demonstrate how a woman can "enjoy the luxury" of her body before masturbating. *Margo* features a bath and a demonstration of mirror self-examination. Both *Shirley* and *Margo* employ voice-over narration by women. These rudimentary instructional narratives can be traced to the privileging of female experience in community and clinical contexts as sexual self-help advice was organizing around the "problem" of female orgasm in the early 1970s. The prototype for the integration of masturbation into heterosexual coupling can be found in *Joy in Her Pleasure,* which shows a woman masturbating to orgasm with a male partner. Significantly, the man strokes her body, but he does not penetrate her; her solo orgasm ends the film. The Forum also produced Severson's *Near the Big Chakra* as well as Honey Lee Cottrell's *Sweet Dreams* (1979), which she made as a film student at San Francisco State University. Featuring Pat Califia, *Sweet Dreams* not only celebrates female masturbation, it also reiterates the floral iconography common to Hammer's films as well as genital portraiture.

The Forum's female masturbation films offer a composite of analytic-dramatic and autobiographic-holistic signifying practices. As in the analytic mode of scientific image making described by Cartwright, close-up shots in these films focus attention on isolated body parts: breasts (nipples and areolae), the face, and genital displays. Like the "primitive" physiological motion study and its popularization of corporeal displays in facial expression films, specific close-up shots serve to signal physiological changes.[65] These isolated anatomic-analytic shots are edited with medium to long shots of the masturbating body, in a rhythm that builds toward a (literal) climax conveyed through longer takes of the orgasmic performance. As both analytic and holistic, each film formally attempts to document the process of arousal and climax for the performer, though not in "real time" as in amateur porn productions.[66] Due to the Forum's connections at the time to local university-based and community-based sex education programs, these films draw on the feminist autobiographic act of masturbation demonstration; indeed, some educators appear in these films.[67] They perform their masturbatory acts in a "presentational" style—aware of the camera, sometimes turning away from it, sometimes directly addressing it. In *Susan,* the woman looks at the camera and smiles after her final act of masturbation, enthusiastically waving her vibrator at the camera. Thus the use of the performers' names as titles and the self-consciousness of their demonstrations point to the autobiographic-holistic aspects of these films. Whereas "natural" body styles predominate in the Forum films, professional sex instruction videos feature more conventionally attractive people, perhaps in keeping with the beauty standards of industrial film production.

Although it is hard to determine how these films have circulated among professional clinicians, they have been regularly used in Forum/Institute courses designed to teach students, including professional clinicians, about sexuality. Some of these clinicians have gone on to make their own tapes. For example, Michael Perry, who received his doctorate from the Forum/Institute, hosts the video series "Sex a Lifelong Pleasure." Although professional clinicians may be familiar with the feminist-inspired practice of masturbation demonstration, they do not use this tactic in their own videos. Instead, in the manner of the popular science documentary, professional clinicians narrate the masturbatory techniques for achieving orgasm as the performers dramatically enact them. Privileging a voyeuristic psychic economy for the sex scenes designed to appeal to men and women, the professional sex instruction video also owes something to the emergence of pornography made to attract women to the genre. Like Candida Royalle's porn movies, the professional sex instruction video signifies female orgasmic performances through medium-long to long shots with longer takes.[68] Three of Royalle's features—*Christine's Secret, Three Daughters,* and *Revelations*—revolve around protagonists for whom masturbation leads to coupling with male partners; the act of masturbation is framed in each case as an important event for the protagonist. In the sex instruction video, successful masturbation by the woman programmatically leads to improved sexual pleasure in a couple relationship.

Representing sexual experience, the performers in the professional sex instruction video function as composite types. Like the objective data preferred by professional clinicians, composite characters serve to dramatize the analytic signifying practice of clinical sexology, which privileges the aggregate over the individual. Following Masters and Johnson's laboratory-based thesis that the woman must give "erotic significance" to naturally occurring sensations, clinicians urge the "preorgasmic" woman to become a self-consciously sexual performer in order to become a naturally orgasmic body. As the title of Dr. Julia Heiman and Dr. Joseph LoPiccolo's "how-to" program "Becoming Orgasmic" implies, this transformation is a performative process. As a companion to the book of the same title, the video *Becoming Orgasmic* (story credited to LoPiccolo) centers on a composite character's sexual self-discovery and is purportedly based on women who have been treated successfully with the program.[69] During this video's sequence of "preorgasmic" exercises, the voice-over narration suggests that the woman try exaggerating what it might be like to experience an orgasm; simultaneous to that advice, the actress-character arches her back, moans, writhes, and clenches her fists. Posing in this "representational" style is familiarly feminine, common to both romantic and pornographic conventions of female sexual agency. However, the simulation exercise cannot be summarily dismissed as a sexist strategy to encourage women to fake it just for male pleasure. In advocating the simulation exercise (which is not unusual for sexual self-help products), *Becoming Orgasmic* suggests that faking an orgasm is one way for women to achieve the real thing. As Lonnie Barbach says, only "you" (the implied woman) can "give" yourself an orgasm.[70] Following Judith Butler, it is possible to read this performative simulation as gender parody: if there is no original female orgasmic performance (and there cannot be for the "preorgasmic" subject), then any performance is a copy for which there is no original.[71] Similarly lacking an original, the aggregate data produced by clinicians function as a baseline of normalcy, but cannot be attributed to any single unit of measurement (i.e., individual participant). In both pornographic and sex instruction conventions, representationally sexy performances serve to dramatize female masturbation as foreplay to the climax of heterosexual intercourse.[72]

Subverting the objective, analytic authority of the professional clinician-narrator, community-based sexperts also address the camera directly, but through an autobiographic-holistic mode. In *Sluts and Goddesses,* Sprinkle parodies the staid role of the professional clinician.[73] Urging women to explore their dual natures, as indicated by the video's provocative title, she proffers her advice in colloquial terms rather than clinical discourse. *Sluts and Goddesses* also spoofs the laboratory documentation of multiple orgasm by staging an extended masturbatory sequence performed by Sprinkle over which is superimposed a graph that charts the multiple peaks of pleasure. Like Sprinkle, many sexperts are interested in reclaiming a historic or mythic role of the female sex teacher (sexpert) or "sacred prostitute," although they might not agree with each other's belief systems.[74] Through their holistic frameworks, these sexperts promote community-based feminist perspectives on the relationship of the clitoris to the body's sensory capacities, rather than relegate the external clitoris to one step in foreplay on the way to orgasm with a partner. Indeed, with the exception of Dodson's tape, sexpert videos privilege a particular kind of masturbatory, clitoral body climax—female ejaculation. For example, in their respective videos, Dorrie Lane and Debi Sundahl refer to diagrams from the Federation of Feminist Women's Health Centers. The federation's book *A New View of a Woman's Body* provides the following definition of the female sexual structure:

> By *clitoris* we mean the whole complex organ, consisting of the glans; shaft and hood; clitoral legs (also called crura); inner lips; hymen; several bodies of erectile tissue, including the clitoral bulbs, urethral sponge, and perineal sponge; muscles; nerve endings; and networks of blood vessels. . . . Once understood and recognized, it is clear that the clitoris is an organ as complex and active as the penis.[75]

By organizing the clitoral body in this synthetic-holistic perspective, the assertion of sexual homology (also documented in clinical sex research) and active potentiality is an important step in reclaiming power that has been culturally assigned to the penis. From this perspective, it can be argued that both the clitoris and the penis are equipped to ejaculate (whether paraurethral or prostatic fluids), though the female glans is arguably superior due to both its ontogenic primacy and its capacity to have successive multiple orgasms.[76]

Although professional sex instruction videos do not explore female ejaculations, the sexual self-help discourse has popularized the theory of the "Grafenberg spot," which some think to be the stimulation point for female ejaculation. In 1982, sex researchers Ladas, Whipple, and Perry published *The G-Spot* for the popular sexual self-help market.[77] Whipple also consulted on the production of an educational film on the topic, *Orgasmic Expulsions of Fluid in the Sexually Stimulated Female* (Focus International, 1981).[78] This short film presents a dramatized clinical session in which a female therapist meets with a client who is concerned about her ejaculations. In the analytic signifying practice, extreme close-up shots of female ejaculations—clinically exhibited by an anonymous performer—are intercut with this dramatic, representational narrative. By contrast, sexpert videos privilege "social actors"—women who are known as community-based sex educators, such as Carol Queen and Shannon Bell—who explain the problems they have experienced due to this fluid production. Through their autobiographic narratives, they seek to validate this type of orgasmic productivity for other women. When they demonstrate masturbation, their bodies are not cut away from the scene, as in the analytic mode, to display the objective performativity of the sex organ. Rather, in an autobiographic-holistic performativity, their bodies perform as rigid, writhing, or standing, depending on the individual's masturbatory tactics. As a counteraesthetics to professional masturbation instruction and industrial pornography, these demonstrations may challenge viewers' preconceptions regarding standards of feminine beauty and sexual performativity.

These "presentational" masturbation demonstrations can be seen to parody pornographic conventions for representing female sexual pleasure while also claiming the ability to perform spectacular orgasms for women. Through her theory of "autobiographics," Leigh Gilmore argues that "confessional technologies" can be used by women in an autobiographic mode that "explores the constrained 'real' for the reworking of identity in the discourses of women's self-representation."[79] In these sexpert videos, the project is to authenticate ejaculation as a female activity known experientially to the amateur experts. Of course, the ejaculation demonstrations could be faked, but proving them real is less important than presenting them counterpornographically and counteranalytically. Through autobiographic-holistic signifying practices, these videos attempt to subvert and challenge the convention of sexing the ejaculation as solely male, as in pornography's "money shot." Indeed, these ejaculatory performances signify like graffiti or peeing in the snow: the autobiographical signature stains the pornographic ground upon which it is written. Shannon Bell, who appears in *Nice Girls Don't Do It* and *How to Female Ejaculate,* advances a political agenda for female ejaculation by claiming that it takes up space ordinarily reserved for men.[80] Although this might strike some readers as a dubious claim, female fluids are marginalized as a novelty in popular pornography.[81] According to Susan Faludi, the male ejaculation performance is the "last bastion of masculinity" in an industry in which men are paid less overall than women to perform; as one male insider says, "The one thing a woman cannot do is ejaculate in the face of her partner."[82] Sexperts not only suggest that women can do this, but also advocate that women learn how to ejaculate to enhance their own orgasmic pleasure.

Erotic Bodies and the Body Politic

According to Giuliana Bruno, "Film is another form of vision that affects the mapping of the body."[83] Introducing her study of the "*corpo*real" aesthetics of Elvira Notari, the first woman filmmaker in Italy, Bruno states, "My study intends to foreground spatial representation and aims at inscribing desire in spatial practice. Reading from a feminist viewpoint means to venture into that erotic geography that exists as an intersubjective site, in-between the filmic texts and the female spectator (and critic)."[84] With this framework in mind, Bruno argues that Notari's films and production fragments articulate a popular "erotics of passion" in response to inscriptive modes of "mapping" the body—most notably the anatomic-analytic signifying practice that dissects the body and the film body.[85] Given my distinction between the dramatic-analytic and autobiographic-holistic modes, we can understand the specular scene of female self-seduction as a technology of sex-gender for mapping the female body in relation to personal and/or communal space. Whereas the professional clinician assumes a private self-mapping within the domestic context of the heterosexual couple, the sexpert pays homage to the community-based tactic of communal genital mappings. Even though genital self-examination as a public ritual has become a feminist cliché, as a symbolic gesture of erotic-corporeal autonomy for women it continues to resonate across sexual self-help advice.[86] How that specular scene has been articulated—through dramatic-analytic or autobiographic-holistic signifying practices—points to very different political effects. Although inscriptive models of social relations grounded in surveillance and *scientia sexualis* may be useful for understanding the dramatic-analytic mode, they fail to account for the autobiographic-holistic mode, or what Bruno defines as an "erotics of passion." For this reason, we need to rethink the concept of counterpractices and resistances in terms of their positively participative social relations.

Having examined the specular scene of female self-seduction, I want to conclude by addressing two questions about the social and political implications of the "*corpo*real" performativities it can produce. First, critics might ask: Does this mirror scene effect such a self-consciousness about the female genitals that they must always be made up fashionably for the potential (male) spectator? After all, the female genitals are almost always styled *before* they pose, regardless of the intent for dramatic-analytic display or autobiographic-holistic portraiture. The "natural" pubic styles in *Near the Big Chakra* are clearly an exception. Thus the specular scene of female self-seduction may perpetuate feminine beauty production: the naked genitals must be dressed up in order to become a performer for an already feminized gaze. However, this raises the issue of accounting for women's agency in creating and/or popularizing pubic fashions. Indeed, Dodson *sees* vulvas differently, subverting clinical categories based on anatomical structures: "The heart shape is not the shape of the heart in our chests—it's the shape of the women's genitals when she opens her lips [labia]."[87] In this way, genital portraiture—through which female sexual performativity begins by styling that "valentine" in the mirror—belongs to the domain of *ars erotica* rather than *scientia sexualis.*

Second, critics might ask: Whose genitals are the focus in the specular scene of female self-seduction? Professional sex instruction videos privilege white bodies. According to Robert Eberwein's analysis of professional sex video marketing, advertisements for these products appear in a wide range of popular magazines, but he located only one such advertisement in a magazine, *Heart and Soul,* targeting African American women.[88] Not surprisingly, this advertisement featured the only black couple in that particular series, "Ordinary Couples, Extraordinary Sex." In comparison, the feminist documentaries and *Near the Big Chakra* bring together racially diverse bodies for genital exhibition. Likewise, sexpert videos offer some variety as far as race, age, and body size are concerned. In the feminist spirit of community-based sex education, the National Black Women's Health Project produced *On Becoming a Woman: Mothers and Daughters* (1987), directed by Cheryl Chisholm. Perhaps due to multigenerational reception or to make sex education more entertaining for teens, the specular self-examination scene is featured in an animated sequence by Ayoka Chenzira. Not only does *On Becoming a Woman* refer to the feminist practice of making the genitals self-representationally significant for women, it also challenges the dominant convention of associating beauty with whiteness. As Judith Butler observes, there are "punitive consequences" for challenging gender-sex performances, and these pivot on how one's gender, race, class, and age are figured in the body politic.[89] For example, actress Jamie Lee Curtis can proudly tell *Entertainment Weekly* that masturbation is her favorite hobby, but Dr. Joycelyn Elders was symbolically fired as surgeon general of the United States following her suggestion that educators consider teaching schoolchildren about masturbation.[90]

Finally, it could be argued that genital portraiture and masturbation demonstration ultimately fail as signifying practices to maintain the most radical impulse associated with a feminist counteraesthetics: the destruction of (male) visual pleasure. However, Lisa Tickner suggests another way of theorizing the visual pleasure genital portraiture and masturbation demonstration might offer women: "Living *in* a female body is different from looking at it, as a man."[91] Indeed, both clinicians and community-based sexperts assume that women will recognize in this specular scene something intrinsic to their embodied experience. If women have been socialized to overlook their genitals or to see them as dirtying the "real," then their unfocused glances need to be redirected through a personal gaze/touch at that "off/scene" corporeal space, thereby bringing it "on/scene" for them.[92] About styling one's pubic area, Dodson writes, "Although this may sound frivolous, it actually enhances the woman's awareness of her genitals."[93] As she intuits, looking and touching are productive not only of sexual knowledges, but also of erotic-aesthetic pleasures. In community-based videos, the autobiographic-holistic mode for elaborating the specular scene might be understood as a performative act of self-love, a visual caress. Western cultures do indeed have their *ars erotica*; this specular scene provides one space in which to locate an erotic, participative corporeality that differs from the discursive-inscriptive corporeality of *scientia sexualis*.[94]

◆──

NOTES

A short version of this essay titled "Romancing the Self: Performing Masturbation in Sexual Self-Help Videos for Women" was presented at the third annual Visible Evidence conference, Carpenter Center, Harvard University, August 1995. My thanks to Henry Jenkins for comments on that conference paper.

1. After many years of community-based work, Dodson earned a doctorate from the Institute for the Advanced Study of Human Sexuality, where Carol Queen has also studied. The institute (formerly the National Sex Forum) began as a community-based sex education center, then developed into a degree-granting school. It has maintained a borderline position between university-based sexual science and community-based sex education and activism.

   Susie Bright's pseudonym is Susie Sexpert, under which she penned an advice column for *On Our Backs*. She was also the first editor of this lesbian sex magazine. As a neologism, *sexpert* functions on two levels: (1) it points to the exclusion of community-based educators from professionalized

discourses about sex, and (2) it seeks to qualify the speaker to her community precisely because of her position outside such discourses.

2. Typically, sexual self-help advice assumes that women have more problems than do men in learning to masturbate or practicing it successfully. Although sexual self-help videos do demonstrate male masturbation, they do not frame it as a problem in the same way; men are usually encouraged to use masturbation to practice prolonging erection.

3. Betty Dodson originally formulated this thesis in her book *Liberating Masturbation* (New York: Bodysex Designs, 1974), later reissued as *Selflove and Orgasm* (New York: Crown, 1983), then as *Sex for One* (New York: Crown, 1987). She reiterates the point in her video *SelfLoving: Video Portrait of a Women's Sexuality Seminar* (Dodson, 1991).

4. As critics have pointed out, sexology has been constructed around crises in heterosexuality; nevertheless, it has also considered a wide range of sexual practices. See Janice Irvine's *Disorders of Desire* (Philadelphia: Temple University Press, 1990); John

D'Emilio and Estelle B. Freedman, *Intimate Matters* (New York: Harper & Row, 1988).

5. Although this gendered mirror scene is not his focus, Robert Eberwein also studies sex instruction films and videos. See his essay "'One Finger on the Pause Button': Sex Instruction Videos," *Jump Cut* 41 (1997): 36–41.

6. Dodson, *Sex for One*, 140–42. Dodson's book addresses women and men, but the process she follows and the techniques she advocates were developed with women in mind.

7. Ibid., 88.

8. Lisa Cartwright, *Screening the Body: Tracing Medicine's Visual Culture* (Minneapolis: University of Minnesota Press, 1995), 4.

9. Ibid., 5.

10. Linda Williams, *Hard Core: Power, Pleasure, and the "Frenzy of the Visible"* (Berkeley: University of California Press, 1989); Cartwright, *Screening the Body*, 1–16; Giuliana Bruno, *Streetwalking on a Ruined Map: Cultural Theory and the City Films of Elvira Notari* (Princeton, N.J.: Princeton University Press, 1993), 58–76.

11. An example of such scientific, sexological imaging occurs in the film *Physiological Responses of the Sexually Stimulated Female in the Laboratory* (1974), made with Dr. Gorm Wagner, Institute of Medical Physiology, Copenhagen University; produced by Christian Hartkopp and Ebbe Preisler; and sponsored by Schering AG Berlin/Bergkamen. This film offers visual documentation of the "responses" explained by Masters and Johnson in their best-selling book *Human Sexual Response* (Boston: Little, Brown, 1966).

12. I am expanding on de Lauretis's "technology of gender" concept. See Teresa de Lauretis, *Technologies of Gender* (Bloomington: Indiana University Press, 1987). Similarly, discussing Notari's films, Bruno engages de Lauretis's project on gender and (self)-representation in *Streetwalking on a Ruined Map*, 234.

13. On the boundary of community-based education and university-based clinical study, Barbach's work is clearly feminist; she argues that women need sexual autonomy. This emphasis on autonomy from men is important to Dodson's advice, too. According to Dodson, Barbach based her women's sexuality groups on Dodson's sex workshops (Betty Dodson, personal interview, October 29, 1995). Because Barbach did not respond to my request for an interview, I can neither speak for her position nor corroborate Dodson's claim. See Lonnie Barbach, *For Yourself: The Fulfillment of Female Sexuality* (New York: Anchor/Doubleday, 1975), which includes one of Dodson's illustrations of the female genitals. My thanks to Betty Dodson for granting me an interview and sharing her work with me.

14. Interestingly, *Better Orgasms* (a British production) takes the bold step of suggesting that men can improve their self-loving experiences following the same exercises demonstrated for women: bathing and mirror gazing. However, the tape focuses problematically on a single performance: a black man poses before a full-length mirror, surveying his body. Whereas the female genitals are typically shown in a portrait shot, his penis remains concealed, which perhaps points to both the association of femininity with sexual display and the Western taboo against revealing the penis. For more on that taboo, see Peter Lehman, *Running Scared* (Philadelphia: Temple University Press, 1994).

15. De Lauretis, *Technologies of Gender*, 5.

16. Jenijoy La Belle, *Herself Beheld: The Literature of the Looking Glass* (Ithaca, N.Y.: Cornell University Press, 1988), 67.

17. Judith Butler, "Performative Acts and Gender Constitutions," in *Performing Feminisms: Feminist Critical Theory and Theater*, ed. Sue-Ellen Case (Baltimore: Johns Hopkins University Press, 1990), 272.

18. De Lauretis, *Technologies of Gender*, 18. I understand "heterosexual social contract" as a discursive inscription here, rather than as a judgment about the way practicing heterosexuals might understand or experience their sexual relationships, which clearly take place at the "local" level, too.

19. Joseph P. LoPiccolo and W. Charles Lobitz, "The Role of Masturbation in the Treatment of Orgasmic Dysfunction," *Archives of Sexual Behavior* 2, no. 2 (1972): 163–71.

20. Ibid., 167.

21. Although Masters and Johnson formulated this theory as a factor to explain male impotence, it has been widely adopted in sexual self-help to address female sexual dysfunction. This theory is especially interesting because it offers a model of (dysfunctional) spectatorship in which a voyeuristic position results in too much distance from the spectacle of one's own body (female or male).

22. William Masters and Virginia Johnson, *Human Sexual Inadequacy* (Boston: Little, Brown, 1970), 297.

23. For example, LoPiccolo and Lobitz recommend that the client compare her genitals to the illustrations in *Sexual Expression in Marriage* (1966). "The Role of Masturbation," 167.

24. In idealizing simultaneous orgasms, the (hetero)sexual self-help discourse shares with pornography the problem of reconciling male and female response cycles. See Cindy Patton, "Hegemony and Orgasm: Or the Instability of Heterosexual Pornography," *Screen* 30, no. 1–2 (winter–spring 1989): 100–112.

25. Raymond Williams, *The Sociology of Culture* (New York: Schocken, 1982), 44–48.

26. Focusing on the specular scene of female self-seduction, the professional sex instruction tapes to be considered here are *Advanced Sexual Techniques Vol. 2* (1992), *Better Orgasms* (1992), *The Female Orgasm* (1992), and *Becoming Orgasmic* (1993). With the exception of *Becoming Orgasmic* (Sinclair Institute), all of these tapes are part of series.

27. On "social actors," see Bill Nichols, *Representing Reality: Issues and Concepts in Documentary* (Bloomington: Indiana University Press, 1991).

28. Some of these pairings may include actual couples. Nevertheless, as Eberwein points out about the "Better Sex Video" series, their identities are "false (for the sake of privacy)." "'One Finger on the Pause Button.'"

29. See Thomas Waugh, "'Acting to Play Oneself': Notes on Performance in Documentary," in *Making Visible the Invisible: An Anthology of Original Essays on Film Acting*, ed. Carole Zucker (Metuchen, N.J.: Scarecrow, 1990), 64–91.

30. David James, "Hardcore: Cultural Resistance in the Postmodern," *Film Quarterly* 42, no. 2 (winter 1988–89): 31–39.

31. Ibid., 34.

32. See Boston Women's Health Book Collective, *Our Bodies, Ourselves* (New York: Simon & Schuster, 1973 [1971]); and *The New Our Bodies, Ourselves* (New York: Simon & Schuster, 1984). My thanks to Cindy Irvine and the Boston Women's Health Book Collective for lending me a copy of *Healthcaring* to study.

33. Julia Lesage, "The Political Aesthetics of the Feminist Documentary Film," *Quarterly Review of Film Studies* 3, no. 4 (fall 1978): 507–23; Julia Lesage, "Feminist Documentary: Aesthetics and Politics," in *"Show Us Life": Toward a History and Aesthetics of Committed Documentary*, ed. Thomas Waugh (Metuchen, N.J.: Scarecrow, 1984); E. Ann Kaplan, "Theories and Strategies of the Feminist Documentary," and Patricia Erens, "Women's Documentary Filmmaking: The Personal Is Political," both in *New Challenges for Documentary*, ed. Alan Rosenthal (Berkeley: University of California Press, 1988).

34. See Stephen Grosz and Bruce McAuley, "Self-Health and Healthcaring," *Camera Obscura* 7 (1981): 129–35. For additional political critique, see Marcia Rothenberg, "Good Vibes vs Preventive Medicine," *Jump Cut* 17 (April 1978). As for Johnston's critique of "women's cinema," her discussion of film's "language" involves issues of realism and/or illusionism that have been given ample space elsewhere. See Claire Johnston, "Women's Cinema as Counter-Cinema," in *Movies and Methods*, ed. Bill Nichols (Berkeley: University

of California Press, 1976), 208–17. Because my argument does not proceed from the same assumption of a monolithic film language, I consider these issues to be outside the range of this essay.

35. Grosz and McAuley, "Self-Health and Healthcaring," 131.

36. Ibid.

37. Lesage, "The Political Aesthetics," 513.

38. That Lesage, as a critic, shares the enthusiasm of the women in these feminist documentaries self-consciously shows both her political alignment with them and her objective to retain the phenomenological experience of (female) gazing during the self-exam, although she does not put it this way. As Dodson remarks in *Liberating Masturbation*, "Many women feel that their genitals are ugly, funny looking, disgusting, smelly, and not at all desirable—certainly not a beautiful part of their bodies" (18).

39. Grosz and McAuley, "Self-Health and Healthcaring," 131.

40. Nichols, *Representing Reality*, 120.

41. Annie Sprinkle's live act, "Public Cervix Announcement," reformulates cervical portraiture as performance art for mixed audiences. According to Terri Kapsalis, this act "professes the beauty of the cervix and the possible pleasures of specularity." Terri Kapsalis, "The Pelvic Exam as Performance: Power, Spectacle, and Gynecology" (Ph.D. diss., Northwestern University, 1994), 113. Kapsalis's dissertation has been published since this essay was written, as *Public Privates: Performing Gynecology from Both Ends of the Speculum* (Durham, N.C.: Duke University Press, 1997). She also discusses Grosz and McAuley's "Self-Health and Healthcaring." However, because my points were formulated before Kapsalis's book was published, I have left discussion of her position out of this revision.

42. See James, "Hardcore."

43. Johnston formulated this phrase—which has been so important to feminist film criticism—in relation to Dorothy Arzner's work. See Claire Johnston, ed., *The Work of Dorothy Arzner* (London: British Film Institute, 1975); see also Judith Mayne, "The Woman at the Keyhole: Women's Cinema and Feminist Criticism," in *Re-Vision: Essays in Feminist Film Criticism*, ed. Mary Ann Doane, Patricia Mellencamp, and Linda Williams (Frederick, Md.: University Publications of America and American Film Institute, 1984).

44. See Scott MacDonald, *A Critical Cinema 2* (Berkeley: University of California Press, 1988). As Severson tells MacDonald, "I had never seen any woman's vagina [vulva is focus in the film] except crotch shots in pornographic films and magazines or close-ups of birth films" (326). My thanks to Scott

MacDonald for suggesting I include this film in my analysis after I presented the first version of this paper at the Visible Evidence conference, 1995. For other discussions of *Near the Big Chakra*, see Richard Dyer's analysis in *Now You See It* (New York: Routledge, 1990). B. Ruby Rich identifies the film as "structural," using P. Adams Sitney's definition, yet she observes that critics refused to accept the film into this category, presumably due to their reactions to the content. B. Ruby Rich, "In the Name of Feminist Film Criticism," in *Issues in Feminist Film Criticism*, ed. Patricia Erens (Bloomington: Indiana University Press, 1990), 276.

45. MacDonald, *A Critical Cinema 2*, 320.
46. Cartwright, *Screening the Body*, 14.
47. Dyer, *Now You See It*, 182.
48. Ibid., 208.
49. Williams, *Hard Core*, 48.
50. Dyer, *Now You See It*, 183.
51. Consider the proliferation of sex manuals and the cultural significance of oral sex in the 1970s, as Linda Williams points out. For example, see Alex Comfort, *The Joy of Sex: A Gourmet Guide to Love Making* (New York: Simon & Schuster, 1972).
52. Dodson made this claim in an interview; see Carol Queen, "Sisters Are Doin' It for Themselves," *On Our Backs*, November–December 1992, 20–22, 38–41. Dodson's visual art is also discussed in Lisa Tickner, "The Body Politic: Female Sexuality and Women Artists since 1970," in *Framing Feminism: Art and the Women's Movement, 1970–1985*, ed. Rozsika Parker and Griselda Pollock (London: Pandora and Routledge & Kegan Paul, 1987), 263–76. In 1971, *Evergreen* magazine featured copies of these drawings and an interview with Dodson by Mary Phillips. In that interview, Dodson attempted to make a feminist case for explicit art: "If all erotic material is degrading to women, that really means that sex is degrading to women" (37). She was not only mounting an argument against censorship, she was challenging the nascent feminist antipornography movement. From that movement's perspective, Dodson was probably seen as toeing the sexist, leftist party line associated with explicit publications and magazines that featured female nudity for male viewing pleasure. Mary Phillips, "The Fine Art of Lovemaking," *Evergreen*, February 1971, 36–43, 73.
53. Dodson, *Liberating Masturbation*, 25.
54. On the "split beaver" convention as a fetish, see Kelly Dennis, "'Leave It to Beaver': The Object of Pornography," *Strategies* 6 (1991): 122–67. Dennis maintains that "the 'beaver shot,' in fact, constitutes in no small way the originary vanishing point of Western perspectival realism" (130). Although I think this is an extraordinary claim, I appreciate her

discussion of exhibitionism in relation to signifying practices and the way she challenges the idea that women are simply objectified in representation, as claimed by some theorists.

55. As a result of Dodson's steadfast position on the significance of erotic art for women, her relationship to the feminist movement was troubled; nevertheless, she always identified herself as a feminist. In the early 1970s, the editors of *Ms.* held back an essay they had solicited from her and significantly reduced it for publication at a later date. However, as Dodson explains, the response to the essay was so great that it prompted her to collect her ideas into a book, hence she created and self-published *Liberating Masturbation* (personal interview).
56. In *Near the Big Chakra*, only the performers' vulvas are shown—there is no sound and no other sense of participation by the performers.
57. Dodson, who appears nude along with her workshop participants, was sixty when this video was shot.
58. Similarly advancing the issue of female sexual agency in a humorous way, Canadian musicians made a video, *We're Talking Vulva*, in which band members were decked out in vulva outfits.
59. Sexpert tapes include *Nice Girls Don't Do It* (Daymond and Bell, 1989–90), featuring Shannon Bell explaining and performing female ejaculation in an avant-garde mode; *Sluts and Goddesses* (Beatty and Sprinkle, 1992), featuring Annie Sprinkle as narrator and performer, along with others; and the following House O'Chicks productions: *The Magic of Female Ejaculation* (1992) and *How to Find Your Goddess Spot* (1993), featuring House-mate Dorrie Lane, and *Masturbation Memoirs, Volume I* and *Masturbation Memoirs, Volume II* (1995), which include Sprinkle, Lane, Guadalupe San Francisco, and Scarlot Harlot. At the border of "artisanal" and "market-professional," *How to Female Ejaculate* (1992) was made by Debi Sundahl with resources generated from her then company, Blush Entertainment, which included *On Our Backs* and Fatale Video. Nevertheless, most of Fatale's videos exhibit an amateur-artisanal quality; moreover, *How to Female Ejaculate* features Sundahl as narrator and performer, along with Shannon Bell and Carol Queen. My thanks to Dorrie Lane for providing the House O'Chicks tapes.
60. Waugh, "'Acting to Play Oneself,'" 68.
61. Masters and Johnson, *Human Sexual Response*, 133.
62. Of course, the control exercised over image and performance is always shaped by social, cultural, and psychic forces beyond the conscious intent of the individual, whether the specific technology in use is film or a mir-

ror. My point is that this specular practice shares with the concept of a women's "countercinema" the aim to give women the opportunity to be image makers.

63. Noting the variety of people who participate in the field of "sexology," Janice Irvine observes, "This emphasis [on medical professionalism] is, however, at odds with the complex nature of this field in which scientists, pornographers, feminists, transvestites, therapists, and others uneasily share the podium." *Disorders of Desire*, 2.

64. The Forum films are still distributed for educational purposes by Multi-Focus, Inc. (formerly Multi-Media Resources), an auxiliary organization that was part of the Glide Methodist Church in San Francisco, through which members were active in sexual consciousness-raising projects. My thanks to Ted McIlvenna and the staff at the Institute for the Advanced Study of Human Sexuality for sharing information and preview copies of tapes.

65. Tom Gunning argues that early physiological films must be understood as a "cinema of attractions," based on exhibitionism rather than voyeurism. Tom Gunning, "The Cinema of Attraction," *Wide Angle* 8, nos. 3–4 (1986): 63–70. In *Screening the Body*, Cartwright advances the point that these films were implicated in a surveillant and analytic practice developed through scientific imaging.

66. See James, "Hardcore."

67. Another Forum film, *Self Loving* (1976), features discussion at a feminist sex consciousness-raising group.

68. As I have argued elsewhere, women's porn videos attempt to authenticate female orgasm through production practices, including the use of medium-long to long shots and longer takes than in conventional porn to show the orgasmic performances. These videos also claim to feature "real-life" lovers or actors who wanted to perform together, which does lend them an autobiographical appeal, at least in the marketing, even though the performances are representational. However, my comparison here to the professional sex instruction video applies mostly to heterosexual porn features by Royalle's Femme Productions, in which masturbation is also foreplay to coupling. For further analysis of form and style in women's pornography, see Eithne Johnson, "Excess and Ecstasy: Constructing Female Pleasure in Porn Movies," *Velvet Light Trap* 32 (fall 1993): 30–49.

69. Given that Heiman's name does not appear in the credits for the video, I assume she was not involved in that production. It should be noted that Mark Schoen, Ph.D., who produced this tape, is also president of Focus International, a sex instruction/self-help tape distribution company. According to sources at the Institute for the Advanced Study of Human Sexuality, its distribution outlet, Multi-Media Resources, changed its name to Multi-Focus, Inc., during negotiations to merge with Schoen's outfit. Though the deal fell through, both distributors retained the word *focus* in their names.

70. Barbach, *For Yourself*, 13.

71. Judith Butler, *Gender Trouble: Feminism and the Subversion of Identity* (New York: Routledge, 1990), 138.

72. Linda Williams reiterates Stephen Ziplow's list of porn genre conventions as of 1977, with masturbation—implicitly female masturbation—ranked number one. *Hard Core*, 126–27.

73. Sprinkle's performance art/porn has been extensively analyzed in Chris Straayer, "The Seduction of Boundaries: Feminist Fluidity in Annie Sprinkle's Art/Education/Sex," and Linda Williams, "A Provoking Agent: The Pornography and Performance Art of Annie Sprinkle," both in *Dirty Looks: Women, Pornography, Power*, ed. Pamela Church Gibson and Roma Gibson (London: British Film Institute, 1993); see also Terri Kapsalis, "Retooling the Speculum: Annie Sprinkle's 'Public Cervix Announcement,'" in *Public Privates*, 113–34.

74. Annie Sprinkle and Dorrie Lane subscribe to the idea of the "sacred prostitute." According to Shannon Bell, "In the modern period *scientia sexualis* absents the prostitute as anything other than a clinical subject; the postmodern discourse of prostitute recovers the prostitute's ancient role as erotic teacher." Theorizing the effects of prostitute performance art by women such as Annie Sprinkle and Scarlot Harlot, Bell argues that they "have produced a new social identity—the prostitute as sexual healer, goddess, teacher, political activist, and feminist—a new social identity which can trace its genealogy to the ancient sacred prostitute." Shannon Bell, *Reading, Writing, and Rewriting the Prostitute Body* (Bloomington: Indiana University Press, 1994), 13, 184.

75. Federation of Feminist Women's Health Centers, *A New View of a Woman's Body*, rev. ed. (West Hollywood, Calif.: Feminist Health Press, 1991), 47.

76. Exactly what constitutes the fluid—whether paraurethral or urine—ejaculated by women continues to be subject to debate.

77. Alice Kahn Ladas, Beverly Whipple, and John D. Perry, *The G Spot and Other Recent Discoveries about Human Sexuality* (New York: Holt, Rinehart & Winston, 1982).

78. That this tape predates the publication of *The G Spot* suggests that it was used in therapy sessions and educational settings at the time that the authors' controversial

research was under way. When the book was published it created quite a public sensation. According to Janice Irvine, the G-spot results also disrupted normal business for sexology, as it had focused on its conception of the clitoris since Masters and Johnson's research: "Not surprisingly, the major emphasis in the profession was less on the implications of the G-spot for female sexuality, and more on the spot's existence." *Disorders of Desire*, 165.

79. Leigh Gilmore, *Autobiographics: A Feminist Theory of Women's Self-Representation* (Ithaca, N.Y.: Cornell University Press, 1994), 239.

80. For more on Bell's argument, see Shannon Bell, "Feminist Ejaculations," in *The Hysterical Male*, ed. Arthur Kroker and Marilouise Kroker (New York: New World Perspectives, 1991), 154–69. Bell's claims about the politics of ejaculation raise many questions: What is to be gained from squirting in the privacy of one's domestic space? How can women's ejaculations take up public space? As an avid promoter of ejaculation, Bell has appeared not only in these videos but in a variety of publications, mostly alternative 'zines. For text and stills from *Nice Girls Don't Do It*, see *Fireweed* 37; for a photo spread with Daymond and Bell, see *Lickerish* 2 (summer 1994). My thanks to Christie Milliken for bringing these 'zines to my attention.

81. As I have argued elsewhere, *The Grafenberg Spot* (1985), a porn film by the Mitchell Brothers, sought to capitalize on the "G-spot" while also revealing it to be a faked performance in the closing credit sequence. Johnson, "Excess and Ecstasy." As her pseudonym implies, Annie Sprinkle earned notice for "golden shower" (urination) performances in porn films, but this act suggests a different type of female sexual pleasure.

82. Susan Faludi, "The Money Shot," *New Yorker*, October 30, 1995, 68.

83. Bruno, *Streetwalking on a Ruined Map*, 242.

84. Ibid., 6.

85. Ibid., 8.

86. For example, in the film *Fried Green Tomatoes* (Avnet, 1991), the protagonist, played by Kathy Bates, makes a humorous, yet dismissive, reference to a women's sexuality workshop she has attended in the process of improving herself.

87. Dodson, *Liberating Masturbation*, 25.

88. Eberwein, "'One Finger on the Pause Button,'" 14.

89. According to Judith Butler, "As a strategy of survival, gender is a performance with clearly punitive consequences." "Performative Acts," 273.

90. In her honor, the House O'Chicks video *Masturbation Memoirs, Volume I* includes footage of Elders's (in)famous speech.

91. Tickner, "The Body Politic," 266.

92. I am borrowing this distinction between "off/scene" or "ob/scene" and "on/scene" from Linda Williams. See her "Pornographies On/Scene or Diff'rent Strokes for Diff'rent Folks," in *Sex Exposed: Sexuality and the Pornography Debate*, ed. L. Segal and M. McIntosh (London: Virago, 1992), 233–65.

93. Dodson, *Liberating Masturbation*, 18.

94. I am developing this thesis in my dissertation. Chris Straayer also suggests further interrogation of Foucault's distinctions and scholarly acceptance of them. See her *Deviant Eyes, Deviant Bodies: Sexual Re-Orientations in Film and Video* (New York: Columbia University Press, 1996), specifically her analysis of *The Virgin Machine* in chap. 2.

VIVIAN SOBCHACK

[**12**] *Toward a Phenomenology of Nonfictional Film Experience*

The term *documentary* designates more than a cinematic *object*. Along with the obvious nomination of a film genre characterized historically by certain objective textual features, the term also—and more radically—designates a particular *subjective relation* to an objective cinematic or televisual text. In other words, documentary is less a *thing* than an *experience*—and the term names not only a cinematic object, but also the experienced "difference" and "sufficiency" of a specific mode of consciousness and identification with the cinematic image. More often than not, however, the particular set of sufficient conditions that constitute what I here will call *documentary consciousness* and the structure of the perceived differences we experience in our engagement with the cinematic image when we see a "documentary" have been subsumed and elided by that foundational theory of cinematic identification based on Lacanian psychoanalysis.[1] Assuming the spectator's regressive "misrecognition" of image for referent, and conflating the "irreal" and the "absent" in the privileged order of the Imaginary, this dominant theoretical model is highly problematic for inquiry into the structure of documentary identification. The reason is that it treats the spectator's phenomenological sense of the "real" as it relates to cinematic representation of *any* kind as essentially phantasmatic in nature and does not seem to allow for the structural differences that distinguish our engagement with cinematic images we regard as documentary representations of "the real" from those we regard as real representations of a "fiction."

In this essay, I want to introduce a *phenomenological* model of cinematic identification—one alternative to the psychoanalytic model in that it does not posit a single and totalizing structure of identification with the cinematic image, but rather differentiates among a variety of subjective spectatorial modes that coconstitute the cinematic object as the kind of cinematic object it is. This model ultimately offers a more dynamic, fluid, and concrete description of film viewing than does its psychoanalytic counter-part. Furthermore, it discloses rather than discounts what I should like to call—for its moral as well as affective connotations—the "charge of the real" that is so central to our experience of documentary cinema. This phenomenology of cinematic identification was published in 1969 by Belgian psychologist Jean-Pierre Meunier, in an undeservedly neglected (and untranslated) volume, *Les Structures de l'experience filmique: L'Identification filmique*.[2] Meunier's little book (only 140 pages in length) gives us, by his own admission, a rather schematic description of cinematic identification, but it also offers the premises and potential for an enriched understanding of how dynamic and fluid our engagement with the cinema really is.

Drawing upon both Maurice Merleau-Ponty's existential phenomenology of embodied perception and European *filmologie*, Meunier not only addresses the necessary conditions that make the cinematic image what it is in general, but also lays out the sufficient conditions that distinguish, in particular, three modes of spectatorial consciousness and their correspondent objective cinematic forms. Within this context, Meunier explicitly addresses our engagement with documentary film—differentiating it from, and seeing it as an intermediate form between, identification with the "home movie" (in French more aptly called the *film-souvenir*) and the fiction film. Thus, although here my primary focus is on documentary, understanding how Meunier differentiates all three modalities in which we subjectively "take up" what is objectively "given" as cinematic data is crucial to an appreciation of his specific description of our identification with—and of—the "documentary" as such.

A summary of Meunier's phenomenological description begins with the apodicticity (or "givenness") of the fact that the necessary condition of all films as they are experienced is their presentation of objects to perception that are not physically present to us except in their form as images. However, in a critical move that does not assume that the cinematic object is irreal merely because it is absent, Meunier points out that this fundamental absence characteristic of all cinematic representation is always *modified* by our personal and cultural knowledge of an object's existential position as it relates to our own. Our consciousness is neither disembodied nor impersonal nor "empty" when we go to the movies—which is to say that, from the first, our personal embodied existence and knowledge give our consciousness an existential "attitude" or "bias" toward what is given for us to see on the screen and how we will take it up. Within the context of an existential experience that is particular and situated, I do not engage the cinematic image of a dog or a dragon similarly even though both may be equivalent in their physical absence from me and in their presence as images in a particular work I engage as a fiction.[3] Furthermore, if the image of a dog happens to be an image of *my* dog, I will not engage its image in the same way that I engage the image of "Lassie," a dog with which I have romped only cinematically, in a fiction, or in the same way I engage the image of "Fala" or "Checkers" as each lolls at the feet of an actual past president of the United States in a documentary newsreel.[4]

The attitude of our consciousness toward the cinematic object simultaneously positions us as existential subjects in relation to the screen and posits the existential status of what we see there in relation to what we have experienced and know of the life-world we inhabit. At one end of the spectrum of identification is the home movie or *film-souvenir* in which we, our families, our dogs, our friends, the places we've been, the things we've done are given to us as images on the screen. According to Meunier, we take these images up as existentially and specifically known to us already—as referring to beings and things and events that exist now or once existed "elsewhere" than solely on the screen. In the spectrum's "intermediate" position is the documentary, which entails not only our existential and cultural knowledge, but also our partial *lack* of it—a lack that modifies the nature of our identification with the image. That is, as we watch images of Fala or John F. Kennedy or the Gulf War, aspects of what we see are taken up by us as unknown in their existential specificity, yet because we have some general cultural knowledge of them, their past or present existence is posited by us nonetheless—if, however, always in a way qualified by our lack of personal knowledge. Finally, at the other end of the experiential spectrum from the *film-souvenir,* Meunier marks our engagement with the fiction film. In the mode of fictional identification, we take up the cinematic object as unknown to us in its specificity. I know *my* dog in the home movie, and I know *the* dog Fala as an existential being in a documentary, but I know the character *Lassie* only from—and in—her screen presence in a narrative. In the case of fiction, according to Meunier, we become increasingly screen dependent for specific knowledge of what we see, and we tend to bracket, rather than to posit, the "real" existence of what we see there. Thus, in fictional consciousness, the cinematic object is perceived as "irreal" (like Lassie) or "imaginary" (like a dragon) rather than "absent" or "elsewhere." Unlike our experience with the home movie or the documentary, Meunier suggests, the images of fiction are experienced as *directly* given to us, and they exist not "elsewhere," but "here" in the virtual world that is "there" before us.

For Meunier, these subjective modifications of objective cinematic "givens" are actualized by the spectator in a progressive and increasingly intense form of attention to the screen that, in its engagement with the cinematic "data," coconstitutes an increasingly autonomous reality differentiated from the reality of the spectator's life-world and existing only in its mediated presence to perception. Furthermore, this progressively intense and subjective form of attention to the screen dynamically coconstitutes with the objective cinematic "data" the particular form or genre of film we perceive: *film-souvenir,* documentary, or fiction.

In sum, Meunier's phenomenology of cinematic identification demonstrates that the more dependent we are on the screen for *specific* knowledge of what we see in the film experience, the less likely we are to see beyond the screen's boundaries and back into our own life-world. Indeed, Meunier suggests that the more the viewer's attention is focused *on*—rather than *through*—the screen object, the more the matter of this object ceases to be generalized and the more it becomes considered in its specificity— that is, in itself rather than for what it evokes. He notes that our attention to screen objects in the *film-souvenir* is far less focused than our attention to screen objects in the documentary—whereas our attention is most focused on screen objects in the fiction film. However, this amplified subjective attention to the screen and the correspondent increasing specificity of the cinematic object as we move from *film-souvenir* to fiction comes with an increasing and parallel reduction in the constitutive activity of spectatorial consciousness. Meunier points out that, in the experience of the *film-souvenir,* consciousness is engaged in a highly constitutive activity, the intentional objective of which is less the apprehension of the specific film image than the general recovery of the memory of a whole person or event.[5] Experience of the documentary, however, is only partially constitutive in structure—for although, as with the *film-souvenir,* our intentional objective is achieving a general recovery of persons and events, unlike with the *film-souvenir,* our constitutive activity is modified and undercut by our only partial existential knowledge of the screen object. Thus, in the documentary experience, our consciousness is more necessarily tied to and determined by the specificity of the images given on the screen and the increased attention that must be paid them. In the experience of the fiction film, we have an even greater need than with the documentary to focus on and "intend" the screen in order to gain specific knowledge and enjoy a significant experience. This increased attention leads to what Meunier describes as a sort of "submission" to the particularity of the singular objects and events on the screen—seen as singular in that they gain their primary meaning from their particular relations to each other rather than from their general relations to known objects and events in our life-world. (In this sense, given the photographic basis of cinema, I apprehend the existential dog that acts as Lassie much more generally than I do Lassie, the irreal dog-character, whom I know only through her particular actions and relations as I see them on-screen in this particular narrative.)

As our attention to the screen progressively increases in our engagement with the *film-souvenir,* the documentary, and the fiction film, Meunier suggests that the status of screen objects also changes. Screen objects gain an increasingly intensified presence as consciousness shifts from a primarily constitutive engagement with the film image to a primarily nonconstitutive and "submissive" engagement. The presence of screen objects comprehended within a generalized form of attention whose horizon includes but extends spatially and temporally beyond the screen, as is the case with the *film-souvenir* and, more mediately, the documentary, is less intense than the presence of screen objects comprehended within a narrowed and particularized form of attention whose horizon is nearly isomorphic with the screen, as is the case with fiction. Insofar as the viewer depends to some degree upon scrutinizing screen objects for knowledge about them, one might say not only that screen objects are increasingly focalized in the move from *film-souvenir* to documentary to fiction, but also that this increased focalization produces them as fetish objects. What comes to mind here as an intriguing example are the various images of the spilled Burger King milkshake in Errol Morris's documentary, *The Thin Blue Line.* Certainly the abstraction of the object by virtue of the close-up does much to constitute this fetishization, but the close-up alone is not sufficient to account for the experiential intensity of our engagement, which, if we follow Meunier, arises in part from the move of consciousness into a structure of attention more characteristic of our hermeneutic engagement with fiction than of our engagement with documentary.

Meunier goes on to describe a number of important variations on our identification with the fiction film dependent upon whether it is perceived as "realist" or presents a world that seems completely autonomous from the spectator's perceived reality. Although limitations of space prevent elaboration of these distinctions, given our focus here on documentary consciousness, it is important to note Meunier's discussion of how filmic consciousness "takes up" the realist fiction film's verisimilitude and indexicality to the spectator's life-world as a generalized and undifferentiated referentiality that exists as an existential echo within the specificity of the autonomous and irreal fiction. Leaves on trees, cityscapes, roads, crowds of people on a street, and dogs who are not Lassie—these are existentially known objects that, on the screen, do not usually solicit the spectator's close scrutiny even as they referentially ground the fiction as "realist." Existentially known, they are apprehended generally while the spectator's consciousness devotes primary attention to the unknown specificities foregrounded by the fiction. In some cases, however, this existential echo can be raised to a shout and fictional consciousness ruptured. Previously, I have written about the death of a rabbit in Jean Renoir's *Rules of the Game* and how the generalized referentiality of the fauna in that film is abruptly transformed by the rabbit's death leap as it is shot, the viewer's extratextual knowledge suddenly positing the rabbit's existence beyond the frame of the fiction into the documentary space of an "elsewhere" where it lived its rabbit life.[6] Indeed, if we think about it, this transformation of fictional consciousness occurs quite often, if less dramatically, in those moments in realist fiction when our consciousness suddenly diverts its primary attention from the specific fictional characters and events to the film's general referentiality to the existential world. Here we might think of how, following the specificity of a fictional character as she walks on a crowded city street, we are drawn on occasion to shift our primary attention from this "character" to those "people" surrounding her to wonder if they know they're in a movie. As we scrutinize their faces for signs of awareness, they no longer are quite "generalized" in status, but they also do not yield up the very specific knowledge afforded us by fictional characters. They become ambiguous—not directly present and "given" to us as is the film's heroine. Thus, for a moment, in the midst of a fiction, we find ourselves in a mode of documentary consciousness: looking both *at* and *through* the screen, dependent upon it for knowledge, but also aware of an excess of existence not contained by it.

Meunier's phenomenology of cinematic identification ultimately challenges both our habit of thinking about home movies, documentaries, and fiction films as completely discrete categories or fixed objects and our tendency to describe cinematic identification as stable enough to maintain a single structuration throughout even a single film experience. Indeed, perhaps the most important of Meunier's conclusions is that the structural form of cinematic identification does not depend necessarily (even if it does sufficiently) on the "type" of film objectively unfolding on the screen. However each type of film may *objectively* and actively solicit our spectatorial consciousness, in the end, we will actively and *subjectively* "take up" the film and position its existence and status *as the kind of film object it is,* based on a personal and cultural knowledge less deliberate than lived. Thus, as I will elaborate below, a fiction can be experienced as a home movie or documentary, a documentary as a home movie or fiction, a home movie as a documentary or fiction. Existential knowledge and forms of attention structure cinematic identification with—and of—the cinematic object. In this regard, given my focus on nonfiction film, I want to explore further the specific structures of cinematic identification that coconstitute our experience of the *film-souvenir* and the documentary.

If we understand cinematic identification as a general comportment and attentive attitude toward the screen that is informed by personal and cultural knowledge, then one woman's irreal situation comedy may be another's home movie. Reminiscing on *Entertainment This Week* about *Laverne & Shirley*, series actress Cindy Williams talked about watching her patently fictional sitcom in syndicated reruns and seeing it as "a diary of my life—when you *[sic]* can remember what went on."[7] For Meunier, the structure of identification in the home-movie attitude is essentially one of *evocation*. That is, the function of the *film-souvenir* for its viewer is incantatory and procurative, and its images are taken up as an intermediary, mnemonic, and channeling device *through* which the viewer evokes and identifies not with the mimetic image, but with an absent person or past event. As suggested earlier, this means that the spectator's identification with—and of—the *film-souvenir* consists essentially of subjectively mobilizing intuitive, synthetic, and personal knowledge of the viewed person or event in a *constitutive actualization* enabled by the objectively specific images on the screen (my son Christopher crawling toward the camera, my cat in the backyard of a house I haven't lived in for more than twenty years, and so on). These objectively specific images, however, are subjectively *generalized* by the spectator in a vain effort to evoke presence—that is, the *whole ensemble* of a well-known person's gestures and comportment or of temporal events surrounding those depicted on the screen. (However unfulfilled it may be, my desire is to evoke my son as he was in his existence as a baby, not just as he was in this one moment of crawling toward the camera; similarly, I want to reexperience his first birthday party not only in the fragmented space and moments imaged specifically before me, but as a whole coherent and affective event merely suggested by the balloons and cake in the image.) Hence Cindy Williams's somewhat plaintive "if you can remember what went on." Thus, even as they retain the specificity from which their motivational power emerges, the images of the *film-souvenir* are not apprehended *for* themselves, but rather *as* the catalyst to a primarily constitutive and generalizing activity that transcends their specificity in an attempt to call up and reactivate the "real" and "whole" person or event that is (or was) elsewhere and at some other time. I do not "intend" the specific image of my son crawling toward the camera, and thus I do not scrutinize the image intensely. Rather, I see my son *through* the image—his smile evoking an ensemble of gestures and looks in excess of the image's specificity, evoking the person I know whose existence and comportment form a general whole that I try to re-member from this image fragment of him. Similarly, the image fragments of the backyard of the house I once lived in do not provoke intense scrutiny, but rather evoke a coherent, eventful, and lived space I wish to recall in excess of what is given me on the screen.[8]

However, while the specific images of our own home movies do not serve as the "end" or intentional object of our perceptual activity (which desires the reactivation of the whole person or event), and thus we do not watch them intently, we nonetheless watch them discretely—with what Meunier calls a "longitudinal consciousness." Viewing our own home movies, we do not usually retrospect on the film's past screen images and scenes, nor do we usually project forward to future ones so as to create meaning and value from a syntagmatic enchaining. That is, the temporal activity of retention and protention that we perform in relation to images and scenes in a fiction film and by which they gain coherence is, in the *film-souvenir* attitude, subordinated to the *present* presence of each set of images and scenes that both catalyze our general memory of existentially known persons and events and exist as fragments of a whole experience we can never fully re-member. This structure of identification in which we are invested primarily in the present scene may well explain why the *film-souvenir* is usually not constructed as narrative (which demands a specific form of attention that gathers up past images to project and orient them ahead toward the future). Rather, the *film-souvenir* tends to be a chronicle of temporal fragments that exists for us as a marker of experience and has little to do with causality.

The piecemeal specificity of the objective fragments of the *film-souvenir* set against our subjective activity of attempting to constitute the whole ensemble of evoked experience as a coherence creates an affective charge effected less by the re-presentation of the real experience than by its irrevocable loss. Watching our own home movies, our intentional objective is to rejoin (and here the word *remember* affectively hyphenates) the real event or person or our real selves "elsewhere" and in other times. The impossibility of realizing this objective, however, leads to what Meunier calls an "empty sympathy"—what we call "nostalgia"—in relation to the screen image. (This is why the French *film-souvenir* seems so much more precise a nomination than *home movie*.) In sum, our relation to the screen image and its function is much the same as our mnemonic relation to seashells we brought home summers ago from a Mediterranean beach.

Given the primarily constitutive activity of consciousness and the mode of identification both solicited by and constituted as the *film-souvenir*, it becomes clear why it is often boring to watch other people's home movies insofar as we are unfamiliar with their cinematic objects and have never experienced their evoked events. For us, the image fragments are neither catalytic nor mnemonic; we neither engage in the constitutive activity of re-membering nor feel the irrevocable loss of an "original" experience that, through its cinematic evocation, creates in us the "empty sympathy" that is nostalgic pleasure. Thus one woman's poignant home movie, at least when it is not also a situation comedy, is another woman's unsatisfying documentary.

For Meunier, the intentional objective of documentary consciousness is *comprehension,* not evocation. In the documentary experience, the spectator engages in a mode that Meunier calls "apprenticeship" to the film object. That is, identification in the documentary experience involves a *process of learning* that occurs *contemporaneously* with viewing the film. Nonetheless, given the cultural knowledge we have of our life-world, which includes the already posited existence of people and events we know (if only through mediation of some type), we still take up the objective specificity of a particular documentary image as a *general* form. As with the *film-souvenir,* we not only posit the existence "elsewhere" and at some "other time" of the people and events we see on the screen, we also—although to a certain and lesser degree—perceive their specificity as part of a more general style of being or of a more expansive occurrence. However, unlike our experience of the *film-souvenir,* we do not usually use the documentary image as incantatory, nor do we see *through* it to the specific comportment or structure of a whole, personally remembered person or event. (Nonetheless, this use of the documentary image is still possible—for, as Meunier points out, what finally determines the specific mode of cinematic identification is the personal situation of each individual viewer in relation to a given film. Many viewers of *Berkeley in the Sixties,* for example, may have identified with it less as a documentary than as a *film-souvenir.*) What is essential to the experience of documentary, as such, is that however much our cultural knowledge informs us that who and what we see on the screen are partial aspects of a "real" and more general existential ensemble, insofar as we do not *ourselves* have existential experience of the persons or events we see on the screen, our *specific* knowledge of these persons and events is contemporaneous with our viewing of the film. Even though we may already have known what Hitler looked like and did from photographs, books, and other films, we do not use the images of *Triumph of the Will* as a channel *through* which we evoke a larger personal memory of Hitler at Nuremberg. Rather, we *learn* Hitler as we watch the film—but to do so we must pay more attention to the screen images than we would to our own (although not Eva Braun's) home movies.

To some degree, then, our identification with documentary film involves the "longitudinal consciousness" that Meunier attributes to our primary engagement with the *film-souvenir*, in which our intentional object is not the specificity of the image in itself, but the whole ensemble that the person or event it represents evokes. Nonetheless, given our lack of prior personal experience of the documentary's subjects and, thus, our correspondingly greater reliance on the screen for perceptual data and knowledge, our identification with documentary also involves some degree of what Meunier calls the "lateral consciousness" that structures our identification with the fiction film.

Lateral consciousness, for Meunier, occurs in the present as it relates to past and future in the activity and structure of retention and protention. Past images are accumulated and inform present meanings that intentionally direct consciousness toward the revelation and significance of future outcomes. Lateral consciousness is thus structured as a temporal progression that usually entails causal logic as well as teleological movement. Documentary identification engages both longitudinal and lateral consciousness—hence, for Meunier, its intermediary position between the *film-souvenir* and the fiction film. Each objective image of a person or event in the documentary is perceived as a specific example or insight into a general comportment or broader occurrence than is seen in the film. In this sense, we are engaged with the image longitudinally, using it in the present to evoke and generalize something more—although not necessarily something future. In this way, as with the *film-souvenir*, our activity is constitutive. However, because we lack personal knowledge of that more general comportment or broader occurrence, we are dependent upon the progression and accumulation of examples and illustrations specified by the images so we may achieve an increasingly general comprehension of them. Unlike the *film-souvenir*, the documentary image is not transcended, but provides the primary basis of our information. In this sense—and despite some degree of constitutive activity—we must, to use Meunier's term, also "submit" to the screen and pay it more attention.

Each documentary image, then, possesses a general existential reality presented across multiple specific views. The specific information in each image is retained and integrated with subsequent images to form our cumulative knowledge of that general reality we know exists or has existed "elsewhere" in our life-world. Thus documentary consciousness is structured as a particular temporal relation between the present and the past. Its activity is both constitutive and retrospective, but it is not necessarily directed toward a future or a specific teleological end. In this sense, lateral consciousness in the documentary experience is only partial. It is "forestalled" to some degree by the longitudinal consciousness that structures the temporal relation we have to the *film-souvenir*. Thus documentary experience can be differentiated in structure from that of the *film-souvenir* (in which a primarily longitudinal consciousness tarries in the present and relates to the specific images before it as a general medium for constitutive reverie) or of the fiction film (in which a primarily lateral consciousness presently re-members the images past with an eye to imaginary future outcomes and relates to the specific images before it in their very specificity).

For Meunier, in the "apprenticeship" learning experience that structures documentary identification, our relation to the filmed person or event remains a relation of otherness and exteriority. In the home-movie experience, I don't have to learn anything about my son from the images. Indeed, I know more of him than the images show me. I don't have to *work* at comprehending him (although I do have to work at evoking him). With the documentary, however, the labor involved in the cumulative comprehension of the person in general or the event in general creates a distance between me and the image of the person or event. Given my dependence upon it for information, the screen is less transparent than it is for me in the home movie—and, by virtue of the increased attention I must pay them so as to comprehend them specifically and accumulate them as a generality, images in the documentary experience gain in autonomy and intensity. Nonetheless, in that I have, from the first, posited the existence of what these images represent and am thus engaged in some degree of constitutive and evocative activity, the documentary image is not completely autonomous, but still connected to and intermediary between myself and what I perceive to be a "real" unknown person or event "in general."

Again, we must remind ourselves that a "documentary" is not a thing, but a subjective relationship to a cinematic object. It is the viewer's consciousness that finally determines what kind of cinematic object it is. In the same way that Cindy Williams can watch *Laverne & Shirley* as a home movie, so we can watch a documentary as a fiction. Presuming a lack of certain cultural knowledges—including those of stylistic cinematic conventions, which are themselves never a guarantor, but only a solicitation, of an image's existential status—as well as a lack of personal experience of what is seen on the screen, there would be no necessary existential connection made between what we see on the screen and what we know of our lifeworld. We would have no basis for positing the cinematic object's existence rather than bracketing it and putting the nature of its existence out of play. As in fiction, all our specific information would come from the screen. Our consciousness would tend to be structured laterally, and screen images would increase in autonomy with the intensity of our attention.

Meunier's elaboration of cinematic identification, in length as well as in progression, tends to privilege experience of the fiction film and its various modes. Documentary identification is seen as an intermediate form between the evocative *film-souvenir* and the narrative fiction. It seems to me, however, that we can recognize the value of Meunier's descriptions and differentiations without embracing the hierarchical aspects of his model. (Indeed, Meunier himself states that cinematic identification is more fluid and less linear than his own brief schematic and progressive description would imply.) Thus we should foreground how often the fiction film experience for us is interrupted by a shift in the structure of our identification to that of identification with the *film-souvenir* or documentary.

Consider, for example, how our bracketing of existence stops and how our temporal relation to the image becomes forestalled and "longitudinal" when in a fiction film we see a known city street or a specific landscape in which we have vacationed. In those moments, the image tends to lose its specificity and becomes evocative, incantatory. The fiction, insofar as we are residually focused on it, is perceived as taking place in our home movie. Consider also how, even more often, watching a fiction film such as *Cleopatra,* we cease to bracket the existence of the performers and suddenly find ourselves watching not Cleopatra but Elizabeth Taylor kiss not Antony but Richard Burton. Although we certainly know Antony and Cleopatra less than we do Burton and Taylor, and should therefore need the more specific information the screen gives us about their historic romance, our cultural knowledge of the Burton/Taylor off-screen romance puts us in a different and less focused relation to the specific images on the screen. We are distanced from the historically based characters and find ourselves not only positing the existence of the "real" performers but also — because we don't have personal knowledge of the latter — "learning" them from the screen, scrutinizing and accumulating images of their embrace less with an eye to their future as historical characters than with an eye to our comprehension of their actual romance. We are, in this instance, in a mode of documentary identification. I might point also to all those moments in fiction films when boredom dilutes our attention to the specificity of the image and our horizon expands beyond what was an autonomous irreality so that we watch actors rather than characters, sets and locations rather than a world, scenes and histrionics rather than significant events and emotions. Again, the structure of temporal relationship that marks identification with the fiction is ruptured and forestalled, and we find ourselves attending to the screen with a documentary rather than fictional consciousness.[9]

In sum, cinematic identification is not only differentiated in modality, it is radically coconstitutive of the film experience. The film that is objectively given to the viewer may be subjectively taken up in a variety of ways, not only in its entirety, but also in its parts. The form of our identification with specific cinematic objects may be solicited, but it is never determined a priori. Indeed, our identification is certainly as fluid, dynamic, and idiosyncratic as it is fixed and conventional. One viewer's fiction may be another's *film-souvenir*; one viewer's documentary, another's fiction. And each viewer may—and probably does—identify with the cinematic object in each of these modalities many times over during a given film experience, only to fix one as dominant by its end. Although the brevity of Meunier's phenomenology lends it a certain schematic quality, his differentiated descriptions of the various temporal and spatial relations we have with the screen open up the possibilities for acknowledging and describing even more closely and with greater nuance the ways in which we engage cinematic existence and invest dynamically in screen images. In sum, a phenomenological model of cinematic identification restores the "charge of the real" to the film experience. It affirms what we know in experience: that not all images are taken up as imaginary or phantasmatic and that the spectator is an active agent in constituting what counts as memory, fiction, or document.

◆──

NOTES

1. I will be using the notion of "engagement" here to stress the active relationship of film spectator and film that involves not only perception and cognition but also affect and value. Given common usage in the field of media studies, insofar as words such as *perception* and *apprehension* tend to be reduced to and naturalized as scientific and cognitive operations, they don't convey the overarching activity of spectator-film relations quite so well as *engagement*.

2. Jean-Pierre Meunier, *Les Structures de l'experience filmique: L'Identification filmique* (Louvain: Librarie Universitaire, 1969).

3. In a photographically based cinematic fiction, I may "take up" both the dog and the dragon as equivalent in their status as "characters," but my own existential and extratextual knowledge makes me also aware that their ontological status is quite different: a "real" existing dog "acts" as the "character," whereas the dragon is an "irreal" construction that "exists" only in and for the film. (Outside the film, it is merely a mechanical model, or an inhabited dragon suit, and so on.)

4. Fala was Franklin D. Roosevelt's Scottie; Checkers was Richard M. Nixon's spaniel.

5. The term *intentional* here relates to the primary phenomenological concept of "intentionality," which posits the irreducible rela-

tion of consciousness to its objects. That is, consciousness is never empty and "in itself"; it always has an object. Furthermore, intentionality is always directed in existence, even if its direction is reversible. That is, in that it always has an object, consciousness is always directed either toward that object or reflexively toward its own activity.

6. Vivian Sobchack, "Inscribing Ethical Space: 10 Propositions on Death, Representation and Documentary," *Quarterly Review of Film Studies* 9, no. 4 (fall 1984): 283–300; and Vivian Sobchack, "On the Death of a Rabbit in Fictional Space: Extratextual Knowledge and Documentary Consciousness," in *Documenting Fictions* (Minneapolis: University of Minnesota Press, forthcoming).

7. Cindy Williams, interviewed on *Entertainment This Week*, NBC, March 7, 1993.

8. Meunier's phenomenologic of this discontinuity in the *film-souvenir* between the image given in its specificity and the more general image we wish to re-member bears some relation to Gilles Deleuze's distinction between the "virtual image" and the "recollection image," which he discusses throughout *Cinema 2: The Time Image*, trans. Hugh Tomlinson and Robert Galeta (Minneapolis: University of Minnesota Press, 1989).

9. A slightly different, but more recent, example occurs in the film *Contact* (Robert Zemeckis,

1997), a work of science fiction that presents several presidential commentaries on a fictitious action (the discovery of a message sent by extraterrestrials) through digitally inserted footage from actual presidential news conferences in which President Clinton was remarking on the discovery of meteorites from Mars. It is clear that the filmmaker is using this footage of a current president speaking actual words that, as edited, "apply" to the fiction to *strengthen* the fantasy, supposedly giving it both veracity and verisimilitude. The great irony, however, given our extratextual knowledge of the figure and voice of President Clinton (and, in some instances, what he really was talking about), is that this footage leads to a documentary mode of engagement and *weakens* the high intensity of our attention to the specifics of the fiction—that is, those characters, things, events we can know only through close attention to the screen. Extratextual knowledge moves us into a more diffuse and less intense state of attention with the image proper and starts us considering the context in which the president's comments were actually made. (Whether we remember that context or not is irrelevant, for we are pretty sure there *is* an extratextual context and that the president did not purposefully take a supporting role in the fiction.)

JAMES M. MORAN

[**13**] *A Bone of Contention:*
Documenting the Prehistoric Subject

In *Letter from Siberia* (1957), an experimental documentary notable for its innovations, Chris Marker's imagination fuses with historical reality to create a text whose representations of the past are necessarily contingent upon techniques available to the filmic medium. For example, in one revealing sequence, which documents Siberia's prehistory as home for the woolly mammoth, Marker resorts to blatantly crude animation for the depiction of these animals, now extinct, unavailable as living profilmic referents, and therefore incapable of photographic reproduction. The comic inflection of the sequence, while it may subvert a definition of documentary as a sober discourse, nevertheless implies that, in the absence of automatically, photochemically, or electronically recorded indexes whose supposed objectivity lends documentary its authority, the animated icon "must do" in their place, its creative manipulations and subjective inaccuracies taken lightly. Such traces of animation's second-rate status in relation to cinematography leave their imprints on documentary theory today.

Marker further problematizes the prehistoric subject by animating ancient hunters representing mammoths in cave drawings. Not only extinct beasts but man himself predates the invention of the camera, and so, too, our ancestors must be rendered pictorially. These impediments to photographic reproduction suggest that prehistory can be reconceived as twin epochs raising problems for any modern historiographic project. The first, marked by an evolutionary break, is the period prior to the appearance of man, an era that escapes the authoritative appeals of ethical proof. The second, marked by a technological break, is the period prior to the appearance of the photographic apparatus, an era that escapes the scientific appeals of indexical proof. Documentary, most often defined as a union of human eye and camera eye, must therefore find the practice of "recording" prehistory a challenge, if not theoretically impossible.

By drawing our attention to the impressionistic evidence of cave drawings, Marker raises the specter of their use value and a pivotal problem of documentary representation. In what ways did the reproduction of a woolly mammoth function for prehistoric men? Did they reference the beast as documentary, as an index of the historical world, as evidence of its existence? Or did they re-create it as fiction, as an icon of an imaginary world, as evidence of their aesthetic ability? Set in opposition, these questions, themselves mammoth and left entirely to speculation, nevertheless identify a fundamental bipolarity structuring critical discourse about documentary, a practice registering the tension between an imperative to record reality and a desire to re-create it.

The status of cave art, of course, is also the status of painting, torn between two ambitions Bazin has described as "one, primarily aesthetic, namely the expression of spiritual reality wherein the symbol transcended its model; the other, purely psychological, namely the duplication of the world outside."[1] Here, the cinema's greatest disciple of art as a mode of preservation would seem, by his second definition, to support the cave drawing as a valid historical document. Describing the origin of the plastic arts as motivated by a "mummy complex" whose function transforms the representation of life into its preservation, Bazin connects the mimetic drives of painting to a fundamental desire of documentary to cheat death, stop time, and restore loss.[2]

The parallels between painting and documentary, however, cannot be sustained within Bazin's critical framework. The invention of the camera, he concludes, marks an epistemic break in the history of the image, an ontological divide reifying photography as unparalleled in its claims as a tool of preservation, and thus of documentary. Because the camera apparatus records the presence of the referent at the moment of production, thus serving as an unmanipulated index of its existence, the photograph's authority lies in the properties the painted icon is said to lack: objectivity, authenticity, and credibility. In Bazin's evolutionary theory of art, whose timeline curiously and inevitably cannibalizes itself as a cyclical myth, the plastic arts become the ersatz of photography, which liberates painting from its subaltern mimetic functions. Thus, by essentializing the photographic image as an intrinsic trace of the "real," Bazin's description of documentary practice carries the prescriptive baggage that his insistence upon ontology packs with it.

Although disputed by scholars of fictional cinema, Bazin's argument in favor of the photographic index over all other signifying strategies has had an immeasurable influence upon documentary theory, which for the most part has presumed that, like neorealist cinema, documentary practice should attend only to subject matter consonant with the camera's capacity as a recorder of life, of what lies before us, of presence. What relation, then, does documentary have to death, of what lies behind us, of absence? Where is its capacity to record prehistory, which escapes photographic signification? How can digital technologies, whose representations are allied as much with pictorialism as with photorealism, reanimate the prehistoric subject and, in the process, instate themselves as instruments of a valid documentary strategy? To answer these questions, we need first summarize documentary's relation to history, photography, and science as typically posited in critical discourse.

▶ ————————————————————————————————

Documentary: History, Photography, and Science

With his typically pithy insight, Roland Barthes has noted that "the same century invented History and Photography."[3] To this pair we might add documentary, whose credibility depends upon the authenticity of the former and the objectivity of the latter. Together, this trinity has stood indivisible in conceptions of documentary as a cinematic means with historiographic ends, or, as Paula Rabinowitz puts it, as a mode of writing history in film: "Documentary is usually a reconstruction—a reenactment of another time or place for a different audience—a graphing of history, in and through the cinematic image and taped sound, onto the present."[4]

Often functioning as historical evidence itself, the documentary wishes to ensure its authenticity by grounding its claims in the historical world in order to avoid the fictional displacements precipitated by the whimsies of human memory.[5] As Bill Nichols asserts, the fundamental difference between expectations prompted by documentary and those prompted by narrative fiction lies in the former's assumption that the profilmic event and the historical referent "are taken to be congruent with one another."[6] Philip Rosen further distinguishes typical discourses of historiography, whose issues arise from the subject's absence from a past reality, from typical discourses of documentary cinema, whose issues arise from the subject's presence in a present reality.[7] When this subject is explicitly identified by Nichols as the filmmaker, whose agency supposedly transports the spectator into the historical world,[8] he reconfirms the "mythical definition" of denotation that insists, as Barthes notes, *the photographer had to be there,*[9] fulfilling the expectation of documentary that its sounds and images will bear an indexical relation to the world. Rosen adds that the automatic effects of the photographic apparatus cannot be disentangled from its presence on the scene: "In cinema, indexicality designates the presence of camera and sound-recording machinery at the profilmic event, which, in turn, guarantees that the profilmic really did exist in the past."[10]

In summarizing these positions, a sanctioned documentary practice would seem to require the presence of man and camera, of human and mechanical eye—witnesses to the referent's contemporaneous existence.[11] According to this view, the credibility of photorealism depends, paradoxically, upon the separation of human eye from camera lens; that is, historical meaning, attributed to human intervention (perception, order, subjective understanding), must be isolated from historical authenticity, attributed to human withdrawal (data, recording, objective representation). As Bazin dictates, between the originating object and its reproduction there can intervene only "the instrumentality of a nonliving agent" (photography).[12]

This celebration of the camera mechanism's automatism subscribes, in the final determination, to a notion of the cinematic apparatus as a tool of scientific inscription. As opposed to animation, a plastic art thought capable only of creating an illusion of life, documentary, like science, would like to claim "real life" as its referent, and authorizes that claim simply by an appeal to its own reproductive technologies. Science and documentary, according to this perspective, share the same configuration and the same epistemological goals: a union of man and technology in search of a "truth" about the historical world. When so grounded within the field of science, the art of cinematography becomes confined to an empirical method, limiting the expressive potential of documentary to "discourses of sobriety" whose relation to the real is imagined as "direct, immediate, transparent."[13]

▶──

Science Fiction: Prehistory, Special Effects, and Speculation

Whereas documentary theory is often dictated by a metaphysics of presence, documentary practice is driven by a fear of absence, by a desire to preserve a fading event, a vanishing custom, a disappearing species.[14] One wonders if, once that event has already faded, that custom already vanished, or that species already disappeared, documentarians must necessarily lose their motivation for preservation, must let bygones be bygones, must record only the history passing in front of the lens and ignore the history that has passed altogether. Prehistory, for example, can never be contained by a documentary practice whose current definition it exceeds. As a period existing prior to all historical accounts and all techniques of reproduction, prehistory can speak only of absence: absence of existing referents, absence of a human being to witness them, absence of a camera to record them. Prehistory is not profilmic; its temporal relation to the camera cannot be measured by a photographic index, and its spatial relation to the filmmaker denies their historical coexistence. The prehistoric subject is extinct, its remains lying nearly beyond the codes of representation themselves. The mammoth, the mastodon, the dinosaur: How can their invisibility signify their existence? How can an object-that-is-not be indexed as a subject-who-once-was? What documentary strategies are necessary to preserve what has already decayed?

Even a tentative answer to these questions will reveal the impossibility of a congruence between prehistoric subjects and current documentary practice, between an absent referent and a mode of representation demanding its presence. Where documentary nags for empirical evidence to secure validation, prehistory begs for reconstruction as a viable object of study. The gap between them, littered only by fossilized traces few and far between, can be bridged only by speculation, a form of interpretation whose historiographic and scientific ends must be compromised by fictive means.

Of course, neither history nor science is void of speculation. Hayden White, in his various applications of narrative theory to historiography, has demonstrated that the historian must interpret his documents by filling in gaps in his information by inference: "In his efforts to reconstruct 'what happened' in any given period of history, the historian inevitably must include in his narrative an account of some event or complex of events for which the facts that would permit a plausible explanation of its occurrence are lacking."[15] Likewise, the historical filmmaker must embroider spare records to document a mise-en-scène whose maintenance of an illusion of historical reality must pretend to show more about the past than its designers could possibly know. As David Herlihy has pointed out: "It is hard to choose appropriate objects, especially for events that occurred in the centuries and millennia before the very recent past. The makers of historical films must then resort to imagination. They must fill the screen with scenes or backgrounds that may or may not be accurate."[16] In this view, prehistory and history are not inevitably torn asunder, divided by their capacities for "authentic" representation, but are linked instead by necessarily (if not equally) fictive historiographic enterprises.

Neither should science be thought of as distinct from fictive modes of representation. As Michel de Certeau suggests, the scientific hypothesis is a species of fiction whose artifacts are judged not in terms of reality, but in terms of the possibilities they generate for producing or transforming reality.[17] Like fiction, science is a system of representation; rather than using language to create life, it uses symbols to describe life, or to produce facts about life rather than life itself. Like fiction, science often works in the conditional mode; cosmology, evolutionary biology, and paleontology, whose objects of study existed millions of years ago and whose causes cannot be repeated, are scientific disciplines that rely on the arts of retrospective prediction and deduction from effects.

When history and science meet with photography, the authorized technology of "truth," the result is deemed documentary. When prehistory and science meet with special effects, the second-order technology of speculation, the result is deemed science fiction. In its very appellation, "science fiction" thrives upon the tension between the real and the imaginary, eloquently described by Siclier and Labarthe as a kind of "prophetic 'neorealism,' which reality corroborates after the fact."[18] A good example of the science fiction genre's indebtedness to the documentary precision of its fictive speculations is *2001: A Space Odyssey* (1968), a text that jettisons the present entirely in its focus on the absent past and the unknown future. For the "Dawn of Man" sequence, director Stanley Kubrick documented anthropoids by use of optics, costumes, and props that simulate a prehistoric world whose photographic effects, of course, are "special" (manipulated rather than automatic). Even though the sequence serves ultimately as a prologue to a fictional narrative, Kubrick's in-depth research and meticulous attention to detail were hailed at the time of the film's release as responsible for the finest representation of prehistoric man yet captured on celluloid. Therefore, although *2001* was not intended as straight documentary, being science fiction, its representations of the past intersect with documentary's epistemological goals, if not its standard or sanctioned means of representation. Although Kubrick's use of special effects seems antithetical to documentary's insistence upon unadulterated photographic recording, such use is more than appropriate, indeed necessary, to the representation of prehistory. The lesson of *2001* may be that, rather than relegate the prehistoric subject inevitably to the genre of science fiction because current strategies cannot accommodate its excess, documentary may do well to revise its practice to include special effects, if for no reason other than that they offer to human view a "document" of the unseen but *not* unreal.

▶

The Bones of Contention: Fossils, Indexicality, and Representation

Perhaps the most famous moment in *2001* is the classic cut on action and graphic match, where the ape/man's bone/weapon thrown spiraling into the earth's primeval atmosphere is transformed into a rotating station in deep space. The transition is subjunctive, moving from a speculative past into a speculative future, linked by a fossil whose interpretation by Kubrick as humankind's first tool constitutes a leap of faith coupling science and imagination. At their juncture is the bone of contention, the signifier of the gap between absence and presence, index and referent, fact and faith, fossil and reconstruction—between the traces of existence and the tracing of representation. Here is the space where documentary can reveal, record, and preserve the prehistoric subject, paradoxically, in the most expressive mode.

In any attempt to discover a signifier that can adequately close the gap of prehistoric signification, one must interrogate a notion of indexicality that excludes fossil-based hypotheses and reconstructions as mere iconography (too often a euphemism for fiction or fantasy). Whereas the documentaries of Trinh T. Minh-ha, Raul Ruiz, and Errol Morris have broadened our notions of discursive truth by employing experimental strategies at the level of narration, documentaries of the prehistoric subject must experiment in the domain of the image, as the unstable nature of the fossil, the subject's only claim to indexicality and scientific truth, necessitates an unconventional means of reimagination and re-presentation. Fragmented, eroded, and unsignified, each newly discovered fossil must await the proper label as part of the Adamic enterprise of paleontology. And, although the fossil may serve as irrefutable testimony to the existence of living beings in the distant past, its semiotic power is diffused. Recalling the semiotic typology of Charles Sanders Peirce, Philip Rosen attests: "In the case of a genuine index, the referent, or what Peirce calls the sign's object, is an existent whose presence is required in the formation of the sign."[19]

If we are to take Rosen literally, how then, in the absence of a living referent, can a fossil serve as a genuine index? How does it function in the representation of, say, a dinosaur itself? Perhaps Carlo Ginzberg's conjectural paradigm based on the interpretation of clues is a place to begin.[20] Paleontologists, after all, are like detectives, following the trail of dinosaur tracks, digging for evidence, and reconstructing the time, place, and "suspects" of the prehistoric scene. Modeling extinct species depends also on skills shared by forensic artists, who reconstruct the faces of unidentified murder victims. But as paleontologist Ian Tattersall notes, forensic artists have the advantage of studying the soft anatomy of living people, whereas he has no living standards for comparison.[21]

What Tattersall is suggesting, and what the Ginzbergian model advocates, is the need for subjective assessment in the reconstruction of any incomplete picture of the past. Because an extinct species like the dinosaur can be identified only morphobiologically, based upon the discovery of new fossils, its representation must be left to the provisional nature of ongoing research and speculation as a series of prehistoric reenactments in a continual process of displacement.[22] In other words, the dinosaur's iconic image can only simulate an indexical bond to its imagined referent.

No wonder the process of dinosaur reconstruction has been fraught with controversy. Two-dimensional drawings; three-dimensional models; animatronics; stop-motion, graphic, or digital animation: What is the proper strategy for representing the dinosaur? Is one technique more indexical, more authentic, more real than another? How should we document dinosaur behavior, unfortunately not preserved along with fossils, which can only suggest possibilities? What about skin color: reptilian green as fancied by the general public, drably colored according to scientists, or wildly colorful beyond the imaginations of both? Lacking evidence, we may never know.

In the absence of scientific solutions, aesthetics must prevail. Tattersall, who curated the American Museum of Natural History's Hall of Human Biology and Evolution, expresses the paleontologist's profound ambivalence between his bias for fossils as more objective evidence than reconstructed models and his keen awareness that nothing brings the past alive in the public's eye like a well-crafted reconstruction: "What I had failed to consider, however, was the extraordinary number of awkward decisions that would become necessary as work progressed. We scientists customarily deal with objective matters, and we are happiest reaching judgments based on testable reality. Untestable speculation makes most of us acutely uncomfortable."[23] Initially fearing that the cumulative result of these unscientific evocations would produce purely fantastic beings, Tattersall finally concludes that speculation is inescapable in any attempt to depict extinct species and may not necessarily sacrifice reasonable scientific accuracy.[24]

One wonders if Tattersall's optimism would have been maintained in the event of the museum's controversial exhibit "The Dinosaurs of *Jurassic Park*," whose insertion of artifacts from a commercial motion picture into a museum space blurred distinctions not only between soft and hard science, but between prehistory and fiction, pop and high culture, entertainment and education. Mark Norell, a paleontologist at the museum and the exhibition's cocurator, registered his own brand of ambivalence between "real science" and its cinematic representation by ticking off the "inaccuracies" in Spielberg's film: "Dilophosaurus did not have a neck frill, and there is no evidence that it could spit. There is no evidence that velociraptors traveled in packs."[25] And from beginning to end, the installation's informational plaques tersely corrected the fanciful science of the film, the last one concluding, "There would be no *Jurassic Park*, no recreated dinosaurs for our entertainment, without science."[26]

One could retort, however, that there would be no Museum of Natural History, no re-created dinosaurs for our scientific education, without fiction. This perspective was more recently investigated at Universal Studios in Hollywood, where the installation of "Behind the Scenes of *Jurassic Park*" even further problematized prehistoric representations by blurring museum and theme park. This exhibition documented how dinosaurs are reconstructed by scientists and by filmmakers, but failed to register the ambivalence of its New York counterpart, because it baldly demonstrated that the processes for both are much the same. Displaying paleontological artifacts from museum collections side by side with profilmic artifacts from the film, the exhibit deconstructed the notion that, in relation to an extinct referent, there is a discernible *visible* difference between a scientific and fictional *representation* of its prior existence, regardless of the means used for its derivation or the context of its final destination. For example, one showcase compared fossilized dinosaur eggs with prop dinosaur eggs. How are we to identify which ones are "real"? Only the informational plaque provided the authority to make the distinction, suggesting that authenticity resides not so much in appearance or in the technique of signification as in a compact between exhibitor and patron, a relationship similar to that between documentarian and spectator.

This compact is nicely illustrated by *Mr. DNA*, an animated short created for the diegesis of *Jurassic Park* but exhibited independently in the Universal Studios installation. In both cases, the cartoon serves as instruction. Within the film, it supports a story line dramatizing a process by which dinosaurs are reconstituted from DNA structures lying dormant in fossilized dinosaur genes, a realization within the narrative that inflects the cartoon as a tool of fiction. Within the installation, the same animated sequence supports a hypothesis that such a process, if not currently realized, remains feasible as genetic experimentation advances in the future, a postulate that inflects the cartoon as a tool of science education. What this comparison teaches are two important lessons for documentary: the first, that animation succeeds as a mode of representation for documenting the unseen, the unseeable, and the foreseen whose existence is at least possible if not provable; the second, that animation in itself is not essentially fictional, but can be interpreted only within the context of and according to the contract of its exhibition.

▶ ───

Animating the Dead: *Jurassic Park* and the Documentary Contract

Turning from installations to the film itself, it is interesting to note that in *Jurassic Park* more than half of the dinosaur shots are a "pigment of a computer imagination."[27] Although initially favoring huge profilmic models on the order of King Kong at the Universal Studios theme park, director Steven Spielberg welcomed digital animation when he realized, paradoxically, that computer graphics more effectively produced a photorealistic appearance for his dinosaurs, which was of primary importance. Michael Crichton, from whose novel the film's screenplay was adapted, staked out similar claims: "A lot of my work has to do with ideas of verisimilitude. . . . So the first thing was to make compelling dinosaurs, and that had a lot to do with how they were conceived and how they behaved and how they were introduced and talked about. That was my overriding concern."[28]

This drive for "dinorealism" motivated the film's entire crew, who acted on a paleontological impulse to get the dinosaurs just right, regardless of the movie's generic categorization as a narrative fantasy. For instance, cinematographer John Alcott noted that, as opposed to, say, a brachiosaur, "E.T. is something that nobody has ever seen, and therefore you can get away with any type of movement."[29] Although dinosaurs, of course, have never literally been seen before either, Alcott's point underlines the film's implicit premise: that dinosaurs may appear in fictional contexts, but they should always appear as nonfictional in and of themselves. Unlike creatures of a mythical past, such as the unicorn or phoenix, the T. rex from the prehistoric past *did* exist, and therein lies its fascination and the desire for its accurate representation within the narrative.

Appropriately, the film's animated dinosaurs were reconstructed the same way that paleontologists reconstruct their own three-dimensional models: first, the skeletal system was put in place, then muscles, skin, and movement were added later. This digital process, wherein bits of computer information filled in the gaps where science ends and imagination begins, oddly paralleled the film's dramatization of the use of frog DNA to fill in the gaps left by inadequate scientific knowledge of dinosaur DNA, both procedures "cheating" in order to restore the dinosaur as "true to life" (at any cost). Production designer Rick Carter explained that he tried "to find the animal in the dinosaur as opposed to the monster in the dinosaur."[30] Working from anatomical breakdowns in scholarly paleontological texts, illustrator Crash McCreery agreed that "the idea was to show that we were up-to-date on the current thinking that dinosaurs were probably warm-blooded and birdlike rather than cold-blooded and lizardlike."[31] In preparation for the completed brachiosaur, the animation team studied elephants, both on film and at wildlife parks; on the set, Jack Horner, a professional paleontologist, advised designers about "authentic" dinosaur behavior.[32]

Spielberg himself provides the best summary of the production team's concerted efforts to achieve documentary credibility:

I did want my dinosaur movie to be the most realistic. . . . I wanted the audience to say, "I really believe this could happen today." *Close Encounters,* in a way, was based on both scientific and popular beliefs that UFOs have existed — or at the very least, *could* exist. And there was a credibility in that film that I drew upon in attacking *Jurassic Park.* I wanted my dinosaurs to be animals. I wouldn't even let anyone call them monsters or creatures. What I was after was kind of like *Nova* meets *Explorer,* with a little bit of *Raiders of the Lost Ark* and *Jaws* mixed in.[33]

"Close Encounters of the Prehistoric Kind," perhaps? Here Spielberg discusses his works not as fantasy, not even precisely as fiction, but as documentary in the subjunctive mode. In a similar vein, Bill Nichols concedes that "documentary is a fiction unlike any other precisely because the images direct us toward the historical world, but if that world is unfamiliar to us, our direction will just as likely be toward a fiction like any other."[34] Although it would be theoretically untenable to conclude that the text of *Jurassic Park* functions as documentary, it is not so far-fetched to suggest that, embedded within a fictional diegesis, the film's representation of dinosaurs participates in a documentary contract.[35] Indeed, for most viewers, authentic dinosaur reconstruction had reached a new apotheosis.

What seems most necessary to the credibility of dinosaur imagery rests not so much upon its perception as an unmediated record of reality as upon the spectator's trust that the images, as documentary, were generated in good faith. Bazin himself recognized that at the heart of photorealism was a psychological drive, a subjective position that Philip Rosen notes "must finally make imagination, fantasy, the illogical a root of any true realism."[36] Our belief in the existence of the prehistoric subject, therefore, may have less to do with its mode of representation than with the mood of its reception: a bond, not so much between image and referent, but joining filmmaker, spectator, and the spaces between them. Useful here is Vivian Sobchack's description of documentary space as indexically constituted by the perceived conjunction of the viewer's life-world and the visible space represented in the text: "As much as documentary space points off-screen to the viewer's world, it is a space also 'pointed to' by the viewer who recognizes and grasps that space as, in some way, contiguous with his or her own."[37]

Of course, the very idea that the space of prehistory, which by definition precludes human beings, could be contiguous with viewer space must always be a fantasy, suggesting that any documentary of the prehistoric subject is as much a discourse of desire as a discourse of sobriety. The space of prehistory, in which we wish to insert ourselves and which, impossibly, we seek to "remember," is a cyberspace, a place of the imaginary where human and dinosaur may roam the earth together. Perhaps no other contemporary medium is better suited than the "movies" (and all this nickname implies) to dissolving the boundaries of prehistoric time and space by inviting us to cross the proscenium of the silver screen. As expressed by Stan Winston, an animator on *Jurassic Park,* this fantasy expresses a documentary impulse, a profilmic desire: "The dinosaurs are there, they are real, and people are going to leave the theater almost believing that dinosaurs are living amongst us—and that somehow Steven Spielberg found them and shot a movie around them."[38]

Jurassic Park was only the first of Spielberg's films in 1993 to participate in a documentary contract. The second was *Schindler's List,* hailed widely as the finest, most authentic narrative of the Holocaust this side of conventional documentary. Spielberg had finally grown up, critics said, leaving fantasy behind in favor of real, adult subject matter. *Schindler's List* swept the Academy Awards' major prestige categories, while *Jurassic Park* was limited to nominations in the special effects and technical categories, rewarded primarily for its digital animation. Why is it that science fiction, the dinosaur, and animation are cast again and again as childish pleasures within popular discourse? Why, also, are these subjects so often the bastards of "legitimate" cinema?

Articulating the problematic between animation and live action, Alan Cholodenko shares his insight into these questions in relation to documentary:

> Like the child, the animated cartoon is what is excluded to allow the live action film to be what it is. Certainly, we speak of the animated cartoon (as we do of the fiction film) to enable us to believe that there is an "outside"—both "within" film and "outside" film—that is not cartoon (or not fictional), that is, "within" film—the documentary—and "outside" film—what the documentary supposedly purchases—the real. The documentary is presumed to be where fantasy and fiction end, where one can gain a purchase on the real (and its correlates: the true, the meaningful, etc.), where the child is finally left behind for the adult.[39]

Ironically, that *Jurassic Park* is not intended for children became the most heatedly debated issue pervading journalistic accounts of the film. Although most parents and critics admitted enjoying the film's scare tactics and amazing dinosaur reconstructions, many insisted that Spielberg's decision to portray the dinosaurs realistically unfairly excluded children from the theater, as if the subject of dinosaurs is somehow naturally or rightfully of more interest to children than to adults, and that, therefore, their threatening aspects should have been domesticated in order to provide suitable entertainment for family members of all ages.

It is most fascinating that dinosaurs, who vanished from the face of the earth more than sixty-five million years ago, can still be perceived as a threat. Perhaps like the Frankenstein myth, the reanimation of dinosaurs has to do with the uncanny, the return of the dead, and the abject confusion of distinctions. An ur-monster of childhood nightmares, perhaps the dinosaur in its too realistic manifestation appears uncanny, returning the fears of childhood to the adult who has repressed them. The dinosaur returned from the dead suggests that the adult is never only adult but always child: "What returns from one's own childhood is allied with what returns from the childhood of the human—our primitive animistic beliefs."[40] Perhaps their current threat is thus a primal threat: the inescapable fact of the dinosaur's extinction, despite the unsurpassed length of its reign on earth, points to a fascination with but abjection of our own inevitable individual and collective demise. The dinosaur becomes an analogy of the human corpse, which, "without God and outside of science, is the utmost of abjection. It is death infecting life."[41] Beckoning to us, its jaws opened wide, the reanimated dinosaur also threatens our sanctified body of documentary theories.

▶──

Animation and the Digital Code: The Abject of Documentary

The example of *Jurassic Park* demonstrates the ambivalent status of digital animation: on one hand, it appears consonant with documentary practice in terms of filmmaker and audience contracts; on the other, it appears antithetical to documentary theory in terms of critical and academic precepts. For example, in the introduction to *Representing Reality,* Bill Nichols assumes, perhaps too hastily, that digital sampling destroys his argument, and thus limits his study to photochemical and electronic imagery.[42] Why does his documentary theory appear unable to accommodate the digitized image? The problem, it would seem, is the digital code's circumvention of analogical recording. The code to break all codes, it is the *gram* that defers presence, and thus makes all the *différance.*[43] This analog/digital polarity returns us again to Bazin's distinction between photography and painting, which taken up by Roland Barthes is upheld precisely in terms of coding. Barthes argues that the photograph, whose message is uncoded, must be opposed to the painting, whose message is coded in two significant ways: (1), it is governed by a set of conventional transpositions; (2), it divides the significant from the insignificant, intervening within the object of representation and thus failing to reproduce everything.[44] This opposition between analogical copy and digital code generates a series of concomitant

oppositions wherein the first term is privileged over the second: referent/
model, representation/simulation, profilmic/postfilmic, live action/animation,
documentary/fiction, fact/speculation.

Several recent theorists have reacted against these distinctions as onto-
logically essentialist. John Tagg has offered a corrective to the conception
of the photographic apparatus as being void of coding: "We have to see
that every photograph is the result of specific and, in every sense, significant distortions which render its relation to any prior reality deeply problematic."[45] He argues that the indexical nature of the photograph guarantees neither meaning nor direct access to a real that can be imagined as
some universal, common, or necessary referent. Rather, photographic representations guarantee only the power of the authority that the privileged
optical and chemical devices of the camera apparatus can command in
their organization of experience. The relation of index to referent is thus
less a relation of existence or essence than a relation of power. Therefore,
we can argue that, though denied the same authority, the digital image
is no more or less authentic a documentary signifier than the photographic
image outside of the institutions in which the latter dictates.[46]

In *The Illusion of Life,* Alan Cholodenko argues for a more complicated articulation between animated and live action film. Breaking down
cinemato-graphy etymologically to point out that its practice can escape
neither its character as drawing nor its technological function as an animator of still photographs, he asserts that animation is the fundamental process of all cinema, which it not only preceded but engendered.[47] He locates
the origin of the separation of live action from animation in the two major
definitions of animation: the endowment of life and the endowment of
movement. Live action jettisons the second definition in favor of the first,
a strategic move Cholodenko deconstructs in Derridean fashion as corresponding to Plato's valorization of organic living truth against mechanical
simulation: "the opposition between the original and the copy, or in its displaced form the good copy (the faithful likeness) and the bad copy (the
ghostly pernicious simulacrum): like soul to body, living to nonliving, speech
to writing."[48] Rather than the inferior term paired against live action, animation should be thought of more as a supplement that "indetermines and
suspends the distinction between representation and simulation."[49]

To complement Cholodenko's analysis, Lisa Trahair unravels yet another definition of animation: as imagery whose illusion of motion is created
rather than recorded. She notes that animation has been most commonly
distinguished from live action by reference to animation's frame-by-frame
filming technique, where movement within the image is created by illusion
rather than recorded through documentation. To deconstruct this opposi-

tion, she points to the protocinematic work of Muybridge, who demonstrated that live action is dependent on the camera's technical ability first to deconstitute movement before it can then be reconstituted by inserting an elliptical gap between two frames that would make the illusion of life possible. Trahair concludes that, despite this dependence of live action on the techniques of animation, a dominant aesthetic reliant upon the technological objectivity of the camera (carried to its limits by Bazin) would ensure "a polarization between live-action as representational or (in a sense) realist and animation as magical or simulacral."[50] In short, the "liveness" of live-action film is conventional rather than inherent to the filmic medium.

Finally, Michael Renov and Linda Williams have broadened documentary theory's horizons in their individual discussions of documentary's fictive aspects. For his part, Renov has reinstated desire into the analysis of documentary spectatorship, cautioning against the assumption that only fiction films appeal to the viewer's Imaginary, the psychic domain of idealized forms, fantasy, and reversible time,[51] primary psychological factors in the motivation to document the prehistoric subject. Williams has advocated a mode of documentary practice whose fictional strategies are designed to choose from among relative and contingent truths without necessarily dispensing with the concept of the real or conflating documentary with fiction. Approaching something like Foucault's "regime of truth," these fictive techniques become a strategy for obtaining truth, rather than for creating an image of truth itself.[52]

▶ ——————————————————————————————

Conclusion

Revisionist positions such as these reopen documentary theory not only to new content, but to new forms as well. Rather than the abject of documentary, prehistory *can* be its object. Rather than the abject of cinematography, digital animation *can* be its supplement. Perpetually provisional, the subjunctive documentary of the prehistoric subject must use every fictive strategy at its command, must not resist the adaptation of new technologies consonant with paleontology's new discoveries. As Renov puts it, "While the instinct for cultural self-preservation remains constant, the markers of documentary authenticity are historically variable."[53]

Digital documentary is no more oxymoronic than Grierson's definition of documentary as the creative treatment of reality. Even Bazin admits that "some measure of reality must always be sacrificed in the effort of achieving it."[54] Whatever the digital image loses as an analogue, it gains as an analogy. It functions as a subjunctive correlative (to twist Eliot's phrase), simulating present realities, projecting the future or—more pertinent to our current concerns—conjuring up the past. Bridging the gap of historio/graphy and cinemato/graphy, the coded images of computer-generated graphics fill in the vacuum in signification produced by the imperfect vision of the human eye, the camera eye, and the limited stretch of history. More pointedly, they reanimate the dinosaur where all other modes of representation fail.[55]

Like Vertov's "kino-eye" that makes use of every possible kind of technique as a means to conquer time and space and to document the invisible world,[56] the "dino-eye" of computer graphics reveals the truth about extinct species that all other eyes cannot see. Digital animation also makes possible a documentary cinema with the ability to reconstruct life forms from inanimate remains. It exploits the "plasmaticness" of the image, a term outlined by Eisenstein as the being in animation that behaves like the primal protoplasm, "not yet possessing a 'stable' form, but capable of assuming any form and which, skipping along the rungs of the evolutionary ladder, attaches itself to any and all forms of animal existence."[57] The authenticity of a digitized dinosaur, more iconic than indexical, hinges not on any unique concrete referent, but on the grounds that such a type of being was likely to exist at a specific time, in a specific place, under specific environmental conditions.

What documentaries of the prehistoric subject are most concerned with, finally, is representing virtual reality, whose claims to credibility must lie outside the technology producing it. For documentary authority never lies *within* the image, but always in the discursive field *around* it: its narration, site of exhibition, reputation, intention, interpretation—even its category at the local video store. Documentary is determined less by apparatus than by filmmaker and audience, is marked less by a techno-ontological arrangement than by a social bond, a relationship based as much upon good faith as good science, upon curiosity as well as sobriety, upon a longing to believe.[58] Prehistory simply foregrounds the space where science and desire meet in all documentary.

◆————————————————————————————————

NOTES

1. André Bazin, "The Ontology of the Photographic Image," in *What Is Cinema?* vol. 1, ed. and trans. Hugh Gray (Berkeley: University of California Press, 1967), 11.
2. For a more in-depth discussion of documentary in the "record/reveal/preserve" mode, see Michael Renov, "Toward a Poetics of Documentary," in *Theorizing Documentary*, ed. Michael Renov (New York: Routledge, 1993), 25–28.
3. Roland Barthes, *Camera Lucida: Reflections on Photography*, trans. Richard Howard (New York: Noonday, 1981), 93.
4. Paula Rabinowitz, "Wreckage upon Wreck-

age: History, Documentary and the Ruins of Memory," *History and Theory* 34, no. 2 (1993): 119–20.

5. See Rea Tajiri's *History and Memory* (1991) for a documentary practice that both uses and questions history and memory as sources of evidence and authority.

6. Bill Nichols, *Representing Reality: Issues and Concepts in Documentary* (Bloomington: Indiana University Press, 1991), 25.

7. Philip Rosen, "Document and Documentary: On the Persistence of Historical Concepts," in *Theorizing Documentary*, ed. Michael Renov (New York: Routledge, 1993), 85.

8. Nichols, *Representing Reality*, 184.

9. Roland Barthes, "The Photographic Message," in *Image/Music/Text*, ed. and trans. Stephen Heath (New York: Noonday, 1977), 30.

10. Rosen, "Document and Documentary," 85.

11. Annette Kuhn, for example, has claimed that documentary's hegemonic discourse informing its practice of observation "hinges upon seeing, which when it involves filmmaking crucially takes place at two points: first, at the eye of the human observer, the camera operator; and second, at the eye of the camera itself." Annette Kuhn, "The Camera I: Observations on Documentary," *Screen* 19, no. 2 (1978): 77.

12. Bazin, "Ontology of the Photographic Image," 13.

13. Nichols, *Representing Reality*, 3–4.

14. Rabinowitz, "Wreckage upon Wreckage," 120.

15. Hayden White, "Interpretation in History," in *Tropics of Discourse: Essays in Cultural Criticism* (Baltimore: Johns Hopkins University Press, 1978), 51.

16. David Herlihy, "Am I a Camera? Other Reflections on Films and History," *American Historical Review* 93, no. 5 (1988): 1189.

17. Michel de Certeau, "History: Science and Fiction," in *Heterologies: Discourse on the Other*, trans. Brian Massumi (Minneapolis: University of Minnesota Press, 1986), 201–2.

18. Translated and quoted by Vivian Sobchack in *Screening Space: The American Science Fiction Film* (New York: Ungar, 1987), 55. *Omni*, a magazine marketed to the reader of both hard science journals and science fiction fanzines, during its early years of publication echoed these very sentiments in its motto: "Yesterday's science fiction is today's science fact."

19. Philip Rosen, "History of Image, Image of History: Subject and Ontology in Bazin," *Wide Angle* 9, no. 4 (1987): 12.

20. See Carlo Ginzberg, "Morelli, Freud and Sherlock Holmes: Clues and Scientific Method," *History Workshop* 9 (spring 1980): 5–36.

21. Ian Tattersall, "Evolution Comes to Life," *Scientific American* 267 (August 1992): 83. The intersection of the science of paleontology with the art of forensics could not be better illustrated than in the exhibit of "La Brea Woman" at the George C. Page Museum of La Brea Discoveries in Los Angeles. Her plaque reads: "The wear on her teeth and newly erupted wisdom teeth suggest that she was about 25 to 30 years old. Evidence indicates that she was a homicide victim. Death was caused by a severe blow to the head with a blunt object, possibly a grinding stone."

22. Although reenactment has often been posited in opposition to credible documentary practice, Michael Renov has suggested that the documentation of the unrecorded history of any subject may in fact require its reconstruction: "The desire to retain the trace of an already absent phenomenon has led the nonfiction artist to supplement behavior or event-in-history with its imagined counterpart." Michael Renov, "*Lost, Lost, Lost*: Mekas as Essayist," in *To Free the Cinema: Jonas Mekas and the New York Underground*, ed. David E. James (Princeton, N.J.: Princeton University Press, 1992), 223.

23. Tattersall, "Evolution Comes to Life," 80–83. Tattersall's bias for scientific objectivity ironically blinds him to the fictive aspects of the paleontological evidence he cites as authentic. For instance, he maintains that "while visitors are looking at the dioramas, they will also have before them *replicas of the actual fossils* on which these recreations are based—the best of both worlds!" (emphasis added).

24. Ibid., 86.

25. Quoted in William Grimes, "Natural History Museum Lets Movie Dinosaurs Stalk behind Real Ones," *New York Times*, June 25, 1993, C28.

26. Quoted in ibid.

27. David A. Kaplan, "Believe in Magic," *Newsweek*, June 14, 1993, 61.

28. Quoted in Don Shay and Jody Duncan, *The Making of Jurassic Park: An Adventure 65 Million Years in the Making* (New York: Ballantine, 1993), 40–41.

29. Quoted in Mitch Tuchman, "An Interview with John Alcott," *American Cinematographer* (March 1985): 66.

30. Quoted in Shay and Duncan, *The Making of Jurassic Park*, 14.

31. Quoted in ibid., 20–21.

32. Ibid., 134, 137.

33. Quoted in ibid., 15–16.

34. Nichols, *Representing Reality*, 160.

35. It might be helpful to compare this idea of a documentary contract that I am developing with the autobiographical pact theorized and later revised by Philippe Lejeune. In trying to define autobiography, Lejeune soon discovered that no catalog of icons, themes,

or conflicts, no narrative technique or image, and no particular style seemed to constitute a true understanding of the autobiographical project. Rather, autobiography could be perceived only when the integrity of authorial intention and the fulfillment of reader expectation coincided in a compact as much ethically as textually based. Thus, because of its extratextual dimensions, autobiography escaped simple generic definition, particularly when intermediary variations of such a pact could be found embedded within or serving as the foundational premise of autobiographical fiction. In short, narrative fictions may contain autobiographical moments. See Paul John Eakin, ed., *On Autobiography*, trans. Katherine Leary (Minneapolis: University of Minnesota Press, 1989), 3–30, 119–37. In a similar fashion, Vivian Sobchack notes that the killing of a real rabbit in Renoir's *The Rules of the Game* (1939) ruptures the film's symbolic representations with an extracinematic indexical referent; in other words, a documentary moment representing an actual death is embedded within a fictional narrative, which gains power from that moment's "ferocious reality." Vivian Sobchack, "Inscribing Ethical Space: 10 Propositions on Death, Representation and Documentary," *Quarterly Review of Film Studies* 9, no. 4 (fall 1984): 293. Because autobiography and documentary may either constitute entire texts or appear only as moments within fictional texts, perhaps they should be conceived less as autonomous genres and more as intentional modes of nonfictional representation contingent upon both social and textual contexts.

36. Rosen, "History of Image," 17. Similarly, in his survey of major film theories, Dudley Andrew interprets Bazin's claims about cinematic realism in the psychological sense that "realism has to do not with the accuracy of the reproduction but with the spectator's belief about the origin of the reproduction" (that is, mechanical, automatic recording). Dudley Andrew, *The Major Film Theories: An Introduction* (New York: Oxford University Press, 1976), 138. In a sense, then, like Lejeune's autobiographical pact, Bazin's conception of photographic realism depends more upon a social contract between producer and spectator than upon the image's internal properties. Here Bill Nichols concurs about this documentary compact between text and historical referent: "The primary importance of this indexical quality to the photographic image . . . is less in the unassailable authenticity of the bond between image and referent than in the *impression of authenticity* it conveys to a viewer." *Representing Reality*, 150.

37. Sobchack, "Inscribing Ethical Space," 294.

38. Quoted in Shay and Duncan, *The Making of Jurassic Park*, 121.

39. Alan Cholodenko, "Introduction," in *The Illusion of Life: Essays on Animation*, ed. Alan Cholodenko (Sydney: Power, 1991), 35.

40. Ibid., 28.

41. Julia Kristeva quoted in Peter Hutchings, "The Work-Shop of Filthy Animation," in *The Illusion of Life: Essays on Animation*, ed. Alan Cholodenko (Sydney: Power, 1991), 165.

42. Nichols, *Representing Reality*, 5. It is never absolutely certain why Nichols would disqualify digital sampling from proper documentary discourse, as various statements throughout *Representing Reality* and other of his published writings would suggest the contrary. For example, in "Style, Grammar, and the Movies," *Film Quarterly* 28, no. 3 (spring 1975): 33, Nichols claims that both analog and digital forms are, rather than in opposition, "basic to all natural systems of communication."

43. For a relatively concise elaboration of these terms, see Jacques Derrida, "Semiology and Grammatology: Interview with Julia Kristeva," in *Positions*, trans. Alan Bass (Chicago: University of Chicago Press, 1981), 15–36.

44. Roland Barthes, "Rhetoric of the Image," in *Image/Music/Text*, ed. and trans. Stephen Heath (New York: Noonday, 1977), 43. Barthes includes the "demands of apprenticeship" as the third significant level of a drawing's coded nature.

45. My summary of John Tagg's position is derived from his introduction to *The Burden of Representation* (Amherst: University of Massachusetts Press, 1988), 1–32.

46. In discussing cybernetic technologies and their cultural effects, Bill Nichols echoes Tagg's argument: "The process of adopting new ways of seeing that consequently propose new forms of social organisation becomes a paradoxical, or dialectical, process when the transformations that spawn new habits, new vision, are themselves engendered and substantially recuperated by the existing form of social organisation which they contain the potential to overcome." Bill Nichols, "The Work of Culture in the Age of Cybernetic Systems," *Screen* 29, no. 1 (winter 1988): 26. Thus, while generally conceding that electronic simulation may constitute a new way of envisioning culture (which includes documentary practice), Nichols himself chooses to recuperate (and ultimately expel) digital sampling within the prior, institutionalized, hegemonic discourses of analog reproduction.

47. See Cholodenko, "Introduction," 9–36.

48. Alan Cholodenko, "Who Framed Roger Rabbit; Or the Framing of Animation," in *The Illusion of Life: Essays on Animation*, ed. Alan Cholodenko (Sydney: Power, 1991), 215.

49. Cholodenko, "Introduction," 21.

50. Lisa Trahair, "For the Noise of a Fly," in *The Illusion of Life: Essays on Animation*, ed. Alan Cholodenko (Sydney: Power, 1991), 189.

51. Michael Renov, "Introduction: The Truth about Non-Fiction," in *Theorizing Documentary*, ed. Michael Renov (New York: Routledge, 1993), 3.

52. Linda Williams, "Mirrors without Memories: Truth, History, and the New Documentary," *Film Quarterly* 46, no. 3 (1993): 14.

53. Renov, "Toward a Poetics of Documentary," 23.

54. André Bazin, "An Aesthetic of Reality: Neorealism," in *What Is Cinema?* vol. 2, ed. and trans. Hugh Gray (Berkeley: University of California Press, 1971), 30.

55. It should come as no surprise that the first, most significant, and most influential animated film is Winsor McCay's *Gertie the Dinosaur* (1914).

56. See Annette Michelson, ed., *Kino-Eye: The Writings of Dziga Vertov*, trans. Kevin O'Brien (Berkeley: University of California Press), 87–88.

57. Quoted in Keith Broadfoot and Rex Butler, "The Illusion of Illusion," in *The Illusion of Life: Essays on Animation*, ed. Alan Cholodenko (Sydney: Power, 1991), 271–72.

58. Again, Bill Nichols concedes that "our willingness to suspend disbelief in the face of the 'living likeness' such images convey supports the fascination, pleasure, and power to persuade that documentary affords; it is also a willingness we tender more often on faith than reason." *Representing Reality*, 153.

MARK J. P. WOLF

[14] Subjunctive Documentary: Computer Imaging and Simulation

Whereas most documentaries are concerned with documenting events that have happened in the past, and attempt to make photographic records of them, computer imaging and simulation are concerned with what *could be, would be,* or *might have been*; they form a subgenre of documentary we might call *subjunctive* documentary, following the use of the term *subjunctive* as a grammatical tense. At first glance such a term might appear to be an oxymoron, but there is no more contradiction here than in any other form of documentary. The last of the above conditionals, *what might have been,* applies to all documentary film and video, because all are subjective and incomplete, reconstructing events to varying degrees through existing objects, documents, and personal recollections. However, by translating invisible entities (beyond the range of human vision) or mathematical ideas into visible analogues, computer simulation has allowed the conceptual world to enter the perceptual one. It has created new ways in which an image can be linked to an actual object or event, with mathematically reconstructed simulacra used as representations, standing in for photographic images. By narrowing and elongating the indexical link and combining it with extrapolation or speculation, computer imaging and simulation may suggest that there is a difference between what is called "documentary film" and "nonfiction film," especially when one is documenting the subjunctive.

In this era of computer simulation, there is a greater willingness to trade close indexical linkage for new knowledge that would otherwise be unattainable within the stricter requirements of indexical linkage that were once needed to validate knowledge empirically. Many of these requirements have to do with observation, the visual verification of one's data. In *Techniques of the Observer,* Jonathan Crary describes transformations in the notion of visuality that occurred in the first half of the nineteenth century. Writing about the relationship between the eye and the optical apparatus, he states:

> During the seventeenth and eighteenth centuries that relationship had been essentially metaphoric; the eye and the camera obscura or the eye and the telescope or microscope were allied by a conceptual similarity, in which the authority of an ideal eye remained unchallenged. Beginning in the nineteenth century, the relation between eye and apparatus becomes one of metonomy: both were now contiguous instruments on the same plane of operation, with varying capabilities and features. The limits and deficiencies of one will be complemented by the other, and vice versa.[1]

The notion that observation could be performed through the mediation of instruments did not find immediate acceptance; Auguste Comte, the founder of positivism, deprecated the microscope, the use of which he did not consider to be direct observation.[2] In *Instrumental Realism*, Don Ihde writes that seventeenth-century Aristotelians objected to Galileo's telescope, and Xavier Bichat, the founder of histology (the study of living tissues), distrusted microscopes and would not allow them into his lab.[3] Ihde points out, however, that some of the objection was due to imperfect technology, which produced blurred images. In one sense, a blurred image is an indication that the technology has reached its limits; sharp images with dubious indexical linkages may be more harmful in that their shortcomings are less noticeable. The instrument does not indicate what it does not see, and so one must take this into account when studying objects viewed with it.

The use of imaging technologies is essential to much of modern science, but the issues regarding the status of the entities studied through them are still a matter of debate. In his discussion of instrumental realism, Ihde describes the work of philosopher Patrick Heelan:

> Heelan's position regarding instrumentation is clearly an enthusiastic endorsement of a "seeing" with instruments, albeit cast in the hermeneutic terms of "reading" a "text" provided by instruments. Nevertheless, this "reading" is held to have all the qualities of a perceptual "seeing." Thus, one can say that Heelan's is a specialized but liberal interpretation of "seeing with" an instrument.[4]

Ihde gives Heelan's example of a measured perception that is both hermeneutical and perceptual: that of reading a thermometer to learn the temperature, an act that requires no knowledge of thermodynamics, but rather an understanding of how the instrument is read. Ihde points out that Robert Ackerman's position is more cautious:

> [Ackerman] argues both for the largest degree of ambiguity relating to what he calls "data domains" which are text-like, and for considerable skepticism

relating to the (hermeneutic) interpretative process. "Instrumental means only produce a data text whose relationship to nature is problematic." And, "the features of the world revealed to experiment cannot be philosophically proven to be revealing of the world's properties." (I am not sure whether Ackerman holds any counterpart thesis that other means of analyzing world properties can be philosophically proven.) Yet, examination of the interpretive result relating to such data domains turns out to be the same as for other knowledge claims.[5]

Thus, along with optical instruments like the microscope and telescope, we could include the camera and the record it produces. Photographic technology and processes, since their invention, have come to be valued as records and evidence in the areas of science, law, and medicine.[6] Most people's reliance on media for knowledge of the world is another instance of belief in the recorded image.

Photography, as a source of instrumental realism, differed from prior instruments because of its ability to store an image. The viewing of entities using telescopes, microscopes, and other optical apparatuses was done in real time, an unbroken link between subject and observer, both physically present on either end of the link. The camera, as a system of lenses, was similar to the telescope and microscope, but it had the ability to record the images seen, saving them for later examination, even after the subject was gone. The photograph's image was not "live" like the images viewed in other optical instruments, but its fixity provided a means of making a record that could be analyzed later, like a scientific journal. The photograph bridged the gap between *observation* and *documentation*.

The documentary value accorded the photograph was due in part to the acceptance of other optical apparatuses as epistemologically sound instruments, and could be seen as an extension of them. Other imaging technologies, such as video, were also accorded similar status. As the computer came to be trusted as a scientific tool, it was only a matter of time before it, too, would be combined with the imaging apparatus, especially in its revolutionization of the idea of the retrievable document. The concept of the stored image is analogous to the concept of the stored program, and the digital image can be seen as the marriage of the two.

Computer imaging, however, is often indexically less direct than film-based photography, due to the active mediation of hardware and software, as well as the storage of the image as a signal instead of a fixed record. Like the magnification produced by the microscope or telescope, computer imaging is often an extension of the camera into realms indirectly available to human experience. One of the functions of the *Voyager* spacecraft, for example, was to send back images of the outer planets of the solar system.

Images of the planets taken by its onboard camera were transmitted electronically back to Earth, composited, and arranged in sequence to produce moving imagery, which contained far more detail than what an Earthbound observer could produce. Physical distance is not the only boundary overcome; many forms of computer imaging record light waves or energies that fall outside the spectrum of visible light—infrared, ultraviolet, radio waves, and so on—and transduce them into the visible portion of the spectrum, creating visual imagery from recorded data. Likewise, forms of medical imaging such as computerized axial tomography (CAT) scans, positron emission tomography (PET) scans, and magnetic resonance imaging (MRI) use radio waves (and ultrasound, which uses sound waves) to construct images or three-dimensional models, with different tones or colors representing different intensities.

The rendering of these transduced waves into the visible spectrum means tones or colors must be assigned to various frequencies to make them visible. The false coloring making up the image, however, is a step into the subjunctive, because the image is not a record of how the subject appears to the observer, but rather how it *might* appear, if such frequencies were substituted for frequencies (light waves) within the visible spectrum. Thus it is the differences between frequencies that are being documented, not the frequencies themselves. Also, false colors in computer imaging are usually assigned to make the data displayed clearer, representing another level of mediation between subject and observer.[7]

In some ways, the false coloring found in computer imaging is only one step removed from black-and-white photography, which shows us things not as they appear to us (in color) but rather as a map of tonal intensities. In this sense, black-and-white photography could also be considered subjunctive, showing us what things would look like if our retinas contained only rods and no cones, making us sensitive to tonality but not to hue and saturation. Ironically, the emphasis on computer imaging processes can lead to neglect of the real, visible colors that exist in the universe. David F. Malin has described how the visible spectrum is often overlooked by astronomers, who often prefer to use charged-coupled devices (CCDs), electronic detectors that collect light far more efficiently than do photographs:

> One of the key advantages [film-based] photography has over electronic imaging is that photographic plates can capture high-resolution, sensitive images over an area of virtually unlimited size, for example, across the entire wide field view of the U. K. Schmidt telescope in Australia. In comparison, the largest CCDs measure only a few centimeters across. Photography therefore offers a superior means for recording images of extended astronomical objects such as nebulae and nearby galaxies.

Furthermore, the photographic layer serves as a compact medium for storing vast amounts of visual information. A single 35.6-by-35.6-centimeter plate from the U. K. Schmidt telescope, which records a patch of sky 6.4 degrees on a side, contains the equivalent of several hundred megabytes of data.

Color images present the information packed into an astronomical photograph in an attractive and intuitively obvious way. Indeed, measuring the colors of nebulae, stars and galaxies is central to understanding their composition and physical state.[8]

In the computer age, film-based photography now seems like a direct process of observation, compared with computer imaging, quite a far cry from the days when the microscope was considered a step beyond direct observation. At the same time, computer imaging technologies have changed the nature of "observation" and what is considered observable.

Many of the entities or energies imaged by the computer are ones that are too small, too large, or too fast to be visible to traditional optical instruments or the unaided eye. In the photographic world, microphotography, time-lapse, and high-speed photography serve similar purposes, although to a much lesser degree; but in several cases they can be seen as precursors of computer imaging techniques. The electron microscope, for example, is an extension of the optical microscope and the camera, using a focused beam of electrons rather than light to create an image; the scanning electron microscope produces an image from scan lines in a manner similar to television images. The scanning tunneling microscope, which uses computer imaging, produces an image by scanning a very small area with a fine, microscopic probe that measures surface charge. The closer the probe is to an atom, the stronger the charge. The charge on the probe changes during the scan, and a reconstructed image of the surface emerges when different colors are assigned to different charge intensities and displayed. Although the process presents a visual image of the atoms, it is not an image in the traditional photographic sense, because traditional photography is impossible on a subatomic scale.[9]

The recording of high-speed events in particle physics also evolved from photographic techniques to computer imaging techniques in which twenty-five billion bits of data are produced in one second. The earliest detectors used for monitoring particle collisions were cloud chambers, bubble chambers, and streamer chambers, all of which were similar in principle. In these chambers, charged particles were detected when they moved through a medium leaving a trail of ionized atoms behind them. These trails (composed of water droplets, bubbles, or sparks, depending on the chamber) could then be recorded on film. Photographic records were highly detailed and could be interpreted easily, and during the late 1960s computers were used in the analyses of the photographs, although more complicated images required human assistance. However, according to a 1991 article in *Scientific American*:

> Capturing events on film became impossible when accelerators were developed that produced thousands of particles in a second. To record particles at this rate, physicists designed complicated electronic detectors. Because information was gathered in electronic form, computers became an essential tool for making quick decisions during data collection.
>
> Yet physicists still cannot rely exclusively on computers to analyze the data. Computers that automatically inspect events are limited by the expectations of programmers. Such systems can selectively suppress information or obscure unusual phenomena. Until scientists invent a pattern recognition program that works better than the human brain, it will be necessary to produce images of the most complicated and interesting events so that physicists can scrutinize the data.[10]

Toward the end of the article, the authors state that "the detectors, like all complex mechanisms, have certain quirks." And they add that during the test runs of the detectors, "the programs occasionally produce images showing inconsistencies between the data and the laws of physics. These inconsistencies can arise because of a malfunction in part of the detector, in the data acquisition system or in the data analysis software."[11] In this instance, the desire for more data and finer detail necessitated a move away from conventional media, which proved to be too limited for scientific purposes. Although the data may not be as reliable, there are several thousand times more data to examine.

Sensor technology is also used on larger scales as well, for tracking and imaging planes with radar, submarines with sonar, or weather patterns imaged by satellite. Electronic signals and sensors have been used to track whole flocks of birds, and even human beings, some of whom owe their lives to these sensors.[12] NASA's Mission to Planet Earth (MPTE) involves sending up nineteen Earth-orbiting satellites over a fifteen-year period (1998–2013) that will collect data on environmental conditions such as the greenhouse effect, desertification, ozone depletion, weather cycles, and other ecological information. Garrett Culhane, writing about these satellites in *Wired*, states:

> One of the largest will generate a terabyte (10^{12} bytes) of data about the earth every ten days—that's enough to fill 2,000 CDs or 500,000,000 pages of text. "The EOS will produce data on the scale of that contained in the Library of Congress about every ten days," says [MPTE director Robert] Price.[13]

The data imaged are collected from all over the globe, and the sheer numbers of them are far too extensive to be represented in any single image or sequence of images; and if the satellites are collecting continuously, the data may be coming in faster than anyone can analyze it.

In this string of examples, computer imaging gradually moves further and further away from conventional photographic methods of documenting events as the phenomena being studied slip out of visibility, because they are too far away, too small, or too quick, or because they lie outside of the visible spectrum. And unlike infrared, ultraviolet, or even X-ray photography, computer imaging involves more interpretation and often must reconstruct objects or events in order to visualize them. Although often displayed in two-dimensional images, the data collected in medical scanning, astronomy, particle physics, and meteorology represent complex events and structures in three dimensions. These reconstructed events can be rendered and viewed from any angle, and replayed repeatedly for further analysis, as computer simulations.

Computer-generated three-dimensional representations that change over time are more than just reconstructions of images, they are reconstructions of a system's behavior. In these reconstructions, still imagery becomes moving imagery, and computer imaging becomes computer simulation; like the photograph as a stored image that can be analyzed in the absence of its subject, a computer simulation made from recorded data allows an event to be reconstructed and analyzed after it has occurred. The data in a computer simulation are a series of measurements combining disparate forms of other data, many of which are nonphotographic. These data are linked to their referents in a variety of ways, recording the values of whatever variables they are programmed to represent.

If computer simulations are documentary, they are subjunctive documentary. Their subjunctive nature lies not only in their flexibility in the imaging of events, but in their staging as well; computer simulations are often made from data taken from the outside world, but not always. Just as the digital image does not always have a real-world referent, computer simulation can be used to image real or imaginary constructs, or some combination of the two. Computer simulations go beyond the mere recording of data; they are frequently used to study the behavior of dynamic systems and become the basis of decisions, predictions, and conclusions made about them. As a simulation is constructed, and the data set becomes larger and more comprehensive, its indexical link to the physical world grows stronger, until the simulation is thought to be sufficiently representative of some portion or aspect of the physical world. The computer allows not only physical indices like visual resemblance but conceptual indices (like gravity or the laws of physics) to govern simulated events. Like the photograph, computer simulation can combine observation and documentation, and as the embodiment of a theory, it can document what *could be, would be,* or *might have been.* In many cases, actual experiments and events are represented as measurements and relationships; these are abstracted into a set of laws governing the phenomena, and these laws become the basis for creating the *potential events* of the simulation. Thus the simulation documents possibilities or probabilities instead of actualities.

Computer simulation has been used in a wide range of applications: for the visualization of purely mathematical constructs, architectural walk-throughs, job training, product design and testing, and experimental scientific research. The basis for all of these simulations is mathematical reconstruction, in which a mechanical, simplified version of the events being studied is created in the computer's memory. Mathematical visualization can give visual form to purely mathematical constructs, such as fractal objects, rotating hypercubes, and other higher-dimensional forms.[14] It can also be used to illustrate the hypothetical; for example, to show how relativistic distortions would appear to an extremely high-speed traveler (buildings would shift in color and appear to lean in toward the observer). A simulation can give the hypothetical an appearance of feasibility, by virtue of its visualization; such concrete imagery can be useful in swaying belief, especially in a society that tends to rely on the image as evidence. Although mathematical visualizations seek to give concrete visual form to abstract ideas, most visualizations seek to re-create objects and situations that are thought to have existed or that could exist in the material world.

Architectural walk-throughs—or fly-throughs, as they are called—are computer simulations of hypothetical buildings that the user can "move through" and view from any angle, under various lighting conditions, and with different styles of decor and furniture. They allow a user to get a sense of what a building and its interior will be like before it is built, to make changes, and to decide on a final design. Architects designing on the computer may work closely with these tools while creating the plans for buildings. The limitations inherent in a simulation program, then, may subtly influence the design of a building, and the way the building is depicted as a three-dimensional space will also influence the choices shaping its design. While computer simulation allows the visualization of possibilities, it limits those possibilities by providing the language of speculation used to create their visual analogues.

Architectural simulations can be used to speculate about the past as well as the future. Structures that are partially destroyed, no longer exist, or were designed but never built can be visually (and aurally) re-created.[15] The Taisei Corporation, Japan's third-largest construction firm, uses computer modeling in the design of large-scale structures, including skyscrapers and power plants. The company has also made a series of architectural fly-throughs of ancient cities, which it reconstructed for the British Museum.[16] Reconstructed from archaeological data, a fly-through of the Sumerian city of Ur begins with a rotating bird's-eye view of the city. The point of view revolves around a ziggurat and over rooftops, and then eventually drops down to street level, moving through an alley, under canopied doors, and finally through the interior of one of the buildings, where pottery and furniture can be seen. The sequence combines a map of the city, architecture of individual buildings, and artifacts such as pottery into one unified illustration. Similarly, computer animation is used to bring a reconstructed city of Tenochtitlan back to life in *500 Nations* (1995), a television series documenting Native American history. Although the virtue of such reconstructions is a more holistic presentation of disparate data, it is difficult to tell from the imagery alone where historical evidence ends and speculation begins; the problem is similar to that faced by paleontologists who reconstruct dinosaur skeletons from incomplete collections of bone fragments. It would seem that computer simulations are not so different, after all, from the constructed interpretations found in documentary film and video, where editing constructs a world and a point of view; they are all representations of partial reconstructions of the past, and can be considered subjunctive to some degree. No simulation or film can ever provide enough information for a reconstruction of past events free of speculation. There are always gaps filled in by the person who constructs the re-creation, as well as by those who study it; and these may range from educated guesses to unacknowledged assumptions.

History, however, is not the only thing at stake; the belief that computer simulations can represent reality is often relied upon to the point that people's lives may depend on the accuracy of those simulations. For example, the flight simulators used in training pilots are deemed close enough to the real experience that pilots can obtain their licenses without ever having left the ground. During an actual flight, weather conditions may produce zero visibility, forcing pilots to fly entirely by their instruments and radar; when this happens, the cockpit completely mediates the experience of the pilots, much as a training simulator would. In such cases, ironically, actual conditions simulate the simulator.

Pilots and their passengers are not the only ones whose lives might depend on the accuracy of simulations. On the ground, surgeons can now perform lifesaving operations without having practiced on animals or cadavers. One medical simulator developed by High Techsplanations of Rockville, Maryland, allows users to open up a digital torso that contains three-dimensional organs such as kidneys, urethra, and prostate, all in vivid color. The organs can even be programmed to simulate various illnesses.[17] The attempt at realism even extends to the purely visual side of the simulation. According to a newsletter from Viewpoint Datalabs:

> For the opening of a new digestive center, Traveling Pictures produced an animation featuring Revo Man, showing the intricacies of the digestive system. Viewpoint's anatomy datasets were implemented to produce a result that was almost too real. "We reached our goal of making the sequence look realistic," says Dave Burton, animation director. "When we showed our clients the initial animation, it made some people ill because of the realism. We had to tone it down a little by using transparent and glassy materials."[18]

Even if the simulations look as real as Burton claims, will these abstractions prepare medical students psychologically for the real thing? Can virtual blood replace real blood, and the cutting of an incision in a human being with a sharp metal tool? No matter how accurately human organs can be simulated, there will always be an *experiential* gap between real and virtual.

Medical simulations are most useful for analysis and visualization when the data used to construct them are taken directly from life. As with an x ray, the data are taken from the patient's body and analyzed on-screen. One simulation, of the treatment of an ocular tumor, was shown at a SIGGraph convention, and some of the methods were described. The clip had the following voice-over:

> The physical form of the eye for this simulation comes from diagnostic ultrasound scans. The shapes of the eye and tumor are captured as digitized slices by using digitized pulse echo ultrasound. The digital slices are stretched into a rectangular format and used as the basis for reconstructing solid models. A typical section is shown indicating the tumor and retina. Sweeping through the volume gives the doctors a feel for the data integrity. The model eye is constructed from the image slices by hand tracing. As data slices are peeled away, outlines of the tumor and retina are shown being converted into polygonal objects. The shape of the other structures in the eye are obtained from standard database structures and B scan ultrasound.[19]

The simulation described above combines data gathered from a real source (the patient) with data from outside the patient ("from standard database structures"). The patient's body has become a series of interchangeable parts, for which standardized structures can be substituted—an instance of filling in the gaps with default assumptions.

The substitution of a generalized, "standard" computer model for a specific existing object is common throughout computer simulation. The general model acts as a stand-in for all specific physical versions of the model. Many industries use computer simulation in designing their products, and an increasing number are doing product testing with computer simulation as well. Originally, the purpose of product testing was to see how well a product stood up to forces in the physical world, so there is perhaps a certain irony in simulating such tests on the computer—today product testing could be done physically in order to test not the product itself, but rather how well the simulation simulates the product.

Computer-simulated product testing is used for everything from simple containers to complex large-scale products like automobiles, where people's lives may be at stake if the product fails. In 1991, "the world's first digital smashup involving two complete automobiles" occurred inside a computer in Germany.[20] Describing it, Gene Bylinsky writes:

> Such simulations are so accurate and economical that engineers at many automakers now conduct most of their crash tests using computers instead of real cars. In one that models a broadside collision of two Opels, the cars appear on the screen as ghostly X-ray images produced by a Cray supercomputer and software from Mecalog of Paris. The crash unfolds in slow motion. The engineers can freeze the action at any point and study the effect of the impact on the bodywork, the key internal parts, and the dummies inside. Such tests yield detailed results at a cost of about $5,000 per crash—vs. roughly $1 million using real cars.[21]

The cars, crashes, and human beings are all simulated by the computer, and now even the test-driving of cars under various conditions is being simulated on the computer.

> Since Renault can't test a new model under real conditions without the risk of leaking its designs to its competitors, it has created a digital testbed for prototyping the aesthetics, road-holding, and drivability of new vehicles.
> The first step is to build a database of virtual driving routes. Then designers mock up a complete virtual car with digitized features: weight, size, shock absorption, steering-lock coefficient, and tire profiles. Using a simulator program, the design team then drives the prototype through the database to find out how it behaves.[22]

Rather than bring the virtual product into a real environment for testing, manufacturers simulate the environment along with the product.

Computer simulations and reconstructions are depended on not only in industry, but in experimental science and law as well, where they are routinely given a status that is almost that of real events. In the courtroom, computer simulations have been admitted as substantive evidence with independent probative value—that is, they may be used as evidence or proof. In 1985, computer simulations were pivotal in the case concerning the crash of Delta Flight 191. This fourteen-month trial was the longest in aviation history, and more than $150 million in claims were at stake.[23] Lawyers from both sides made extensive use of computer simulation to support their case, and they were able to establish a precise chronology of events and replay them from multiple perspectives. Most crucial were the films made from the digital onboard flight recorder that survived the crash. These "black boxes" record flight path and instruments, audio of pilots' voices, and airborne radar imagery; newer versions can log as many as seven hundred different variables, including the positions of five hundred switches. When these data are combined with a map of the terrain, simulations can be made from whatever point of view is desired.[24]

Simulations used to reconstruct events are sometimes used even to reconstruct the crime itself, resulting in a bizarre form of visible evidence. Since 1992, Alexander Jason, an expert witness in ballistic events, has been producing computer-generated reconstructions that are used as evidence during criminal proceedings. Ralph Rugoff describes Jason's productions:

> The Mitchell video, which reconstructs the movements of a homicide victim during a sequence of eight gunshots, looks like a primitive video game: the protagonist resembles a faceless robot with orange hair, while bullets appear as bright-red spikes identifying entry and exit wounds. Terse data flash on the screen following each gunshot, but the aura of scientific investigation is occasionally punctured by oddly realistic details—like the way a beer bottle bounces and rolls when it's dropped by the victim. The result is an unnerving viewing experience where a relatively innocent cultural form—the cartoon— is made to serve within a grisly documentary context.
> . . . In other videos, some figures are depicted with clothing, and in a few cases race is also indicated, yet this realism is tempered by the use of uncanny effects: a torso may abruptly dissolve to reveal the underlying skeletal structure, tracing a bullet's path through the body. In one stunning cinematic flourish, Jason creates a shot from the bullet's point of view, taking us from a policeman's gun, through the victim's chest, and into the wall beyond.[25]

Despite the strange iconic and geometrical appearances of the simulations, people's unquestioning faith in both the documentary quality of the presentations and the scientific and mathematical means of producing them make it necessary for judges to remind jurors of the unreal and speculatory nature of such simulations. In this sense, some of the abstractions of computer graphics are desirable, because they can act as a reminder of the simulation's construction. They can also be used to distance the jury from the events, in the same way that judges will often allow black-and-white photographs of a victim's injuries to be used but will not allow color photos because they are felt to unduly influence a jury.

Simulations like Jason's may look nothing like the actual crime, but they are believed to represent the events of the crime. Similarly, in experimental science, abstract representations are made to represent events— in many cases, events that never even happened. In chemistry, computer simulation is used to model such things as molecular bond energies and enzyme catalysis; the objects being modeled are molecules, atoms, and particles, whose individual properties can be satisfactorily defined with a small number of variables, and are visually represented in a variety of ways, one of the more familiar being a three-dimensional array of balls and sticks, similar to the wooden or plastic physical models used before the development of computer modeling. Here, the generalized models used in the simulations come closest to what they represent, because individual atoms have no specificity apart from position (like pixels and phonemes, they too are subject to "double articulation").

Experiments simulated on a computer come a long way from traditional means of documentation, such as the photograph or eyewitness reports, and one may ask what indexical connection to the real-world referent remains. It certainly isn't one of visual resemblance, because molecules don't really look like wiggling balls and sticks, as they are so often depicted. Nor are the simulated reactions reconstructions of specific reactions that actually took place; they are only possible scenarios based on chemical properties and the laws of physics. Molecular simulations are based on such things as bond angles, binding energies, and other elementary data, and are used to test and develop theories in a manner similar to physical experiments. In effect, the re-creation of dynamics and behavior is their only link to the outside world and the only thing being documented; the referents are not objects, but laws of physics and descriptions.

In this indexical shift, as mentioned above, actual experiments and observations have been reduced to measurements and relationships, which are in turn abstracted into a set of laws. These laws then become the basis for the *potential events* seen in the simulation. Theories based on these laws, which fill in incomplete data and understanding of the laws of physics, stretch the indexical link even further. There is a shift from the *perceptual* to the *conceptual*; the image has become an illustration constructed from data, often representing an idea or speculation as much as or more than existing objects or actual events.

All simulations are subjunctive to some degree, subjective, and prone to ideological manipulation. Yet in science and in many public sectors, as well as in the public's imagination, the mathematical basis behind computer simulation has given it a status similar to (or greater than) photography, despite the often much more tenuous indexical linkage. One of the reasons is computer simulation's obscuring of point of view. Documentary theory has shown, in a wide array of writings, how the camera is not objective but subjective, because every image contains an inherent point of view. Simulations, however, do not come with an inherent visual point of view; they can be rendered and replayed from any angle, and reconstructed events can be seen from any point of view desired, including from the insides of objects. Although this omniscience lends an air of objectivity to the displays, it effaces the fact that *point of view* more importantly refers to the programs, theories, and assumptions controlling the simulations, in much the same way that a particular theoretical stance may steer an authorial voice in a photographic documentary. The "point of view" is not visual or perceptual, but conceptual and theoretical, the speculation behind the simulation structuring how everything is seen. As Albert Einstein is said to have remarked, "So far as the laws of mathematics refer to reality, they are not certain. And so far as they are certain, they do not refer to reality."

No simulated "virtual world" can be free of a worldview, and the assumptions behind such a world are often difficult to discern, given only the visuals. Even barring digital legerdemain and computer simulations deliberately slanted in one direction or another, assumptions and speculations will be shaping the results they produce. Indeed, due to the complexity of the science, mathematics, and program code involved, it may be the case that no single person is aware of all the assumptions involved in a particular simulation. The simulation's subjectivity is a multiple one, layered with the assumptions of multiple people and disciplines: the designers, the programmers, the company that sells it, and the field expert who uses it. And, of course, the potential for deliberate manipulations will always remain. It is usually assumed that computer simulations are at least unfolding on a sound mathematical basis, but how can anyone but the programmers be sure?

Computer simulation's speculative nature blurs the line between fiction and nonfiction and complicates the question of how far an indexical link can be stretched and displaced and still be considered valid in society, as facts get skewed, left out, misinterpreted, or filled in by theory and speculation. As Jack Weber cautions:

> Precisely because it allows you to see the invisible, the capabilities of visualization, with its pizzazz and drama, can also blind you to what it reveals. To watch the dynamic ebb and flow of market forces or to reach out and touch an enzyme molecule is a seductive experience—so seductive that you can easily forget the approximations and interpolations that went into it.
>
> "One of the problems with data exploration and visualization," says Paul Velleman, president of Data Description (Ithaca, NY), a maker of visualization software, "is that these technologies make it easy to find patterns that may or may not be real." Color, shading, sound, and other dimensions that add realism to visualization are equally capable of making the unreal seem more plausible.[26]

Even the most honest and accurate computer simulations can suc-
cumb to software glitches, hardware flaws, and human or computer error,
making them unreliable and sometimes potentially dangerous. As in the examples of car testing, medical simulations, court cases, and pilot training,
people's lives can depend on computer simulations.[27] And, as Theodore
Roszak points out, political leaders often make decisions based on computerized representations and simulations of situations, complete with pre-
dicted outcomes, so world affairs may actually depend on software intri-
cacy and accuracy, and the way the software develops the user's worldview
of the events the simulation supposedly represents.[28]

Computer simulations and systems are enormously long chains, and
they are only as strong as their weakest links. The interconnectedness of
computer systems means that errors can propagate to enormous size before
they are corrected. Peter Neumann, the moderator of RISKS-forum on the
Internet (which is a compendium of reports of disasters due to computer
error), describes the collapse of the ARPANET in 1980:

> There was a combination of problems: You had a couple of design flaws, and
> you had a couple of dropped bits in the hardware. You wound up with a node
> contaminating all of its neighbors. After a few minutes, every node in the entire
> network ran out of memory, and it brought the entire network down to its
> knees. This is a marvelous example because it shows how one simple problem
> can propagate. That case was very similar to the AT10:52 AMT collapse of
> 1990, which had exactly the same mechanism: A bug caused a control signal to
> propagate that eventually brought down every node in the network repeatedly.[29]

Software glitches can occur due to small errors in source code; in one
case, a string of failures at a telephone company resulted from three faulty
instructions in several million lines of code.[30] Complexity is one of the main
reasons for software bugs; there may be thousands or even several million
lines of code and thousands of decisions and alternate paths of execution,
making it nearly impossible to test everything before the program is put
into operation. And with multiple programmers working over long periods
of time, human error is also a likelihood.[31] According to the authors of an
article published in 1992 in *Scientific American,* the very nature of digital
technology itself is partly responsible for the computer's vulnerability:

> The intrinsic behavior of digital systems also hinders the creation of com-
> pletely reliable software. Many physical systems are fundamentally continuous
> in that they are described by "well-behaved" functions—that is, very small
> changes in stimuli produce very small differences in responses. In contrast, the
> smallest possible perturbation to the state of a digital computer (changing a
> bit from 0 to 1, for instance), may produce a radical response. A single incor-
> rect character in the specification of a control program for an Atlas rocket,

carrying the first U.S. interplanetary spacecraft, Mariner I, ultimately caused the vehicle to veer off course. Both rocket and spacecraft had to be destroyed shortly after launch.[32]

Not only is computer source code ultrasensitive to error, but the creation of software is, according to some, not yet even a science. Even after fifty years of refinement, the NATO Science Committee's goal of a field of "software engineering," defined as "the application of a systematic, disciplined, quantifiable approach to the development, operation and maintenance of software," has yet to emerge fully. "It's like musket making was before Eli Whitney," says Brad J. Cox, a professor at George Mason University.[33]

In the computer industry, the design of integrated circuits and micro-chips has grown so complex that much of it is done on—or by—computers. As in so many other industries, testing of the designs is also done on the computer.[34] Computers are being used to simulate computers; thus, if errors occur and go undetected during the design phase, software glitches in to-day's computers could become hardware flaws in tomorrow's computers. Of course, this doesn't mean the process would be more error-free without computers; the chips are simply too complex to be manufactured perfectly in any event. For example, Intel Corporation's Pentium microprocessor received sudden media attention when Thomas Nicely, a mathematics professor in Lynchburg, Virginia, discovered that the chip had a flaw in its floating point divider.[35] The story got a lot of press and inspired some jokes in the computer community (Q: What's another name for the "Intel Inside" sticker they put on Pentiums? A: Warning label), but Intel's promise to replace the chip seemed to quell any fears that might have arisen; the "new" replacement chip, by virtue of its being the "replacement," was seen as being better. But can anyone prove that it is really more error-free than the chip it replaces?

At any rate, computer imaging and simulation represent a shift from the *perceptual* to the *conceptual,* a shift that underscores a willingness to exchange direct experience for abstractions that open up the wide vistas not directly available to the senses. As subjunctive documentary, computer simulation reconstructs and preserves, but not without speculation; several layers of assumptions (concerning the computer hardware, the software, the expert witness, and the applied theories) will always be present. The data used in simulations are often much more selective and abstract than the images and sound of conventional film documentary, which take in background scenery and sound, recording the subject's milieu along with the subject. Thus a lack of context may occur in some simulations, limiting the means of cross-checking data and limiting the data to only what was thought to be important at the time—or, worse, what could be afforded. The epistemological problems of computer simulation can shed new light on the speculative nature of documentary film and video, when they are viewed as "simulations" of events. However, unlike film and video, computer simulations are relied upon in medicine, science, industry, law, and other institutions in which human lives may depend on decisions based on computer simulations.

Through its translation of the invisible into a visible analogue, computer simulation has allowed the conceptual world to enter the perceptual one, by concretizing the imaginary or speculatory through visualizations. It has created new ways in which an image can be linked to an actual object or event and ways to make that link as flexible and selective as the user wishes to program it. Mathematically reconstructed simulacra are used as representations, standing in for photographic images, and the faith in logic accorded to mathematics may well spill over into the simulations, making them seem more credible in the process. In any event, computer simulations are routinely given the same status as real events, and are relied upon as such. Thus it makes sense to consider computer simulation as a special form of documentary, albeit a subjunctive one. By limiting and elongating the indexical link and combining it with extrapolation or speculation, computer imaging and simulation may suggest that there is a difference between "documentary film" and "nonfiction film," especially when one is documenting the subjunctive.

◆————————————————————————————

NOTES

1. Jonathan Crary, *Techniques of the Observer* (Cambridge: MIT Press, 1990), 129.
2. From the "Positivism" entry by George Boas in *Collier's Encyclopedia*, vol. 19, *Phyfe to Reni* (New York: P. F. Collier, 1993), 292.
3. Don Ihde, *Instrumental Realism: The Interface between Philosophy of Science and Philosophy of Technology* (Bloomington: Indiana University Press, 1991), 87–88.
4. Ibid., 85.
5. Ibid., 107–8. The Ackerman quotes come from Robert Ackerman, *Data, Instruments, and Theory* (Princeton, N.J.: Princeton University Press, 1985), 31, 9.
6. The video camera has likewise been given the status of reliable witness, in the courtroom as well as in psychotherapy sessions, where it has been shown to help mental patients whose responses and behavior are recorded and analyzed. As early as 1977, video's potential was recognized, as in Dr. Arthur Parkinson's "Videocassettes Used as Diagnostic Tools for the Mentally Ill," *Millimeter* (June 1977): 28. Not only were patients recorded, but a computer was then used to analyze their behavior: "It permits us to compare facial expression and physical attitude with specific responses."
7. According to Ihde, an early use of false coloring was for the study of transparent tissue, in order to make cells more visible. *Instrumental Realism*, 88.
8. David F. Malin, "A Universe of Color," *Scientific American*, August 1993, 73, 75.
9. The useful magnification power of the light-based microscope is limited by the wavelength of light in the visible spectrum, which cannot be used to image objects smaller than the light waves themselves, any more than a person could determine much about the shape of a small porcelain figurine while wearing boxing gloves. Because traditional photography also is light based, it suffers the same limitations.

10. Horst Breuker, Hans Dreverman, Christoph Grab, Alphonse A. Rademakers, and Howard Stone, "Tracking and Imaging Elementary Particles," *Scientific American*, August 1991, 58–63. The illustration on p. 61 is especially interesting, as it shows images from three different types of image technologies side by side.

11. Ibid., 63.

12. Brad Warren, "The Winged Wired," *Wired*, August 1994, 36; Kevin M. Baerson, "NOAA Aids in Global Search and Rescue," *Federal Computer Week* 6, no. 3 (February 3, 1992): 8(2). According to Baerson, some 2,262 individuals owe their lives to the Cospas/Sarsat, a satellite tracking system used for locating downed aircraft and sinking boats and ships.

13. Garrett Culhane, "Mission to Planet Earth," *Wired*, December 1993, 94.

14. Of course, there is no way to represent objects of more than three dimensions adequately in visual form; only the "shadow" of a hypercube can be represented in three dimensions. In order to represent more than three dimensions, one must apply some set of visual conventions, placing such images further into the symbolic realm than the iconic. For a discussion of some of these conventions, see Lloyd A. Treinish, "Inside Multidimensional Data," *Byte*, April 1993, 132–35.

15. B. J. Novitski, "Visiting Lost Cities: Using 3D CAD and Rendering Tools, Archaeologists and Architects Are Making Famous Buildings and Cities Accessible to a Wide Audience of 'Travelers,'" *Computer Graphics World* 16, no. 1 (January 1993): 48. On the aural recreation of architectural spaces, see Mark Frauenfelder, "Listening to a Blueprint," *Wired*, February 1995, 47.

16. The fly-throughs of ancient cities are shown on a demo tape produced by the Taisei Corporation. For a description of the Taisei Corporation, see Paul Gillin, "Mixing High Tech and High Rises," *Computerworld* 24, no. 33 (August 13, 1990): S25(2).

17. Gene Bylinsky, "The Payoff from 3-D Computing," *Fortune*, autumn 1993, 40.

18. From "Take the Guesswork Out of Modeling," *Exchange*, spring 1994, 12. *Exchange* is a newsletter produced by Viewpoint Datalabs, and is available from the company.

19. From "Simulated Treatment of an Ocular Tumor," *SIGGraph Video Review* no. 9849 *Visualization in Scientific Computing*, (contact: Wayne Lytle, Cornell National Supercomputer Facility, B49, Caldwell Hall, Garden Avenue, Ithaca, NY 14853).

20. Bylinsky, "The Payoff from 3-D Computing," 34.

21. Ibid., 40.

22. Andrew Joscelyne, "A Totally Unreal Car," *Wired*, August 1994, 35.

23. Paul Marcotte, "Animated Evidence: Delta 191 Crash Recreated through Computer Simulations at Trial," *ABA Journal* (December 1989): 52–56. This article was the journal's cover story. Marcotte describes a number of other cases in which computer simulations of events became the deciding factors in the case outcomes and also tells of a company, Graphic Evidence of L.A., that specializes in producing computer-simulated evidence for the courtroom.

24. Daniel Clery, "Black Box Flight Recorder 'Film' of Crashes," *New Scientist*, October 7, 1992, 19.

25. Ralph Rugoff, "Crime Storyboard: Welcome to the Post-rational World," *L.A. Weekly*, December 2–8, 1994, 39. For other examples of the use of computer simulations in the courtroom, see David Sims, "Virtual Evidence on Trial," *IEEE Computer Graphics and Applications* (March 1993): 11–13. On Legal Video Services, a company producing products for video and computer use in the courtroom, see Jordan Gruber, "Persuasion on the Fly," *Wired*, April 1995, 48.

26. Jack Weber, "Visualization: Seeing is Believing; Grasp and Analyze the Meaning of Your Data by Displaying It Graphically," *Byte*, April 1993, 128.

27. For more examples of dangers to public safety caused by software glitches, see Bev Littlewood and Lorenzo Strigini, "The Risks of Software," *Scientific American*, November 1992, 62; W. Wayt Gibbs, "Software's Chronic Crisis," *Scientific American*, September 1994, 86.

28. Theodore Roszak, *The Cult of Information: A Neo-Luddite Treatise on High Tech, Artificial Intelligence, and the True Art of Thinking*, 2d ed. (Berkeley: University of California Press, 1994). Computer simulation-based decision making has being going on for some time; for a look at what it was like more than twenty-five years ago, see U.S. General Accounting Office, *Advantages and Limitations of Computer Simulation in Decisionmaking* (report to the Congress by the Comptroller General of the United States) (Washington, D.C.: U.S. Department of Defense, 1973).

29. Quoted in Simson L. Garfinkel's interview with Peter G. Neumann, "The Dean of Disaster," *Wired*, December 1993, 46.

30. See "Faulting the Numbers," *Science News*, August 24, 1991, 127.

31. Littlewood and Strigini, "The Risks of Software," 62.

32. Ibid., 63.

33. Quoted in Gibbs, "Software's Chronic Crisis," 86–87.

34. Jozef Kalisz, "General-Purpose Languages Simulate Simple Circuits," *EDN* 35 (September 17, 1990): 205–14.

35. Peter Baker, "Flawed Chip Brings Fame," *Milwaukee Journal*, December 17, 1994, 1.

MARK WILLIAMS

[**15**] *History in a Flash:*
Notes on the Myth of TV "Liveness"

The potential relevance of televisual "liveness" to documentary studies
seems apparent. *Liveness,* a term derived from the technological capacity
of electronic media to carry an event virtually simultaneous to the event's
occurrence, suggests an immediacy of the indexical representation of an object (the mediation from protelevisual to text), but also the capacity for a
roughly immediate distribution and exhibition of that representation. When
addressing issues of TV's documentary potential and relation to the real,
however, one must recognize that television, especially as we know it in the
United States, has become a mature but still protean industry, apparatus,
and social institution, and cannot be considered merely as visual broadcast
technology. Liveness, although long considered to be a defining and natural
characteristic of this technology, may best be recognized as a historically
specific and perhaps even situational affect that continues to play a crucial
role in delineating TV's mediation of the real and the real world. In this
essay I will suggest the importance of historicizing the trajectories of U.S.
television's appropriation of, reliance on, and fetishization of liveness by focusing on a specific moment in these trajectories: the April 1952 telecast of
an A-bomb test in Nevada, which was produced regionally by independent
Los Angeles station KTLA but carried nationally by the major networks.

▶

Is It "Live," or Is It TV?

Work in critical television studies has pointed out the extent to which *liveness* has become an expansive and saturated term of sliding, paradoxical
signification regarding contemporary U.S. television, key to what has been
called television's "timeless now." Stephen Heath and Gillian Skirrow,
writing about British TV, have proposed that through a complex negotia-

KTLA camera, equipped with specially filtered Zoomar lens, as seen before the second televised test.

tion of signifying practices and broadcast flow, television seems to identify its every emanantion as "live," regardless of program format. In other words, beyond the description of technological capacity, "liveness" as a mode of televisual address pertains even to the various uses of prerecorded material. Television has become imbued with an institutionalized sense of coexistence and interdependence with the everyday, which suggests "a permanently alive view on the world."[1]

Beverle Houston, in an analysis of televisual desire, posits that liveness pervades U.S. television as an apparatus even when the set isn't on. For Houston, the palpable sense that television is always already available is the "promise" of television, derived from its schedule, coverage, and site of consumption:

> The flow of American television goes on for twenty-four hours a day, which is crucial in producing the idea that the text issues from an endless supply that is sourceless, natural, inexhaustible, and coextensive with psychological reality itself. . . . Thus television's promise is intensified by a certain relation to materiality. Not only does it lean on the world's body—that is to say, in its liveness—but it is available domestically at all moments—that is to say, in its *livedness*.[2]

These studies indicate the complex epistemological and ontological status of contemporary U.S. television—a kind of virtual "presence" that is characterized by sliding notions of "presentness." TV is "present" in its seemingly pervasive spatiality, both in its assumed access to world events and culture and in the saturated availability of TV sets and monitors in both domestic and nondomestic spaces. TV is likewise "present" in its seemingly immediate temporality, via the standard assumptions of "live" electronic representations of events, but also in providing contemporary, market-driven information and knowledges (which it both determines and is determined by), or acting as the de facto curator of visually recorded and mediated culture—its "collection" continually amended, though placed on display according to market concerns such as generational demographics and network brand-name recognition (e.g., the periodic recycling of World War II film footage on cable "history" channels; the stylish use of antiquated network logos, or clips from "rare" TV programs not in the current rerun cycle; the plumbing of news archives in order to create programming that promises cultural memory "flashbacks").

Studies of specific textual dynamics and signifying practices have afforded additional critical distance regarding televisual liveness and its approximation of the real. Jane Feuer has extended the ideological study of liveness, suggesting that TV's presumed ontology of technological simultaneity is often posited as a condition if not a guarantor of objectivity, even as it functions to smooth over television's characteristic discontinuity and "segmentation without closure."[3] Recent work by Claus-Dieter Rath, Mary Ann Doane, and Patricia Mellencamp has emphasized the crucial role that coverage of social discontinuities—crises and catastrophes—plays in anchoring TV "liveness" to the "real."[4] Such telecasts are suggested to reaffirm, through their shock value and proximity to death, TV's distinctive access to the Real, but also function as a denial of the processes of television's economic project to sell audiences to advertisers. They are also significant as they serve in part to demarcate the valuation of different formats of liveness (e.g., breaking news of humanistic import versus the Home Shopping Channel).

Just as television can be seen to have configured to its benefit the relationship of liveness to the present/Real, so does it configure the relationship of liveness to the past. Mimi White has delineated the semantic play regarding TV's usage of the term *history*, which she suggests is invoked on TV as another kind of meaningful (culturally weighted) term even as it is employed in ways that are fragmentary and multiple. Most relevant to the present essay is her point that even though liveness and immediacy are in most conventional senses implicitly opposed to history (as closed, absent, or past), contemporary U.S. television invokes the term *history* in such dispersed and contradictory ways as to conflate liveness and history as equally mystified concepts, if not precisely a conceptual equivalence. The specificity of temporal relations implied by traditional notions of history is relativized within televisual practices, which denote as "historic" a melange of non-complementary "events," each of which is cast as "live" in the televisual flow. For example, an event to be broadcast on TV may be politically or socially momentous; that TV is covering an event, perhaps merely a popular event, may be unprecedented; or a "classic" but as yet unaired program episode may premiere. In addition, the *mise-en-abyme* of intertextual references on TV can serve to cavalierly reconfigure or absolutely confound historical principles regarding TV series histories, reruns, and so on (e.g., Pam's infamous "dream" on *Dallas*, which most problematically recharacterized an entire season's episodes and events).

▶

Television, History, and Con/Textuality

Each of the aforementioned studies makes a distinct contribution toward an understanding of "liveness" in its elaborate and various contemporary modalities and demonstrates that liveness cannot be posited as "naturally" derived from electronic technology. Attention to the rise and development of these modalities can augment and help to refine our understanding of television's relationship to the Real. Because contemporary television insists on and propagates its sense of "presence," and because it plays with contradictory practices of historicism, issues related to television's own history can potentially widen the range of questions regarding the televisual "real."

An important tool in this project can be textual analysis. Television's protean, market-driven changes make its signifying practices almost inevitably doomed to someday become conspicuously antiquated (or surprisingly consistent). As a result, an examination of television texts from prior periods can afford otherwise unavailable insights about current television practices, particularly if those texts are placed in larger industrial and institutional contexts.

A valuable indication of this kind of study is provided by Robert Vianello's investigation of liveness as a specific network strategy of dominance in the United States, achieved first in the radio industry and then in television. Vianello introduces a significant gradation of liveness based on the "quality" of spectacle and coverage: the networks, he suggests, constructed and relied upon an enhanced kind of programmed "live" that only they could afford, essentially delineating categorizations of "network live" versus "local live," which was a less desirable or alluring proximation of the technology. The lower production values of local programming, in other words, contributed to the distinction between local and national as represented in broadcast technologies.

Although Vianello does not analyze individual program texts, his attention to textual issues as they correspond to the appropriation of "liveness" in determining relations of power in these industries is noteworthy. My chief reservation about Vianello's analysis is that it ultimately also posits the local as merely a bad or inferior object, and so revalidates network practices as perhaps singularly important in this history. Although networks of course have been and remain crucial forces of economic determination and viewer identification in U.S. broadcast media, and historical work on them is most valuable, it is also important to recognize that a lack of attention to nonnetwork practices can lead to a homology of, in this case, networks and television, which, as Vianello's study ultimately suggests, networks themselves have had an interest in promoting.

In this essay, then, I will suggest an intervention to the historicized understanding of "liveness" and its significance to the televisual "real" through textual analysis but also through attention to nonnetwork practices.[5] I adopt a brand of historical inquiry additionally distanced from that typically deployed by television itself. As Colin McArthur points out, television, when self-consciously engaged in historical work, represents history as positivistic, unproblematic, linear, and evenly developmental.[6] This is especially true when television represents its own history. Critical work about television history should endeavor to recognize the uneven and differential temporalities that characterize the emerging strategies and configurations of power in this history.

▶
The Context of Local Los Angeles Television

Early Los Angeles TV can serve as a singular and important object for critical U.S. television history. As a region, L.A. emerged from World War II as an established but still burgeoning metropolis. As a television market, it was physically displaced from the network administrations and webs in the East. A strongly independent television market, Los Angeles had featured experimental TV broadcasts since 1931. By September 1949, the city had what was at the time a full complement of seven TV stations, even though the network affiliates were the last of these to receive their commercial licenses. The predominant station in this period was KTLA, the first commercial station west of the Mississippi, owned and operated by Paramount Pictures.

KTLA flourished in these early years under the stewardship of television pioneer Klaus Landsberg, a German émigré who was hired by Paramount to head the studio's experimental Los Angeles station W6XYZ in 1941. The station was maintained through the war years and received its commercial license as KTLA in January 1947, one full year before any of the local competing stations and two years before any Los Angeles network affiliate. Partially due to this head start, Landsberg was able to establish KTLA as the region's leading station and chief competition to the networks.

As was the case at most stations in this period, Landsberg programmed a staple of available movies and various low-budget studio shows. But remote telecasts were central to KTLA's popularity and notoriety, and were developed into a practice that effectively served as a kind of station identification. Landsberg realized that telecasts featuring mobile pickups "solved" certain industrial, economic, and programming limitations endemic to local stations, while at the same time capitalizing on opportunities in the burgeoning community for both "entertainment" and "public service" programming. Working to stimulate local interest in KTLA by marrying the topicality of television to that of events within the city, remotes also helped to profile the station as a leading participant in a community medium.

Landsberg had experimented with remote telecasts at the station since 1942, and had utilized an operational mobile unit since 1943. In the postwar years, KTLA (as well as the other local stations) most often featured remotes of sporting events in the area. But Landsberg also contracted for regular nonstudio telecasts of musical entertainers and other popular fare. Perhaps the defining event of KTLA's "remote" identity was its 27.5-hour coverage of the attempted rescue of Kathy Fiscus, a three-year-old child who ultimately did not survive a fall down a narrow San Marino well. The impact of this April 1949 event and telecast is legendary in Southern California; it brought the region to a virtual standstill and changed for many the popular perception of television. (As a news event, it also garnered national and even international attention.)

By documenting and providing arresting access to a disruption in the social "real," the Fiscus telecast can be seen to have helped to instill a desire for what Doane calls television's "lure of referentiality." In establishing, at the local level, an alleged access to the Real, it led to a popular reassessment of television as a "good object," able to offer a variety of topicalities and identifications. It helped to establish for L.A. television a promise to be an eye on the world—or at least the region. It functioned, in other words, not to "solve" television's paradoxes of discontinuity, but to help establish them and their allure. It also foregrounded KTLA as the leading station for local "coverage" within months of the network affiliates' coming on the air in Los Angeles.

The "discontinuity" particular to the Fiscus telecast should be further positioned historically, for it was not especially enhanced by its interruption of the regular TV programming schedule, as Doane and Mellencamp suggest is true of crisis coverage today. The extant TV schedule—television's continuity—was experienced by too few and was too partial and undeveloped to be considered, in Nick Browne's important formulation, as a "supertext":[7] television's relationship to the larger social Symbolic was only partial and fragmentary; its "logic and rhythm" had not yet had significant impact on (that is, had only begun to "naturalize") the social order.

Indeed, the disruptibility of the televisual flow was endemic to this era, and in such a state of imbalance as to render typically only "unpleasure." The programs broadcast were often not those listed in the newspaper; rudimentary technical skills and aesthetics were in process of standardization; the degree of professionalism for on-air performers was decidedly uneven; mawkishness and hype characterized advertisements (though in this instance we may find a distinct continuity with today). To some degree, these aspects of early televisual address were received as humorous, or perhaps tolerable when positioned as part of the medium's "novelty" status. But the still-modest revenues from advertisers, which would not increase before full employment of the coast-to-coast "link" and the end of the FCC freeze on stations in 1952 ensured a further saturation of sets (and genuine national ad rates), virtually ensured a lack of preparation and rehearsal time as well as persistent gaffes. The move from novelty to institution would depend to some extent on a demonstration of television's access to the Real.

By the spring of 1952, when KTLA's "feed" of the A-bomb test was nationally carried, institutional, technological, and programming developments had transformed much of the early television landscape, and KTLA's position within it. The completion of the transcontinental microwave and coaxial relay enabled the national coverage of the tests, but more significantly enhanced the threat of network domination of the Los Angeles market. A sign of the times to come was the ongoing construction of large state-of-the-art West Coast production facilities by both NBC and CBS.[8] What's more, the competition for local news coverage had grown considerably, the result of development in the local TV industry but also of increased demand for TV news—a condition more ideological than merely industrial.

According to a study conducted by James Rue for the Department of Radio-Television at USC, the "spark" for this interest was the outbreak of the Korean War in late June 1950 (nine months after Truman had announced the Soviet Union's atomic capabilities).[9] Television news was at this time temporally disadvantaged compared with both radio and newspapers because of its reliance on teletype, wirephoto, and less immediate film and newsreel coverage of nonlocal events. Nevertheless, the war induced an almost immediate increase in the number of TV news programs and news personnel, a growth rate much accelerated in comparison with that of the rest of local television. The TV broadcast day was slowly expanding: at the time the war began, only two independent stations, KFI (channel 9) and KLAC (channel 13), programmed shows during the morning, afternoon, and evening. All other stations broadcast only in the evening, though schedules of many were set to expand in the fall.[10] Even with such attenuated schedules, there was an empirical jump in the number of newscasts:

> In early June, 1950, just before the war broke out in Korea, three of the seven TV stations in the Los Angeles area had no regularly scheduled news programs on the air. Soon, all seven outlets frequently supplied war news headlines. By the end of August, eighty-seven news presentations were available as compared to fifty-six before the war.[11]

As this suggests, regional socioeconomic developments (and associated ideological parameters) are also important to consider in contextualizing the A-bomb telecasts, which demonstrate both celebration and wariness toward these spectacles of power. Local interest in the Korean effort was pervasive, as it affected not only nationalistic sentiments but also various regional economic and security concerns. Many troops and reserves lived in Southern California, and the ports in Long Beach and San Diego were active points of departure and arrival during the war. The renewal of military and munitions manufacturing also proved a widespread boon to local Los Angeles industry. A related, growing fear of nuclear attack and devastation was part of a larger civic and socioeconomic contradiction, whereby California cities courted new military-industrial investments while decrying the threat such investments incurred.[12]

Anti-red sentiments and suspicions, already prevalent, were newly fueled and expanded upon. The House Un-American Activities Committee (HUAC) continued its second, more sweeping probe of the motion picture industry. By February 1952, the committee was announcing that Hollywood was "the Communists' greatest financial angel," and was cautioning the television industry against similar "infiltration." Apparently as a public response to such charged implications, Landsberg—who of course worked for a television station owned and operated by a movie studio—

distanced television from motion pictures by offering an industrially based rationale to deflect the committee's suspicions. Suggesting that "the very nature" of the television industry would act as a "safeguard" against such political infiltration, he added: "We don't employ people just for one show. . . . Our producers, directors and writers are part of a permanent staff, and therefore better known to us than people in a media who are hired per job."[13]

Televising the Nevada A-bomb tests, the planning of which began about five weeks after Landsberg's comments, fit squarely within all of the dynamics detailed above: it provided KTLA a newsworthy coup through which the station transcended local and network competition (furnishing the "feed" for every L.A. station and the major networks); it served as a nationalistic bellwether through its demonstration of U.S. prowess during a wartime political environment;[14] it celebrated U.S. defense interests and developments, which were important to the region's economy as well as to its clout in Washington; and it provided the ultimate imagery for dystopic fears and Los Angeles's catastrophic imaginary.

▶

History in a Flash: The Nevada A-Bomb Test

Especially in the case of the first sanctioned televised test on April 22, 1952,[15] KTLA occupied a unique televisual role, positioned centrally within both the local and national broadcasts of the tests—a kind of technological/industrial discursive "shifter," because its "feed" was employed in every possible communicative act of the blanketed televising of this event.[16] Landsberg and the station reached a pinnacle of apparatus-hood that day, at the cutting edge of most all that television as an industry and as an emerging cultural institution could hope to be. Landsberg was the only industry representative willing to undertake the preparations necessary for these telecasts, organizing and building in less than three weeks a complete microwave relay system to Las Vegas via four line-of-sight mountain peaks. KTLA and Paramount had gambled the entire cost of the enterprise, which would pay off only if successful. With the cooperation of the Atomic Energy Commission (AEC), especially the use of a Marine helicopter, the relay was achieved in time so that the telecast could be received nationally.[17]

This logistical accomplishment is the dominant profile of the incident still maintained by the station in its self-histories and publicity materials. Although the considerable efforts of Landsberg and his crew should certainly be recognized, given that they evidenced an ingenuity and determination remarkable for that time or any other, my concerns in this essay do not rest with these achievements. Indeed, such an emphasis on the very act of "communicating"—on the technological and discursive processes and accomplishments in "covering" the tests—can be seen to suffuse this coverage, and to serve as one important mode of "containing" the underlying threats and contradictions that the tests made manifest. The historical significance of KTLA's activities that day exceeds the phatic role that the station played and resonates with the ideological charge that almost all of the television industry was both tapping into and helping to disseminate.

It should be stressed that the tests were to some degree "staged" and prearranged, ploys for publicity and ideology dissemination by the Atomic Energy Commission. Although fully "expected," the performance of the tests themselves mixed what Doane and Mellencamp refer to as "crisis" and "catastrophe" modes of temporality. Prior to the countdown to explosion (itself a crisis-laden temporality, emphasizing limited amounts of time), the coverage consisted largely of surveying the tools and preparations for the tests and the telecasts—underscoring the deadline-like qualities of this event and its coverage. The crucial moment of detonation can be seen to evoke catastrophe not only by its characteristic "instantaneous" occurrence, but also of course by its spectacle of devastating power. Unlike genuine catastrophe coverage, these telecasts did not mediate an unexpected interruption of the everyday, a sudden shock that therefore allows the potential for new configurations of meaning. They nevertheless displayed and considered at length the "sign" of a genuine threat of catastrophe—one with the capacity to destabilize comfortable everyday "knowledges"—and ultimately treated that sign as a fetish in an effort to contain and control its meaning.

The A-bomb telecasts were extreme in their display of both dread and military prowess. The bomb's capacity for widespread destruction was genuine and awe-inspiring—very real and yet too much to imagine. In addition, there existed deep ambivalence pervading the spectacle of the mushroom cloud—an image so ominous and yet so nebulous as to allow any number of potential (and contradictory) meanings to be aligned with it. Doane suggests that catastrophe, especially in the postindustrial age, always has to do with technology and its potential collapse, "the failure of the escalating technological desire to conquer nature."[18] In the case of catastrophes, she points out, terms of description and analysis can resonate with culturally gendered assignations, as a masculinist discourse "attempts to reestablish control over a failed masculinized technology."[19] The descriptions provided in the first A-bomb telecast by newsmen Grant Holcomb and Fred Henry, who provided brief but telling voice-over commentary for

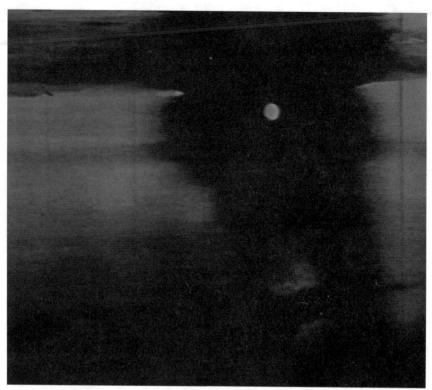

The explosion renders a negative effect, via lens flare.

this landmark event, establish a telling "range" of possible readings or interpretations of the imagery of this spectacle, generally oscillating between aesthetic beauty and devastating effects. They nevertheless also indicate the futility of such an attempted semantic containment.

As the cameras focus on a blurry terrain, Holcomb announces, "Bombs away." He counts off increments of five seconds in a regular, metric pacing. Suddenly, the sight of the explosion briefly overexposes and blacks out the entire screen. Soon a ball of white near the horizon line peers out from within the black circle enshrouding it. Another faint announcement reports that a shock wave will arrive in thirty seconds. Only then, a full half minute after the detonation, does Holcomb offer a laconic comment:

GH: Well, there it is. The first public demonstration, and the biggest continental atomic detonation in the history of the world.

Shortly thereafter, Henry begins to describe the mushroom cloud the detonation has produced. (The following quotes are excerpted from the telecast, but maintain the continuity of the commentaries; breaks indicated are breaks in the correspondents' own speech.)

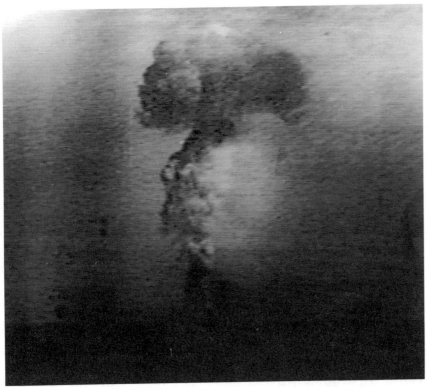

Full image of the bomb blast, from the second test televised by KTLA.

FH: . . . exploded into not the flashy red, brilliant red that we had been led to believe. But it just seemed to hover there for a moment, and then it went up and now it is pouring into the . . . like a donut completely unfolding itself. . . . a huge puff on a pipe almost, and the red and the brown is now tumbling under, as white smoke comes down from the top, and the dust across this entire basin goes up almost like a battleship. It looks very much like there's a battleship in this basin, with a huge white smoketrail above it, and then this tremendous donut up there that goes higher and higher—it's an absolutely fabulous sight.

GH: Fred, just looking away from the beautiful mushroom that's turning into that fabulous white now, and down to that ugly gray all across the floor of this valley, you can't help but realize that you could put—right inside this proving ground, from where we are—the entire island of Manhattan, New York City. And if you look at that dirty, ugly gray base, you see what that particular weapon can do. And certainly as we've been told here many times during the past few days by Mr. Gordon Dean, the chairman of the Atomic Energy Commission [and] General Joseph Mills, who is in charge of the air-drop today, the enemy certainly has similar weapons.

Henry's description in particular, with almost surreal juxtapositions of images and metaphors (e.g., a donut and a battleship), but also its evocation of fluidity and ephemerality, emphasizes the event's refusal of concrete and universal meanings. Important in this regard is how several ambiguous yet acculturated gender codes may be seen to underlie the more "aesthetic" renderings of the mushroom cloud: daunting in size and extremely colorful, the cloud is described as "unfolding itself," "tumbling under," and perhaps most evocatively as "a huge puff on a pipe." (A description in a second telecast suggests that the cloud resembles a "giant stalk" as well as "a big ball of cotton.") Such a combination of latent female and phallic imagery, supplemented by imagery that is merely incongruous, reveals the imaginary threat that the bomb instills.[20] Holcomb's subsequent envisioning of the Nevada test site transposed upon "the island of Manhattan" functions in a quasi "call-response" fashion, as an ultimate image of catastrophe and nationally symbolic devastation that displaces the trope of (threatening) fluidity manifest in the previous descriptions. This displacement also evidences a key defensive maneuver of historical repression consistent in all of the A-bomb telecasts, as an imagined (defensive) vision of future domestic devastation stands in for any reference to the actual devastation and suffering experienced by the Japanese in 1945.

As this analysis indicates, gendered "informational" discourse, deployed in the attempt to contain the threats endemic to the A-bomb tests, is one key to understanding the depth and specific characteristics of these threats. If, as Doane suggests, the goal of technology is to master nature, the poles of this linear narrative of mastery are transposed and blurred in the case of these nuclear tests. The bomb, as an "advance" in technological evolution, suggests in its moment of detonation the potential instant eradication of that historical line. Its "technology" works not to control nature so much as to "unleash" it, because the bomb's power paradoxically resides in what the scientific discourse of the period referred to as the most basic energy of nature itself.

This gendered discourse moves toward a more decidedly masculinist perspective in Holcomb's subsequent discussion/interview with United Press correspondent Hugh Baillie, one of the "seasoned" and "expert" (national) journalists upon whom much of the rest of the TV coverage relied. Notable here is an emphasis on the physical experience of the event, which is placed into terms resonant with hard-boiled literature: an act of "witnessing" inflected by bravado.

The clip begins with both Holcomb and Baillie looking off toward the distance, surveying what is left of the mushroom cloud.

> GH: Well ladies and gentlemen, this is Mr. Hugh Baillie, a gentleman that I'm apt to run into most anyplace in the world. [Baillie smiles] His byline is

familiar to all of you—he's the president of the United Press. And like yourself and myself, he, too, saw his first atomic detonation this morning. Hugh, what did you think of it?

HB: Well, it was of course one of the most tremendous things the eye of man could witness. And if we were sitting out there now [he looks back], instead of just being a few smoke plumes here and there it would be devastated—filled with dead people. Not many dying people, most of them would be dead, I expect.

GH: That's right. What did you think of that shock wave? Did that catch you unawares, as it did me? [laughs]

HB: The heat wave did. That was the first one. Because that came almost immediately after the fireball. I expected to feel the shock shortly after the fireball, but you remember we saw the fireball . . .

GH: Yes.

HB: . . . and almost at the same time, it was just like opening the door of a furnace, and you felt yourself slapped in the face of that heat wave.

GH: Well after that heat wave, I forgot all about the shock wave, and it really caught me unawares . . . [laughs]

HB: Yes, if you weren't looking for it, it might give you quite a shove. It did me—I sat back up against the table there, and most of [us] were pretty well braced around where I was sitting, and of course they gave us a warning of its arrival over the loudspeaker here, down where I was, but when it came it was as if someone had given you a combination shove and slap.

The commentators represent the bomb, first of all, as an impressive object to be seen by "the eyes of man." The carnage they are quick to imagine seems to coalesce the masculinist perspective implicit to that initial remark, as it serves as an attempt to valorize the act of (passive) witnessing by positioning it in terms of extreme and "unflinching" experience—again invoking but displacing the recent experiences of World War II. Such a constructed emphasis foregrounds the significance of their "actual" experience of the test, especially as their attention to the physicality of the bomb's effects renders an opposing "body" constructed in counterpoint to the masculinist discourse that describes it. This implicitly figures the bomb as "female," complementing the standard masculinist dichotomy between technology and nature to which Doane refers. In light of the rugged journalistic tone that Baillie affects, it might even be suggested that the bomb is discussed as if it were a kind of "femme fatale"—duplicitous yet powerful, slapping and shoving the (male) reporters sent to witness it.

The symbolic positionings of this device are nevertheless fraught with contradictions, perhaps endemic to attempts to transform the threat that the bomb represents into "defense." One sign of this is an "unforced error" that later arises in Henry and Baillie's discussion of the drifting atomic cloud. Their casual indication of the potential for radioactive fallout—a topic that the AEC strongly wished to avoid and downplay—points out how tenuous the "proper" and ideologically supportive discourse could be. Such ideological "leakage" is especially of interest to audiences today, as information about the actual effects of such fallout continues to trickle into public consciousness nearly fifty years after the tests themselves. But it also indicates a centrally important aspect of the marked interest in the tests at that time. One quality pervading the tests and telecasts—easy to ignore from our contemporary perspective—is how secretive and mysterious the development of the bomb had been. Evelyn Fox Keller suggests that the "making of the bomb was perhaps the biggest and best-kept secret that science ever harbored."[21]

Secrets, according to Keller, are important social constructs that "function to articulate a boundary: an interior not visible to outsiders, the demarcation of a separate domain, a sphere of autonomous power."[22] Certainly such a description applies to the AEC, and to the nationalistic security surrounding its activities. But Keller's discussion of "secrecy" and science, which specifically addresses aspects of nuclear research, offers an additional insight into the dynamic of gendered discourse detailed above in the coverage of the nuclear tests. Carrying further the "boundary" of interior/exterior suggested by secrets, Keller suggests that science's "ferreting out of nature's secrets" is from this perspective "understood as the illumination of a female interior, or the tearing of nature's veil."[23]

The allure and impact of the tests—and the containment of that impact—can therefore be seen to rely in part on the "secrecy" of this previous history. The telecasts offered a newly emergent opportunity to tap into this magically powerful, yet previously clandestine, "heritage" of power and prowess, as well as a forbidden, voyeuristic register with which to supplement the dread and awe that the tests continued to inspire. Prior to detonation, for example, the focus on how successful the TV apparatus might be is not only crisislike (e.g., "Will it work at the time we need it?") but also fetishistic, constructing a temporal and visual "keyhole effect" in its suggestion that the much-desired view that we anticipate is so "charged" as to potentially obscure itself from our access.

Joyce Nelson has suggested that the telecasts of A-bomb tests were in part a public relations ploy by the AEC to capitalize on television's tremendous growth and popularity: "Its pleasurable entertainment function in the home could 'rub off,' so to speak, onto the spectacle of bomb-blasts imaged on its screens."[24] Although such a dynamic is conceivable, at least in the homes of those enthralled by nuclear detonations, the reverse impact seems to me more likely. Certainly the AEC was attempting by these tests to instill renewed popularity for its programs in the light of comparatively waning interest and potential budget cuts. But the impact was more dependent on secrecy and danger than on a simplistic favorable gloss. Not unlike the television cameras at Eniwetok for nonpublic A-bomb testing in 1948, the TV apparatus provided visual access to this menacing and unknowable, destructively powerful device, but from a position that ensured a fetishistic pleasure: close enough for viewers to appreciate its threatening splendor, yet far enough away to both preclude any real danger and maintain prolonged visual contact.

This fetishistic dynamic of course enhanced the "spectacle" qualities of the tests and reinforced their "gendered" positioning. It also could be employed to sustain their mystery, as is evidenced in Holcomb's inteview with *New York Times* reporter William L. Laurence during the aftermath of the first televised test. The only reporter present at the initial A-bomb detonation at Alamogordo in 1945, Laurence had been a consistent promoter of nuclear power and nuclear weapons since 1940.[25] Suggested by historian Paul Boyer to be "in effect functioning as the Manhattan Project's public-relations man," Laurence had become the most prominent (and cheerleading) correspondent on the "atomic" beat, even writing *The Hell Bomb* in 1950—a book widely excerpted in popular magazines—in support of expanded weapons testing as a means of speeding development of the more powerful hydrogen bomb.[26] In conversation with Holcomb, Laurence's "seasoned" description of the test blast positions it classically as a fetish, before drifting into a more rational scientific explanation of the explosion:

> GH: Tell me, what's your reaction having seen the first atomic detonation in history, the first nuclear detonation, and then the preceding ones and then this final one today—what's . . .
>
> WL: Well, my reaction, Grant, is really that you never see a second atomic blast. You always, it's always a first. No matter, I think, how many you see, you always have a new experience, as though you have never seen it before. And you stand there, and you gaze at it, and you look at it, and you say, "Am I seeing things, am I dreaming? Is this real, is this possible?" Your senses tell you that it is, but when you think . . . what there is in it. Inside the bomb is a very small amount of material, either plutonium (which is a man-made material, it doesn't exist in nature), or a natural material that exists in nature in very small amounts, called uranium 235. Now the amount actually exploded is so small . . .

Most astonishing in this response is the lethal irony of Laurence's first statement ("you never see a second atomic blast"), which emphasizes the importance of positionality regarding the viewing of the tests: in the case of

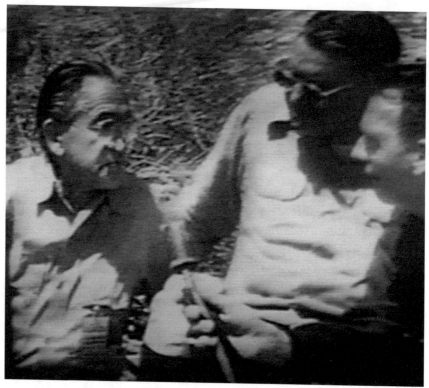

New York Times reporter William Laurence (left) is interviewed after the first televised test.

a nuclear attack, one indeed never sees a second blast. That this irony goes unrecognized is indicative of the haphazard foreclosure of the effects of nuclear devices in this coverage. Whereas other reporters only "imagine" scenes of destruction, Laurence fixates on the spectacle of the device and its detonation, virtually ignoring potential effects. An even more extreme example in the telecasts is a statement by newsman Gil Martyn from the second televised test:

> Words almost fail to describe what we see, and it is with the most inadequate words that we pay tribute to this fearsome creature that we sincerely hope will be used only in a peaceful effort, and not in other ways.

Not only words fail in this instance, but memory and history as well. Laurence's description of the blast as dreamlike and fantastic relates not only to the empirical experience of those present at the test, it also renders a most obvious culmination of the gendering of the bomb, figuring it literally as a psychic fetish in its magical balancing of knowledge and belief. On one level, this balance seems to suggest a "belief" in the bomb's nationalistic symbolic qualities, at the cost of the "knowledge" of the many lives

A-bombs had already taken. On another level of Laurence's description, the bomb is a fetish in its metaphoric association with the mother's (castrated) body. Positioning the bomb as yet one more masculinist substitute for what is perceived as woman's "lack," Laurence reconfirms the "secretive" boundary line, maintaining the bomb's (female) mystery even as he goes on to explain its scientific principles.

The boundaries ascribed to atomic weapons in this broadcast induce a fascination that limits questions of personal and social agency regarding this "power," and even an effacement of the bomb's history. Exemplary of catastrophic events (even virtual or staged ones, as in this instance), the tests offered no simple, readily definable reassurance or rearticulation of traditional values. In the "live" mediation of these events, what the telecasts most provide is a valorization of top-down hierarchies of knowledge and power (of course complementary to the masculinist discourses above) and a merger of containments or appeasements to this display of problematic nationalistic power: the reliance on traditional and official arbiters of "coverage" of the event, who were significantly "national" in their reputations, scope of experience, and resources.

The marked public, nationalistic interest in the A-bomb tests was of course the primary determinant of the telecast's anticipated allure, so much so that this first broadcast might be considered a nascent "media event," in the terms of Daniel Dayan and Elihu Katz's study of this television genre.[27] This telecast conforms to many of the criteria found in the Dayan and Katz studies: the event to be represented was widely anticipated and prearranged, its importance was seen to be sufficient to dominate and preempt regular broadcast practices and schedules, and the success of the staged act was historically and socially charged. But the test and its telecast were resolutely "spectacular," refusing any genuinely participatory or interactive response, save a mixture of awe and dread. (It is interesting to note, however, that in Los Angeles the interest level was so high that the Orpheum theater screened the telecast to a full house via theater television.) Varied in audience response probably to the extent of cultural contradiction, the A-bomb telecast ultimately is akin to media events only in its apparent ideological intentions, which, as Dayan and Katz explain, generally "are salutes to the status quo, legitimations of elites, and reiterations of the national well-being . . . undoubtedly reinforcing of the existing power structure, even if they open delicate, potentially subversive questions."[28] As close analysis of the A-bomb telecast reveals, such problematic "questions" did indeed arise, even in the course of "live," "objective" coverage implicitly supportive of the AEC.

►

Conclusion

Industrially and institutionally, Landsberg's notable efforts were an attempt to transcend the impending threats to KTLA's stature and market strength by "tapping into" both local and national interest in the tests. The telecasts can be seen, however, ultimately to have contributed to the enhancement of TV's access to a national Symbolic, a quality central to the development of a "liveness" that the networks would appropriate in their consolidation of televisual address and power. (The culminating experience of this mediated Symbolic would be coverage of the JFK assassination and funeral in 1963.)[29] Nevertheless, the telecast remains instructive as to a historicized understanding of TV liveness, especially in relation to issues of local versus national television. It is worth noting that through industrial and regulatory shifts, the status of these latter terms has grown toward an almost paradoxical complexity. KTLA, for example, which was created as an arm of Paramount Pictures and remains the major independent television station in Los Angeles, is today owned by the Chicago Tribune and exists as a nationally available superstation, affiliated to the recently formed Warner Bros. "network."

More directly relevant to the telecast analyzed here is KTLA's famous role as the source for a more recent and notorious local/national news story: the dissemination via satellite of George Holliday's camcorder videotape recording of the Rodney King beating. Although similar to the role the station played in the first A-bomb telecast, this latter example might best be seen as indicative of a trope of less centralized sources and arbiters of the televisual "real"—a different hierarchy of access, a different display of power, but producing a nevertheless critical impact on popular memory and national consciousness.

Contemporary television continues to afford, and often relies upon, constructions of "live" through its coverage of news and events (e.g., the Gulf War; the O.J. chase, trials, and verdicts; the death and funeral of Princess Diana). But as John Caldwell suggests, in the age of cable and satellite channel proliferation and especially digital effects, television's affect of and for the moment has become as much or more a question of aesthetics and pictorialism as it is news.[30] The performance of specifically televisual cutting-edge style (graphics, editing, animation, and so on) may be seen to be as determinant of TV's market-driven "now" as is any breaking event or new information that a station or network might report. But even the coverage and construction of such events and information tend to reveal new modalities of temporality increasingly beholden to dictates of entertainment economics. Examples range from syndicated infomercials that feature count-down clocks in order to stimulate sales to NBC's coinage of the phrase "plausibly live" to describe the network's time-shifted prime-time coverage of the 1996 Summer Olympics. The complexities and paradoxes of liveness indeed seem to lie continuously at the core of television's impetus to transform itself as it keeps hold of our attention. The study of historically specific appropriations of power, which both afford and are afforded by the institutionalized but dynamic practices of the empirical and virtual "real worlds" linked by the televisual "live," will continue to suggest more thorough understandings of television as a force in American and global cultures.

◆ ──────────────────────────────────

NOTES

1. Stephen Heath and Gillian Skirrow, "Television: A World in Action," *Screen* 18, no. 2 (summer 1977): 54.
2. Beverle Houston, "Viewing Television: The Metapsychology of Endless Consumption," *Quarterly Review of Film Studies* 9, no. 3 (summer 1984): 184.
3. Jane Feuer, "The Concept of Live Television: Ontology as Ideology," in *Regarding Television*, ed. E. Ann Kaplan (Frederick, Md.: University Publications of America, 1983), 12–22.
4. See Claus-Dieter Rath, "Live Television and Its Audiences: Challenges of Media Reality," in *Remote Control: Television, Audiences and Cultural Power*, ed. Ellen Seiter, Hans Borchers, Gabrielle Kreutzner, and Eva-Maria Warth (New York: Routledge, 1989), 79–95; Mary Ann Doane, "Information, Crisis, Catastrophe," and Patricia Mellencamp, "TV Time and Catastrophe, or *Beyond the Pleasure Principle* of Television," both in *Logics of Television*, ed. Patricia Mellencamp (Bloomington: Indiana University Press, 1990).
5. It should be noted that because contemporary context affects any writing of history, the current climate of U.S. television, with hegemonic networks facing continuous and critical loss of audience and sway, may provide an additional degree of interest in historical issues of local and independent programming.
6. Colin McArthur, *BFI Television Monograph 8: Television and History* (London: British Film Institute, 1980).
7. Nick Browne, "The Political Economy of the Television (Super) Text," *Quarterly Review of Film Studies* 9, no. 3 (summer 1984): 174–83.
8. The CBS studio, located at Beverly and Fairfax and deemed "Television City," was estimated to be more than 30 percent complete in February 1952. The actual construction of NBC's new studio was begun on July 7, but was completed more quickly through the use of "tilt-up slab techniques." Both were partially operational and in use by October 1952, in time for the fall season. See "Teevee Plant Opens Oct. 1," *Los Angeles Herald Examiner*, February 5, 1952; "Southland Gains as Tele Center for U.S.," *Los Angeles Herald Examiner*, October 5, 1952.
9. James Joseph Rue, "Analysis of Television News Techniques in the Los Angeles Area" (master's thesis, University of Southern California, January 1951).
10. Ibid., 4. Rue also details the procedures of independent TV news producer Sam Hayes, who prepared complete nightly or weekly news packages on a freelance basis. The extent to which his material was aired is unclear.
11. Ibid., 54.
12. For a thorough examination of the history of this dynamic, see Roger W. Lotchin, *Fortress California 1910-1961: From Warfare to Welfare* (New York: Oxford University Press, 1992).
13. Quoted in "House Group Asks Spy Death Penalty in Time of Peace," *New York Times*, February 17, 1952, 4. A related response from Harry Ackerman, vice president in charge of CBS television, confirmed that his network employed a loyalty questionnaire for each prospective employee.
14. Truman's approval of domestic testing of atomic bombs had occurred months after the Korean conflict began. See Howard Ball, *Justice Downwind: America's Atomic Testing Program in the 1950's* (New York: Oxford University Press, 1986), 20–31.
15. KTLA and KTTV had fashioned an ad hoc

telecast of a test more than a year earlier. In the predawn hours of February 6, 1951, they pointed their cameras toward Las Vegas to capture the "flash" of the final explosion of the "Ranger Series" of tests. See Walter Ames, "Blast of Atom Bomb Thrills Audience; Ferrer, Swanson Talk Radio Series," *Los Angeles Times*, February 7, 1951, 26.

16. Shifters are linguistic units, the meaning of which depends upon the situation of address or the context of utterance—such as the words *I* and *you*, which "shift" in meaning depending on who is speaking. I use the term here to emphasize both the historical specificity of this unprecedented configuration and its geographic and industrial characteristics.

17. The most detailed report on the production of these telecasts is the May 9, 1952, speech by Charter Heslep to the Georgia Radio and Television Institute: "They Said It Couldn't Be Done," in *New Horizons in Journalism, 1951–52* (Athens: University of Georgia, 1952), 62–73.

18. Doane, "Information, Crisis, Catastrophe," 231.

19. Ibid., 239.

20. It may prove useful to consider the bomb as indeed a "queer" object, especially regarding these properties of fluidity and the overall strategies of "othering" its perceived threat. See Diana Fuss, "Inside/Out," in *Inside/Out: Lesbian Theories, Gay Theories*, ed. Diana Fuss (New York: Routledge, 1991), 1–10.

21. Evelyn Fox Keller, "From Secrets of Life to Secrets of Death," in *Body/Politics: Women and the Discourses of Science*, ed. Mary Jacobus, Evelyn Fox Keller, and Sally Shuttleworth (New York: Routledge, 1990): 180.

22. Ibid, 178.

23. Ibid., 178–79.

24. Joyce Nelson, *The Perfect Machine: TV in the Nuclear Age* (Toronto: Between the Lines, 1987): 42.

25. See William L. Laurence, "The Atom Gives Up," *Saturday Evening Post*, September 7, 1940, 12–13, 60–63.

26. Paul Boyer, *By the Bomb's Early Light* (New York: Pantheon, 1985): 187. See also William L. Laurence, *The Hell Bomb* (New York: Alfred A. Knopf, 1951).

27. See Daniel Dayan and Elihu Katz, "Electronic Ceremonies: Television Performs a Royal Wedding," in *On Signs*, ed. Marshall Blonsky (Baltimore: Johns Hopkins University Press, 1985), 16–32; Daniel Dayan and Elihu Katz, *Media Events: The Live Broadcasting of History* (Cambridge: Harvard University Press, 1992).

28. Dayan and Katz, *Media Events*, 224–25.

29. See especially Mellencamp, "TV Time and Catastrophe"; Philip Rosen, "Document and Documentary: On the Persistence of Historical Concepts," in *Theorizing Documentary*, ed. Michael Renov (New York: Routledge, 1993), 58–89.

30. See John Caldwell, *Televisuality: Style, Crisis, and Authority in American Television* (New Brunswick, N.J.: Rutgers University Press, 1995). Caldwell decries theoretical work on "liveness" because it has so often been posited in the service of denigrating the aesthetics, production values, and even the very act of viewing television. Although I agree with the underlying motivation for his argument, it seems to me that dismissing liveness study altogether is throwing the baby out with the bathwater. Through the present essay I of course hope to advocate future work in liveness studies.

MICHAEL RENOV

[16]   *Documentary Horizons: An Afterword*

Not too many years ago, as I was deciding on a title for a collection of essays on nonfiction film, I tried out *Rethinking Documentary* on a documentary filmmaker friend. His somewhat flippant rejoinder was that documentary had yet to be "thought" for the first time, let alone "rethought." At the time, I had trouble arguing the point. Not so today. In what follows I will survey the current conditions of documentary research at a moment of expansion and redefinition and suggest some of the most productive directions that research might take in the years ahead.[1]

The 1998 Society for Cinema Studies conference featured no fewer than nine panels or workshops devoted to documentary topics. Many of these panels' themes might once have missed the documentary studies "radar" entirely:

Spectator studies specific to the documentary
Analyses of sex education films
The role of documentary in the construction of "nation"
Representations of the everyday in 1950s television
Explorations of autobiographical practices
The analysis of irony in documentary film

This roster of topics indicates that a number of the most compelling research questions alive in media studies today are now being posed in relation to nonfiction film and video. What is largely missing from the SCS sessions is a hagiographic focus on the documentary patriarchs—Flaherty, Grierson, Rouch, Leacock—an approach largely consistent with an older auteurist emphasis.

This is not to suggest that there have been no significant revisionist histories written in the 1990s, for indeed there have been. The two best may be those of Brian Winston, who, in his *Claiming the Real*, argues that the Griersonian documentary project, long considered a model for documentary advocacy, in fact constituted a monumental retreat from radical aims (a "running away from social meaning"), and Fatimah Tobing Rony, author of *The Third Eye,* who, as Jane Gaines notes in the introduction to this book, delivers a devastating critique of Flaherty's *Nanook of the North* as an exercise in "ethnographic taxidermy," the romanticized preservation of an exoticized Other.[2] The appearance of two such books in the mid-1990s combining biting ideological critique with historiographic ambition demonstrates documentary's current vibrancy and breadth. They are the work of a British scholar and longtime documentary practitioner on the one hand and of a young Asian American feminist—part scholar, part independent filmmaker—on the other. But there can be little doubt that the new directions in documentary studies are being forged by a generation of scholars who have far less interest in revisiting the canon than in appropriating theoretical principles derived from the study of documentary for their own purposes.

This tendency, far from provoking the scorn of the elders, should be understood for what it is: documentary's long-overdue "discovery" by the American academy and hence its reinvention. The emergence of new research topics such as those featured at the recent SCS meeting threaten to recast documentary studies to such a degree that the standard historical survey, Erik Barnouw's *Documentary: A History of the Non-Fiction Film,* may soon cease to set a sufficient or fully historicizing agenda for the advanced student.[3] Barnouw is nothing less than a totemic ancestor; in these circumstances, patricide should be recognized as a symptom of the field's vitality.

▶

A Critical Survey

In fact, the most recent forays into nonfiction scholarship appear in the wake of a significant number of documentary-themed books published in English in the 1990s. In the front ranks must be the twin efforts of Bill Nichols, *Representing Reality* (1991) and *Blurred Boundaries* (1994), the first of which has established itself as the single most significant and influential book on documentary film.[4] Interestingly, the two volumes contain somewhat complementary insights, with *Representing Reality* laying out a series of taxonomic grids within which all documentary can presumably be located and the latter book exploring the outer limits of current practice and its altered epistemic underpinnings. In *Blurred Boundaries,* for example,

Nichols explores the new documentary's recourse to situated or embodied knowledge rather than universalizable abstraction and the tendency toward the performative in place of the sober discursivity that served as the defining condition of documentary in the earlier book. *Theorizing Documentary* (1993), a collection that I edited, called by Noel Carroll "a state-of-the-art compendium of received thinking about the documentary film," did indeed attempt to situate documentary within diverse currents of contemporary thought, ranging from postcolonial discourse to ordinary language philosophy, queer theory, and historical poetics.[5] It was the first collection of essays exclusively devoted to theoretical questions arising in the study of documentary film and video, though without sacrifice of historiographic concerns, as evidenced in essays by Philip Rosen, Brian Winston, and Paul Arthur.

Both John Corner's *The Art of Record: A Critical Introduction to Documentary* and Richard Kilborn and John Izod's *An Introduction to Television Documentary* provide close and careful analysis of documentary television in Britain.[6] Although Corner's book does include a chapter on *Roger & Me*, it, like Kilborn and Izod's volume, is almost exclusively British in its focus. This national specificity, although limiting for American audiences, is the source of the books' strength, given their attention to the questions confronting makers, critics, and audiences of the documentary film in the United Kingdom today. Both books make it crystal clear that no meaningful forum for documentary practice exists in Britain outside of television. A comparable examination of the relations between U.S. broadcast institutions and contemporary documentary practices has yet to be undertaken and would be of enormous significance in a culture that presumes that maverick practitioners of any sort can always beat the odds. Given the scant options of the film festival circuit and fast-disappearing nontheatrical distribution, it is increasingly the case that American independent documentarists find few exhibition outlets outside television. The one new book that situates American documentary practices in relation to broadcast institutions is Deirdre Boyle's *Subject to Change: Guerrilla Television Revisited*, which provides the definitive account of that moment in the late 1960s and early 1970s when collectives of young men and women attempted to reinvent television with their Sony portapaks, their anger, and their commitment.[7] By writing the history of these grassroots alternatives and their coverage of dissent, community building, and wacky Americana, Boyle has helped to fill a crucial gap in our understanding of this century's documentary landscape.

Paula Rabinowitz's *They Must Be Represented*, although not exclusively devoted to documentary film, is at its best when it focuses on the interweaving of multiple discursive registers and rhetorical figures drawn from Depression-era America.[8] The discussions of such key documentary films as *The River* and *The Plow That Broke the Plains* are strengthened by the attention given to contemporaneous efforts by Farm Security Administration photographers and populist writers as well as the practitioners of Hollywood cinema. Carl Plantinga's *Rhetoric and Representation in Nonfiction Film* is a work of a dramatically different order; Plantinga seeks to offer an original and globalizing theory of nonfiction discourse based on a philosophy of "possible worlds."[9] In so doing, he seeks to bypass the traditional and now oversaturated documentary debates around "truth" and "reality." While it remains to be seen how fruitful this tack will prove to be, Plantinga's book makes a significant contribution to an increasing theoretical/methodological pluralism discernible in current documentary studies, a condition requisite to any field of study.

In a rather more combative tone, Noel Carroll has issued his own challenge to what he deems the postmodernist branch of documentary studies that emerged in the early 1990s (his references are to the work of Bill Nichols, Brian Winston, and myself). An acknowledged "epistemic conservative," Carroll inveighs against "postmodernist film theorists" whom he claims are attracted to philosophical positions that are "either shallow or . . . superficially understood."[10] Carroll wishes to cleanse the Augean stables of documentary theory, which he sees as dominated by "arrogant sloganeering" rather than sound thinking. Because of its frequently ad hominem attacks, Carroll's essay seems far removed from the guiding principle of the book in which it is featured, *Post-Theory: Reconstructing Film Studies,* which is to encourage the field to become "more dialectical."[11] At the very least, Carroll's essay demonstrates that documentary film theory has sufficiently constituted itself so as to attract the ire generally reserved for psychoanalytic film theory, the book's bête noire.

A final volume deserves mention in this survey of the new critical literature: *Beyond Document: Essays on Nonfiction Film,* edited by Charles Warren.[12] Composed primarily of pieces by a distinguished roster of novelists, poets, and essayists, the book also features a foreword by Stanley Cavell and contributions from other Harvard-based or -influenced scholars—Vlada Petric, William Rothman, Robert Gardner, and Warren himself. With some notable exceptions, *Beyond Document* is the combined effort of artists and critics whose chief concerns have heretofore not included documentary film. That said, it is also the case that these essays are suffused with a cinephilia rarely found in academic texts, a desire to share the pleasures and revelations of enlightened viewing. There are long and passionate studies of individual filmmakers (Vertov, Makaveyev, Marker) as well as extended reflections upon such underdeveloped topics as the essay film and the representation of death in documentary. While the book feels better suited to the nonspecialist, this alone is neither vice nor virtue. The question remains as to whether or not this book (or, more precisely, this *kind* of book) is capable of engendering additional further research.

▶

A Mighty Recasting of Representational Forms

In the world of film and television studies, then, documentary has entered a new era. As evidenced by the 1998 Society for Cinema Studies panel offerings and the outpouring of recent books, no longer is the documentary treated as a marginalized genre of little interest to mainstream film scholars, irrelevant to the most fertile areas of inquiry.[13] Indeed, given that the separation between fictional and nonfictional media forms has become progressively more difficult to uphold, it makes sense that a broad range of specialized subfields should look to the documentary for its objects of study with a level of interest equal to that accorded fiction. This blurring of the fiction/nonfiction divide is consistent with the challenging of other historic and hierarchical dyads—as, for example, those of male and female, white and black, the cultural "high and low"—and the embrace, even celebration, of a hybridized, mutable, and "impure" model of social life.

But the blurred boundaries we hear so much about are really nothing new. More than sixty years ago, it was Walter Benjamin who, in his essay "The Author as Producer," wrote of "a mighty recasting of literary forms, a melting-down in which many of the opposites in which we have been accustomed to think [science and *belles lettres,* criticism and production, education and politics] may lose their force." Optimistic even in the face of fascist advances, Benjamin singled out the newspaper as that literary vehicle capable of replacing depth with breadth and of dissolving the conventional distinction between author and public.[14] As always, Benjamin captures both sides of the equation at once, both blessing and curse: yes, breadth might displace depth—a significant loss for intellectual life—but that circumstance was balanced by heightened public access to the means of production. In the newspaper, letters to the editor and opinion pieces could mingle freely with professional news coverage; literary qualification could begin to become public property. The newspaper was the "theatre of the unbridled debasement of the word" but also its salvation. Now, these many decades later, it is the camcorder and the Internet that lower the bar of professional authorship and afford the opportunity for what Benjamin calls "the literarization of the conditions of living." To the antinomies superseded as described by Benjamin, we must add those of the public versus private spheres and of the professionalized, taxonomically discrete domains of fiction and nonfiction. New methods for representing the self in everyday life (home video, Web pages) have begun to wear away the distinction between home use and public display, just as the traditional modes of documentary exposition (as outlined by Nichols: expository, observational, interactive, reflexive)[15] no longer prove adequate for comprehending the contemporary nonfiction environment. As Nichols writes in his description of a fifth mode, the performative: "Things change. The four modes of documentary production that presented themselves as an exhaustive survey of the field no longer suffice."[16] I would argue that the performative mode, an important addition for its correspondence to the exciting new work of independent film- and videomakers in the late 1980s and 1990s, leaves an expanding site of reality-based representation still unimagined.

In a more traditional broadcast setting, the attack on the stable fiction/nonfiction distinction is evidenced by the rapid expansion of televisual forms that couple documentary with fiction, the educative with the entertaining: talk shows, prime-time magazine shows, docudramas, hours-long morning news programs mixing traffic reports with cheesy human interest stories, infomercials, home shopping formats, and that most globalizing label for all such fabricated TV formats, edutainment. What these highly commodified forms have in common is the marketplace: they are relatively cheap to produce and generate handsome profits. The new generation of documentary researchers has begun to examine this important feature of the media environment with tools borrowed from the documentary studies tradition.

The emergent media landscape is an increasingly uncharted one; such borrowings are necessary. Standards and points of reference are no longer in their place. As such recent films as *Wag the Dog* so wickedly illustrate, the presumed border between the real and the fabricated in the world of mass-mediated representation, never so intact, is currently in serious disrepair. For the skilled digital compositors in *Wag the Dog* who concoct a "newsreel" clip of an Albanian girl—white kitten clutched, scrambling across a burning bridge, bombed-out village in the background—there are no limits to the authorship of a plausible "real." As digital imaging techniques proliferate, the fiction/nonfiction border will become an ever more active site of contestation and play. The insights regarding the ontological, epistemological, and ethical status of the image derived from documentary studies will become increasingly more pertinent. What I have described above, through reference to new broadcast forms and emerging technologies, domestic and industrial, is less an argument for the onset of a postmodern condition than a description of current practices and a call for documentary theory to catch up with those practices. This collection and the work upon which it draws suggest that this process is well under way.

▶

Making Evidence Visible

Clearly, documentary scholars have expanded their critical horizons in important ways in this decade. The Visible Evidence conference has been the most significant venue for the wide-ranging study of nonfiction media, serving as a vital and increasingly international nexus for new documentary research. Conceived in the aftermath of the 1990 Ohio University conference on documentary organized by Jeanne Hall, the first Visible Evidence conference was convened at Duke University in September 1993. For the first several years, the question was raised as to whether or not there was sufficient interest to warrant an annual rather than a biannual meeting. After successive events at the University of Southern California, Harvard University, University of Wales-Cardiff, Northwestern University, and San Francisco State University, there can be little question that the international community of documentary scholars has established for itself a permanent beachhead. The strength of these meetings has been their interdisciplinarity; besides media specialists, the conferences have attracted sociologists, philosophers, anthropologists, art historians, musicologists, and legal and literary scholars. The conferences have also provided valuable opportunities for dialogue between scholars and practitioners, a place for makers to screen new and unfinished work and to solicit critical response. The Visible Evidence meetings have, above all, become a barometer of documentary's vitality, its potential for renewal, its ability to generate new work and new questions. At a time when, as scholars of postmodernity argue, affect is on the wane, Visible Evidence continues to attract scholars and makers who care passionately about their work precisely because it represents a charged encounter with the social world and because, to paraphrase Bill Nichols's powerful notion, it packs a "double whammy" (the documentary shares the indexical status of all cinematic signs but distinguishes itself by sharing the same plane of existence as lived reality).

Of course, the profusion of interest in the documentary is far richer and more variegated than can be represented in one series of conferences. However, one important outgrowth of the Visible Evidence event has been the creation of a book series, edited by Jane Gaines, Faye Ginsburg, and myself, published by the University of Minnesota Press (of which the present volume is a part), to serve as an ongoing and contextualizing venue for some of the most compelling new documentary research. This collection assembles some of the many significant papers presented at the first three conferences, but there have been other books whose genesis can be traced to these meetings, for example, Chon Noriega and Ana López's *The Ethnic Eye: Latino Media Arts*, which began as a cochaired panel at the first Visible Evidence conference.[17] Like *The Ethnic Eye*, the first volume of the Visible Evidence series, *Between the Sheets, In the Streets: Queer, Lesbian, Gay Documentary*, edited by Chris Holmlund and Cynthia Fuchs, began as a panel at the 1993 Visible Evidence conference at Duke. It reminds us that many of the 1990s art world staples—the gender-bending body, queer performativity, and AIDS advocacy—find their most eloquent vehicles in the documentary form. *Between the Sheets* is attracting a wide readership from well beyond the film studies ranks in part because it offers critical insights into the new queer cinema of Derek Jarman, Marlon Riggs, Su Friedrich, Sadie Benning, and John Greyson, work of tremendous invention and panache. Another Visible Evidence volume, Diane Waldman and Janet Walker's edited collection *Feminism and Documentary*, offers testimony to the centrality of the documentary impulse to three decades of feminist film practice. Issues of gender and sexuality have been at the core of film theory for twenty-five years; at last these central concerns have become the basis for serious attention by scholars of nonfiction.

The new momentum achieved within documentary studies has also begun to level the old disciplinary barriers that have historically separated the study of film and photography, to the disadvantage of both. Andrea Liss's book *Trespassing through Shadows: Memory, Photography, and the Holocaust*, the third volume of the Visible Evidence series, effectively intervenes in the debates surrounding such Holocaust-themed films as *Shoah* and *Schindler's List* while reinforcing the overlapping ontologies of film and photography foundationally argued by André Bazin, Roland Barthes, Christian Metz, and others. In a book that joyously tramples on carefully tended hierarchies and taste cultures, Toby Miller's *Technologies of Truth: Cultural Citizenship and the Popular Media*, Visible Evidence volume 2, interrogates the cultural construction of discourses of "truth." In so doing, Miller mines global popular culture for its assertive, knowledge-producing effects with attention given culture's ever-greater role in the making of nations, economies and individual identities. A freewheeling critique of the disciplinary procedures of cultural capitalism, the book crosscuts from Fred Wiseman's *Titicut Follies* (1967) to Australia's Fremantle Prison, from a film about a prison to a prison recently transformed into a museum, to talk about ethics and contesting cultures of incarceration.

If the first volumes of the Visible Evidence series are any indicator of the times (and I think they are), we are now beginning to see documentary studies jettison its once single-minded focus on documentary film history, aesthetics, and ideological criticism in favor of producing a kind of *situated knowledge* in which cultural representation is linked to larger social and historical forces. The emphasis is thus on documentary film, video, and photography *in relation to* queerness, the Holocaust, and cultural citizenship. This is a documentary studies responsive to the best of cultural studies' attention both to the micro level of social phenomena and to the broader contextual map.

▶

Fiction Hides, Nonfiction Seeks

I would like to close by turning briefly to one area of inquiry unrelated to the cultural studies trend alluded to above that continues to hold significant promise for nonfiction scholarship: psychoanalysis. I want to be categorical in my resistance to a straightforward annexation of documentary for some doctrinal variety of psychoanalytic theory. It is, however, my strong belief that there are certain ideas developed within a century of psychoanalytic theory that can help us understand the resonances and deep impacts of certain nonfiction film and video works on audiences. I am thinking of the simmering debate that lingers around the notion of a special kind of fascinated documentary looking, what Bill Nichols has chosen to term *epistephilia* in opposition to the scopophilia affixed to fiction film spectatorship by Metz, Mulvey, and others.[18] In his contribution to this book, Tom Gunning adds a historical dimension to Nichols's idea by tracing out a precinematic theme of "curiositas," an intense need to inspect and dissect the visual world, in nineteenth-century detective photography. I find the refusal to articulate this epistephilia in relation to desire unduly rationalist in its alignment of documentary wholly with consciousness rather than in traffic with unconscious processes. I challenge that position's preference for knowledge effects over pleasurable or ecstatic looking and for its enthronement of sobriety at the expense of the evocative and delirious. I would argue for the documentary gaze as constitutively multiform, embroiled with conscious motives and unconscious desires, driven by curiosity no more than by terror and fascination.[19]

If the above sounds like the sort of dry-as-dust academic disagreement that amounts to very little, I would have to disagree, because I think it matters when we try to talk intelligently about the depth of our engagement with documentary films and tapes. I recently had the experience of showing Su Friedrich's newest film, *Hide and Seek,* to students in a seminar on documentary. This piece is an unusual amalgam of fictional and nonfictional elements in that it mixes interviews with adult lesbians recalling the complexities of their young erotic lives with a fictional tale of girlhood angst. In the narrative portion of the film, a youthful protagonist struggles inchoately to sort out her deep attachment to her best friend alongside a growing awareness that same-sex passions can be socially damaging. The interviews as excerpted and intercut into the film seem at times to comment on the diegetic development whereas at other times they remain autonomous and intellectually freestanding. Two films, a well-acted female bildungsroman and a talking-heads documentary, become one. (Perhaps the fiction "hides" while the nonfiction "seeks"?)

Because *Hide and Seek* maintains such a careful structural balance between interviews and story time, it seemed the ideal occasion to investigate identificatory ties, to ask if the connectedness to the fictional portion "felt" qualitatively different to that of the nonfiction. No one had a definitive answer, but the very asking of the question seemed to sound a false note for the group. There were differences of opinion as to whether or not the union of the two discursive systems "worked" on the screen and which of the two domains was preferred. Some people found themselves wanting more depth and duration from the interviews, whereas others had felt them to be a diversion from the main event. But nobody could dredge up anything remotely resembling an affective "shifting of gears" as Friedrich moved so fluidly between fiction and nonfiction. For many of the women in the audience, gay and straight, there were moments of identification with the unnamed women interview subjects as they spoke about their deep affection for childhood girlfriends or their difficulties in meshing with the hegemonic sexuality of adolescence. But there were also strong emotional ties felt to the pony-tailed narrative protagonist. Epistephilia seemed too arid a term for what was driving our interest in these on-screen, self-narrating women, just as it would have been for the fiction with which they colluded.

I do not pin a great deal on this single classroom experience. But I don't discount it either. If I have argued for the documentary gaze as constitutively multiform, bound up with conscious motives such as intellectual curiosity as well as less conscious ones aligned with fantasy, memory, or longing, Friedrich's *Hide and Seek* provides a useful testing ground through its consistent oscillation between fictional and nonfictional realms. What is the source of our fascination as we watch and listen to the film? Is our reception of the acted versus the interview-based segments distinctive and in pieces, or is the source of our desirous gaze a fluid and mobile one? It seems to me that the leveling of disciplinary boundaries that characterizes current documentary scholarship ought to find its counterpart in our conceptualizing of models for documentary spectatorship. The pleasure principle is too seldom invoked as a feature of our reception, but can it be argued that such documentary classics as *Rain* (1929), *Man with a Movie Camera* (1929), *A propos de Nice* (1930), *Las Hurdes* (1932), and *Le Sang des bêtes* (1949) conjure a full range of emotions, from eroticism to melancholy and even disgust? If we are here at times beyond the pleasure principle, we are decidedly beyond the bounds of a rigorously enforced reality principle, which is where documentary theory has too often relegated its object.

▶

Parochialism Is Dead

Bill Nichols's *Representing Reality,* the early 1990s book that kicked off the resurgence of interest in the documentary, treated documentary film and video to the exclusion of digitally based forms, which raised ontological and epistemological questions of a different order. Given the ground to be covered, the exclusion was strategic. Less than a decade later, the focus on the photochemical at the expense of the computer-based begins to bind. Too many practices get excluded; too many theoretical questions remain unaddressed. Documentary scholarship as the province of film studies specialists has begun to feel unduly exclusionary in its own way. Documentary studies, vibrant and multidisciplinary, now attracts to itself scholars *and* practitioners, social scientists *and* art historians, graying educators *and* twenty-something video artists. Wherever one looks, the pattern repeats: realignment, reinvention, reinvestment.

Devotees of the documentary have tended to be motivated by a sense of political urgency, as evidenced by the titles of such neoclassic volumes as Alan Rosenthal's *The Documentary Conscience* (1980), Bill Nichols's *Ideology and the Image* (1981), and Tom Waugh's *"Show Us Life": Toward a History and Aesthetic of the Committed Documentary* (1984).[20] As we career toward the twenty-first century, the sites for radical political inquiry have shifted and expanded, attuned no doubt to late capitalism's chameleon successes. Now we have left-wing scholars such as Julia Lesage arguing persuasively that it is right-wing media that must be the focus of our critical attention. Documentary studies has learned the same lesson, that parochialism is dead.

Question: In moving on, have we simply replaced one master narrative (the documentary film as the hammer of social change) for another (documentary media as the open-sesame for cultural reinvention)? Books are now being written that chart the changes wrought by documentary practices around sexual identities, the formation of the new global order, and the struggle for the creation of popular memory. But have our critical goals become too diffuse in the aftermath of the galvanizing social movements of the 1960s, have we given ground too readily to hegemonic forces? What's left of "the documentary tradition," whose scholars once championed the concrete and the historical, now that postmodernity has witnessed a decay of referentiality and ideological anchorage? If there is a consensus emerging among the newest generation of documentary scholars, it may just be that representations of the real have more rather than less power to shape our world than heretofore, that the production and control of the flow of historically based images is increasingly the arena of social power that matters most. It's just that the sites and situations of documentary culture have exploded exponentially — on cable TV twenty-four hours a day, on urban billboards and big-screen displays, in museums and on the Internet. As our perceptual world moves toward oversaturation, our critical responses must strain to equal the speed, density, and contradictoriness of the media environment. Fluidity, intellectual diversity, breadth of application, invention — these must be the new watchwords for the documentary scholar of the twenty-first century. The documentary horizon is a virtual terra incognita, studded with promise and peril for the resourceful analyst. And the stakes have never been higher.

◆ ——

NOTES

1. There is a perpetual "naming" problem for the documentary that speaks to the taxonomic confusions that surround this mode of film and video practice. In literature, *nonfiction* refers to many kinds of discursive writing, from the student composition to journalistic reportage, the essay, biography, and autobiography. This is far from a stable category and one never free of the "taint" of fiction. Autobiography, in particular, is notorious for its fictive elements ("the fiction of the self"), and the essay is the possessor of a complex genealogy that encompasses the philosophical writings of Locke and Bacon as well as the digressive meditations of Montaigne, Nietzsche, Adorno, and Barthes. There is no simple or necessary correspondence between the domains of nonfiction literature and documentary film. Over the years, various labels have been attached to the nonfiction film, including *actualité, the film of fact,* and *documentary.* The last term has been decisively affiliated with the writing and production practices of John Grierson,

a circumstance that has tended to narrow its meaning in the direction of a kind of earnest didacticism from which some have felt the need to distance themselves. In an open letter to the the Academy of Motion Picture Arts and Sciences executive director, Miramax Films (distributors of several popular films such as *Truth or Dare* that had been overlooked by the Academy) went so far as to suggest that the Academy Award in the documentary category become an award for "best nonfiction film," so that the "negative connotations" of the word *documentary* could be avoided. Robert Epstein, "Academy's Latest Film Stir-Fry," *Los Angeles Times,* March 12, 1992, F9.

In the scholarly world, the situation is no less conflicted. There is no institutionalized world of "documentary studies," although in this essay I argue for the emergence of just such an interdisciplinary field of inquiry, in which a range of theoretical and methodological approaches converge and in which the object can be photography, film, video, and the digital arts as vehicles of historical representation. Although it is essential to retain a sense of the specificity of each of these media forms, it is equally important to develop a sufficiently inclusive rubric and critical community capable of embracing them all.

2. Brian Winston, *Claiming the Real: The Griersonian Documentary and Its Legitimations* (London: British Film Institute, 1995); Fatimah Tobing Rony, *The Third Eye: Race, Cinema, and Ethnographic Spectacle* (Durham, N.C.: Duke University Press, 1996).

3. Erik Barnouw, *Documentary: A History of the Non-Fiction Film* (Oxford: Oxford University Press, 1974; rev. eds. 1983, 1993).

4. Bill Nichols, *Representing Reality: Issues and Concepts in Documentary* (Bloomington: Indiana University Press, 1991); Bill Nichols, *Blurred Boundaries: Questions of Meaning in Contemporary Culture* (Bloomington: Indiana University Press, 1994).

5. Michael Renov, *Theorizing Documentary* (New York: Routledge, 1993); Noel Carroll, "Nonfiction Film and Postmodernist Skepticism," in *Post-Theory: Reconstructing Film Studies*, ed. David Bordwell and Noel Carroll (Madison: University of Wisconsin Press, 1996), 285. Carroll's description was not intended as praise but rather as a denunciation of the book for its preference for what he took to be "fashionable" theory rather than sound philosophical thinking—of which he is, predictably, the single best exemplar.

6. John Corner, *The Art of Record: A Critical Introduction to Documentary* (New York: St. Martin's, 1996); Richard Kilborn and John Izod, *An Introduction to Television Documentary* (New York: St. Martin's, 1997).

7. Deirdre Boyle, *Subject to Change: Guerrilla Television Revisited* (New York: Oxford University Press, 1997).

8. Paula Rabinowitz, *They Must Be Represented: The Politics of Documentary* (London: Verso, 1994).

9. Carl Plantinga, *Rhetoric and Representation in Nonfiction Film* (New York: Cambridge University Press, 1997).

10. Carroll, "Nonfiction Film and Postmodernist Skepticism," 302.

11. David Bordwell, "Introduction," in *Post-Theory: Reconstructing Film Studies*, ed. David Bordwell and Noel Carroll (Madison: University of Wisconsin Press, 1996), xiv.

12. Charles Warren, ed., *Beyond Document: Essays on Nonfiction Film* (Hanover, N.H.: University Press of New England, 1996).

13. Here I have in mind such diverse research orientations as those associated with cultural studies, queer studies, feminist theory, television studies, reception theory, new historicism, postcolonial studies, psychoanalysis, ethics, and studies of new technologies. Documentary studies in the late 1990s has engaged with all of these domains of research in the humanities.

14. Walter Benjamin, "The Author as Producer," in *The Essential Frankfurt School Reader*, ed. Andrew Arato and Eike Gebhardt (New York: Continuum, 1982), 258–59.

15. Bill Nichols, "Documentary Modes of Representation," in *Representing Reality*, 32–75.

16. Nichols, *Blurred Boundaries*, 93.

17. Chon Noriega and Ana M. Lopez, *The Ethnic Eye: Latino Media Arts* (Minneapolis: University of Minnesota Press, 1996).

18. Nichols, *Representing Reality*, 178–80.

19. I have developed this critique at greater length in "Charged Vision: The Place of Desire in Documentary Film Theory" (in Swedish), *Aura* 3, nos. 3–4 (1997): 93–101. An English-language version of the essay will appear in my forthcoming book, *Documenting Subjectivity* (Minneapolis: University of Minnesota Press).

20. Alan Rosenthal, *The Documentary Conscience: A Casebook in Film-Making* (Berkeley: University of California Press, 1980); Bill Nichols, *Ideology and the Image: Social Representation in the Cinema and Other Media* (Bloomington: Indiana University Press, 1981; Thomas Waugh, ed., *"Show Us Life": Toward a History and Aesthetics of Committed Documentary* (Metuchen, N.J.: Scarecrow, 1984).

Contributors

JENNY COOL is an ethnographic filmmaker and Internet media producer in San Francisco. She is currently working on a doctorate in anthropology at the University of California, Berkeley, where her research focuses on telecommunities and technocultures.

ELIZABETH COWIE is senior lecturer in film studies at the University of Kent, Canterbury, England. She is founding editor of *m/f*, a journal of feminist theory, and coedited *The Woman in Question*. She has published on psychoanalysis, film noir, classical Hollywood narrative, and documentary, and is the author of *Representing the Woman* (Minnesota, 1997).

JANE M. GAINES is associate professor of literature and English and director of the Program in Film and Video at Duke University. She is the author of *Contested Culture: The Image, the Voice, and the Law* and the forthcoming *Other/Race/Desire: Mixed Blood Relations in Early Cinema*.

FAYE GINSBURG is director of the Center for Media, Culture, and History at New York University, where she is also professor of anthropology. Author and editor of a number of books on gender and reproduction, she is currently completing *Mediating Culture*, a book based on the development of indigenous media and the challenges it poses to visual anthropology.

TOM GUNNING is professor in the Department of Art History and the Cinema and Media Program of the University of Chicago. He has published widely on early cinema and its origins and is the author of *D. W. Griffith and the Origins of American Narrative Film* and of a forthcoming study of the films of Fritz Lang.

EITHNE JOHNSON is instructor in media and cultural studies in the Department of Sociology at Wellesley College. Her previous essays on sexually explicit films and videos have appeared in *The Velvet Light Trap* and the *Journal of Film and Video*.

ALEXANDRA JUHASZ is associate professor of media studies at Pitzer College. She makes and writes about activist media, and her works include the book *AIDS TV: Identity, Community, and Alternative Video*, numerous AIDS activist videos, the feature film *The Watermelon Woman*, and the book and feature documentary *Women of Vision: 18 Histories in Feminist Film and Video*.

NEIL LERNER is assistant professor of music at Davidson College. He received his Ph.D. in musicology from Duke University. His essay in this volume is part of his dissertation, "The Classical Documentary Score in American Films of Persuasion: Contexts and Case Studies, 1936–1945."

AKIRA MIZUTA LIPPIT is assistant professor of film studies and critical theory in the Department of Cinema at San Francisco State University. His work has appeared in *1985, Afterimage, Assemblage, Camerawork, Criticism, MLN, Paragraph,* and *Poliphile*. His study of animality titled *Electric Animal: Toward a Rhetoric of Wildlife* is forthcoming (Minnesota, 2000).

NANCY LUTKEHAUS is associate professor in the Department of Anthropology and codirector of the Center for Visual Anthropology at the University of Southern California. In addition to her ethnography *Zaria's Fire: Engendered Moments in Manam Ethnography, Papua New Guinea* she has completed a video, *Finishing 'Apui's Name: Death and Remembrance on Manam Island*. She is currently working on a book titled *Margaret Mead and the Media*, which explores the development of Mead as a cultural icon.

JAMES M. MORAN, a former professional wedding videographer, recently completed his doctorate at the University of Southern California in the School of Cinema-Television. His dissertation, "There's No Place Like Home Video," explores critical and cultural questions about video's specificity as a medium and as a practice.

MICHAEL RENOV, professor of critical studies at the School of Cinema-Television, University of Southern California, is the editor of *Theorizing Documentary*, coeditor of *Resolutions: Essays in Contemporary Video Practices*, and author of the forthcoming *Documenting Subjectivity*.

VIVIAN SOBCHACK is associate dean and professor of film and television studies at the UCLA School of Theater, Film, and Television and was the first woman elected president of the Society for Cinema Studies. Her books include *Screening Space: The American Science Fiction Film, The Address of the Eye: A Phenomenology of Film Experience,* and the edited anthologies *The Persistence of History: Cinema, Television, and the Modern Event* and *Meta-Morphing: Visual Transformation and the Culture of Quick-Change* (Minnesota, 2000). A collection of her own essays, *Carnal Thoughts: Bodies, Texts, Scenes, and Screens,* is forthcoming.

LINDA WILLIAMS is professor of rhetoric and film studies at the University of California, Berkeley. She is the author of *Hard Core: Power, Pleasure, and the Frenzy of the Visible* and the editor of *Viewing Positions: Ways of Seeing Film.*

MARK WILLIAMS is assistant professor in the Department of Film Studies at Dartmouth College, where he teaches courses in film and television history and theory. His book on early Los Angeles television, *Remote Possibilities,* is forthcoming.

MARK J. P. WOLF has a Ph.D. from the School of Cinema-Television at the University of Southern California. He teaches in the Communication Department at Concordia University Wisconsin, and his interests include the study of technology and culture and the interaction between them.

Index

A propos de Nice, 323
Ackerman, Robert, 275
Actuality, 8, 19, 27, 47, 91; constitutive, 247; spectacle of, 26
Adair, John, 162
Adorno, Theodor, 67, 141
Advanced Sexual Techniques, Vol. 2, 222
Aesthetics, 157; corporeal, 233
"AIDS and Postmodernism," 211
Alaska Native Heritage Project, 163
Alcott, John, 264
Alterity, 140, 153n2
Althusser, Louis, 2, 199
Amateur, 56, 59; footage, 95
American Amateur Photographer, 48–49, 59
Anthropology, 15, 52, 116–17, 119, 122, 157, 164; critiques of, 131; reverse, 169
Antonia, Portrait of a Woman, 200
Appadurai, Arjun, 160–61
Ars erotica, 234–35
Art of Record, The: A Critical Introduction to Documentary, 315
Artaud, Antonin, 79
Arthur, Paul, 315
Asch, Patsy, 120, 133
Asch, Timothy, 118, 120, 130, 133
Atomic bomb test in Nevada: photograph of, 293, 302–3, 308
Atomic Cafe, 85
Atomic Energy Commission (AEC), 300–301, 306, 309
Attendant, The, 172
Audience, 89, 90, 159, 165, 270; activism, 89; politicized, 99; production of, 88–89. *See also* Spectator; Viewer
Aumont, Jacques, 88
Author as Producer, The, 317
Avant-garde, feminist, 87, 191–92
Ax Fight, The, 120

BabaKiueria, 15, 167–69
Baby the Stork Brought Home, The, 125–26
Bacon, Francis, 72

Baillie, Hugh, 304–5
Balzac, Honoré de, 70
Barbach, Lonnie, 218, 230, 236n13
Barbash, Ilisa, 128
Barnouw, Erik, 132, 314
Barthes, Roland, 6, 72, 110, 199, 257, 267, 320
Basquiat, Jean-Michel, 71
Battle of Chile, The, 91, 177
Battle of the Somme, The, 40
Battleship Potemkin, The, 86
Batty, David, 170
Baudrillard, Jean, 19, 128, 163–64
Baudry, Jean-Louis, 78
Bazin, André, 2–7, 41n8, 41n12, 256, 258, 265, 267, 269, 320
Becoming Orgasmic, 222, 230
Bell, Shannon, 227, 232
Benjamin, Walter, 29, 43n32, 53, 76–77, 140, 317–18
Benning, Sadie, 320
Berkeley in the Sixties, 91, 249
Better Orgasms, 222
Between the Sheets, In the Streets: Queer, Lesbian, Gay Documentary, 320
Beyond Document: Essays on Nonfiction Film, 316
Bichat, Xavier, 275
Birri, Fernando, 211
Birth Film, 204
Birth of a Nation, The, 40
Birth of a Nation: 4/29/92, 96; image from, 97
Black Audio Collective, 91
Blurred Boundaries, 156, 314
Bobby's Kodak, 61; advertisement for, 62
Bodies That Matter, 11
Body, 90, 93–94; and the political film, 89; as visual indices, 66; control, 58; existence, 57; genre, 90; human, 66; language, 61; limits of, 67; on screen, 90; politicized, 88, 90; propriety, 47, 54; sensationalized, 90
Bohannan, Laura, 119
Bonus March, 91
Bordwell, David, 105
Borinage, 86–87

Bottomore, Stephen, 46, 61
Bouillion, Victor, 69
Box of Treasures, 164
Boyd, Todd, 93
Boyer, Paul, 307
Boyle, Deirdre, 95, 315
Brady, Mathew, 55
Brant, Henry, 110
Brecht, Bertolt, 88, 184, 186–87
Breuer, Josef, 75
Bright, Susie, 216
Browne, Nick, 298
Bruno, Giuliana, 218, 233
Bui Doi, 123–24
Burch, Noël, 42n25
Butler, Judith, 3, 11, 220, 230, 234

Cahiers du Cinéma, 2, 11
Caldwell, John, 310
Califia, Pat, 228
Camera ethics, 61
Camera obscura, 22–24
Candid Camera, 29
Carelli, Vincent, 163
Carroll, Noel, 315–16
Carter, Kevin, 176, 187
Carter, Rick, 264
Cartwright, Lisa, 68, 75, 81n13, 217–18, 225, 229
Cassirer, Ernst, 67
Catastrophe, 16
Causality, narrative, 30
Cavell, Stanley, 316
Center for Visual Anthropology, University of
    Southern California, 117–18, 130, 133
Centro de Trabalho Indigenista, 163
Certeau, Michel de, 5, 259
Chagnon, Napoleon, 120, 133
Chancer, Lynn Sharon, 184
Charcot, Jean-Martin, 35, 76, 148
Chauvin, Rémy, 74
Chenzira, Ayoka, 234
Chief in Two Worlds, A, 128–29
Chisholm, Cheryl, 234
Cholodenko, Alan, 266, 268
Choy, Christine, 92
Christine's Secret, 230
Chronophotography, 77–78
Cinema of attractions, 26, 28
Cinema verité, 12, 120, 133, 180, 191, 194, 201
Cinématographe, 74
Cinematography, 258, 268–70
Claiming the Real, 84, 314
Cleopatra, 252
Clifford, James, 14, 116, 121, 140
Cohen, Keith, 123
Colonial mirror, 96, 98
Colonialism, Shamanism, and the Wild Man, 123
Columbia Revolt, 91; still from, 91
Comolli, Jean-Luc, 2, 22–23
Comte, Auguste, 275
Coniston Story, 170
Connor, Linda, 120–21
Consciousness, 245; documentary, 241, 246,

249–50; lateral, 250; longitudinal, 248–49;
    political, 89; spectatorial, 242, 244, 246
Cook, Pam, 200–201
Cool, Jenny, 14, 116–39
Corner, John, 315
Corporeal performativity, 220
Cottrell, Honey Lee, 228
Counterporn, 15
Cowie, Elizabeth, 8, 19–45
Cowtipping, 172
Cox, Brad J., 289
Cox, Kirwin, 85
Crapanzano, Vincent, 119
Crary, Jonathan, 24–26, 41n10, 42n18, 274
Crichton, Michael, 264
Culhane, Garrett, 279
Curtis, Jamie Lee, 234

Dagognet, François, 74, 77
Daguerre, Louis-Jacques-Mandé, 22–23, 41n7, 61
Daguerreotype, 22, 70
Daly, Mary, 201
Dargis, Manohla, 192, 199, 206
Dayan, Daniel, 309
Dedeheiwa Washes His Children, 133
Dedeheiwa Weeds His Garden, 133
Deleuze, Gilles, 65, 67, 78, 80
Delirium, 14, 147–49
Derrida, Jacques, 2, 156n16, 163
Desire, 140, 142–43; for the real, 32; televisual,
    293
Detective camera, 9, 13, 47–48, 50–51, 53–54,
    58–60, 63; advertisement for, 50; illustration
    from, 60. *See also* Hand camera
Dialogism, 121, 136, 173
Diana, Princess of Wales, 310
Diasporic communities, 157
Diawara, Manthia, 100, 169
Dinosaurs of Jurassic Park, The, 262
Discourse, 3, 11, 204, 207, 211, 255; about media
    representation and production, 164; anthropo-
    logical, 140; cinematic, 103, 107; critical, 256;
    ethnographic, 142, 143; ideologically support-
    ive, 306; insider, 147; machine, 90; masculinist,
    305–6, 308–9; musical, 107; of desire, 265; of
    psychiatric medicine, 39; of sobriety, 258, 265;
    of the sex clinic, 222; popular, 266; power to
    shape, 148; public, 203; self-help, 219–20;
    social, 51; violence, 97–98
Distribution, 16
Do the Right Thing, 93
Doane, Mary Ann, 23, 191, 199, 294, 297–98, 301,
    304–5
Documentary, 171, 194, 241, 244, 246–47, 249,
    251–52, 255–57, 260, 263, 265, 269, 274, 280,
    290; *A History of the Non-Fiction Film*, 314; and
    science, 258; British, 85; cinema verité, 193;
    classical, 99; committed, 86–87; conventional
    film, 289; discourse of, 9–10; experimental,
    255; feminist, 211; government, 104; Grierson-
    ian, 314; mythology, 90; observational, 29, 31;
    observational mode of, 177; political, 194, 197,
    209; radical, 99; realist feminist, 196, 213;

rhetoric of, 92; social, 51, 133; studies of, 1; subjunctive, 16, 289; talking-heads, 192, 322; television, 31, 84–85; traditional, 99; truth, 176, 183

Documentary Conscience, The, 323

Dodson, Betty, 216–17, 225–27, 231, 234–35

Doring, Jef, 132

Doring, Su, 132

"Dream of Irma's injection," 65–66, 75, 79, 80

Dream screen, 78–80

Dream work, 65

Drifters, 84, 86

DuBowski, Sandi, 14, 146–47

Dulac, Germaine, 76–77, 79

Dumont, Jean-Paul, 119

Dwyer, Kevin, 119

Dyer, Richard, 225

Eastman, George, 48

Eberwein, Robert, 234

Eckstein, Emma, 65

Edison, Thomas A., 75

Eighteenth Brumaire of Louis Bonaparte, The, 146

Einstein, Albert, 287

Eisenstein, Sergei, 84, 86–91, 94, 112, 270

Elder, Sarah, 163

Elders, Joycelyn, 234

Empiricism, 12

Enlightenment, 67, 74, 76, 80, 94, 116–17, 129, 136

Entertainment This Week, 247

Entertainment Weekly, 234

Epistemology, 117, 157, 174n18; and problems of computer simulation, 290; arrogance of, 146; movement, 67; of the inside, 71; of the real, 16; realist, 211

Epistephilia, 17, 28, 43n29, 142, 165, 321–22

Erens, Patricia, 223

"Ethics of the Hand Camera," 59

Ethnic Eye, The: Latino Media Arts, 320

Ethnography, 117; as a genre, 121; domestic, 14, 141, 144, 146, 149–50, 152–53; experimental, 119; new, 117, 121, 123–24, 130, 133; postmodern, 128, 141; realist, 119; reverse, 15; traditional, 117; voice in, 123; written, 118

Ethnoscapes, 160

Evidence, 6, 13, 35, 39, 46, 51, 53, 61, 92, 284; documentary, 51; empirical, 259; image as, 281; objective, 262

Evocation, 141, 247

Exhibitionism, 31

Faber, Mindy, 14, 147–48

Fabian, Johannes, 116, 121, 153

Faludi, Susan, 232

Fanon, Frantz, 96–97, 100

Farm Security Administration, 316

Featherstone, Don, 167

Female Orgasm, The, 222

Feminine Fascinations: Forms of Identification in Star-Audience Relations, 206

Feminism and Documentary, 320

Feminist Film Criticism: An Introduction, 191

Fetish, 292, 301, 306–9; objects, 245

Feuer, Jane, 294

Fictions of Feminist Ethnography, 119

Film and Photo League, 86, 91

Filmmaking: ethnographic, 6, 12, 14, 164; experimental, 12; fiction, 40, 47; historical, 259; interventional mode of, 188

Films Are Dreams That Wander in the Light of Day, 122

Film-souvenir. See Home movies

Fischer, Michael, 116, 121, 128

Fiscus, Kathy, 297–98

500 Nations, 282

Fizeau, Hippolyte, 70

Flaherty, Robert, 6–7, 12, 14, 87, 313–14

Fleming, Toby, 125

For Here or To-Go?, 128–29

For Yourself, 218

Formalism, 192

Foster, George G., 52

Foucault, J. B. Léon, 70

Foucault, Michel, 4–5, 269

Fraser, Nancy, 164

Freud, Sigmund, 20, 25, 27, 35, 65–66, 71, 75–76, 78–79, 80n4; death drive, 21; hypnosis, 75; theory of repression, 65; theory of the unconscious, 20

Freud's Psychology of the Unconscious, 20

Friedrich, Paul, 119

Friedrich, Su, 14, 143–45, 148, 320–22

Frizot, Michel, 70–71

From Object to Subject: Documents and Documentaries from the Women's Movement, 192

Frota, Monica, 127

Fuchs, Cynthia, 320

Fung, Richard, 172

Gaines, Jane M., 1–18, 84–102, 165, 314, 319

Gallery of Illustrious Americans, 55

Gang Cops, 125

Gardner, Robert, 14, 316

Gaze, 27, 29, 141; accidental, 177; anatomic-analytic, 224; camera, 30, 58, 152, 179, 183; clinical, 177; documentary, 177–79, 321–22; endangered, 177; ethnographic, 125; exploitative, 180; female, 226, 234; helpless, 177; humane, 177; imperialist, 13, 53; interventional, 177, 182; male, 184; Nichols's taxonomy of, 177; participatory, 179; professional, 177; urban spectator, 53; Western, 173

Geertz, Clifford, 116, 121, 129, 142

Gelles, Paul, 128

Genital portraiture, 225–28, 234

Gilmore, Leigh, 232

Ginsburg, Faye, 14–15, 124, 156–75, 319

Ginzberg, Carlo, 261

Glasser, Otto, 71

Gledhill, Christine, 211

Godard, Jean-Luc, 87–88, 98

Godmilow, Jill, 10

Goldfarb, Brian, 75

Good Woman of Bangkok, The, 15, 176, 187–88

Good Woman of Setzuan, The, 186

Gorbman, Claudia, 104
Goslinga, Gillian, 123, 125, 138n26
Green, Vanalyne, 142
Greyson, John, 320
Grierson, John, 13, 84–87, 269, 313
Griersonian tradition, 87, 99–100, 165
Griffith, D. W., 40
Grosz, Stephen, 223–24
Growing Up Female, 200
G-Spot, The, 231
Guerrilla video tactics, 95
Gulf War, 310
Gunabibi, 133
Gunning, Tom, 9, 13, 26, 42n26, 46–64, 321

Hall, Jeanne, 319
Hammer, Barbara, 71, 225, 228
Hand camera, 47–49, 54, 57, 59–61; advertisement
    for, 48. See also Detective camera
Handsworth Songs, 91
Handvoice, 228
Haraway, Donna, 6
Harlan County, U.S.A., 10, 85, 177
Harris, Thomas Allen, 150, 152
Harron, Bobby, 61
Headman and I, The, 119
Healthcaring: From Our End of the Speculum, 204,
    223
Heart and Soul, 234
Heath, Stephen, 30, 292
Heelan, Patrick, 275
Heidegger, Martin, 71
Heiman, Julia, 230
Hell Bomb, The, 307
Henderson, Linda Dalrymple, 67–68, 75
Henry, Fred, 301–3
Herlihy, David, 259
Hide and Seek, 321–22
Higgins, Gary, 71
Hiley, Nicholas, 55
Hines, Lewis, 54
Hiroshima, 68, 70, 72, 80; photograph of, 79
Historiography, 259, 270
History and Memory, 172
HIV TV, 207
Holcomb, Grant, 301–2, 304, 307
Holliday, George, 310
Holmes, Burton, 51
Holmlund, Chris, 320
Holocaust, 266
Home Economics, 14, 118, 126, 130–34
Home movies, 8, 15, 143–44, 146, 242–53; on video,
    63, 318
Horkheimer, Max, 67
Horner, Jack, 264
House Un-American Activities Committee
    (HUAC), 299
Housing Problems, 84
Houston, Beverle, 293
How to Female Ejaculate, 232
How to Find Your Goddess Spot, 226
Hurst, A. F., 34
Hymes, Dell, 116

Ichioka, Yasuko, 132
Identification, 29, 31–33, 105, 145, 191, 193–96,
    203, 206–7, 209–10, 213, 241, 243, 245, 247–48,
    250, 252–53, 322; cinematic, 241–42, 244,
    246–47, 251–53; cultural, 171; documentary,
    241, 250–52; fictional, 243; of queerness, 151;
    spectator, 247; station, 297; viewer, 296
Identity, 127–29, 142, 149, 153, 196, 201–5, 208,
    211, 213; collective, 201; construction of, 152,
    171; feminist, 204; formation of, 172; gender,
    219; individual, 209; multiple, 128; nature of,
    212; of subject, 129; personal, 128
Ideology, 2–3, 51, 103, 110, 191, 301; and musical
    instruments, 110, 115n26; and sound track,
    14, 114n10; bourgeois, 193; criticism of, 321;
    manipulation by, 286
Ideology and the Image, 323
Ihde, Don, 275
Illusion of Life, The, 268
Illustrated Manners Book, 58
Imaginary, 3, 32–33, 241
Imperialism, 52
In and Out of Africa, 128–29
In Her Own Time, 120–21, 125
In the Name of Feminist Film Criticism, 198
In the Year of the Pig, 91
Indexicality, 5–6, 16, 95, 245
Instrumental Realism, 275
Intertextual cinema, 165
Intervention, 181–83, 185–86; ethics of, 176
Interview, 31, 178–79
Intolerance, 61
Introduction to Television Documentary, An, 315
It Happens to Us, 203
Ivens, Joris, 86–87
Izod, John, 315

Jaguar, 119, 120
James, C. L. R., 87
James, David, 222
Jameson, Fredric, 128
Janie's Janie, 199–202, 207
Jarman, Derek, 320
Jason, Alexander, 285
Jero on Jero: "A Balinese Trance Séance Observed,"
    120–21
Johnson, Eithne, 15, 216–40
Johnston, Claire, 10, 15, 190, 200, 205–6, 210, 223
Joy in Her Pleasure, 228
Juhasz, Alexandra, 10–11, 93, 190–215
Julien, Isaac, 92, 100, 172
Jurassic Park, 262–63, 265–67

Kamerling, Leonard, 163
Kaplan, E. Ann, 191, 198–200, 202, 207, 223
Kasson, John F., 52, 58
Katz, Elihu, 309
Kayapo: Out of the Forest, 127
Kayapo Video Project, 163
Keller, Evelyn Fox, 306
Kelly, Frances Jupurrurla, 170
Keyhole effect, 306
Kilborn, Richard, 315

Killing Time, The, 170
King, E. J., 106
King, Rodney, 1, 95–98, 177, 310
King Kong, 264
Kino pravda, 12
Kino-eye, 11–13, 270
Klein, Bonnie, 185–86
Klein, Jim, 13
Knowledge, 8, 19, 29, 61, 202, 274; ethnographic, 118, 120, 169; self, 142; sensory, 24; situated, 321
Kodak, 48, 50, 61
Korean War, 299
Kracauer, Siegfried, 2–4, 7
Kristeva, Julia, 199
Kubrick, Stanley, 260
Kula, 132
Kunuk, Zacharias, 163, 169
Kurdungurlu, 170

L'Amateur Photographe, 49, 56, 57
La Belle, Jenijoy, 220
La Nature, 76
Lacan, Jacques, 21, 32–34, 44, 66, 199
Landsberg, Klaus, 297, 299–300, 310
Lane, Dorrie, 226–27, 231
Langton, Marcia, 163, 166
Lantern lecture, 55
Las Hurdes, 323
Last of the Cuiva, 132
Laurence, William L., 307–9
Lauretis, Teresa de, 220
Laverne & Shirley, 247, 251
Le Sang des bêtes, 323
Lee, Spike, 93
Lerner, Jessie, 125
Lerner, Neil, 14, 92, 103–15
Les Maîtres Fous, 119
Les Structures de l'Experience filmique: L'Identification filmique, 242
Lesage, Julia, 3, 192, 202, 223–24, 323
Letter from Siberia, 255
Letterman, David, 98
Lévi-Strauss, Claude, 121, 135, 140, 153, 199
Levinas, Emmanuel, 140, 153n2
Lewin, Bertram, 78, 80
Life and Times of Rosie the Riveter, The, 99
Lippit, Akira Mizuta, 13, 65–83
Liss, Andrea, 320
Littman, Lynne, 120
Liveness, 16, 292–96, 310–11
Lobitz, W. Charles, 221
Logic of Sense, The, 65
Londe, Albert, 76
Looking for Langston, 172
López, Ana, 320
LoPiccolo, Joseph, 221, 230
Lorentz, Pare, 14, 86, 103–5, 108–11, 113
Lost Horizons, 122
Luhrmann, Tanya, 119, 124
Lumière brothers, 13, 74
Lumière, Louis, 20, 74, 75
Lutkehaus, Nancy, 14, 116–39

MacDonald, Scott, 224
MacDougall, David, 119–20, 132–33, 165
MacDougall, Judith, 119–20, 133
Making Love Alone, 217
Malin, David F., 277
Man with a Movie Camera, 323
Manyu Wana, 169–70
Marcus, George, 116, 121, 123–24, 128, 141
Marey, Etienne-Jules, 20, 28, 74, 76–78
Margo, 228
Marker, Chris, 255–56, 316
Marks, Daniel, 125
Marshall, John, 123
Martin, Emily, 124
Martineau, Barbara Halpern, 206
Martinez, Wilton, 122, 128
Martyn, Gil, 308
Marx, Karl, 88, 146
Marxism, 3, 92
Mason, Lowell, 107
Mason, Peter, 140, 153n3
Masters and Johnson, 221, 227–28, 230
McArthur, Colin, 296
McAuley, Bruce, 223–24
McCreery, Crash, 264
McDaniels, Matthew, 96, 102n37
McGarry, Eileen, 191, 200
McIlvenna, Ted, 228
McLuhan, Marshall, 71
Media: activism, 93; and multiculturalism, 172; broadcast, 296; circulation of, 172; electronic, 292; ethnographic, 6, 200; fictional, 317; indigenous, 126, 157, 160, 164–65, 171–72; nonfictional, 317; photographic, 68–69
Medium Cool, 177
Méliès, Georges, 20
Mellencamp, Patricia, 191, 199, 294, 298, 301
Mensel, Robert E., 55
Mentor, The, 54
Merleau-Ponty, Maurice, 242
Metaphysics: of presence, 258
Metz, Christian, 199, 320–21
Meunier, Jean-Pierre, 15, 242, 243, 245–53
Meyer, James, 211
Michaels, Eric, 170–71
Miller, Toby, 320
Mimesis, 93–94, 96–98; aesthetic, 99; mimetic faculty, 94–95, 100, 140–41; mimetic style, 194; political, 90, 99, 100
Mimesis and Alterity, 93
Mimicry, political, 92
Minh-ha, Trinh T., 1, 10, 43, 124, 140, 156, 162, 261
Mirror, 216, 220; effect, 90; stage, 33, 43n36
Mise-en-scène, 30; reflexive, 219
Mishan, Ahrin, 123–24
Modernism, literary, 123
"Modernist Event, The," 17
Moffatt, Tracey, 171
Moholy-Nagy, László, 72, 75
Moi, Un Noir, 119
Monophonic theme, 108
Montage, 123, 134; intellectual, 123, 125; of attractions, 88

"Montage of Film Attraction, The," 84
Montgomery, Alan, 71
Moran, James M., 6, 16, 255–73
Moroccan Dialogues, 119
Morris, Errol, 92, 183, 186, 261
Moser, Brian, 132
"Mountain theme," 108–9; illustration of, 109–10
Mr. DNA, 263
Multiple Orgasms, 225
Mulvey, Laura, 192, 199, 201, 206, 321
Mummy complex, 256
Music, 91, 103–5; track, 92. *See also* Sound track
Muybridge, Eadweard James, 28, 76–78, 269
My Husband's Families, 127
Myerhoff, Barbara, 118, 120–21, 125, 130, 133

N!ai: The Story of a !Kung Woman, 123, 160
Nagasaki, 68, 70, 72, 80
Nanook of the North, 6, 8, 10, 160, 314; illustration of exhibition for, 9; still of, 7
Narboni, Jean, 2
NASA's Mission to Planet Earth, 279
Nation Erupts, The, 95, 98–100
National Sex Forum, 228
Natives, 125
NATO Science Committee, 289
"NCZ's Top 11 Reasons to Loot or Riot," 98
Near the Big Chakra, 224–26, 228, 234
Nelson, Joyce, 306
Neumann, Peter, 288
New Day, 86, 91
New View of a Woman's Body, A, 231
New York by Gaslight, 52
New York Times, 307–8
Newsreel, 86, 89, 91; California, 85; Third World, 85, 91
Nice Girls Don't Do It, 232
Nicely, Thomas, 289
Nichols, Bill, 3–4, 6, 16, 19, 41n1, 90, 99, 155n17, 156, 177–79, 181–82, 257, 265, 267, 314–16, 318–19, 321, 323
Niépce, Joseph Nicéphore, 23
Night Cries, 171
Night Mail, 13, 84
Norell, Mark, 262
Noriega, Chon, 320
Not a Love Story, 185
Not Channel Zero, 95–96, 98–99
Notari, Elvira, 233
Number Our Days, 120, 125
Nykino, 86

Objectivity, 12, 23, 122, 218, 255–56, 286–87; technological, 269
Observer, 176. *See also* Spectator; Viewer
O'Conner, Lynn, 202
On Becoming a Woman: Mothers and Daughters, 234
Ordinary Couples, Extraordinary Sex, 234
Orgasmic Expulsion of Fluids in the Sexually Stimulated Female, 232
Orientalism, 146
O'Rourke, Dennis, 15, 176–82, 184–87

Panopticon, 46, 54
Parallax, 164; definition of, 156; effect, 158, 165, 171, 173
Paramount Pictures, 113, 297, 300, 310
Pathé Frères, 34
Pedagogy, 157
Peirce, Charles Sanders, 261
Penny Pictorial Magazine, 55
Pepino Mango Nance, 123
Perry, Michael, 229, 231
Persuasions of the Witch's Craft, 119, 124
Peters, Frances, 160
Petit a Petit, 169
Petric, Vlada, 316
Phenomenology, 75, 241–42, 244, 246, 253; of the imperceptible, 77
Photography, 23–24, 47, 56, 60, 68, 70–71, 74, 77, 256–58, 260, 320; black and white, 277; colonial, 164; documentary, 60, 176; film based, 278; high speed, 278; instantaneous, 47, 63; time lapse, 278; travel, 49; x-ray, 280
Photophobia, 70, 81n20
Plantinga, Carl, 316
Plato, 268
Plow That Broke the Plains, The, 86, 103, 106, 108, 110, 316
Poe, Edgar Allan, 53
Political Aesthetics of the Feminist Documentary Film, The, 192
Pornography, 72, 224, 229
Postcolonialism, 184, 200, 315
Postmodernism, 2–3, 116, 122, 130–31, 184, 211, 316; radical, 212
Poststructuralism, 2–3, 196
Post-Theory: Reconstructing Film Studies, 316
Princes of Naranja, The, 119
Pringle, Andrew, 59
Privacy, 56–57
Psychiatry, 35, 39
Psychoanalysis, 20, 25, 65–67, 75–76, 79, 321; Lacanian, 241
Public Culture, 161
Pudovkin, Vsevolod, 112
Punch, 46, 58

Qallunaat: Oral History as Inuit Anthropology, 169
Queen, Carol, 216, 232

Rabinow, Paul, 119
Rabinowitz, Paula, 257, 315
Rain, 323
Rainbow Diary, The, 142
Rapp, Rayna, 124
Rat, 89
Rath, Claus-Dieter, 294
Realism, 4, 75, 93, 95, 98–99, 191–92, 194, 196, 202, 210, 213, 283; aesthetic, 92–93; and the body, 95; bourgeois, 219; cinematic, 1, 6; codes of, 193, 207; critique of, 8, 11; documentary, 92–93; epistemological, 22; instrumental, 275; naive, 93; neo, 260; photo, 258, 265; photographic, 5; rhetoric of, 11

Realist Debate in the Feminist Film, The, 198

Realpolitik, 204

Reconstruction: computer, 284

Reenactment, 8, 39–40; prehistoric, 261, 271n22

Referent, 258–59, 261, 265, 268

Reflections on Fieldwork in Morocco, 119

Reflexivity, 119–21, 133–34, 136

Regards compares, 159

Reichert, Julia, 11, 13

Renoir, Jean, 246

Renov, Michael, 14, 16, 127, 140–55, 269, 313–25

Representation, 3, 6, 40, 94, 116–17, 122, 129, 157, 162, 164–65, 172, 184, 195–97, 202, 208–9, 213, 248, 259, 261, 270, 290; abstract, 285; and feminist filmmakers, 10; anthropological, 14, 130; authentic, 259; authored nature of, 133; authors of, 166; catoptric self, 217–18; cinematic, 241, 262; codes of, 259; collective identity through, 204; crisis of, 116, 118, 130, 136; cultural, 117, 135, 173, 321; documentary, 256; Enlightenment modes of, 135; ethnographic, 116, 122; female self, 218; fictional, 263; First World, 15; issues of, 135; live-action, 269; media, 163, 167; mode of, 263, 265; objective, 75; of actuality, 19; of an object, 292; of cultural differences, 130, 158, 165, 171; of death, 317; of events, 285; of interiority, 69; of life, 256; of partial reconstruction of the past, 282; of prostitutes, 183; of self, 127, 129, 166, 223, 318; of sex worker, 186; of the body, 67, 217; of the familial, 149; of the other, 141; of the physical world, 280; of the real, 324; of the unseen, 16; of women in self-help films, 15; photographic, 268; politics of, 191, 204; prehistoric, 255, 263, 265; realist, 117, 122, 192; scientific, 263; screen, 158; tools of, 146; verbal, 123; visual, 126, 129

Representing Reality, 177, 267, 314, 323

Resemblance, 4–5, 7–8; as attraction, 8

Rethinking Documentary, 313

Return to Laughter, 119

Revelations, 230

Revisionism, historiographic, 144

Rhetoric and Representation in Nonfiction Film, 316

Rich, Adrienne, 201

Rich, B. Ruby, 198, 200

Richter, Hans, 26

Ricouer, Paul, 146

Riddles of the Sphinx, 200

Riggs, Marlon, 320

Riis, Jacob, 51–52, 56

Riots, 90; Brixton, 87; Los Angeles, 1, 96, 98

RISKS, 288

Ritual Clowns, 169, 172

River, The, 14, 86, 92, 103–13, 316

Rivers, W. H., 20

Roe, So Yun, 127

Roger & Me, 85, 315

Röntgen, Wilhelm Conrad, 13, 67–71, 74

Rony, Fatimah Tobing, 6–7, 314

Rosen, Philip, 5, 257, 261, 265, 315

Rosenthal, Alan, 323

Rosler, Martha, 11

Roszak, Theodore, 288

Rothenberg, Nicholas, 123–124

Rothman, William, 316

Rouch in Reverse, 169

Rouch, Jean, 12, 117, 119–20, 124, 133, 137n13, 158–59, 174n3, 313

Roy, Bann, 123, 128, 138n34

Royalle, Candida, 229–30

Ruby, Jay, 135, 136n3

Rue, James, 298

Rugoff, Ralph, 285

Ruiz, Raul, 261

Rules of the Game, 246

Ryn, Micah van der, 128

Sacred Harp, 106

Sadoul, Georges, 12

Safer and Sexier: A College Student's Guide to Safer Sex, 207

Said, Edward, 116, 146

Sandall, Roger, 133

Sankofa, 91

Satterfield, Ann Duncan, 71

Schindler's List, 266, 320

Schlemihl, Peter, 59

Scientia sexualis, 233, 234–35

Scientific American, 279, 288

Scopophilia, 17, 27, 43n29, 321; pleasures of, 29

Screening the Body, 217

Secrets of Nature, The, 28

Self-Health, 192, 223

SelfLoving, 216, 227; *Video Portrait of a Women's Sexuality Seminar,* 226

Sensiper, Sylvia, 121–22

Sesame Street, 170

Severson, Anne, 224, 228

Shared camera, 14

Shirley, 228

Shoah, 320

Shohat, Ella, 157, 159, 165, 172

"Show Us Life": Toward a History and Aesthetic of the Committed Documentary, 85, 323

Shulman, Alix, 204

Sigmund Freud's Dora, 200

Signification: photographic, 257; prehistoric, 261

Signifier, 141

Simpson, O. J., 310

Simulation, 274, 281–87, 290; and assumptions, 287; computer, 274, 280, 282–84, 286–90; documentary quality, 285; subjectivity, 287

Sink or Swim, 14, 143–45; image from, 144–45

Skirrow, Gillian, 30, 292

"Slum Life in Our Great Cities," 56; photograph of, 55

Sluts and Goddesses, 231

Sobchack, Vivian, 8, 15, 177–79, 181–82, 241–54, 265

Social action, 84, 161, 166–67, 171

Social actors, 30–31, 222, 224, 226, 232

Social change, 85–87, 97

Society for Cinema Studies, 313–14, 317

Sound track, 99, 103, 143. *See also* Music

Southern Harmony and Musical Companion, The, 106, 112; illustration of, 106

Soviet Union, 299

Space: private and public, 46–47

Spectacle, 19, 65, 70; agitational, 88; as a popular form, 25–26; film as, 19; of knowledge, 21; of reality, 27

Spectator, 9, 29, 34, 75, 88, 90, 164, 207, 213, 221, 224, 243–44, 249, 253, 257, 263; as knowing subject, 32; female, 209–10; politicization of, 13; politicized, 88; trust of, 265

Spectatorship, 89, 159–60, 210, 323; documentary, 269; fiction film, 321

Spielberg, Steven, 262, 264–66

Sprinkle, Anne, 226–27, 231

Stacey, Jackie, 206, 209–10

Stam, Robert, 157, 159, 165, 172

Steiner, Christopher, 128

Stereopticon, 51

Stereoscope, 24, 42n15

Sterling, Scott, 125

Stoddard, John, 51

Stoney, George, 99

Storck, Henri, 86

Strange, Maren, 51–52

Strathern, Marilyn, 121, 124

Strike, 90

Struggle for the Film, The, 26

Studies on Hysteria, 75

Subject to Change: Guerrilla Television Revisited, 315

Subjectivity, 12, 286; of sight, 23

Subjunctive, 274, 277, 280, 286, 290

Sun, Moon, and Feather, 172

Sundahl, Debi, 226, 231

Supertext, 298

Surname Viet Given Name Nam, 124

Surveillance, 13, 46–47, 53, 61, 233

Susan, 228–29

Susan, Barbara, 201

Sutton, Laird, 228

Sweet Dreams, 228

Symbolic, 32, 34

Symns, J. L., 34

Symphony on a Hymn Tune, 105

Tagg, John, 268

Tahimik, Kidlat, 142

Tajima, Renee, 92

Tajiri, Rea, 172

Taking Aim, 127

Taking Our Bodies Back, 223

Talbot, William Henry Fox, 22–23, 74

Talking about Our Lives and Experiences: Some Thoughts about Feminism, Documentary, and Talking Heads, 206

Talking heads, 205, 209–10, 222; interviews, 203; style, 203

Tattersall, Ian, 261–62

Taubin, Amy, 203–4, 206

Taussig, Michael, 4, 93–94, 100, 102n35, 123, 140

Taxidermy, ethnographic, 6–7, 314

Taylor, Lucien, 128

Techniques of the Observer, 274

Technologies of Truth: Cultural Citizenship and the Popular Media, 320

Television, 292–95, 300; documentary, 84; documentary potential, 292

Territories, 91–92, 100

Theorizing Documentary, 315

Theory: anthropological, 122; apparatus, 2; cultural, 165; documentary, 15–16, 255, 267, 269, 319, 323; European, 160; feminist film, 10, 15, 191, 198–99, 204, 219, 320; feminist film, 89; film, 320; French, 196; media, 94; narrative, 259; psychoanalytic, 316, 321; queer, 315; semiotic, 5; social, 159; Western political, 87

They Must Be Represented, 315

Thin Blue Line, The, 92, 186, 245

Third Cinema, 200, 211

Third Eye, The, 314

Thompson, Kristin, 105

Thomson, Virgil, 14, 92, 103–6, 108–13

Three Daughters, 230

Thriller, 200

Through Navajo Eyes, 162

Tickner, Lisa, 235

Tidikawa and Friends, 132

Titicut Follies, 320

To Live with Herds, 132

Tomboychik, 14, 146–47

Topology, 72, 75

Tracy, Linda Lee, 185–86

Trahair, Lisa, 268–69

Transnational Fiesta: 1992, 128–29

Trespassing through Shadows: Memory, Photography, and the Holocaust, 320

Trick or Drink, 142

Tristes Tropiques, 140

Triumph of the Will, 249

Truman, Harry, 299

Tuhami, 119

Turkana Conversations, 119

Turner, Terence, 127, 163, 171, 175n33

2001: A Space Odyssey, 260

Tyler, Stephen A., 141

Unconscious, 40, 65–66, 76, 78

Union Maids, 13, 86, 91–92, 99, 207

Universal Studios, 263–64

Unthinking Eurocentrism, 157, 159

Uprising of '34, 99–100

Variety, 134

Verisimilitude, 30, 32, 40, 245, 264

Vertov, Dziga, 11–13, 86–87, 270, 316

Vianello, Robert, 295–96

Viewer, 30, 46, 89, 93, 143, 166, 207, 209; attention of, 244; politicized, 91; stereotypes, 122

Viewing Cultures, 122

Vintage: Families of Value, 150–52; photograph from, 151

Violence, 100; revolutionary, 97; screen, 97

VIP Video Group, 197

Virtual reality, 6, 270

Visible Evidence Conference, 1, 319–20

Visual pleasure, 21. *See also* Scopophilia
Visweswaran, Kamala, 119
Voice-over, 104, 124–25, 131–32, 150, 201, 222, 230
Voyager (spacecraft), 276–77
Voyeurism, 15, 28, 56, 224; urban, 53

Wag the Dog, 318
Waldman, Diane, 320
Walker, Billy, 106
Walker, Janet, 320
Walkowitz, Judith, 52
Wallace, Michele, 97
War Neuroses: Netley, 1917, Seale Hayne Military Hospital, 1918, 20–22, 32, 34, 39–40; stills from, 36–39
Warner Bros., 310
Warren, Charles, 316
Waugh, Tom, 3, 85–87, 227, 323
Way to My Father's House, The, 172
We Care: A Video for Care Providers of People Affected by AIDS, 191, 195, 206–7; photographs from, 193, 195, 198, 203, 205, 208, 210, 212
Weber, Jack, 287
West, Cornel, 211
Weston, Kath, 149
When the Moon Waxes Red, 1, 156
White, Benjamin Franklin, 106
White, Hayden, 17n3, 143, 259
White, Mimi, 294
Who Killed Colin Roach?, 92
Who Killed Vincent Chin?, 92

Williams, Cindy, 247, 251
Williams, Linda, 15, 90, 92, 176–89, 191, 199, 218, 269
Williams, Mark, 16, 292–312
Williams, Raymond, 221
Winston, Brian, 3, 84–86, 105, 314–16
Winston, Stan, 266
Wired, 279
Wiseman, Fred, 320
With Babies and Banners, 99
Wobblies, The, 99
Wolf, Mark J. P., 6, 16, 274–91
Woman's Film, The, 200, 204
Women I Love, 225
Women's Cinema as Counter Cinema, 190
Women's movement, 93, 199
Wondrous Vulva Puppet, 226
Word Is Out, 91
"Work of Art in the Age of Mechanical Reproduction, The," 76
Worlds Incomplete: From Nation to Person, 127
Worth, Sol, 162
Wright, Basil, 86
Wu, Ju-hua, 127

x ray, 13, 67–76, 78–80, 81n18, 283; photograph of, 69, 73

You've Been Framed, 29–30

Zimmermann, Patricia, 12